CICERO

II

LCL 386

CICERO

DE INVENTIONE

DE OPTIMO GENERE ORATORUM

TOPICA

WITH AN ENGLISH TRANSLATION BY

H. M. HUBBELL

HARVARD UNIVERSITY PRESS

CAMBRIDGE, MASSACHUSETTS

LONDON, ENGLAND

First published 1949

LOEB CLASSICAL LIBRARY® is a registered trademark
of the President and Fellows of Harvard College

ISBN 978-0-674-99425-6

*Printed on acid-free paper and bound by
The Maple-Vail Book Manufacturing Group*

CONTENTS

INTRODUCTION

THE treatise *de Inventione* is a youthful work of
Cicero, which was probably written while he was
studying the elements of oratory, and is in fact
hardly more than an elaborate note-book in which he
recorded the dictation of his teacher. To this he later
added conventional introductions when he decided
to publish. It is an immature work, stiff, didactic
and formal, and shows, except in the introductions,
no promise of the opulence of style and breadth
of thought which were to characterize the rhetorical
works of his later years. We are not surprised,
then, that when he composed the *de Oratore* at the
height of his career as an advocate, Cicero spoke
slightingly of the *de Inventione*, and in fact used
language which might be interpreted to mean that
the publication was an accident.[a]

Of the date of composition we know nothing
beyond Cicero's own statement (*v.* note *a*) that it
was written when he was a boy or youth (*puer aut
adulescentulus*)—two words which, vague in themselves, do not gain precision by being combined.

---

[a] *de Orat.* I, 5. . . . quae pueris aut adulescentulis nobis
ex commentariolis nostris incohata ac rudia exciderunt, vix
hac aetate digna et hoc usu sunt quem ex causis quas diximus
tot tantisque consecuti sumus. " The incomplete work—
merely a rough draft—which escaped from my note-books
between boyhood and youth is hardly worthy of my age and
of the experience that I have acquired from the many important cases in which I have appeared."

Many attempts have been made to determine a more exact date, but none have met with general acceptance. The most that can be said is that it contains no reference to any event later than 91 B.C., though references to all earlier periods of Roman history are common. This does not prove that it was written before that date, but does suggest strongly that its composition cannot belong to a much later period. Cicero was fifteen years old in 91. If the *de Inventione* was published in 87, at the age of 19, he might well describe himself at that time as *puer aut adulescentulus*.

Equally elusive is the relationship of the *de Inventione* to the other rhetorical work of the same period which has come down to us in the Ciceronian corpus, but which is certainly by another hand. This work is dedicated to one Gaius Herennius, and because of the lack of certainty as to its authorship, is now generally referred to as *Auctor ad Herennium*. It is a complete treatise on rhetoric, whereas the *de Inventione* is unfinished. In the parts which they have in common, the two treatises have a high degree of similarity which necessitates the assumption of common origin. When one endeavours to make the relationship clearer, however, the problem becomes involved, and no definite agreement has been reached. No one, nowadays, attempts to prove that Cicero copied the *Auctor*, or served as his source. Parallels have been cited which indicate that each author copied the other, and the net result is that the arguments cancel out. They do prove, however, that both derive ultimately from Greek τέχναι or text-books of rhetoric, and probably from the same one, that this τέχνη was interpreted and adapted for Roman students by the teacher

INTRODUCTION

whom Cicero and the *Auctor* followed, and that in
so doing they used a more or less uniform technical
terminology in Latin which had become current in
Rome.[a]

The authorship of these Greek τέχναι cannot be
determined, but it has been shown conclusively
that the important part of the book, the doctrine of
constitutio causae, or determination of the " issue ",
is derived with some modifications from Hermagoras
of Temnos, a rhetorician of the second century B.C.
who first formulated the principles. Hermagoras
leaned heavily on Stoic logic, and Stoic ideas appear
frequently in the *de Inventione*, but no Stoic is mentioned. On the other hand, there are frequent
references to Peripatetics, and this fact suggests that
Cicero's source combined Hermagorean and Peripatetic doctrine. Further than that one cannot go
with confidence.

A modern text-book of rhetoric deals largely with
style—choice of words, figures of speech, formation
of sentences, arrangement of paragraphs—and has in
view the practice of writing fully as much as of speaking. An ancient Rhetoric trained men entirely
for speaking, and almost exclusively for speaking
in the law court. It is a doctrine of controversy and
debate. Furthermore, it is concerned with matter
as well as with style. Invention, or the discovery
of ideas and subject matter, was the first and perhaps
the most important section of any formal treatise
on rhetoric. In developing " invention " the authors
are of necessity busied with the concepts and pro-

---

[a] Both authors, for example, translate στάσις as *constitutio*, by no means the only way of rendering it, for Cicero in
his later rhetorical works uses *status*.

INTRODUCTION

cedure of the court-room. A rhetoric thus becomes a "Practical Pleader's Guide." Hence much of the *de Inventione* reads like a law book.

"Invention" was the first of five parts in a rhetorical treatise. It was followed by chapters on Arrangement, Expression or Style, Memory and Delivery. Cicero intended to write a complete Rhetoric, but only the section on Invention was finished. This accounts for the title *de Inventione* which has clung to it for centuries, though the original title *Rhetorici Libri* gave a better indication of the original plan of the work.

A brief outline of the *de Inventione* follows:

Book I

1. General introduction: defence of eloquence, §§ 1–5.

2. The function, end, materials and divisions of eloquence, §§ 5–9.

3. *a.* The four issues, *coniecturalis, definitiva, generalis, translativa* defined, §§ 10–16.

b. The case may be simple or complex, § 17.

c. Cases arising out of a written document, §§ 17–18.

d. Further analysis of the *constitutiones*, §§ 18–19.

4. The parts of an oration:

a. Exordium, §§ 20–26.

b. Narrative, §§ 27–30.

c. Partition, §§ 31–33.

d. Confirmation, §§ 34–77.

e. Refutation, §§ 78–96.

f. Digression, §§ 97.

g. Peroration, §§ 98–109.

5. Conclusion, § 109.

INTRODUCTION

Book II

1. Introduction: eclectic nature of this book, §§ 1–10.

2. Subject matter of Book II: the arguments appropriate to each " issue " and to each kind of speech, §§ 11–13.

3. Forensic speeches (genus iudiciale).

> (Under each heading a similar plan of presentation is followed: brief statement of the facts in a typical case; the charge, answer and point of decision; the arguments available for the prosecution and defence; the " common topics.")

a. Cases involving general reasoning:

Issue of fact (constitutio coniecturalis), §§ 14–51.
Issue of definition (constitutio definitiva), §§ 52–56.
Issue of competence (constitutio translativa), §§ 57–61.
Issue of quality (constitutio generalis), §§ 62–115.

b. Cases involving interpretation of a document:

Ambiguity, §§ 116–120.
Letter and intent, §§ 121–143.
Conflict of laws, §§ 144–147.
Reasoning by analogy, §§ 148–153.
Definition, §§ 153–154.

4. Political speeches (genus deliberativum), §§ 155–176.

5. Epideictic speeches (genus demonstrativum), §§ 176–177.

6. Conclusion, § 178.

INTRODUCTION

The war has made it impossible to examine the manuscripts in preparation for this edition. I have therefore been compelled to rely on the testimony of Weidner, Ströbel and others, particularly of Ströbel, who gives in his edition (Teubner, Leipzig, 1915) the fullest *apparatus criticus*. As my text is essentially that of Ströbel, I have cited manuscript readings only where I differ from him, or in the few instances where a variant seemed likely to interest the reader.

The manuscripts used in the apparatus with their sigla, following the scheme of Ströbel, are:

CODICES MUTILI

H. Codex Herbipolitanus Mp. m. f. 3.
P. Codex Parisinus 7774 A.
S. Codex Sangallensis 820.
L. Codex Leidensis Vossianus LXX.
R. Codex Corbeiensis (Petropolitanus) F vel. 8 auct. class. Latin.
M. the consensus of H P S L R or of H P.

CODICES INTEGRI

b. Codex Bambergensis 423 MV 8.
l. Codex Leidensis Gronovianus 22.
s. Codex Sangallensis Vadianus 313.
u. Codex Urbinas 1144.
v_2. Codex Vaticanus 1698.
v_7. Codex Vaticanus 3236.
J. all or most of the Codices Integri.
i. some of the Codices Integri.
C. consensus of M and J.

ω_1. editions of Omnibonus (1470), Manutius (1540) Lambinus (1566), Ernesti (1774), Schütz (1804), Lindemann (1828).

STEMMA

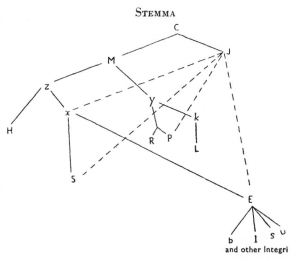

This stemma represents approximately the relation of the manuscripts as worked out by Ströbel. Of a complete MS. (earlier than the ninth century) two copies were made, M and J. The original and both copies are now lost. M was mutilated by the loss of several leaves (from I, 62 *quod enim* to I, 76 *hoc est. tum inductione*, and from II, 170 *huius modi necessitudines* to II, 174 *exspectare oportebit* are missing), and from this mutilated copy H S P R L are ultimately derived. Both P and S show signs of having been

corrected from a manuscript of the J class. E is another descendant of M with the lacunae filled from J. It is now lost, but from it were derived the great mass of complete MSS., of which I cite b, l, d, s, u, v_2, v_7.

In general the M recension is more reliable than J, but not sufficiently superior to justify an editor in following it exclusively.

BIBLIOGRAPHY

THE principal modern editions are:

TEXT

Johann Kaspar von Orelli, M. Tullii Ciceronis opera quae supersunt omnia. Vol. I. Zürich, 1826.

id. and Johann Georg Baiter, editio altera. Zürich, 1845.

Reinhold Klotz, M. Tullii Ciceronis scripta quae manserunt omnia. Vol. I. Leipzig, 1851.

id. Editio altera. Leipzig, 1863.

Carl Ludwig Kayser, M. Tullii Ciceronis opera quae supersunt omnia, ed. J. G. Baiter, C. L. Kayser. Vol. I. M. Tullii Ciceronis opera rhetorica, rec. C. L. Kayser. Leipzig, 1860.

Andreas Weidner, M. Tullii Ciceronis artis rhetoricae libri duo. Berlin, 1878.

Wilhelm Friedrich, M. Tullii Ciceronis scripta quae manserunt omnia, rec. C. F. W. Mueller. Pars I, vol. I. Opera rhetorica, rec. Gulielmus Friedrich. Leipzig, 1884.

Eduard Ströbel, M. Tullii Ciceronis scripta quae manserunt omnia, Fasc. 2, Rhetorici libri duo qui vocantur De Inventione, rec. Eduardus Stroebel. Leipzig, 1915.

TEXT AND TRANSLATION

Henri Bornecque, Cicero, De l'invention, édit et traduit par Henri Bornecque. Paris, 1932.

BIBLIOGRAPHY

TRANSLATIONS

Bornecque, v. above.

Charles Duke Yonge, The Orations of Marcus Tullius
Cicero. Vol. IV, containing the fourteen orations
against Marcus Antonius, to which are appended
the Treatise on Rhetorical Invention, etc.
London, 1852.

BOOKS AND ARTICLES ABOUT THE *DE INVENTIONE* [a]

Karl Aulitzky, Apsines περὶ ἐλέου. Wiener Studien
xxxix, 1, pp. 26–49. Discussion of the source
of the passages on Pity (I, 98).

K. Barwick, Die Gliederung der Narratio in der
rhetorischen Theorie und die Bedeutung für
die Geschichte des antiken Romans. Hermes
lxiii (1928), pp. 261–287. Discussion of I, 27.

Emilio Costa, Cicerone giureconsulto, 2 vols. Bologna,
1927.

G. Herbolzheimer, Ciceros rhetorici libri und die
Lehrschrift des Auctor. Philologus lxxxi (1925–
26), pp. 391–426. Herbolzheimer thinks that
both Cicero and the Auctor drew from a
rhetorical treatise in Latin.

Werner Hofrichter, Studien zur Entwicklungs-
geschichte der Deklamation. Diss. Breslau,
1935. A good discussion of the history of some
of the illustrative cases used by Cicero.

Wilbur Samuel Howell, The Rhetoric of Alcuin and
Charlemagne. Princeton, 1941. Has an interest-
ing introduction on the use of the de Inventione
as a source by later rhetoricians.

---

[a] This list is supplementary to the bibliography of
Ströbel, but includes a few of the works there mentioned
which may be useful to the reader.

BIBLIOGRAPHY

Walter Jaeneke, De statuum doctrina ab Hermogene tradita. Diss. Leipzig, 1904. Corrects and extends the investigations of Thiele.

Wilhelm Kroll, Das Epicheirema. Sitzungsberichte der Academie der Wissenschaften in Wien, Phil.-hist. Klasse, vol. 216. 2. Vienna and Leipzig, 1937.

Wilhelm Kroll, Rhetorik, in Pauly-Wissowa-Kroll R. E., Supplementband 7.

L. Laurand, De M. T. Ciceronis studiis rhetoricis. Paris, 1907.

Claus Peters, De rationibus inter artem rhetoricam quarti et primi saeculi intercedentibus. Diss. Kiel, 1907.

Torsten Petersson, Cicero: a Biography. Berkeley, University of California, 1920. Contains a good chapter on rhetoric.

Friedrich Pfister, Isokrates und die spätere Gliederung der Narratio. Hermes lxviii (1933), pp. 457–460.

Rudolph Preiswerk, De inventione orationum Ciceronianarum. Diss. Basel, 1905.

Maximilian Schamberger, De declamationum Romanarum argumentis observationes selectae. Diss. Halle, 1917. On declamations based on de Inv. II, 87, and II, 144.

Hans Kurt Schulte, Orator. Untersuchungen über das ciceronianische Bildungsideal. Frankfurt, 1935. On Poseidonius as the source of de Inv. I, 1–5. Cf. R. Philippson, Ciceroniana in Jahrbücher für classische Philologie cxxxiii (1886), pp. 417–425. Berliner philologische Wochenschrift xxxviii (1918), pp. 630 ff.

Friedrich Solmsen, Aristotle and Cicero on the orator's

BIBLIOGRAPHY

playing on the feelings. Classical Philology xxxiii (1938), pp. 390–404.

Friedrich Solmsen, The Aristotelian tradition in ancient rhetoric. American Journal of Philology lxii (1941), pp. 35–50, 169–190. Shows that Aristotle's principles had more currency in the practical treatises on rhetoric than is generally believed.

Friedrich Solmsen, Drei Rekonstruktionen. III, Hermes lxvii (1932), pp. 151–154.

Johannes Stroux, Aus der Status-Lehre (zu Quintilian III, xi, 15–17). Philologus lxxxv (1929–30), 342–346.

Georg Thiele, Hermagoras: Ein Beitrag zur Geschichte der Rhetorik. Strassburg, 1893. This is the classic work on the doctrine of *status* or *constitutio* (determination of the " issue "). It has been corrected and extended by later scholars, but is still the best source.

Philip Thielmann, De sermonis proprietatibus quae leguntur apud Cornificium et in primis Ciceronis libris. Strassburg, 1879. The most important work on the language of the de Inventione.

Hermann Throm, Die Thesis, Ein Beitrag zu ihrer Entstehung und Geschichte (Rhetorische Studien, 17. Heft). Paderborn, 1932. Beginning with the history of θέσις (quaestio) and ὑπόθεσις (causa) discusses many aspects of the Hermagorean tradition to be found in Cicero.

Richard Weidner, Ciceros Verhältnis zur griechisch-römischen Schulrhetorik seiner Zeit. Diss. Erlangen, 1925.

LIST OF CICERO'S WORKS
SHOWING ARRANGEMENT
IN THIS EDITION

LIST OF CICERO'S WORKS

TWO BOOKS ON RHETORIC
DE INVENTIONE

BOOK I

M. TULLI CICERONIS

RHETORICI LIBRI DUO

QUI VOCANTUR DE INVENTIONE

LIBER PRIMUS

1   I. SAEPE et multum hoc mecum cogitavi, bonine an
mali plus attulerit hominibus et civitatibus copia dicendi ac summum eloquentiae studium. Nam cum
et nostrae rei publicae detrimenta considero et maximarum civitatum veteres animo calamitates colligo,
non minimam video per disertissimos homines in-
vectam partem incommodorum; cum autem res ab
nostra memoria propter vetustatem remotas ex litterarum monumentis repetere instituo, multas urbes
constitutas, plurima bella restincta, firmissimas socie-
tates, sanctissimas amicitias intellego cum animi ratione tum facilius eloquentia comparatas. Ac me
quidem diu cogitantem ratio ipsa in hanc potissimum
sententiam ducit, ut existimem sapientiam sine eloquentia parum prodesse civitatibus, eloquentiam vero
sine sapientia nimium obesse plerumque, prodesse
nunquam. Quare si quis omissis rectissimis atque

2

MARCUS TULLIUS CICERO

TWO BOOKS ON RHETORIC

COMMONLY CALLED ON INVENTION

BOOK I

1   I. I HAVE often seriously debated with myself
whether men and communities have received more
good or evil from oratory and a consuming devotion
to eloquence.   For when I ponder the troubles in our
commonwealth, and run over in my mind the ancient
misfortunes of mighty cities, I see that no little part
of the disasters was brought about by men of eloquence.   When, on the other hand, I begin to
search in the records of literature for events which
occurred before the period which our generation can
remember, I find that many cities have been founded,
that the flames of a multitude of wars have been
extinguished, and that the strongest alliances and
most sacred friendships have been formed not only
by the use of the reason but also more easily by the
help of eloquence.   For my own part, after long
thought, I have been led by reason itself to hold
this opinion first and foremost, that wisdom without eloquence does too little for the good of states,
but that eloquence without wisdom is generally
highly disadvantageous and is never helpful.   Therefore if anyone neglects the study of philosophy and

3

honestissimis studiis rationis et offici consumit omnem operam in exercitatione dicendi, is inutilis sibi, perniciosus patriae civis alitur; qui vero ita sese armat eloquentia, ut non oppugnare commoda patriae, sed pro his propugnare possit, is mihi vir et suis et publicis rationibus utilissimus atque amicissimus civis fore videtur.

2 Ac si volumus huius rei quae vocatur eloquentia, sive artis sive studi sive exercitationis cuiusdam sive facultatis ab natura profectae considerare principium, reperiemus id ex honestissimis causis natum atque optimis rationibus profectum. II. Nam fuit quoddam tempus cum in agris homines passim bestiarum modo vagabantur et sibi victu fero vitam propagabant, nec ratione animi quicquam, sed pleraque viribus corporis administrabant; nondum divinae religionis, non humani offici ratio colebatur, nemo nuptias viderat legitimas, non certos quisquam aspexerat liberos, non, ius aequabile quid utilitatis haberet, acceperat. Ita propter errorem atque inscientiam caeca ac temeraria dominatrix animi cupiditas ad se explendam viribus corporis abutebatur, perniciosissimis satellitibus.

Quo tempore quidam magnus videlicet vir et sapiens cognovit quae materia esset et quanta ad

---

^a The exact nature of rhetoric was the subject of long and acrimonious debate in antiquity, and this debate was reflected in the definitions with which the handbooks usually began and of which we have an extended discussion in the second book of Philodemus, *de Rhetorica*. Hailed as an art or even as a science by its advocates, it was dismissed as a mere " knack " or " skill " by its opponents, or as a natural gift which needed little or no guidance. *Studium*, here translated " study," is unusual in definitions of rhetoric; so unusual that the text

moral conduct, which is the highest and most honourable of pursuits, and devotes his whole energy to the practice of oratory, his civic life is nurtured into something useless to himself and harmful to his country; but the man who equips himself with the weapons of eloquence, not to be able to attack the welfare of his country but to defend it, he, I think, will be a citizen most helpful and most devoted both to his own interests and those of his community.

2   Moreover, if we wish to consider the origin of this thing we call eloquence—whether it be an art, a study, a skill, or a gift of nature [a]—we shall find that it arose from most honourable causes and continued on its way from the best of reasons. II. For there was a time when men wandered at large in the fields like animals and lived on wild fare; they did nothing by the guidance of reason, but relied chiefly on physical strength; there was as yet no ordered system of religious worship nor of social duties; no one had seen legitimate marriage nor had anyone looked upon children whom he knew to be his own; nor had they learned the advantages of an equitable code of law. And so through their ignorance and error blind and unreasoning passion satisfied itself by misuse of bodily strength, which is a very dangerous servant.

At this juncture a man—great and wise I am sure—became aware of the power latent in man and the wide

has been questioned. It is apparently Cicero's translation of the Greek ἄσκησις, meaning pursuit or study, which is used particularly of devotion to and practice of the tenets of a philosophical sect. It is essentially equivalent to *ars* (cf. *de Oratore* II, 232: natura, studio, exercitatione). Cicero may have had in mind such a definition as that given in *Rhet. Graec.* VII, 49, ῥητορική ἐστιν ἄσκησις λόγου ἐν ἰσοσθένεσι τὸν ῥήτορα γυμνάζουσα λόγοις.

maximas res opportunitas in animis inesset hominum, si quis eam posset elicere et praecipiendo meliorem reddere; qui dispersos homines in agros et in tectis silvestribus abditos ratione quadam compulit unum in locum et congregavit et eos in unam quamque rem inducens utilem atque honestam primo propter insolentiam reclamantes, deinde propter rationem atque orationem studiosius audientes ex feris et immanibus mites reddidit et mansuetos.

3 Ac mihi quidem videtur hoc nec tacita nec inops dicendi sapientia perficere potuisse ut homines a consuetudine subito converteret et ad diversas rationes vitae traduceret. Age vero, urbibus constitutis, ut fidem colere et iustitiam retinere discerent et aliis parere sua voluntate consuescerent ac non modo labores excipiendos communis commodi causa, sed etiam vitam amittendam existimarent, qui tandem fieri potuit, nisi homines ea quae ratione invenissent eloquentia persuadere potuissent? Profecto nemo nisi gravi ac suavi commotus oratione, cum viribus plurimum posset, ad ius voluisset sine vi descendere, ut inter quos posset excellere, cum eis se pateretur aequari et sua voluntate a iucundissima consuetudine recederet quae praesertim iam naturae vim obtineret propter vetustatem.

Ac primo quidem sic et nata et progressa longius eloquentia videtur et item postea maximis in rebus pacis et belli cum summis hominum utilitatibus esse

---

ᵃ For parallels to the thought of this section, see the discussion by F. Solmsen in *Hermes* lxvii (1932), pp. 151–154.

field offered by his mind for great achievements if one could develop this power and improve it by instruction. Men were scattered in the fields and hidden in sylvan retreats when he assembled and gathered them in accordance with a plan; he introduced them to every useful and honourable occupation, though they cried out against it at first because of its novelty, and then when through reason and eloquence they had listened with greater attention, he transformed them from wild savages into a kind and gentle folk.[a]

3   To me, at least, it does not seem possible that a mute and voiceless wisdom could have turned men suddenly from their habits and introduced them to different patterns of life. Consider another point; after cities had been established how could it have been brought to pass that men should learn to keep faith and observe justice and become accustomed to obey others voluntarily and believe not only that they must work for the common good but even sacrifice life itself, unless men had been able by eloquence to persuade their fellows of the truth of what they had discovered by reason? Certainly only a speech at the same time powerful and entrancing could have induced one who had great physical strength to submit to justice without violence, so that he suffered himself to be put on a par with those among whom he could excel, and abandoned voluntarily a most agreeable custom, especially since this custom had already acquired through lapse of time the force of a natural right.

This was the way in which at first eloquence came into being and advanced to greater development, and likewise afterward in the greatest undertakings of peace and war it served the highest interests of

versata; postquam vero commoditas quaedam, prava
virtutis imitatrix, sine ratione offici, dicendi copiam
consecuta est, tum ingenio freta malitia pervertere
urbes et vitas hominum labefactare assuevit.

4   III. Atque huius quoque exordium mali, quoniam
principium boni diximus, explicemus. Veri simillimum mihi videtur quodam tempore neque in publicis
rebus infantes et insipientes homines solitos esse
versari nec vero ad privatas causas magnos ac disertos
homines accedere, sed cum a summis viris maximae
res administrarentur, arbitror alios fuisse non incallidos homines qui ad parvas controversias privatorum
accederent. Quibus in controversiis cum saepe a
mendacio contra verum stare homines consuescerent,
dicendi assiduitas induit audaciam, ut necessario
superiores illi propter iniurias civium resistere audacibus et opitulari suis quisque necessariis cogeretur.
Itaque cum in dicendo saepe par, nonnunquam etiam
superior, visus esset is qui omisso studio sapientiae
nihil sibi praeter eloquentiam comparasset, fiebat ut
et multitudinis et suo iudicio dignus qui rem publicam
gereret videretur. Hinc nimirum non iniuria, cum
ad gubernacula rei publicae temerarii atque audaces
homines accesserant, maxima ac miserrima naufragia fiebant. Quibus rebus tantum odi atque
invidiae suscepit eloquentia ut homines ingenio-

mankind. But when a certain agreeableness of manner—a depraved imitation of virtue—acquired the power of eloquence unaccompanied by any consideration of moral duty, then low cunning supported by talent grew accustomed to corrupt cities and undermine the lives of men.

4   III. Let me now set forth the origin of this evil also, since I have explained the beginning of the good done by eloquence. It seems to me very probable that there was a time when those who lacked eloquence and wisdom were not accustomed to meddle with public affairs, and when on the other hand great and eloquent men did not concern themselves with private suits at law, but while matters of the greatest importance were managed by men of the highest distinction, there were, I think, other men not without shrewdness who concerned themselves with the petty disputes of private citizens. Since in these disputes men grew accustomed to stand on the side of falsehood against the truth, constant practice in speaking led them to assume a bold front; the inevitable result was that the better class was compelled because of injuries to their fellow citizens to resist the audacious and help their own kin and friends. And so, because one who had acquired eloquence alone to the neglect of the study of philosophy often appeared equal in power of speech and sometimes even superior, such a one seemed in his own opinion and that of the mob to be fit to govern the state. Therefore it was not undeserved, I am sure, that whenever rash and audacious men had taken the helm of the ship of state great and disastrous wrecks occurred. These events brought eloquence into such odium and unpopularity that men of the

sissimi, quasi ex aliqua turbida tempestate in portum,
sic ex seditiosa ac tumultuosa vita se in studium
aliquod traderent quietum. Quare mihi videntur
postea cetera studia recta atque honesta per otium
concelebrata ab optimis enituisse, hoc vero a plerisque
eorum desertum obsolevisse tempore quo multo
vehementius erat retinendum et studiosius ad-
5 augendum. Nam quo indignius rem honestissimam
et rectissimam violabat stultorum et improborum te-
meritas et audacia summo cum rei publicae detrimento, eo studiosius et illis resistendum fuit et rei
publicae consulendum.

IV. Quod nostrum illum non fugit Catonem neque
Laelium neque Africanum neque eorum, ut vere
dicam, discipulos Gracchos Africani nepotes : [1] quibus
in hominibus erat summa virtus et summa virtute
amplificata auctoritas et, quae et his rebus orna-
mento et rei publicae praesidio esset, eloquentia.
Quare meo quidem animo nihilo minus eloquentiae
studendum est, etsi ea quidam et privatim et publice
abutuntur ; sed eo quidem vehementius, ne mali

---

[1] neque eorum ut vere dicam discipulum Africanum neque
Gracchos Africani nepotes *J* : Africanum. Neque *M* : neque
. . . nepotes *omitted by Victorinus, questioned by Friedrich.*
Ammon proposes to bracket Gracchos, *Ströbel to bracket*
Africani nepotes. *The reading in the text is the conjecture of
Martha.*

---

[a] Marcus Porcius Cato the Censor, consul 195 B.C.
[b] Gaius Laelius (Sapiens) consul 140 B.C. He was the close
friend of Scipio (note *c*).
[c] Publius Cornelius Scipio Aemilianus Africanus, consul
147 and 134 B.C., destroyed Carthage. He and Laelius were
the chief members of the " Scipionic circle."
[d] Tiberius Sempronius Gracchus, tribune 133 B.C., and
Gaius Sempronius Gracchus, tribune 123 B.C., popular leaders

greatest talent left a life of strife and tumult for some quiet pursuit, as sailors seek refuge in port from a raging storm. For this reason, I think, at a later period the other worthy and honourable studies were prosecuted vigorously in quiet seclusion by the men of highest virtue and were brought to a brilliant development, while this study of eloquence was abandoned by most of them and fell into disuse at a time when it needed to be maintained more earnestly 5 and extended with greater effort. For the more shamefully an honourable and worthy profession was abused by the folly and audacity of dull-witted and unprincipled men with the direst consequences to the state, the more earnestly should the better citizens have put up a resistance to them and taken thought for the welfare of the republic.

IV. This was well known to our Cato,[a] to Laelius,[b] and Africanus [c] and to their pupils—as I may rightfully call them—the Gracchi,[d] the grandsons of Africanus. These men possessed the highest virtue and an authority strengthened by their virtue, and also eloquence to adorn these qualities and protect the state. Therefore, in my opinion at least, men ought none the less to devote themselves to the study of eloquence although some misuse it both in private and in public affairs. And they should study it the more earnestly in

and reformers. They were the sons of Cornelia the daughter of Scipio Africanus the Elder, who defeated Hannibal at Zama in 202 B.C. Cicero generally expresses an unfavourable opinion of the Gracchi as subverters of the state. The phrase *ut vere dicam* is intended as an apology for including them with such patriots as Cato and Africanus, just as he excuses a similar favourable reference to the reformers in the speech on the Agrarian Law (II, 5, 10).

magno cum detrimento bonorum et communi omnium pernicie plurimum possint; cum praesertim hoc sit unum, quod ad omnes res et privatas et publicas maxime pertineat, hoc tuta, hoc honesta, hoc illustris, hoc eodem vita iucunda fiat. Nam hinc ad rem publicam plurima commoda veniunt, si moderatrix omnium rerum praesto est sapientia; hinc ad ipsos qui eam adepti sunt laus, honos, dignitas confluit; hinc amicis quoque eorum certissimum et tutissimum praesidium comparatur. Ac mihi quidem videntur homines, cum multis rebus humiliores et infirmiores sint, hac re maxime bestiis praestare, quod loqui possunt. Quare praeclarum mihi quiddam videtur adeptus is qui qua re homines bestiis praestent ea in re hominibus ipsis antecellat. Hoc si forte non natura modo neque exercitatione conficitur, verum etiam artificio quodam comparatur, non alienum est videre, quae dicant ei qui quaedam eius rei praecepta nobis reliquerunt.

Sed antequam de praeceptis oratoriis dicimus, videtur dicendum de genere ipsius artis, de officio, de fine, de materia, de partibus. Nam his rebus cognitis facilius et expeditius animus unius cuius- que ipsam rationem ac viam artis considerare poterit.

6 V. Civilis quaedam ratio est, quae multis et magnis ex rebus constat. Eius quaedam magna et ampla

---

a The passage in sections 2–5 in praise of eloquence and its function in promoting civilization is a commonplace at least as old as Isocrates. It may be compared to Cicero, *de Oratore* I, 32 f.; *de Natura Deorum* II, 148, *Tusc. Disp.* V, 5, where a similar rôle is attributed to philosophy; Isocrates *Nicocles* 5 (=*Antidosis* 253). Cf. also Hubbell, *The Influence of Isocrates on Cicero, Dionysius and Aristides*, pp. 27–30, and Reinhardt,

order that evil men may not obtain great power to
the detriment of good citizens and the common
disaster of the community; especially since this is
the only thing which has a very close relation to both
private and public affairs, this renders life safe,
honourable, glorious and even agreeable. For from
eloquence the state receives many benefits, provided
only it is accompanied by wisdom, the guide of all
human affairs. From eloquence those who have
acquired it obtain glory and honour and high esteem.
From eloquence comes the surest and safest pro-
tection for one's friends. Furthermore, I think that
men, although lower and weaker than animals in
many respects, excel them most by having the power
of speech. Therefore that man appears to me to
have won a splendid possession who excels men themselves in that ability by which men excel beasts.
And if, as it happens, this is not brought about by
nature alone nor by practice, but is also acquired
from some systematic instruction, it is not out of
place to see what those say who have left us some
directions for the study of oratory.[a]

But before I speak of the rules of oratory I think I
should say something about the nature of the art
itself, about its function, its end, its materials,
and its divisions. For if these are understood the
mind of each reader will be able more easily and
readily to grasp the outline and method of the
subject.

6   V. There is a scientific system of politics which
includes many important departments. One of these
departments—a large and important one—is elo-

Hekataios von Abdera und Demokrit, *Hermes* xlvii (1912),
pp. 492–513.

pars est artificiosa eloquentia quam rhetoricam vocant. Nam neque cum eis sentimus qui civilem scientiam eloquentia non putant indigere, et ab eis qui eam putant omnem rhetoris vi et artificio contineri magnopere dissentimus. Quare hanc oratoriam facultatem in eo genere ponemus, ut eam civilis scientiae partem esse dicamus. Officium autem eius facultatis videtur esse dicere apposite ad persuasionem; finis persuadere dictione. Inter officium et finem hoc interest quod in officio quid fieri, in fine quid effici conveniat consideratur. Ut medici officium dicimus esse curare ad sanandum apposite, finem sanare curatione, item, oratoris quid officium et quid finem esse dicamus, intellegimus, cum id quod facere debet officium esse dicimus, illud cuius causa facere debet finem appellamus.

7 Materiam artis eam dicimus in qua omnis ars et ea facultas quae conficitur ex arte versatur. Ut si medicinae materiam dicamus morbos ac vulnera, quod in his omnis medicina versetur, item, quibus in rebus versatur ars et facultas oratoria, eas res materiam artis rhetoricae nominamus. Has autem res alii plures, alii pauciores existimarunt. Nam Gorgias Leontinus, antiquissimus fere rhetor, omnibus de rebus oratorem optime posse dicere existimavit. Hic infinitam et immensam huic artificio materiam subicere videtur. Aristoteles autem, qui huic arti plurima adiumenta atque ornamenta subministravit,

---

a Famous sophist of the fifth century B.C.
b Aristotle, *Rhetoric* 1358b 7.

quence based on the rules of art, which they call
rhetoric. For I do not agree with those who think
that political science has no need of eloquence, and I
violently disagree with those who think that it is
wholly comprehended in the power and skill of the
rhetorician. Therefore we will classify oratorical
ability as a part of political science. The function of
eloquence seems to be to speak in a manner suited to
persuade an audience, the end is to persuade by
speech. There is this difference between function and
end: in the case of the function we consider what
should be done, in the case of the end what result
should be produced. For example, we say that the
function of the physician is to treat the patient in a
manner suited to heal him, the end is to heal by
treatment. So in the case of the orator we may
understand what is meant by function and end when
we call what he ought to do the function, and the
purpose for which he ought to do it, the end.

7   By the material of the art I mean that with which
the art as a whole and the power produced by the art
are concerned. For example, we say the material of
medicine is diseases and wounds because medicine is
wholly concerned with these; in the same way we
call the material of the art of rhetoric those subjects
with which the art and power of oratory are concerned. However, some have thought that there are
more and some less of these subjects. To cite one
example, Gorgias of Leontini,[a] almost the earliest
teacher of oratory, held that the orator could speak
better than anyone else on all subjects. Apparently he
assigned to the profession a vast—and in fact infinite
—material. Aristotle,[b] on the other hand, who did
much to improve and adorn this art, thought that the

tribus in generibus rerum versari rhetoris officium
putavit, demonstrativo, deliberativo, iudiciali. Demonstrativum est quod tribuitur in alicuius certae
personae laudem aut vituperationem; deliberativum,
quod positum in disceptatione civili habet in se
sententiae dictionem; iudiciale, quod positum in
iudicio habet in se accusationem et defensionem aut
petitionem et recusationem. Et, quemadmodum
nostra quidem fert opinio, oratoris ars et facultas in
hac materia tripertita versari existimanda est.

8 VI. Nam Hermagoras quidem nec quid dicat
attendere nec quid polliceatur intellegere videtur,
qui oratoris materiam in causam et in quaestionem
dividat, causam esse dicat rem quae habeat in se
controversiam in dicendo positam cum personarum
certarum interpositione; quam nos quoque oratori
dicimus esse attributam (nam tres eas partes, quas
ante diximus, supponimus, iudicialem, deliberativam,
demonstrativam).

Quaestionem autem eam appellat quae habeat in
se controversiam in dicendo positam sine certarum
personarum interpositione, ad hunc modum: " Ecquid
sit bonum praeter honestatem?" " Verine sint
sensus?" " Quae sit mundi forma?" " Quae sit
solis magnitudo?" Quas quaestiones procul ab
oratoris officio remotas facile omnes intellegere
existimamus. Nam quibus in rebus summa ingenia
philosophorum plurimo cum labore consumpta intelle-

function of the orator was concerned with three classes of subjects, the epideictic, the deliberative, and the judicial. The epideictic is devoted to the praise or censure of a particular individual; the deliberative is at home in a political debate and involves the expression of an opinion; the judicial is at home in a court of law and involves accusation and defence or a claim and counter-plea. According to my opinion, at least, the art and faculty of the orator must be thought of as concerned with this threefold material.

8 VI. For Hermagoras [a] indeed does not seem to notice what he says or understand what he promises when he divides the material of the orator into " special cases " and " general questions," and defines " special cases " as a matter involving a controversy conducted by a speech with the introduction of definite individuals (this we too say is assigned to the orator, for we give him the three parts which we have already mentioned: judicial, deliberative, epideictic).

" General question " he defines as a matter involving a controversy conducted by a speech without the introduction of definite individuals, as for example, " Is there any good except honour ? " " Can the senses be trusted ? " " What is the shape of the world ? " " How large is the sun ? " I think that everyone understands perfectly that these questions are far removed from the business of an orator. It seems the height of folly to assign to an orator as if they were trifles these subjects in which

---

[a] Hermagoras of Temnos, rhetorician of the second century B.C.

gimus, eas sicut aliquas parvas res oratori attribuere
magna amentia videtur.

Quodsi magnam in his Hermagoras habuisset
facultatem studio et disciplina comparatam, videretur
fretus sua scientia falsum quiddam constituisse de
oratoris artificio et non quid ars, sed quid ipse
posset, exposuisse. Nunc vero ea vis est in homine,
ut ei multo rhetoricam citius quis ademerit quam
philosophiam concesserit: neque eo, quod eius ars
quam edidit, mihi mendosissime scripta videatur;
nam satis in ea videtur ex antiquis artibus ingeniose
et diligenter electas res collocasse et nonnihil ipse
quoque novi protulisse; verum oratori minimum est
de arte loqui, quod hic fecit, multo maximum ex
arte dicere, quod eum minime potuisse omnes
videmus.

9   VII. Quare materia quidem nobis rhetoricae
videtur artis ea quam Aristoteli visam esse diximus;
partes autem eae quas plerique dixerunt, inventio,
dispositio, elocutio, memoria, pronuntiatio. Inventio
est excogitatio rerum verarum aut veri similium quae
causam probabilem reddant; dispositio est rerum
inventarum in ordinem distributio; elocutio est

ᵃ It is likely that Cicero or his source misunderstood
Hermagoras' meaning. As the textbook of Hermagoras has
perished, we have no sure means of determining his position, but
other authorities (Sextus Empiricus, *adversus Math.* II, 62,
Augustine, *de Rhetorica*, RLM fr. 139. 29, and Hermogenes,
RG II, p. 17 S) imply that he claimed for rhetoric the right
to discuss moral and philosophical questions of general
interest, but excluded technical questions requiring specialized
knowledge of a scientific field. Even so Hermagoras was
undoubtedly trying to extend the field of rhetoric and was
trespassing on territory claimed by philosophers. The first
and third questions here propounded were Stoic problems,

we know that the sublime genius of philosophers has spent so much labour.[a]

But if Hermagoras had possessed great skill in dealing with these subjects—a skill acquired by study and training—he would seem to have laid down a false principle about the profession of the orator through confidence in his own knowledge, and to have described not what the art, but what he himself could accomplish. But as a matter of fact the man's ability is such that one will more readily deny him the power of rhetoric than grant him acquaintance with philosophy. Not that I think the text-book which he published is very faulty, for he seems to have done well enough at arranging topics which he had chosen with ingenuity and care from earlier authors, and to have added something new himself; [b] but for an orator it is a very slight thing to talk about his art, as he has done; by far the most important thing is to speak in accordance with the principles of his art, which we all see he was wholly incapable of doing.

9 VII. Therefore the material of the art of rhetoric seems to me to be that which we said Aristotle approved. The parts of it, as most authorities have stated, are Invention, Arrangement, Expression, Memory, Delivery. Invention is the discovery of valid or seemingly valid arguments to render one's cause plausible. Arrangement is the distribution of arguments thus discovered in the proper order.

the others were favourite problems of the Epicureans. *Quaestio* translated "general question" is Hermagoras' θέσις; *causa* or "special case" is ὑπόθεσις.

[b] Ungenerous of Cicero, for Hermagoras was the inventor of the doctrine of "status" which forms the backbone of the *de Inventione*.

idoneorum verborum[1] ad inventionem accommodatio; memoria est firma animi rerum ac verborum [2] perceptio; pronuntiatio est ex rerum et verborum dignitate vocis et corporis moderatio.

Nunc his rebus breviter constitutis eas rationes quibus ostendere possimus genus et finem et officium huius artis aliud in tempus differemus. Nam et multorum verborum indigent et non tanto opere ad artis descriptionem et praecepta tradenda pertinent. Eum autem qui artem rhetoricam scribat de duabus reliquis rebus, materia artis ac partibus, scribere oportere existimamus. Ac mihi quidem videtur coniuncte agendum de materia ac partibus. Quare inventio, quae princeps est omnium partium, potissimum in omni causarum genere, qualis debeat esse, consideretur.

10   VIII. Omnis res quae habet in se positam in dictione ac disceptatione aliquam controversiam, aut facti aut nominis aut generis aut actionis continet quaestionem. Eam igitur quaestionem ex qua causa nascitur constitutionem appellamus. Constitutio est prima conflictio causarum ex depulsione intentionis profecta, hoc modo: " Fecisti." " Non feci," aut: " Iure feci." Cum facti controversia est, quoniam coniecturis causa firmatur, constitutio coniecturalis appellatur. Cum autem nominis, quia vis vocabuli

---

[1] After verborum the MSS. except M[1] insert et sententiarum.

[2] ad inventionem, after verborum is omitted by Cassiodorus, bracketed by Lambinus. Strōbel keeps the phrase, understanding retinendam.

---

[a] Constitutio is a translation of the Greek στάσις, and was supplanted in Cicero's later writings by status. It denotes the basis or ground for dispute.

Expression is the fitting of the proper language to the invented matter. Memory is the firm mental grasp of matter and words. Delivery is the control of voice and body in a manner suitable to the dignity of the subject matter and the style.

Now that these terms have been defined briefly we shall postpone to another time the discussion in which we could explain the nature, the end and the function of this art; for they require lengthy treatment and are not so intimately connected with the description of the art and the transmission of rules. But we think that one who is to write a text-book of rhetoric ought to write about the other two subjects, the material of the art and its divisions. And I think I should treat material and divisions together. Therefore let us consider what the character of invention should be; this is the most important of all the divisions, and above all is used in every kind of pleading.

10   VIII. Every subject which contains in itself a controversy to be resolved by speech and debate involves a question about a fact, or about a definition, or about the nature of an act, or about legal processes. This question, then, from which the whole case arises, is called *constitutio* or the " issue." [a] The " issue " is the first conflict of pleas which arises from the defence or answer to our accusation, in this way: " You did it "; " I did not do it," or " I was justified in doing it." When the dispute is about a fact, the issue is said to be conjectural (*coniecturalis*),[b] because the plea is supported by conjectures or inferences. When the issue is about a definition, it

[b] In the terms of our law, the *constitutio coniecturalis* is an issue of fact, the others are issues of law.

definienda verbis est, constitutio definitiva nominatur.
Cum vero qualis res sit quaeritur, quia et de vi et de
genere negoti controversia est, constitutio generalis
vocatur. At cum causa ex eo pendet, quia non aut is
agere videtur quem oportet, aut non cum eo quicum
oportet, aut non apud quos, quo tempore, qua lege,
quo crimine, qua poena oportet, translativa dicitur
constitutio, quia actio translationis et commutationis
indigere videtur. Atque harum aliquam in omne
causae genus incidere necesse est. Nam in quam
rem non inciderit, in ea nihil esse poterit controversiae; quare eam ne causam quidem convenit putari.

11   Ac facti quidem controversia in omnia tempora
potest tribui. Nam quid factum sit potest quaeri,
hoc modo: Occideritne Aiacem Ulixes; et quid fiat,
hoc modo: Bonone animo sint erga populum Romanum Fregellani; et quid futurum sit, hoc modo: Si
Karthaginem reliquerimus incolumem, num quid sit
incommodi ad rem publicam perventurum.

Nominis est controversia, cum de facto convenit et
quaeritur, id quod factum est quo nomine appelletur.
Quo in genere necesse est ideo nominis esse controversiam, quod de re ipsa non conveniat; non quod
de facto non constet, sed quod id quod factum sit
aliud alii videatur esse et idcirco alius alio nomine id

---

a This fictitious case is stated more fully in *ad Herennium*
I, 18: When Ajax learned what he had done in his fit of
madness, he went into the forest and fell on his sword. Ulysses
chanced to pass by, saw that Ajax was dead and drew the
blood-stained sword from the corpse. Teucer came by, saw
his brother dead and his brother's enemy holding the blood-
stained sword. He charges Ulysses with murder. Quintilian (IV, ii, 13), who gives the story in greater detail, says
that it was taken from the tragic stage (*ex tragoediis*), but

is called the definitional issue, because the force of
the term must be defined in words. When, however,
the nature of the act is examined, the issue is said
to be qualitative, because the controversy concerns
the value of the act and its class or quality. But
when the case depends on the circumstance that
it appears that the right person does not bring the
suit, or that he brings it against the wrong person, or
before the wrong tribunal, or at a wrong time, under
the wrong statute, or the wrong charge, or with a
wrong penalty, the issue is called translative because the action seems to require a transfer to
another court or alteration in the form of pleading.
There will always be one of these issues applicable
to every kind of case; for where none applies, there
can be no controversy. Therefore it is not fitting
to regard it as a case at all.

11   As to the dispute about a fact, this can be assigned
to any time. For the question can be " What has
been done ? " *e.g.* " Did Ulysses kill Ajax ? " [a] and
" What is being done ?," *e.g.* "Are the Fregellans
friendly to the Roman people ?," and what is going
to occur, *e.g.* " If we leave Carthage untouched, will
any harm come to the Roman state ? "

The controversy about a definition arises when
there is agreement as to the fact and the question is
by what word that which has been done is to be
described. In this case there must be a dispute
about the definition, because there is no agreement
about the essential point, not because the fact is not
certain, but because the deed appears differently to
different people, and for that reason different people

the source has not been identified, and it is more likely that
the story is the invention of a rhetorician.

appellet. Quare in eiusmodi generibus definienda res erit verbis et breviter describenda, ut, si quis sacrum ex privato surripuerit, utrum fur an sacrilegus sit iudicandus. Nam id cum quaeritur, necesse erit definire utrumque, quid sit fur, quid sacrilegus, et sua descriptione ostendere alio nomine illam rem de qua agitur appellari oportere atque adversarii dicunt.

12   IX. Generis est controversia, cum et quid factum sit convenit, et quo id factum nomine appellari oporteat constat et tamen quantum et cuiusmodi et omnino quale sit quaeritur, hoc modo: Iustum an iniustum, utile an inutile, et omnia in quibus, quale sit id quod factum est, quaeritur sine ulla nominis controversia. Huic generi Hermagoras partes quattuor supposuit, deliberativam, demonstrativam, iuridicialem, negotialem. Quod eius, ut nos putamus, non mediocre peccatum reprehendendum videtur, verum brevi, ne aut si taciti praeterierimus, sine causa non secuti putemur, aut si diutius in hoc constiterimus, moram atque impedimentum reliquis praeceptis intulisse videamur.

Si deliberatio et demonstratio genera sunt causarum, non possunt recte partes alicuius generis causae putari. Eadem enim res alii genus esse, alii pars potest, eidem genus esse et pars non potest. Deliberatio autem et demonstratio genera sunt

---

ᵃ For the problem which Cicero here dicusses see Excursus, p. 346.

describe it in different terms. Therefore in cases of
this kind the matter must be defined in words and
briefly described. For example, if a sacred article is
purloined from a private house, is the act to be
adjudged theft or sacrilege? For when this question
is asked, it will be necessary to define both theft and
sacrilege, and to show by one's own description that
the act in dispute should be called by a different name
from that used by the opponents.

12   IX. There is a controversy about the nature or
character of an act when there is both agreement as
to what has been done and certainty as to how the
act should be defined, but there is a question nevertheless about how important it is or of what kind,
or in general about its quality, *e.g.* was it just or unjust, profitable or unprofitable? It includes all such
cases in which there is a question about the quality
of an act without any controversy about definition.
Hermagoras divided this genus into four species:
deliberative, epideictic, equitable, and legal. I
think I ought to criticize this error of his—no in-
considerable error as I think—but briefly lest if we
pass it by in silence we be thought to have failed
to follow him without good reason, or if we linger
on the point too long, we seem to have hindered and
delayed the presentation of the rules to be laid down
in the rest of the book.[a]

If deliberative and epideictic are genera of argument they cannot rightly be thought to be species of
any one genus of argument. For the same thing can
be genus in relation to one thing and species in relation to another, but cannot be both genus and species
in relation to the same thing. Moreover the deliberative and epideictic are genera of arguments. For

25

causarum. Nam aut nullum causae genus est aut
iudiciale solum aut et iudiciale et demonstrativum et
deliberativum. Nullum dicere causae esse genus,
cum causas esse multas dicat et in eas praecepta det,
amentia est; unum iudiciale autem solum esse qui
potest, cum deliberatio et demonstratio neque ipsae
similes inter se sint et ab iudiciali genere plurimum
dissideant et suum quaeque finem habeat quo referri
debeat? Relinquitur ergo ut omnia tria genera
sint causarum. Deliberatio et demonstratio non
possunt recte partes alicuius generis causae putari.
Male igitur eas generalis constitutionis partes esse
dixit.

13   X. Quodsi generis causae partes non possunt recte
putari, multo minus recte partis causae partes putabuntur. Pars autem causae est constitutio omnis,
non enim causa ad constitutionem, sed constitutio ad
causam accommodatur. At demonstratio et deliberatio generis causae partes non possunt recte
putari quod ipsa sunt genera; multo igitur minus
recte partis eius quae hic dicitur partes putabuntur.
Deinde si constitutio et ipsa et pars eius quaelibet
intentionis depulsio est, quae intentionis depulsio non
est, ea nec constitutio nec pars constitutionis est; at
si, quae intentionis depulsio non est, ea nec constitutio
nec pars constitutionis est, deliberatio et demonstratio neque constitutio nec pars constitutionis est.
Si igitur constitutio et ipsa et pars eius intentionis

either there is no classification of arguments or there are only forensic arguments, or there are three genera, forensic, epideictic, and deliberative. To say that there is no classification of arguments when he says that there are many and gives rules for them, is madness. How can there be only one genus—the forensic—when deliberative and epideictic are not similar to each other and are far different from the forensic kind and each has its own end to which it may be referred? It follows, therefore, that there are, in all, three genera of arguments. Deliberative and epideictic cannot rightly be regarded as species of any kind of argument. He was wrong, then, in saying that they are species of the qualitative issue.

13 X. Wherefore if they cannot rightly be regarded as species of a genus of argument, there will be much less justification for regarding them as sub-heads of a species of argument. But the " issue " is nothing but a sub-head of argument. For the argument is not subsumed under the issue but the issue is subsumed under the argument. But epideictic and deliberative cannot rightly be regarded as species of a genus of argument, because they are themselves the genera of argument; there will be much less justification for regarding them as sub-heads of this species which is here described. In the second place, if the issue, either entire or any part of it, is an answer to an accusation, then that which is not an answer to an accusation cannot be either an issue or a sub-head of an issue. But if what is not an answer to an accusation is neither an issue or a sub-head of an issue, deliberative and epideictic speeches are not an issue or a sub-head of an issue. If, then, the issue, either entire or any part of it, is the answer to an

depulsio est, deliberatio et demonstratio neque
constitutio neque pars constitutionis est. Placet
autem ipsi constitutionem intentionis esse depul-
sionem; placeat igitur oportet demonstrationem et
deliberationem non esse constitutionem nec partem
constitutionis. Atque hoc eodem urguebitur, sive
constitutionem primam causae accusatoris confirmationem dixerit sive defensoris primam deprecationem; nam eum eadem omnia incommoda
sequentur.

14 Deinde coniecturalis causa non potest simul ex
eadem parte eodem in genere et coniecturalis esse et
definitiva. Nec definitiva causa potest simul ex
eadem parte eodem in genere et definitiva esse et
translativa. Et omnino nulla constitutio nec pars
constitutionis potest simul et suam habere et alterius
in se vim continere, ideo quod una quaeque ex se et ex
sua natura simpliciter consideratur; altera assumpta
numerus constitutionum duplicatur, non vis constitutionis augetur. At deliberativa causa simul ex eadem
parte eodem in genere et coniecturalem et generalem
et definitivam et translativam solet habere constitutionem et unam aliquam et plures nonnunquam.
Ergo ipsa neque constitutio est nec pars constitutionis.
Idem in demonstratione solet usu venire. Genera
igitur, ut ante diximus, haec causarum putanda sunt,
non partes alicuius constitutionis.

accusation, deliberative and epideictic speeches cannot be either an issue or a sub-head of an issue. But he himself is of the opinion that the issue is the answer to an accusation. He ought, therefore, to be of the opinion that epideictic and deliberative speeches are not the issue or a sub-head of the issue. And he will be pressed by the same argument whether he defines issue as the first assertion of his cause by the accuser or the first plea of the defendant. For all the same difficulties will attend him.

14 Furthermore a conjectural argument cannot at one and the same time and from the same point of view and under the same system of classification be both conjectural and definitive, nor can a definitive argument be at one and the same time and from the same point of view and under the same system of classification both definitive and translative. And, to put it generally, no issue or sub-head of an issue can have its own scope and also include the scope of another issue, because each one is studied directly by itself and in its own nature, and if another is added, the number of issues is doubled but the scope of any one issue is not increased. But a deliberative argument generally includes at one and the same time and from the same point of view and under the same system of classification an issue, or *constitutio*, the conjectural, qualitative, definitional, or translative, either any one of these or at times more than one. Therefore it is not itself an issue or a sub-head of an issue. The same thing is wont to occur in the demonstrative (or epideictic) speech. These, then, as we said before, are to be regarded as the genera of oratory and not as sub-heads under any issue.

XI. Haec ergo constitutio, quam generalem nominamus, partes videtur nobis duas habere, iuridicialem
et negotialem. Iuridicialis est in qua aequi et recti
natura aut praemi aut poenae ratio quaeritur; negotialis, in qua, quid iuris ex civili more et aequitate
sit, consideratur; cui diligentiae praeesse apud nos
15 iure consulti existimantur. Ac iuridicialis quidem
ipsa[1] in duas tribuitur partes, absolutam et assumptivam. Absoluta est quae ipsa in se continet
iuris et iniuriae quaestionem; assumptiva, quae ipsa
ex se nihil dat firmi ad recusationem, foris autem
aliquid defensionis assumit. Eius partes sunt quattuor, concessio, remotio criminis, relatio criminis,
comparatio. Concessio est cum reus non id quod
factum est defendit, sed ut ignoscatur postulat.
Haec in duas partes dividitur, purgationem et
deprecationem. Purgatio est cum factum conceditur, culpa removetur. Haec partes habet tres,
imprudentiam, casum, necessitatem. Deprecatio
est cum et peccasse et consulto peccasse reus se
confitetur et tamen ut ignoscatur postulat; quod
genus perraro potest accidere. Remotio criminis
est cum id crimen quod infertur ab se et ab sua culpa
et potestate[2] in alium reus removere conatur. Id
dupliciter fieri poterit, si aut causa aut factum in alium
transferetur. Causa transfertur, cum aliena dicitur

---

[1] ipsa *P²J Victorinus* ipsa et *M* et ipsa *i*.
[2] culpa vi et potestate *P²J. Victorinus, Cassiodorus,
omit* vi *from the text: Kayser brackets* vi et potestate.

---

[a] See Quintilian, III, vi, 57–60, for a discussion of Cicero's
faulty interpretation of Hermagoras' doctrine at this point.
[b] *Purgatio* is very nearly "justification," but in Anglo-
American law justification would include at least *relatio
criminis* and probably *comparatio*.

XI. Therefore this issue, which we call the qualitative issue, seems to us to have two subdivisions, equitable and legal. The equitable is that in which there is a question about the nature of justice and right or the reasonableness of reward or punishment. The legal is that in which we examine what the law is according to the custom of the community and according to justice: at Rome the jurisconsults are thought to be in charge of the 15 study of this subject.[a] The equitable is itself divided into two parts, the absolute and the assumptive. The absolute is that which contains in itself the question of right and wrong done. The assumptive is that which of itself provides no basis for a counter plea, but seeks some defence from extraneous circumstances. It has four divisions, *concessio* (confession and avoidance), *remotio criminis* (shifting the charge), *relatio criminis* (retort of the accusation), and *comparatio* (comparison). Confession and avoidance is used when the accused does not defend the deed but asks for pardon. This is divided into two parts: *purgatio* and *deprecatio.*[b] It is *purgatio* when the deed is acknowledged but *intent* is denied; it has three parts, ignorance, accident, necessity. *Deprecatio* is used when the defendant acknowledges that he has given offence and has done so intentionally, and still asks to be forgiven; this can very rarely occur. It is shifting of the charge when the defendant tries to shift to another the charge brought against himself by transferring to another either the act or the intent or the power to perform the act. This can be done in two ways: either the cause or the act itself is attributed to another. The cause is attributed when the deed is said to have been done because of the

vi et potestate factum; factum autem, cum alius aut
debuisse aut potuisse facere dicitur. Relatio criminis
est cum ideo iure factum dicitur, quod aliquis ante
iniuria lacessierit. Comparatio est cum aliud aliquod
factum rectum aut utile contenditur, quod ut fieret,
illud quod arguitur dicitur esse commissum.

16 In quarta constitutione, quam translativam nominamus, eius constitutionis est controversia, cum aut
quem aut quicum aut quomodo aut apud quos aut
quo iure aut quo tempore agere oporteat quaeritur
aut omnino aliquid de commutatione aut infirmatione
actionis agitur. Huius constitutionis Hermagoras
inventor esse existimatur, non quo non usi sint ea
veteres oratores saepe multi, sed quia non animad-
verterunt artis scriptores eam superiores nec rettulerunt in numerum constitutionum. Post autem ab hoc
inventam multi reprehenderunt, quos non tam imprudentia falli putamus (res enim perspicua est) quam
invidia atque obtrectatione quadam impediri.

XII. Et constitutiones quidem et earum partes
exposuimus; exempla autem cuiusque generis tum
commodius expositori videamur cum in unum
quodque eorum argumentorum copiam dabimus.
Nam argumentandi ratio dilucidior erit cum et ad
genus et ad exemplum causae statim poterit
accommodari.

---

[a] *I.e.* the case of an official accused of nonfeasance, where
the defence is that the failure to perform the act was due to
the negligence of another official.

[b] In *Auct. ad Her.* I, 25, this is stated as a case where
the defendant claims that he chose the lesser of two evils.

power and authority of another; the deed is transferred when it is alleged that another should have
done it or could have done it.[a] The retort of the
charge is used when the defendant claims that the
deed was done lawfully because some one had first
illegally provoked him. Comparison is used when
it is argued that some other action was lawful and
advantageous, and then it is pleaded that the mis-
demeanour which is charged was committed in order
to make possible this advantageous act.[b]

16 In the fourth issue which we call the translative
there is a controversy when the question arises as
to who ought to bring the action or against whom,
or in what manner or before what court or under
what law or at what time, and in general when there
is some argument about changing or invalidating the
form of procedure. Hermagoras is thought to be
the inventor of this issue, not that orators did
not use it before his day—many did use it frequently
—but because earlier writers of text-books did not
notice it nor include it with the issues. Since his
invention of the term many have found fault with
it, not misled by ignorance, I think, for the case
is perfectly plain, so much as they have been kept
from adopting it by a spirit of envy and a desire to
disparage a rival.

XII. We have explained the issues and their
divisions, but it would seem that we can give instances
of each kind more conveniently when we give a store
of arguments for each of them, for the principles of
argumentation will be plainer if they can be applied
immediately both to the general classification and to
the particular instance.[c]

c This is done in Book II.

17 Constitutione causae reperta statim placet considerare utrum causa sit simplex an iuncta; et si iuncta erit, utrum sit ex pluribus quaestionibus iuncta an ex aliqua comparatione. Simplex est quae absolutam in se continet unam quaestionem, hoc modo: " Corinthiis bellum indicamus an non ? " Coniuncta, ex pluribus quaestionibus in qua plura quaeruntur, hoc pacto: " Utrum Karthago diruatur an Karthaginiensibus reddatur an eo colonia deducatur." Ex comparatione, in qua per contentionem, utrum potius aut quid potissimum sit quaeritur, ad hunc modum: " Utrum exercitus in Macedoniam contra Philippum mittatur qui sociis sit auxilio, an teneatur in Italia ut quam maximae contra Hannibalem copiae sint."

Deinde considerandum est, in ratione an in scripto sit controversia. Nam scripti controversia est ea quae ex scriptionis genere nascitur. XIII. Eius autem genera, quae separata sunt a constitutionibus, quinque sunt. Nam tum verba ipsa videntur cum sententia scriptoris dissidere, tum inter se duae leges aut plures discrepare, tum id quod scriptum est duas aut plures res significare; tum ex eo quod scriptum est aliud quod non scriptum est inveniri; tum vis verbi quasi in definitiva constitutione, in quo posita sit, quaeri. Quare primum genus de scripto et sententia, secundum ex contrariis legibus, tertium ambiguum, quartum ratiocinativum, quintum definiti-

---

[a] Or, reasoning, inference. For a definition v. II, 148.

17 When the issue in the case has been determined, it is well to consider whether the case is simple or complex, and if complex, whether it involves several questions or a comparison. A simple case is one which contains in itself one plain question, such as " Shall we declare war on Corinth or not ? " A complex case is made up of several questions ; in which several inquiries are made, such as : " Should Carthage be destroyed, or handed back to the Carthaginians, or should a colony be established there ? " The case involves comparison when various actions are contrasted and the question is which one is more desirable or which is most desirable to perform, in this fashion : " Should an army be sent to Macedonia against Philip to support our allies, or should it be kept in Italy so that the greatest possible force may oppose Hannibal ? "

In the second place one must consider whether the dispute turns on general reasoning or on written documents. For a dispute about a document is one which arises from the nature of a written document. XIII. Of this there are five kinds, which are separate from the " issues." In one case it seems that there is a variance between the actual words and the intent of the author ; in another, that two or more laws disagree ; again, that what is written has two or more meanings ; again, that from what has been written something is discovered which has not been written ; finally, that there is a question about the meaning of a word, *i.e.*, on what the meaning depends, as if it were in the definitional issue. Therefore the first class is said to be concerned with the letter and the intent, the second with the conflict of laws, the third with ambiguity, the fourth with reasoning by analogy,[a]

18 vum nominamus. Ratio est autem, cum omnis quaestio non in scriptione, sed in aliqua argumentatione consistit.

Ac tum, considerato genere causae,[1] cum simplexne an iuncta sit intellexeris et scripti an rationis habeat controversiam videris, deinceps erit videndum, quae quaestio, quae ratio, quae iudicatio, quod firmamentum causae sit; quae omnia a constitutione proficiscantur oportet. Quaestio est ea quae ex conflictione causarum gignitur controversia, hoc modo: " Non iure fecisti." " Iure feci." Causarum autem est conflictio in qua constitutio constat. Ex ea igitur nascitur controversia quam quaestionem dicimus haec: " Iurene fecerit? " Ratio est ea quae continet causam, quae si sublata sit, nihil in causa controversiae relinquatur, hoc modo, ut docendi causa in facili et pervulgato exemplo consistamus: Orestes si accusetur matricidi, nisi hoc dicat " Iure feci, illa enim patrem meum occiderat," non habet defensionem. Qua ratione sublata omnis controversia quoque sublata sit. Ergo eius causae ratio est, quod illa Agamemnonem occiderit. Iudicatio est quae ex infirmatione et confirmatione[2] rationis nascitur controversia. Nam sit ea nobis exposita ratio quam paulo ante exposuimus: " Illa

---

[1] *After* causae *the MSS. have* cognita constitutione (*having determined the issue*).

[2] et confirmatione *omitted by* P[1]: *bracketed by Kayser and Ströbel.*

18 and the fifth with definition. There is a case of general reasoning on the other hand when the whole question turns, not on a written document, but on some logical proof.

And then, after considering the nature of the case, when you have found out whether it is simple or complex, and you have seen whether it discusses a written document or involves general reasoning, then you must see what the question in the case is (*quaestio*), and the excuse or reason (*ratio*), the point for the judge's decision (*iudicatio*) and the foundation or supporting argument (*firmamentum*). All of these should develop out of the determination of the issue. The question (*quaestio*) is the subject of debate which arises from the conflict of pleas, in this way: " You were not justified in doing it." " I was justified in doing it." It is the conflict of pleas, moreover, which determines the issue. From this then comes the subject of debate which we call the question (*quaestio*), as follows: " Was he justified in doing it ? " The reason or excuse is that which holds the case together: if this were taken away there would be no debate left about the case. For instance, to make my meaning clear, let me dwell on a simple and well-known example: If Orestes be accused of murdering his mother, unless he say, " I was justified; for she had killed my father," he has no defence. If this excuse were taken away, the whole debate would be taken away, too. Therefore the excuse in this case is that she killed Agamemnon. The point for the judge's decision (*iudicatio*) is that which arises from the denial and assertion of the reason or excuse. Suppose, for example, that the excuse has been set up which we mentioned a little while ago. " For she," he says,

enim meum,"inquit, "patrem occiderat." "At non,"
inquiet adversarius, "abs te filio matrem necari
oportuit; potuit enim sine tuo scelere illius factum
puniri." XIV. Ex hac diductione rationis illa summa
nascitur controversia quam iudicationem appellamus.
Ea est huiusmodi: Rectumne fuerit ab Oreste
matrem occidi cum illa Orestis patrem occidisset.

19 Firmamentum est firmissima argumentatio defensoris
et appositissima ad iudicationem: ut si velit Orestes
dicere eiusmodi animum matris suae fuisse in patrem
suum, in se ipsum ac sorores, in regnum, in famam
generis et familiae, ut ab ea poenas liberi sui potissimum petere debuerint.

Et in ceteris quidem constitutionibus ad hunc
modum iudicationes reperiuntur; in coniecturali
autem constitutione, quia ratio non est (factum enim
non conceditur), non potest ex diductione rationis
nasci iudicatio. Quare necesse est eandem esse
quaestionem et iudicationem: factum est, non est
factum, factumne sit? Quot autem in causa constitutiones aut earum partes erunt, totidem necesse
erit quaestiones, rationes, iudicationes, firmamenta
reperiri.

Tum his omnibus in causa repertis denique singulae
partes totius causae considerandae sunt. Nam
non ut quidque dicendum primum est, ita primum
animadvertendum videtur; ideo quod illa quae prima

---

^a Nearly equal to *speech.*

" had killed my father." " But," the opponent will say, " your mother ought not to have been killed by you, her son; her act could have been punished without your committing a crime." XIV. From this narrowing or limitation of the excuse the chief dispute arises, which we call *iudicatio* or point for the judge's decision. It is as follows: " Was it right for Orestes to kill his mother because she had killed Orestes'
19 father? " The *foundation* is the strongest argument of the defence, and the one most relevant to the point for the judge's decision; for example, if Orestes should choose to say that his mother had shown such disposition towards his father, himself, and his sisters, the kingdom, the good name of the clan and household that her own children were of all people in the world most bound to exact the penalty from her.

In all the other issues the points for the judge's decision are found in this way; but in the conjectural issue, because there is no excuse alleged in defence—for the defendant does not admit that he did the deed—the point for the judge's decision cannot arise from the narrowing of the excuse. Therefore in that case the question and the point for the judge's decision must be the same: "It was done;" " It was not done." " Was it done? " Moreover it will be necessary to find the same number of questions, excuses, points for the judge's decision and foundations as there are issues or parts of issues in the case.

Then, after all these points about the case have been discovered, the separate divisions of the whole case [a] must be considered. For it does not follow that everything which is to be said first must be studied first; for the reason that, if you wish the first part of

dicuntur, si vehementer velis congruere et cohaerere cum causa, ex eis ducas oportet quae post dicenda sunt. Quare cum iudicatio et ea quae ad iudicationem oportet argumenta inveniri diligenter erunt artificio reperta, cura et cogitatione pertractata, tum denique ordinandae sunt ceterae partes orationis. Eae partes sex esse omnino nobis videntur: exordium, narratio, partitio, confirmatio, reprehensio, conclusio.

Nunc quoniam exordium princeps debet esse, nos quoque primum in rationem exordiendi praecepta
20 dabimus. XV. Exordium est oratio animum auditoris idonee comparans ad reliquam dictionem; quod eveniet si eum benivolum, attentum, docilem confecerit. Quare qui bene exordiri causam volet eum necesse est genus suae causae diligenter ante cognoscere. Genera causarum quinque sunt: honestum, admirabile, humile, anceps, obscurum. Honestum causae genus est cui statim sine oratione nostra favet auditoris animus; admirabile, a quo est alienatus animus eorum qui audituri sunt; humile, quod neglegitur ab auditore et non magnopere attendendum videtur; anceps, in quo aut iudicatio dubia est aut causa et honestatis et turpitudinis particeps, ut et benivolentiam pariat et offensionem; obscurum, in quo aut tardi auditores sunt aut difficilioribus ad

---

^a Or, ready to receive instruction.
^b *Admirabilis*, here translated " difficult," is equivalent to the Greek παράδοξος, " marvellous," apparently from the point of view of the juror, who thinks it strange that anyone should speak in behalf of such a defendant. It is therefore a " difficult " case to present.

the speech to have a close agreement and connexion
with the main statement of the case, you must
derive it from the matters which are to be discussed
afterward. Therefore when the point for decision
and the arguments which must be devised for the
purpose of reaching a decision have been diligently
discovered by the rules of art, and studied with
careful thought, then, and not till then, the other
parts of the oration are to be arranged in proper order.
These seem to me to be just six in number : exordium,
narrative, partition, confirmation, refutation, peroration.

Now since the exordium has to come first, we shall
likewise give first the rule for a systematic treatment
20 of the exordium. XV. An exordium is a passage
which brings the mind of the auditor into a proper
condition to receive the rest of the speech. This
will be accomplished if he becomes well-disposed,
attentive, and receptive.[a] Therefore one who wishes
his speech to have a good exordium must make a
careful study beforehand of the kind of case which he
has to present. There are five kinds of cases :
honourable, difficult,[b] mean, ambiguous, obscure.
An honourable case is one which wins favour in the
mind of the auditor at once without any speech of
ours : the difficult is one which has alienated the
sympathy of those who are about to listen to the
speech. The mean is one which the auditor makes
light of and thinks unworthy of serious attention ;
the ambiguous is one in which the point for decision
is doubtful, or the case is partly honourable and
partly discreditable so that it engenders both good-
will and ill-will ; the obscure case is one in which
either the auditors are slow of wit, or the case

cognoscendum negotiis causa est implicata. Quare
cum tam diversa sint genera causarum, exordiri
quoque dispari ratione in uno quoque genere necesse
est. Igitur exordium in duas partes dividitur,
principium et insinuationem. Principium est oratio
perspicue et protinus perficiens auditorem benivolum
aut docilem aut attentum. Insinuatio est oratio
quadam dissimulatione et circumitione obscure
subiens auditoris animum.

21   In admirabili genere causae, si non omnino infesti
auditores erunt, principio benivolentiam comparare
licebit. Sin erunt vehementer abalienati, confugere
necesse erit ad insinuationem. Nam ab iratis si
perspicue pax et benivolentia petitur, non modo ea
non invenitur, sed augetur atque inflammatur odium.
In humili autem genere causae contemptionis tollen-
dae causa necesse est attentum efficere auditorem.
Anceps genus causae si dubiam iudicationem habebit,
ab ipsa iudicatione exordiendum est. Sin autem
partem turpitudinis, partem honestatis habebit,
benivolentiam captare oportebit, ut in genus honestum
causa translata videatur. Cum autem erit honestum
causae genus, vel praeteriri principium poterit vel, si
commodum fuerit, aut a narratione incipiemus aut a
lege aut ab aliqua firmissima ratione nostrae dictionis;
sin uti principio placebit, benivolentiae partibus
utendum est, ut id quod est augeatur. XVI. In

involves matters which are rather difficult to grasp. Hence, since the kinds of cases are so diverse, it is necessary to construct the exordium on a different plan in each kind of case. The exordium is, then, divided into two species, *introduction* and *insinuation*. An introduction is an address which directly and in plain language makes the auditor well-disposed, receptive, and attentive. Insinuation is an address which by dissimulation and indirection unobtrusively steals into the mind of the auditor.

21   In the difficult case, if the auditors are not completely hostile, it will be permissible to try to win their good-will by an introduction; if they are violently opposed it will be necessary to have recourse to the insinuation. For if amity and good-will are sought from auditors who are in a rage, not only is the desired result not obtained, but their hatred is increased and fanned into a flame. In the mean case, on the other hand, it is necessary to make the audience attentive in order to remove their disdain. If an ambiguous case has a doubtful point for the judge's decision, the exordium must begin with a discussion of this very point. But if the case is partly honourable and partly discreditable, it will be proper to try to win good-will so that the case may seem to be transferred to the honourable class. When, however, the case is really in the honourable class, it will be possible either to pass over the introduction or, if it is convenient, we shall begin with the narrative or with a law or some very strong argument which supports our plea: if, on the contrary, it is desirable to use the introduction, we must use the topics designed to produce good-will, that the advantage which already exists may be increased. XVI. In a case of the

obscuro causae genere per principium dociles auditores efficere oportebit.

Nunc quoniam quas res exordio conficere oporteat dictum est, reliquum est ut ostendatur quibus quaeque rationibus res confici possit.

22 Benivolentia quattuor ex locis comparatur: ab nostra, ab adversariorum, ab iudicum persona, a causa. Ab nostra, si de nostris factis et officiis sine arrogantia dicemus; si crimina illata et aliquas minus honestas suspiciones iniectas diluemus; si, quae incommoda acciderint aut quae instent difficultates, proferemus; si prece et obsecratione humili ac supplici utemur. Ab adversariorum autem, si eos aut in odium aut in invidiam aut in contemptionem adducemus. In odium ducentur si quod eorum spurce, superbe, crudeliter, malitiose factum proferetur; in invidiam, si vis eorum, potentia, divitiae, cognatio,[1] proferentur atque eorum usus arrogans et intolerabilis, ut his rebus magis videantur quam causae suae confidere; in contemptionem adducentur si eorum inertia, neglegentia, ignavia, desidiosum studium et luxuriosum otium proferetur. Ab auditorum persona benivolentia captabitur si res ab eis fortiter, sapienter, mansuete gestae proferentur, ut ne qua assentatio nimia significetur, si de eis quam honesta existimatio

---

[1] *After* cognatio *the MSS. read* pecuniae (*money*); *bracketed by Ströbel.*

obscure kind the introduction must be used to make the audience receptive.

Now that it has been stated what results the orator ought to accomplish by the exordium, it remains to show by what means each result can be obtained.

22 Good-will is to be had from four quarters: from our own person, from the person of the opponents, from the persons of the jury, and from the case itself. We shall win good-will from our own person if we refer to our own acts and services without arrogance; if we weaken the effect of charges that have been preferred, or of some suspicion of less honourable dealing which has been cast upon us; if we dilate on the misfortunes which have befallen us or the difficulties which still beset us; if we use prayers and entreaties with a humble and submissive spirit. Good-will is acquired from the person of the opponents if we can bring them into hatred, unpopularity, or contempt. They will be hated if some act of theirs is presented which is base, haughty, cruel, or malicious; they will become unpopular if we present their power, political influence, wealth, family connexions, and their arrogant and intolerable use of these advantages, so that they seem to rely on these rather than on the justice of their case. They will be brought into contempt if we reveal their laziness, carelessness, sloth, indolent pursuits or luxurious idleness. Good-will will be sought from the persons of the auditors if an account is given of acts which they have performed with courage, wisdom, and mercy, but so as not to show excessive flattery: and if it is shown in what honourable esteem they are held and how eagerly their

quantaque eorum iudici et auctoritatis exspectatio sit
ostendetur; ab rebus, si nostram causam laudando
extollemus, adversariorum causam per contemptionem deprimemus.

23 Attentos autem faciemus si demonstrabimus ea
quae dicturi erimus magna, nova, incredibilia esse,
aut ad omnes aut ad eos qui audient, aut ad aliquos
illustres homines aut ad deos immortales aut ad
summam rem publicam pertinere; et si pollicebimur
nos brevi nostram causam demonstraturos atque
exponemus iudicationem aut iudicationes si plures
erunt. Dociles auditores faciemus si aperte et
breviter summam causae exponemus, hoc est, in quo
consistat controversia. Nam et, cum docilem velis
facere, simul attentum facias oportet. Nam is est
maxime docilis qui attentissime est paratus audire.

XVII. Nunc insinuationes quemadmodum tractari
conveniat, deinceps dicendum videtur. Insinuatione
igitur utendum est cum admirabile genus causae est,
hoc est, ut ante diximus, cum animus auditoris infestus
est. Id autem tribus ex causis fit maxime: si aut
inest in ipsa causa quaedam turpitudo aut ab eis qui
ante dixerunt iam quiddam auditori persuasum
videtur aut eo tempore locus dicendi datur cum iam
illi quos audire oportet defessi sunt audiendo. Nam
ex hac quoque re non minus quam ex primis duabus
in oratore nonnunquam animus auditoris offenditur.

---

^a Perhaps Cicero is mistaken in bringing in this definition.
The statement of the *issue* properly belongs in the Partition,
and Cicero or his teacher mistook the words of Hermagoras.
By *summam causae* must have been meant originally a brief
outline of the case, not a statement of the exact issue. *v.*
Peters, *De rationibus inter artem rhetoricam quarti et primi
saeculi intercedentibus*, p. 32.

^b The heading " receptive " seems hardly necessary, as it

judgement and opinion are awaited. Good-will may come from the circumstances themselves if we praise and exalt our own case, and depreciate our opponent's with contemptuous allusions.

23   We shall make our audience attentive if we show that the matters which we are about to discuss are important, novel, or incredible, or that they concern all humanity or those in the audience or some illustrious men or the immortal gods or the general interest of the state; also if we promise to prove our own case briefly and explain the point to be decided or the several points if there are to be more than one. We shall make the auditors receptive if we explain the essence of the case briefly and in plain language, that is, the point on which the controversy turns.[a] For when you wish to make an auditor receptive, you should also at the same time render him attentive. For he is most receptive who is prepared to listen most attentively.[b]

XVII. Now I think that we should discuss secondly the proper method of handling insinuations. The insinuation, then, is to be used when the case is difficult, that is, as I said above, when the spirit of the audience is hostile. This hostility arises principally from three causes: if there is something scandalous in the case, or if those who have spoken first seem to have convinced the auditor on some point, or if the chance to speak comes at a time when those who ought to listen have been wearied by listening. For sometimes the mind of the auditor takes offence at an orator no less from this last

can be included under "attentive." Anaximenes' division seems better—the exordium should *instruct* the audience and make them *well-disposed* and *attentive*.

24 Si causae turpitudo contrahit offensionem aut pro eo
homine in quo offenditur alium hominem qui diligitur
interponi oportet; aut pro re in qua offenditur,
aliam rem quae probatur; aut pro re hominem aut
pro homine rem, ut ab eo quod odit ad id quod diligit
auditoris animus traducatur; et dissimulare te id
defensurum quod existimeris; deinde, cum iam
mitior factus erit auditor, ingredi pedetemptim in
defensionem et dicere ea quae indignentur adversarii tibi quoque indigna videri: deinde, cum lenieris
eum qui audiet, demonstrare nihil eorum ad te
pertinere et negare quicquam de adversariis esse
dicturum, neque hoc neque illud, ut neque aperte
laedas eos qui diliguntur, et tamen id obscure faciens,
quoad possis, alienes ab eis auditorum voluntatem; et
aliquorum iudicium simili de re aut auctoritatem
proferre imitatione dignam; deinde eandem aut
consimilem aut maiorem aut minorem agi rem in
praesenti demonstrare.

25 Sin oratio adversariorum fidem videbitur auditori-
bus fecisse—id quod ei qui intelliget quibus rebus
fides fiat facile erit cognitu—oportet aut de eo quod
adversarii firmissimum sibi putarint et maxime ei qui
audient probarint, primum te dicturum polliceri, aut
ab adversari dicto exordiri et ab eo potissimum quod
ille nuperrime dixerit, aut dubitatione uti quid

24 cause than from the first two. If the scandalous nature of the case occasions offence, it is necessary to substitute for the person at whom offence is taken another who is favoured, or for a thing at which offence is taken, another which is approved, or a person for a thing or a thing for a person, in order that the attention of the auditor may be shifted from what he hates to what he favours. Also, you must conceal your intention of defending the point which you are expected to defend. After that, when the audience has now become more tractable, approach the defence little by little and say that the things which displease your opponents are also displeasing to you. Next, after pacifying the audience, show that none of these charges apply to you and assert that you will say nothing about your opponents, neither this nor that, so as not openly to attack those who are favoured, and yet, by working imperceptibly, as far as possible to win the good-will of the audience away from your opponents. Also you may offer a decision or opinion of some authorities in a similar case as worthy of imitation; then show that in the present case the same question is to be decided, or one like it or one of greater or less importance.

25 On the other hand, if the speeches of your opponents seem to have won conviction among the audience —a result which will easily be apprehended by one who knows the means by which conviction is won—it behoves you to promise to discuss first the argument which the opponents thought was their strongest and which the audience have especially approved. Or you may begin by a reference to what has been said by your opponent, preferably to something that he has said recently. Or you may express doubt as

primum dicas aut cui potissimum loco respondeas,
cum admiratione. Nam auditor cum eum quem
adversarii perturbatum putavit oratione videt animo
firmissimo contra dicere paratum, plerumque se
potius temere assensisse quam illum sine causa
confidere arbitratur. Sin auditoris studium defati-
gatio abalienavit a causa, te brevius quam paratus
fueris esse dicturum commodum est polliceri; non
imitaturum adversarium.

Sin res dabit, non inutile est ab aliqua re nova aut
ridicula incipere aut ex tempore quae nata sit, quod
genus strepitu acclamatione; aut iam parata, quae
vel apologum vel fabulam vel aliquam contineat
irrisionem; aut si rei dignitas adimet iocandi facultatem, aliquid triste, novum, horribile statim non
incommodum est inicere. Nam, ut cibi satietas et
fastidium aut subamara aliqua re relevatur aut dulci
mitigatur, sic animus defessus audiendo aut admiratione integratur aut risu novatur.

XVIII. Ac separatim quidem quae de principio et
de insinuatione dicenda videbantur haec fere sunt;
nunc quidem brevi communiter de utroque praecipiendum videtur.

Exordium sententiarum et gravitatis plurimum
debet habere et omnino omnia quae pertinent ad

to what to say first, or which passage to answer before all others, at the same time showing perplexity and astonishment. For when the audience see that he whom they think is shaken by the opponent's speech is ready to speak in reply with confidence and assurance, they generally think that they have assented too readily rather than that he is confident without good cause. If, in the third place, weariness has alienated the sympathy of the auditor from your case, it is a help to promise that you will speak more briefly than you were prepared to speak; that you will not imitate your opponent.

If the case permits, it is not unprofitable to begin with some new topic, or a jest, either one which is extemporaneous—a kind which meets with uproarious applause and shouts of approval—or one already prepared containing a fable, or a story, or some laughable incident. Or, if the seriousness of the occasion denies an opportunity for a jest, it is not disadvantageous to insert something appalling, unheard of, or terrible at the very beginning. For, just as a loathing and distaste for food is relieved by some morsel with a bit of a tang, or appeased by a sweet, so a mind wearied by listening is strengthened by astonishment or refreshed by laughter.

XVIII. This is about all that it seemed necessary to say concerning the introduction and the insinuation separately: now it seems desirable to state some brief rules which will apply to both alike.

The *exordium* ought to be sententious to a marked degree and of a high seriousness, and, to put it generally, should contain everything which con-

dignitatem in se continere, propterea quod id optime faciendum est quod oratorem auditori maxime commendat; splendoris et festivitatis et concinnitudinis minimum, propterea quod ex his suspicio quaedam apparationis atque artificiosae diligentiae nascitur, quae maxime orationi fidem, oratori adimit auctoritatem.

26 Vitia vero haec sunt certissima exordiorum quae summopere vitare oportebit: vulgare, commune, commutabile, longum, separatum, translatum, contra praecepta. Vulgare est quod in plures causas potest accommodari, ut convenire videatur. Commune, quod nihilo minus in hanc, quam in contrariam partem causae, potest convenire. Commutabile, quod ab adversario potest leviter mutatum ex contraria parte dici. Longum est quod pluribus verbis aut sententiis ultra quam satis est producitur. Separatum, quod non ex ipsa causa ductum est nec sicut aliquod membrum annexum orationi. Translatum est quod aliud conficit quam causae genus postulat: ut si qui docilem faciat auditorem, cum benivolentiam causa desideret, aut si principio utatur, cum insinuationem res postulet. Contra praecepta est quod nihil eorum efficit quorum causa de exordiis praecepta traduntur; hoc est, quod eum qui audit neque benivolum neque attentum neque docilem efficit, aut, quo nihil profecto peius est, ut contra sit, facit. Ac de exordio quidem satis dictum est.

tributes to dignity, because the best thing to do is that which especially commends the speaker to his audience. It should contain very little brilliance, vivacity, or finish of style, because these give rise to a suspicion of preparation and excessive ingenuity. As a result of this most of all the speech loses conviction and the speaker, authority.

26   The following are surely the most obvious faults of *exordia*, which are by all means to be avoided: it should not be general, common, interchangeable, tedious, unconnected, out of place, or contrary to the fundamental principles. A *general* exordium is one which can be tacked to many cases, so as to seem to suit them all. A *common* exordium is one equally applicable to both sides of the case. The *interchangeable* can with slight changes be used by the opponent in a speech on the other side. The *tedious* exordium is one which is spun out beyond all need with a superabundance of words or ideas. The *unconnected* is one which is not derived from the circumstances of the case nor closely knit with the rest of the speech, as a limb to a body. It is *out of place* if it produces a result different from what the nature of the case requires: for example, if it makes the audience receptive when the case calls for goodwill, or uses an introduction when the situation demands an insinuation. It is contrary to fundamental principles when it achieves none of the purposes for which rules are given about exordia, that is, when it renders the audience neither well-disposed, nor attentive, nor receptive, or produces the opposite result; and nothing surely can be worse than that. This is enough to say about the exordium.

CICERO

27   XIX. Narratio est rerum gestarum aut ut gestarum expositio. Narrationum genera tria sunt: unum genus est in quo ipsa causa et omnis ratio controversiae continetur; alterum, in quo digressio aliqua extra causam aut criminationis aut similitudinis aut delectationis non alienae ab eo negotio quo de agitur aut amplificationis causa interponitur. Tertium genus est remotum a civilibus causis quod delectationis causa non inutili cum exercitatione dicitur et scribitur. Eius partes sunt duae, quarum altera in negotiis, altera in personis maxime versatur. Ea quae in negotiorum expositione posita est tres habet partes: fabulam, historiam, argumentum. Fabula est in qua nec verae nec veri similes res continentur, cuiusmodi est:

   Angues ingentes alites, iuncti iugo . . .

Historia est gesta res, ab aetatis nostrae memoria remota; quod genus:

   Appius indixit Karthaginiensibus bellum.

Argumentum est ficta res, quae tamen fieri potuit. Huiusmodi apud Terentium:

   Nam is postquam excessit ex ephebis . . .

Illa autem narratio quae versatur in personis eiusmodi

ᵃ Pacuvius frg. 397 R². ROL ii, p. 254 line 242.

27 XIX. The *narrative* is an exposition of events that
have occurred or are supposed to have occurred.
There are three kinds : one which contains just the
case and the whole reason for the dispute ; a second
in which a digression is made beyond the strict limits
of the case for the purpose of attacking somebody, or
of making a comparison, or of amusing the audience
in a way not incongruous with the business in hand,
or for amplification. The third kind is wholly
unconnected with public issues, which is recited or
written solely for amusement but at the same time
provides valuable training. It is subdivided into
two classes : one concerned with events, the other
principally with persons. That which consists of an
exposition of events has three forms : *fabula, historia,
argumentum. Fabula* is the term applied to a narrative
in which the events are not true and have no verisimilitude, for example :

" Huge winged dragons yoked to a car." [a]

Historia is an account of actual occurrences remote
from the recollection of·our own age, as :

" War on men of Carthage Appius decreed." [b]

Argumentum is a fictitious narrative which nevertheless
could have occurred. An example may be quoted
from Terence : [c]

" For after he had left the school of youth."

But the form of narrative which is concerned with
persons is of such a sort that in it can be seen not only

---

[b] Ennius, *Annals*, vii, 223 V³.   ROL i, p. 86, line 238.
[c] *Andria*, 51.

est, ut in ea simul cum rebus ipsis personarum sermones et animi perspici possint, hoc modo :

Venit ad me saepe clamans [1] : Quid agis, Micio?
Cur perdis adulescentem nobis? cur amat?
Cur potat? cur tu his rebus sumptum suggeris?
Vestitu nimio indulges, nimium ineptus es.
Nimium ipse est durus praeter aequumque et bonum.

Hoc in genere narrationis multa debet inesse festivitas confecta ex rerum varietate, animorum dissimilitudine, gravitate, lenitate, spe, metu, suspicione, desiderio, dissimulatione, errore, misericordia, fortunae commutatione, insperato incommodo, subita laetitia, iucundo exitu rerum. Verum haec ex eis quae postea de elocutione praecipientur ornamenta sumentur.

28   XX. Nunc de narratione ea quae causae continet expositionem dicendum videtur. Oportet igitur eam tres habere res : ut brevis, ut aperta, ut probabilis sit. Brevis erit, si unde necesse est inde initium sumetur et non ab ultimo repetetur, et si, cuius rei satis erit summam dixisse, eius partes non dicentur—nam saepe satis est quid factum sit dicere, ut ne narres quemadmodum sit factum—et si non longius, quam quo opus est, in narrando procedetur, et si nullam in rem

---

[1] clamans *Bentley*: clamitans *C*.

a Terence, *Adelphoe*, 60–64. Tr. by Sargeaunt, LCL.
b Or, from a variety of materials, *i.e.* . . . But compare *ad Her.* I, 13.
c The last form of narrative is illustrated by a quotation from comedy, but may also be found in other genres, the mime, some types of elegy, and romance. The writing of such exercises in character drawing (prosopopoeiae) formed

events but also the conversation and mental attitude of the characters. For example : " He comes to me perpetually, crying, ' What are you about, Micio ? Why are you bringing the boy to ruin on our hands ? Why this licence ? Why these drinking parties ? Why do you pile him up the guineas for such a life and let him spend so much at the tailor's ? It's extremely silly of you.' He himself is extremely hard, past right and sense." [a] This form of narrative should possess great vivacity, resulting from fluctuations of fortune,[b] contrast of characters, severity, gentleness, hope, fear, suspicion, desire, dissimulation, delusion, pity, sudden change of fortune, unexpected disaster, sudden pleasure, a happy ending to the story. But these embellishments will be drawn from what will be said later about the rules of style.[c]

28   XX. Now it seems necessary to speak of that form of narrative which contains an exposition of a case at law. It ought to possess three qualities : it should be brief, clear, and plausible. It will be brief if it begins with what needs to be said, and is not carried back to the most remote events ; if it does not include details when it is sufficient to have stated the substance of the story—for often it is sufficient to say what happened, so that you do not need to tell how it happened—and if the narrative is not carried farther than is needed, and if it does not digress to

part of the preliminary training in composition, useful alike to orator and poet. (For a different interpretation of this puzzling and oft discussed passage, v. Barwick, K., Die Gliederung der Narratio und seine Bedeutung, *Hermes* lxiii (1928), pp. 261–287.) Cf. also Pfister, F., Isokrates und die spätere Gliederung der Narratio, *Hermes* lxviii (1933), pp. 457–460.

aliam transibitur; et si ita dicetur, ut nonnunquam
ex eo quod dictum est id quod non est dictum
intellegatur; et si non modo id quod obest verum
etiam id quod nec obest nec adiuvat praeteribitur;
et si semel unum quidque dicetur; et si non ab eo
quo in proxime desitum erit deinceps incipietur. Ac
multos imitatio brevitatis decipit, ut, cum se breves
putent esse, longissimi sint; cum dent operam ut res
multas brevi dicant, non ut omnino paucas res dicant
et non plures quam necesse sit. Nam plerisque
breviter videtur dicere qui ita dicit: "Accessi ad
aedes. Puerum vocavi. Respondit. Quaesivi domi-
num. Domi negavit esse." Hic, tametsi tot res
brevius non potuit dicere, tamen quia satis fuit
dixisse: "Domi negavit esse," fit rerum multitudine
longus. Quare hoc quoque in genere vitanda est
brevitatis imitatio et non minus rerum non necessaria-
rum quam verborum multitudine supersedendum est.

29　　Aperta autem narratio poterit esse, si ut quidque
primum gestum erit ita primum exponetur, et rerum
ac temporum ordo servabitur, ut ita narrentur ut
gestae res erunt aut ut potuisse geri videbuntur. Hic
erit considerandum ne quid perturbate, ne quid
contorte dicatur, ne quam in aliam rem transeatur, ne
ab ultimo repetatur, ne ad extremum prodeatur, ne
quid quod ad rem pertineat praetereatur; et omnino
quae praecepta de brevitate sunt hoc quoque in genere
sunt conservanda. Nam saepe res parum est intellecta

another story. Brevity may be gained if the story is told in such a way that at times something which has not been mentioned can be gathered from what has been said; also if not only what is prejudicial is omitted but also what is neither prejudicial nor helpful; and if each thing is mentioned once and once only, and if it does not begin all over again at the point at which it has just stopped. Many are deceived by an appearance of brevity so that they are prolix when they think they are brief. This occurs when they try to say many things in a brief compass, rather than saying very few or not more than is necessary. Many, for example, think that one is speaking briefly who speaks as follows: " I went to his house, I called the slave. He answered. I asked for his master. He said that he was not at home." Here, although so many things could not be said more briefly, still because it was sufficient to say, " He said he was not at home," it is made too long by the abundance of details. Therefore in this section of the speech too, a false brevity is to be avoided, and one must refrain no less from an excess of superfluous facts than from an excess of words.

29   It will be possible to make the narrative clear if the events are presented one after another as they occurred, and the order of events in time is preserved so that the story is told as it will prove to have happened or will seem possible to have happened. On this point care must be taken not to say anything in a confused and intricate style, not to shift to another subject, not to go back to ultimate beginnings nor to go on too far, and not to omit anything pertinent to the case. In general the rules about brevity are to be followed in seeking clarity also. For often a case

longitudine magis quam obscuritate narrationis. Ac verbis quoque dilucidis utendum est; quo de genere dicendum est in praeceptis elocutionis.

XXI. Probabilis erit narratio, si in ea videbuntur inesse ea quae solent apparere in veritate; si personarum dignitates servabuntur; si causae factorum exstabunt; si fuisse facultates faciendi videbuntur; si tempus idoneum, si spati satis, si locus opportunus ad eandem rem qua de re narrabitur fuisse ostendetur; si res et ad eorum qui agent naturam et ad vulgi morem et ad eorum qui audient opinionem accommodabitur. Ac veri quidem similis ex his rationibus esse poterit.

30 Illud autem praeterea considerare oportebit, ne, aut cum obsit narratio aut cum nihil prosit, tamen interponatur; aut non loco aut non, quemadmodum causa postulet, narretur. Obest tum, cum ipsius rei gestae expositio magnam excipit offensionem quam argumentando et causam agendo leniri oportebit. Quod cum accidet, membratim oportebit partes rei gestae dispergere in causam et ad unam quamque confestim rationem accommodare, ut vulneri praesto medicamentum sit et odium statim defensio mitiget. Nihil prodest narratio tum, cum ab adversariis re exposita nostra nihil interest iterum aut alio modo narrare; aut ab eis qui audiunt ita tenetur negotium,

---

a *I.e.* a consul should be made to act and speak like a consul, not like a clown.

60

is misunderstood more from excessive length of the narrative than from obscurity. The diction must also be perspicuous; this topic must be discussed among the rules for style.

XXI. The narrative will be plausible if it seems to embody characteristics which are accustomed to appear in real life; if the proper qualities of the character are maintained,[a] if reasons for their actions are plain, if there seems to have been ability to do the deed, if it can be shown that the time was opportune, the space sufficient and the place suitable for the events about to be narrated; if the story fits in with the nature of the actors in it, the habits of ordinary people and the beliefs of the audience. Verisimilitude can be secured by following these principles.

30   In addition to observing these precepts, one must also be on guard not to insert a narrative when it will be a hindrance or of no advantage, and also not to have it out of place or in a manner other than that which the case requires. A narrative can be a hindrance when a presentation of the events alone and by themselves gives great offence, which it will be necessary to mitigate in arguing and pleading the case. When this situation arises, it will be necessary to distribute the narrative piecemeal throughout the speech and to add an explanation directly after each section so that the remedy may heal the wound and the defence may immediately lessen the animosity. A narrative is of no advantage when the facts have been explained by the opponents and it is of no importance to us to tell the story again or in a different way. The narrative is also useless when the audience has grasped the facts so thoroughly that it is of no advantage to us to instruct

ut nostra nihil intersit eos alio pacto docere. Quod
cum accidit, omnino narratione supersedendum est.
Non loco dicitur, cum non in ea parte orationis col-
locatur in qua res postulat; quo de genere agemus
tum, cum de dispositione dicemus; nam hoc ad
dispositionem pertinet. Non quemadmodum causa
postulat, narratur, cum aut id quod adversario prodest
dilucide et ornate exponitur aut id quod ipsum adiuvat
obscure dicitur et neglegenter. Quare, ut hoc
vitium vitetur, omnia torquenda sunt ad commodum
suae causae, contraria quae praeteriri poterunt
praetereundo, quae dicenda erunt leviter attingendo,
sua diligenter et enodate narrando.

Ac de narratione quidem satis dictum videtur;
deinceps ad partitionem transeamus.

31   XXII. Recte habita in causa partitio illustrem et
perspicuam totam efficit orationem. Partes eius sunt
duae, quarum utraque magno opere ad aperiendam
causam et constituendam pertinet controversiam.
Una pars est quae quid cum adversariis conveniat et
quid in controversia relinquatur ostendit; ex qua
certum quiddam destinatur auditori in quo animum
debeat habere occupatum. Altera est in qua rerum
earum de quibus erimus dicturi breviter expositio
ponitur distributa; ex qua conficitur ut certas animo
res teneat auditor, quibus dictis intellegat fore
peroratum.

Nunc utroque genere partitionis quemadmodum
conveniat uti, breviter dicendum videtur. Quae
partitio, quid conveniat aut quid non conveniat,
ostendit, haec debet illud quod convenit inclinare ad

them in a different fashion. In such a case one must dispense with narrative altogether. The narrative is out of place when it is not set in that part of the speech which the situation demands; this topic we shall take up when we discuss arrangement, for it affects the arrangement. The narrative is not presented in the manner required by the case when a point which helps the opponent is explained clearly and elegantly, or a point which helps the speaker is presented obscurely and carelessly. Therefore, to avoid this fault, the speaker must bend everything to the advantage of his case, by passing over all things that make against it which can be passed over, by touching lightly on what must be mentioned, and by telling his own side of the story carefully and clearly.

Sufficient has, I think, been said about narrative; let us now pass to the *partition*.

31 XXII. In an argument a partition correctly made renders the whole speech clear and perspicuous. It takes two forms, both of which greatly contribute to clarifying the case and determining the nature of the controversy. One form shows in what we agree with our opponents and what is left in dispute; as a result of this some definite problem is set for the auditor on which he ought to have his attention fixed. In the second form the matters which we intend to discuss are briefly set forth in a methodical way. This leads the auditor to hold definite points in his mind, and to understand that when these have been discussed the oration will be over.

Now I think I ought to present briefly the method of using each form of partition. A partition which shows what is agreed upon, and what is not, should turn the subject of agreement to the advantage of

suae causae commodum, hoc modo: " Interfectam
matrem esse a filio convenit mihi cum adversariis."
Item contra: " Interfectum esse a Clytaemestra
Agamemnonem convenit." Nam hic uterque et id
posuit quod conveniebat et tamen suae causae
commodo consuluit. Deinde quid controversiae sit
ponendum est in iudicationis expositione; quae
quemadmodum inveniretur ante dictum est.

32   Quae partitio rerum distributam continet expositionem, haec habere debet: brevitatem, absolu-
tionem, paucitatem. Brevitas est, cum nisi necessarium nullum assumitur verbum. Haec in hoc
genere idcirco est utilis quod rebus ipsis et partibus
causae, non verbis neque extraneis ornamentis
animus auditoris tenendus est. Absolutio est per
quam omnia quae incidunt in causam genera de
quibus dicendum est amplectimur in partitione, ne
aut aliquod genus utile relinquatur aut sero extra
partitionem, id quod vitiosissimum ac turpissimum
est, inferatur. Paucitas in partitione servatur, si
genera ipsa rerum ponuntur neque permixte cum
partibus implicantur. Nam genus est quod plures
partes amplectitur, ut animal. Pars est quae subest
generi, ut equus. Sed saepe eadem res alii genus,
alii pars est. Nam homo animalis pars est, Thebani
aut Troiani genus. XXIII. Haec ideo diligentius

---

[a] In *ad Her.* I, 17, where both examples are given, it is
made clearer that the first statement is made by Orestes'
prosecutor, the second by Orestes: " I agree with the
opponents that Orestes killed his mother: whether he was
justified in doing so is the question." " It is granted that
Agamemnon was killed by Clytemnestra: though this is so,
they say I ought not to have avenged my father."
[b] As is done in the passage from the *ad Her.* quoted in
note *a*.

the speaker's case, in the following manner: " I agree with my opponents that the mother was killed by her son." In the same way on the other side of the case, " It is agreed that Agamemnon was killed by Clytemnestra." [a] For here each speaker stated what was agreed upon, yet was mindful of the advantage of his own side of the case. Secondly, what is in controversy should be set forth in explaining the point for the judge's decision; [b] how this is discovered has been stated above.[c]

32 The form of partition which contains a methodical statement of topics to be discussed ought to have the following qualities: brevity, completeness, conciseness. Brevity is secured when no word is used unless necessary. It is useful in this place because the attention of the auditor should be attracted by the facts and topics of the case, and not by extraneous embellishments of style. Completeness is the quality by which we embrace in the partition all forms of argument which apply to the case, and about which we ought to speak, taking care that no useful argument be omitted or be introduced late as an addition to the plan of the speech, for this is faulty and unseemly in the highest degree. Conciseness in the partition is secured if only *genera* of things are given and they are not confused and mixed with their *species*. To explain: a *genus* is a class that embraces several *species*, as *animal*. A *species* is that which is a part of a *genus*, as *horse*. But often the same thing is a genus in relation to one thing and a species in relation to another. For example, man is a species of animal, but a genus of which Thebans or Trojans are species. XXIII. I have given this description with

[c] § 18.

inducitur discriptio, ut aperte intellecta [1] generum et
partium ratione paucitas generum in partitione
servari possit. Nam qui ita partitur: " Ostendam
propter cupiditatem et audaciam et avaritiam adversariorum omnia incommoda ad rem publicam per-
venisse," is non intellexit in partitione, exposito
genere, partem se generis admiscuisse. Nam genus
est omnium nimirum libidinum cupiditas: eius autem
33 generis sine dubio pars est avaritia. Hoc igitur
vitandum est, ne cuius genus posueris eius aliquam
sicuti diversam [2] ac dissimilem partem ponas in eadem
partitione. Quodsi quod in genus plures incident
partes, id cum in prima causae partitione erit simpliciter expositum, distribuetur tempore eo commodissime, cum ad ipsum ventum erit explicandum in
causae dictione post partitionem. Atque illud quoque
pertinet ad paucitatem, ne aut plura quam satis est
demonstraturos nos dicamus, hoc modo: " Ostendam
adversarios quod arguamus et potuisse facere et
voluisse et fecisse "; nam fecisse satis est ostendere:
aut, cum in causa partitio nulla sit,[3] cum simplex
quiddam agatur, tamen utamur distributione, id quod
perraro potest accidere.

Ac sunt alia quoque praecepta partitionum quae ad
hunc usum oratorium non tanto opere pertineant quae
versantur in philosophia ex quibus haec ipsa trans-
tulimus quae convenire viderentur quorum nihil in
ceteris artibus inveniebamus.

---

[1] aperte intellecta *C*: aperta *H*: aperta [intellecta]
Weidner, Ströbel.
[2] aliquam sicuti diversam *Schuetz*: sicuti aliquam diversam
P²Ri: secuti aliquam diversam *H¹P¹*: secum *H²S*: sicuti
eius * sicuti aliquam diversam *Ströbel.*
[3] *After* sit *the MSS. have* et. *Bracketed by Weidner.*

some care so that when the theory of classification is clearly understood, conciseness in dealing with classes may be secured in the partition. For one who divides his speech as follows: "I shall show that through the covetousness, audacity and avarice of my opponents all disasters have come upon the state," was not aware that in his partition he mentioned a genus and then combined it with a species of that genus. For covetousness or desire certainly is the genus of all appetites, and of this genus avarice is 33 without doubt a species. You should therefore be on your guard lest after mentioning a genus you mention a species of it in the same partition, as if it were different and dissimilar. But if a genus has several species, after stating it straightforwardly in the first partition, the division into species may be most conveniently made when one comes to explain that particular point in the course of the speech after the partition. It also contributes to conciseness not to say that we shall prove more than is necessary, as is done in the following example: "I shall show that my opponents were able to commit the crime with which we charge them, that they wished to, and that they did commit it;" for it would have been enough to prove that they did commit the crime; nor, when there is no partition in the case, because a single question is being debated (but this is a very rare occurrence), to use in spite of that fact a careful distribution.

There are other rules for the partition not so closely connected with oratorical practice; they are used in philosophy, and from them we have chosen the particular rules which seemed to apply and which we did not find in the other textbooks.

Atque his de partitione praeceptis in omni dictione meminisse oportebit, ut et prima quaeque pars, ut exposita est in partitione, sic ordine transigatur et omnibus explicatis peroratum sit,[1] ut ne quid posterius praeter conclusionem inferatur. Partitur apud Terentium breviter et commode senex in Andria quae cognoscere libertum velit:

> Eo pacto et gnati vitam et consilium meum
> Cognosces et quid facere in hac re te velim.

Itaque quemadmodum in partitione proposuit, ita narrat, primum nati vitam:

> Nam is postquam excessit ex ephebis . . .

Deinde suum consilium:

> Et nunc id operam do . . .

Deinde quid Sosiam velit facere, id quod postremum posuit in partitione, postremum dicit:

> Nunc tuum est officium . . .

Quemadmodum igitur hic et ad primam quamque partem primum accessit et omnibus absolutis finem dicendi fecit, sic nobis placet et ad singulas partes accedere et omnibus absolutis perorare.

Nunc de confirmatione deinceps, ita ut ordo ipse 34 postulat, praecipiendum videtur. XXIV. Confirmatio est per quam argumentando nostrae causae fidem et auctoritatem et firmamentum adiungit oratio. Huius partis certa sunt praecepta quae in singula causarum genera dividentur. Verumtamen

---

[1] *After* sit *the MSS. have* hoc modo. *Bracketed by Kayser.*

Now that the rules for partition have been stated, it is necessary to remind the orator that throughout the speech he should bear in mind to complete the sections in order one after another as they have been planned in the partition, and that after all have been dispatched he should bring the speech to a close so that nothing be introduced after the conclusion. The old man in the Andria of Terence makes a brief and neat partition of what he wishes his freedman to know: " In this way you will learn my son's manner of life, my plan, and what I wish you to do in the matter." And his narrative follows the plan laid down in the partition: first, his son's manner of life,

" For after he had left the school of youth . . ."

then his plan:

"And now I am anxious . . ."

then what he wishes Sosia to do, which was the last point in the partition, is stated last:

" Now your task is . . ."

Just as he turned his attention first to each point as it arose, and after dispatching them all stopped speaking, so I favour turning our attention to each topic and when all have been dispatched, winding up the speech.

Now it seems desirable to give in turn the rules about *confirmation* as is demanded by the regular 34 order of the speech. XXIV. Confirmation or proof is the part of the oration which by marshalling arguments lends credit, authority, and support to our case. For this section of the speech there are definite rules which will be divided among the different kinds of cases. But I think that it will

non incommodum videtur quandam silvam atque
materiam universam ante permixtim et confuse
exponere omnium argumentationum, post autem
tradere quemadmodum unum quodque causae genus
hinc omnibus argumentandi rationibus tractis confirmari oporteat.

Omnes res argumentando confirmantur aut ex eo
quod personis aut ex eo quod negotiis est attributum.
Ac personis has res attributas putamus: nomen,
naturam, victum, fortunam, habitum, affectionem,
studia, consilia, facta, casus, orationes.

Nomen est quod uni cuique personae datur quo
suo quaeque proprio et certo vocabulo appellatur.

Naturam ipsam definire difficile est; partes autem
eius enumerare eas quarum indigemus ad hanc
35 praeceptionem facilius est. Eae autem partim divino,
partim mortali in genere versantur. Mortalium
autem pars in hominum, pars in bestiarum genere
numerantur. Atque hominum genus et in sexu
consideratur, virile an muliebre sit, et in natione,
patria, cognatione, aetate. Natione, Graius an
barbarus; patria, Atheniensis an Lacedaemonius;
cognatione, quibus maioribus, quibus consanguineis;
aetate, puer an adulescens, natu grandior an senex.
Praeterea commoda et incommoda considerantur ab
natura data animo aut corpori, hoc modo: valens an
imbecillus, longus an brevis, formosus an deformis,
velox an tardus sit, acutus an hebetior, memor an

---

[a] Habit, as shown by the definitions given below (36, and
II, 30), means an *acquired* mental or physical constitution,
character, disposition, way of acting.

not be inconvenient to set forth in the beginning, without any attempt at order or arrangement, a kind of raw material for general use from which all arguments are drawn, and then later to present the way in which each kind of case should be supported by all the forms of argumentation derived from this general store.

All propositions are supported in argument by attributes of persons or of actions. We hold the following to be the attributes of persons: name, nature, manner of life, fortune, habit,[a] feeling, interests, purposes, achievements, accidents, speeches made.

Name is that which is given to each person, whereby he is addressed by his own proper and definite appellation.

It is hard to give a simple definition of *nature*. It is easier to enumerate the parts of it which are neces-
35 sary for laying down rules here. And these concern partly divine and partly mortal beings. Of those concerned with mortal beings, part are reckoned as belonging to human beings, and part to beasts. And in respect to human beings, their nature is considered first as to sex whether male or female, and as to race, place of birth, family, and age. As to race, whether one is a Greek or a foreigner; as to place of birth, whether an Athenian or a Lacedaemonian; as to family, what are one's ancestors and kin; as to age, whether one is a boy, or youth, of middle age, or an old man. Besides, we take into consideration such advantages and disadvantages as are given to mind and body by nature, as, for example: whether one is strong or weak, tall or short, handsome or ugly, swift or slow; whether bright or

obliviosus, comis [1] an infacetus, pudens, patiens an contra. Et omnino quae a natura dantur animo et corpori considerabuntur.[2] Nam quae industria comparantur, ad habitum pertinent, de quo posterius est dicendum.

XXV. In victu considerare oportet, apud quem et quo more et cuius arbitratu sit educatus, quos habuerit artium liberalium magistros, quos vivendi praeceptores, quibus amicis utatur, quo in negotio, quaestu, artificio sit occupatus, quo modo rem familiarem administret, qua consuetudine domestica sit.

In fortuna quaeritur, servus sit an liber, pecuniosus an tenuis, privatus an cum potestate : si cum potestate, iure an iniuria ; felix, clarus an contra ; quales liberos habeat. Ac si de non vivo quaereretur, etiam quali morte sit affectus erit considerandum.

36 Habitum autem [3] appellamus animi aut corporis constantem et absolutam aliqua in re perfectionem, ut virtutis aut artis alicuius perceptionem aut quamvis scientiam et item corporis aliquam commoditatem non natura datam, sed studio et industria partam.

Affectio est animi aut corporis ex tempore aliqua de causa commutatio, ut laetitia, cupiditas, metus, molestia, morbus, debilitas et alia quae in eodem genere reperiuntur.

Studium est autem animi assidua et vehementer ad aliquam rem applicata magna cum voluptate

---

[1] *After* comis *the MSS. have* officiosus (*courteous*). *Bracketed by Schuetz.*

[2] *After* considerabuntur *the MSS. have* et haec in natura consideranda (*and this ought to be considered under nature*) *with some variation in individual words. The passage was first bracketed by Kayser.*

[3] Habitum autem hunc *C.*

dull, retentive or forgetful, affable or unmannerly, modest, long-suffering, or the contrary; and in short we shall take into consideration all qualities of mind and body that are bestowed by nature. For the qualities acquired by one's own industry have to do with habit, which is to be discussed below.

XXV. Under *manner of life* should be considered with whom he was reared, in what tradition and under whose direction, what teachers he had in the liberal arts, what instructors in the art of living, with whom he associates on terms of friendship, in what occupation, trade, or profession he is engaged, how he manages his private fortune, and what is the character of his home life.

Under *fortune* one inquires whether the person is a slave or free, rich or poor, a private citizen or an official with authority, and if he is an official, whether he acquired his position justly or unjustly, whether he is successful, famous, or the opposite; what sort of children he has. And if the inquiry is about one no longer alive, weight must be also given to the nature of his death.

36   By *habit* we mean a stable and absolute constitution of mind or body in some particular, as, for example, the acquisition of some capacity or of an art, or again some special knowledge, or some bodily dexterity not given by nature but won by careful training and practice.

Feeling is a temporary change in mind or body due to some cause: for example, joy, desire, fear, vexation, illness, weakness, and other things which are found in the same category.

Interest is unremitting mental activity ardently devoted to some subject and accompanied by intense

CICERO

occupatio, ut philosophiae, poëticae, geometricae,
litterarum.

Consilium est aliquid faciendi aut non faciendi
excogitata ratio.

Facta autem et casus et orationes tribus ex temporibus considerabuntur: quid fecerit,[1] quid ipsi
acciderit, quid dixerit; aut quid faciat, quid ipsi
accidat, quid dicat; aut quid facturus sit, quid ipsi
casurum sit, qua sit usurus oratione. Ac personis
quidem haec videntur esse attributa.

37   XXVI. Negotiis autem quae sunt attributa, partim
sunt continentia cum ipso negotio, partim in gestione
negoti considerantur, partim adiuncta negotio sunt,
partim gestum negotium consequuntur.

Continentia cum ipso negotio sunt ea quae semper
affixa esse videntur ad rem neque ab ea possunt
separari. Ex his prima est brevis complexio totius
negoti quae summam continet facti, hoc modo:
parentis occisio, patriae proditio; deinde causa eius
summae per quam et quam ob rem et cuius rei causa
factum sit quaeritur; deinde ante gestam rem quae
facta sint continenter usque ad ipsum negotium;
deinde, in ipso gerendo negotio quid actum sit;
deinde, quid postea factum sit.

38   In gestione autem negoti, qui locus secundus erat
de eis quae negotiis attributa sunt, quaereretur [2]
locus, tempus, occasio, modus, facultas. Locus consideratur, in quo res gesta sit, ex opportunitate quam

---

[1] *After* fecerit *and* acciderit *the MSS. have* aut. *Bracketed
by Kayser.*
[2] quaeritur *M²J.*

74

pleasure, for example interest in philosophy, poetry, geometry, literature.

Purpose is a deliberate plan for doing or not doing something.

Achievements, accidents, and *speech* will be considered under three tenses of the verb: what he did, what happened to him, what he said: or what he is doing, what is happening to him, what he is saying; or what he is going to do, what is going to happen to him, what language he is going to use. These are the accepted attributes of persons.

37 XXVI. The attributes of actions are partly coherent with the action itself, partly considered in connexion with the performance of it, partly adjunct to it and partly consequent upon its performance.

Coherent with the action itself are those things which seem always connected with it and which cannot be separated from it. The first of these is a brief summary of the whole action comprising the sum of the matter, for example, " murder of parent," " betrayal of country." Then inquiry is made as to the reason for this whole matter, *i.e.,* by what means, and why, and for what purpose the act was done. In the next place we inquire what happened before the event right down to the actual deed; then what was done in the performance of the act, and again what was done afterwards.

38 In connexion with the performance of the act (which was the second topic under the heading of attributes of actions) inquiry will be made about place, time, occasion, manner, and facilities. In considering the *place* where the act was performed, account is taken of what opportunity the place seems

videatur habuisse ad negotium administrandum. Ea autem opportunitas quaeritur ex magnitudine, intervallo, longinquitate, propinquitate, solitudine, celebritate, natura ipsius loci et vicinitatis et totius regionis; ex his etiam attributionibus: sacer an profanus, publicus anne privatus, alienus an ipsius de quo agitur locus sit aut fuerit.

39   Tempus autem est—id quo nunc utimur, nam ipsum quidem generaliter definire difficile est—pars quaedam aeternitatis cum alicuius annui, menstrui, diurni, nocturnive spati certa significatione. In hoc et quae praeterierint, considerantur; et eorum ipsorum, quae aut propter vetustatem obsoleverint aut incredibilia videantur, ut iam in fabularum numerum reponantur; et quae iam diu gesta et a memoria nostra remota, tamen faciant fidem vere tradita esse, quia eorum monumenta certa in litteris exstent; et quae nuper gesta sint quae scire plerique possint; et item quae instent in praesentia et cum maxime fiant et quae consequantur. In quibus potest considerari quid ocius et quid serius futurum sit. Et item communiter in tempore perspiciendo longinquitas eius est consideranda. Nam saepe oportet commetiri cum tempore negotium et videre potueritne aut magnitudo negoti aut multitudo rerum in eo transigi tempore. Consideratur autem tempus et

to have afforded for its performance. *Opportunity*, moreover, is a question of the size of the place, its distance from other places, *i.e.*, whether remote or near at hand, whether it is a solitary spot or one much frequented, and finally it is a question of the nature of the place, of the actual site, of the vicinity and of the whole district. The following attributes are also to be considered: whether the place is or was sacred or profane, public or private, the property of the person in question or of another.

39   *Time* in the sense in which we now use it—for to define it absolutely and in general terms is difficult —time is a part of eternity definitely indicated as being of a certain length, a year, month, day, or night. Under this category not only are past events examined, and of these past events those which have either lost their significance through lapse of time or seem incredible so that now they are regarded as fabulous, and those which though they occurred long ago and are remote from our recollection still impress us as having been correctly reported because definite records of them are extant in literature, and those which have occurred recently so that most people can know them, but also those things which exist at the present moment and are most certainly going on, and thirdly actions which are to follow, of which it is possible to consider what will come to pass sooner and what later. Likewise, generally, in examining time the length of time has to be taken into consideration. For often it is proper to measure the action in terms of time, and to see whether such an important action or such a number of undertakings could be accomplished in the given time. One also

anni et mensis et diei et noctis et vigiliae et horae et
in aliqua parte alicuius horum.[1]

40   XXVII. Occasio autem est pars temporis habens
in se alicuius rei idoneam faciendi aut non faciendi
opportunitatem. Quare cum tempore hoc differt :
nam genere quidem utrumque idem esse intellegitur,
verum in tempore spatium quodam modo declaratur
quod in annis aut in anno aut in aliqua anni parte
spectatur, in occasione ad spatium temporis faciendi
quaedam opportunitas intellegitur adiuncta. Quare
cum genere idem sit, fit aliud quod parte quadam et
specie, ut diximus, differat. Haec distribuitur in tria
genera : publicum, commune, singulare. Publicum
est quod civitas universa aliqua de causa frequentat,
ut ludi, dies festus, bellum. Commune, quod accidit
omnibus eodem fere tempore, ut messis, vindemia,
calor, frigus. Singulare autem est quod aliqua de
causa privatim alicui solet accidere, ut nuptiae,
sacrificium, funus, convivium, somnus.

41   Modus autem est in quo, quemadmodum et quo
animo factum sit, quaeritur. Eius partes sunt
prudentia et imprudentia. Prudentiae autem[2] ratio
quaeritur ex eis, quae clam, palam, vi, persuasione
fecerit. Imprudentia autem in purgationem confer-
tur, cuius partes sunt inscientia, casus, necessitas,

---

[1] Consideratur . . . horum *omitted by Anonymus (RLM
309, 7)*: *bracketed by Knackstedt, Weidner and Ströbel.*
[2] autem *bracketed by Ernesti.*

---

[a] This apparent contradiction is cleared up by the fuller
statement of Fortunatianus (RLM 104, 23–27): acts performed
openly are characterized by violence, passion and daring,
secret acts by deceit, fraud, etc.

takes into account the time of the year, of the month,
the day, the night, the watch, the hour, and any
part of any of these.

40   XXVII. An *occasion* is a period of time offering a
convenient opportunity for doing or not doing something.   And it is on the matter of opportunity that
occasion differs from time: for both seem to be the
same in genus, but under the category of time a space
is fixed and limited in some way because the action
is viewed as occurring in a period of time, several
years, one year, or some part of a year, but under the
category of occasion it is understood that to the space
of time there is added the concept of an opportunity
for performing the action. Therefore though *occasion*
is of the same genus as *time*, it is something else,
because it differs from it in some respect and, as we
have said, belongs to a different species. *Occasion*
falls into three classes, public, general, particular.
A public occasion is one in which for some reason the
whole community takes part, as games, a holiday,
or war.   A general occasion is one which affects all
people at about the same time, as harvest, vintage,
hot weather, or cold weather.   A particular occasion,
finally, is one which for some reason affects some one
individually. as a wedding, a sacrifice, a funeral, a
banquet, or sleep.

41   *Manner*, again, is the category under which one
inquires how and in what state of mind the act was
performed. Its parts are intention and lack of
intention.   Now we seek to calculate one's intention from the acts which one performed secretly or
openly,[a] by the use of force or by persuasion.   Lack
of intention, on the other hand, is related to justification, the sub-heads of which are ignorance,

in affectionem animi, hoc est, molestiam, iracundiam, amorem et cetera quae in simili genere versantur.

Facultates sunt aut quibus facilius fit aut sine quibus aliquid confici non potest.

XXVIII. Adiunctum negotio autem id intellegitur quod maius et quod minus et quod aeque magnum et quod simile erit ei negotio quo de agitur, et quod contrarium et quod disparatum, et genus et pars et eventus. Maius et minus et aeque magnum ex vi et ex numero et ex figura negoti, sicut ex statura 42 corporis, consideratur. Simile autem ex specie comparabili aut ex conferenda atque assimilanda natura iudicatur. Contrarium est quod positum in genere diverso ab eo cui contrarium dicitur, plurimum distat, ut frigus calori, vitae mors. Disparatum autem est id quod ab aliqua re praepositione negationis separatur, hoc modo: sapere et non sapere. Genus est quod partes aliquas amplectitur, ut cupiditas. Pars est quae subest generi, ut amor, avaritia. Eventus est exitus alicuius negoti, in quo quaeri solet quid ex quaque re evenerit, eveniat, eventurum sit. Quare hoc in genere, ut commode quid eventurum sit ante animo colligi possit, quid quaque ex re soleat evenire

---

a Examples given by Victorinus in his commentary on the *de Inventione* (RLM, p. 227) may throw some light on what Cicero meant by this obscure passage. Quoting from the first Catilinarian the sentence, "Publius Scipio the Pontifex Maximus though a private citizen killed Tiberius Gracchus who was only slightly weakening the stability of the state; shall we, the consuls, put up with Catiline who is trying to lay waste the whole world with fire and sword," he then illustrates "values" of words and of person. "Lay waste" is "greater" than "weaken," "world" is "greater" than

accident and necessity, and to emotions, such as
annoyance, anger, love, and the others belonging to
the same class.

Facilities are the conditions which make something
easier to do, or without which it cannot be accomplished.

XXVIII. By *adjunct* of an action we mean something
that is greater or less than the action in question or of
equal magnitude or similar to it, also its contrary and
negative, and anything bearing the relation of genus
or species or result. The concept of greater and less
and of equality of size is derived from an examination
of the values and numbers involved, and from the
form of the action, just as if we were considering the
42 stature of a body. *Similarity* is decided on the basis
of comparable appearance and natural characteristics
which can be set side by side and likened one to
another.[a] *Contrary* is that which, placed in a class
different from that to which it is said to be contrary,
is as far as possible removed from it, for example hot
and cold, life and death. *Negative* is that which is
distinguished from something by a prefix meaning
"not," as intelligent, unintelligent. *Genus* is a
term embracing several *species*, for example, desire.
A *species* is a subdivision of a genus, for example, love,
avarice. *Result* is the outcome of any action; in
this connexion it is customary to inquire what
happened after each thing, what is happening, and
what will happen. Therefore, in order that it may be
possible to reason accurately beforehand as to what is
going to happen, it is necessary to consider under

"state," and "Catiline" is more to be feared than "Gracchus." As regards numbers, "two consuls" are "greater"
than "Scipio."

considerandum est, hoc modo : Ex arrogantia odium,
ex insolentia arrogantia.

43   Quarta autem pars est ex eis [1] quas negotiis
dicebamus esse attributas consecutio. In hac eae
res quaeruntur, quae gestum negotium consequuntur :
primum, quod factum est, quo id nomine appellari
conveniat ; deinde eius facti qui sint principes et
inventores, qui denique auctoritatis eius et inventionis comprobatores atque aemuli ; deinde ecquae
de ea re aut eius rei sit lex, consuetudo, pactio,
iudicium, scientia, artificium ; deinde natura eius,
evenire vulgo soleat an insolenter et raro ; postea
homines id sua auctoritate comprobare an offendere in
eis consueverint ; et cetera quae factum aliquid
similiter confestim aut ex intervallo solent consequi.
Deinde postremo attendendum est, num quae res ex
eis rebus quae positae sunt in partibus honestatis aut
utilitatis consequantur ; de quibus in deliberativo
genere causae distinctius erit dicendum. Ac negotiis
quidem fere res haec, quas commemoravimus, sunt
attributae.

44   XXIX. Omnis autem argumentatio quae ex eis
locis quos commemoravimus sumetur, aut probabilis
aut necessaria debebit esse. Etenim, ut breviter
describamus, argumentatio videtur esse inventum
aliquo ex genere rem aliquam aut probabiliter
ostendens aut necessarie demonstrans.

Necessarie demonstrantur ea quae aliter ac dicuntur
nec fieri nec probari possunt, hoc modo : " Si peperit,
cum viro concubuit." Hoc genus argumentandi,

_____
[1] *After* eis *Oudendorp and Ströbel add* rebus.

this head what is the usual result of each thing; for example, arrogance begets hatred, and pride begets arrogance.

43 The fourth class of what are called attributes of actions, is *consequence*. Under this category those things are sought which ensue from an action being performed. First, by what name shall the act be designated? Secondly, who are the chief agents and the originators of this undertaking, and who approve or emulate this example and innovation? Again, is there any law about this, any custom, compact, judicial decision, scientific knowledge or set of rules? Then the nature of the event, whether it is wont to occur frequently or rarely and exceptionally? Furthermore, have men been in the habit of giving such a case the approval of their authority, or of taking offence at it? And all other things are to be considered which are wont to follow an action in the same way, either immediately or after an interval. Finally, it should be noted whether any of the things which are classed under honour or advantage ensue. A more detailed account of this will have to be given in connexion with the deliberative style of oratory. The list which I have given covers approximately the attributes of actions.

44 XXIX. All argumentation drawn from these topics which we have mentioned will have to be either probable or irrefutable. For, to define it briefly, an argument seems to be a device of some sort to demonstrate with probability or prove irrefutably.

Those things are proved irrefutably which cannot happen or be proved otherwise than as stated; for example, " If she has borne a child, she has lain with a man." This style of argument which is used for

83

quod in necessaria demonstratione versatur, maxime
tractatur in dicendo aut per complexionem aut per
enumerationem aut per simplicem conclusionem.
45 Complexio est in qua, utrum concesseris, reprehenditur, ad hunc modum: " Si improbus est, cur
uteris? si probus, cur accusas? " Enumeratio est in
qua pluribus rebus expositis et ceteris infirmatis una
reliqua necessario confirmatur, hoc pacto: " Necesse
est aut inimicitiarum causa ab hoc esse occisum aut
metus aut spei aut alicuius amici gratia aut, si horum
nihil est, ab hoc non esse occisum; nam sine causa
maleficium susceptum non potest esse: si neque
inimicitiae fuerunt nec metus ullus nec spes ex
morte illius alicuius commodi neque ad amicum
huius aliquem mors illius pertinebat, relinquitur
igitur ut ab hoc non sit occisus." Simplex autem
conclusio ex necessaria consecutione conficitur, hoc
modo: " Si vos me istuc eo tempore fecisse dicitis,
ego autem eo ipso tempore trans mare fui, relinquitur
ut id quod dicitis non modo non fecerim, sed ne
potuerim quidem facere." Atque hoc diligenter
oportebit videre, ne quo pacto genus hoc refelli possit,
ut ne confirmatio modum in se argumentationis
solum [1] habeat et quandam similitudinem necessariae conclusionis, verum ipsa argumentatio ex
necessaria ratione consistat.
46 Probabile autem est id quod fere solet fieri aut
quod in opinione positum est aut quod habet in se
ad haec quandam similitudinem, sive id falsum est

---

[1] solum *before* modum *S*: *before* habeat P^2: *in margin J*:
bracketed by Weidner: omitted by Ströbel.

---

[a] For illustrations of this form of argument see Cicero, *in
Verrem* I, 36, and Antiphon, *On the Murder of Herodes*, 57.

rigorous proof, generally in speaking takes the form
of a dilemma, or of an enumeration or of a simple

45 inference. A dilemma is a form of argument in
which you are refuted, whichever alternative you
grant, after this fashion: " If he is a scoundrel, why
are you intimate with him? If he is an honest man,
why accuse him?" Enumeration is a form of
argument in which several possibilities are stated,
and when all but one have been disproved, this one is
irrefutably demonstrated; the following is an
example: " He must have been killed by the
defendant either because of his enmity to him, or
through fear or hope or to gratify a friend; if none of
these statements is true, he cannot have been killed
by the defendant. For a crime cannot be committed
without a motive. If there was no enmity, and no
fear, and no hope of any advantages from his death
and his death was of no interest to any friend of the
defendant, it therefore follows that the defendant
did not kill him." [a] A simple inference arises from a
necessary consequence, as follows: " If you say that
I did this at that time, but at that particular time I
was overseas, it follows that I not only did not do
what you say, but that I was not even in a position
to do it." And it will be necessary to keep a sharp
watch that this kind of argument cannot be refuted
in any way, so that the proof may not contain in
itself only a form of argument and a mere appearance of a necessary conclusion, but rather that
the argument may rest on rigorous reasoning.

46   That is probable which for the most part usually
comes to pass, or which is a part of the ordinary
beliefs of mankind, or which contains in itself some
resemblance to these qualities, whether such re-

sive verum. In eo genere quod fere fieri solet
probabile huiusmodi est: "Si mater est, diligit
filium: si avarus est, neglegit ius iurandum." In eo
autem quod in opinione positum est, huiusmodi sunt
probabilia: Impiis apud inferos poenas esse praepara-
tas; eos qui philosophiae dent operam non arbitrari
deos esse. XXX. Similitudo autem in contrariis,
et ex paribus, in eis rebus quae sub eandem
rationem cadunt maxime spectatur. In contrariis,
hoc modo: "Nam si eis qui imprudentes laeserunt
ignosci convenit, eis qui necessario profuerunt haberi
47 gratiam non oportet." Ex pari, sic: "Nam ut locus
sine portu navibus esse non potest tutus, sic animus
sine fide stabilis amicis non potest esse." In eis rebus
quae sub eandem rationem cadunt hoc modo probabile
consideratur: "Nam si Rhodiis turpe non est por-
torium locare, ne Hermocreonti quidem turpe est
conducere." Haec tum vera sunt, hoc pacto:
"Quoniam cicatrix est, fuit vulnus"; tum veri similia,
hoc modo: "Si multus erat in calceis pulvis, ex itinere
eum venire oportebat."

Omne autem (ut certas quasdam in partes tribua-
mus) probabile quod sumitur ad argumentationem
aut signum est aut credibile aut iudicatum aut
48 comparabile. Signum est quod sub sensum aliquem
cadit et quiddam significat quod ex ipso profectum
videtur, quod aut ante fuerit aut in ipso negotio aut

---

a Quoted by Aristotle, *Rhet.* 1397a, 13 ff. from an unknown
poet (possibly Agathon or Theodectas).

b The latter half of this parallel is given in Aristotle,
Eudemian Ethics, 1237b, 12.

c The same example, but with the name Diomedon, is given
in Aristotle's *Rhet.* 1397a, 25.

86

semblance be true or false. In the class of things
which for the most part usually come to pass are
probabilities of this sort : " If she is his mother, she
loves him." " If he is avaricious, he disregards his
oath." Under the head of ordinary beliefs or opinions
come probabilities of this sort : " Punishment awaits
the wicked in the next world." " Philosophers are
atheists." XXX. Resemblance is seen mostly in
contraries, in analogies, and in those things which
fall under the same principle. In contraries, as
follows : " For if it is right for me to pardon those who
have wronged me unintentionally, I ought not to be
grateful to those who have assisted me because they
47 could not help it." [a] In analogies, thus : " For as a
place without a harbour cannot be safe for ships, so
a mind without integrity cannot be relied on by
friends." [b] In the case of those things which fall
under the same principle, probability is considered
after this fashion : " For if it is not disgraceful for the
Rhodians to farm out their customs-duties, neither is
it disgraceful for Hermocreon to take the contract." [c]
Arguments of this kind are sometimes rigorous—for
example : " Since there is a scar, there has been a
wound "—sometimes they are only plausible, for
instance : " If there was much dust on his shoes, he
must have been on a journey."

For the sake of making definite subdivision we may
say that all *probability* that is used in argument is
either a *sign*, or something *credible*, or a point on
which *judgement* has been given, or something which
48 affords an opportunity for *comparison*. A *sign* is
something apprehended by one of the senses and
indicating something that seems to follow logically
as a result of it : the sign may have occurred before

87

post sit consecutum, et tamen indiget testimoni et gravioris confirmationis, ut cruor, fuga, pallor, pulvis, et quae his sunt similia. Credibile est quod sine ullo teste auditoris opinione firmatur, hoc modo: " Nemo est qui non liberos suos incolumes et beatos esse cupiat." Iudicatum est res assensione aut auctoritate aut iudicio alicuius aut aliquorum comprobata. Id tribus in generibus spectatur, religioso, communi, approbato. Religiosum est quod iurati legibus iudicarunt. Commune est quod homines vulgo probarunt et secuti sunt, huiusmodi: ut maioribus natu assurgatur, ut supplicum misereatur. Approbatum est quod homines, cum dubium esset quale haberi oporteret, sua constituerunt auctoritate, velut Gracchi patris factum populus Romanus qui eum[1] eo quod insciente collega in censura nihil[2] gessit post censuram consulem fecit. Comparabile autem est quod in rebus diversis similem aliquam rationem continet. Eius partes sunt tres: imago, collatio, exemplum. Imago est oratio demonstrans corporum aut naturarum similitudinem. Collatio est oratio rem cum re ex similitudine conferens. Exemplum est quod rem auctoritate aut casu alicuius hominis aut negoti

49

[1] *After* eum *the MSS. have* ob id factum; *bracketed by Oudendorp.* eo *is omitted by J.*
[2] nonnihil *Schuetz, Ströbel.*

---

[a] *Cf.* [Aristotle] *Rhet. ad Alex.* 13, 1430b.
[b] Tiberius Sempronius Gracchus, consul 177 and 163, censor 169 B.C. with Gaius Claudius Pulcher. Their strict use of the censorial power aroused vigorous opposition, and they were charged with treason. Claudius was about to be convicted and Gracchus acquitted, but he refused to accept a divided verdict, and both were acquitted. Details of the story vary in different versions. The text here given is obscure and may be corrupt.

the event or in immediate connexion with it, or have followed after it, and yet needs further evidence and corroboration; examples might be, blood, flight, pallor, dust, and the like.[a] A statement is *credible* which is supported by the opinion of the auditor without corroborating evidence: for example, " There is no one who does not wish his children to be safe and happy." *Judgement* is the approval of an act by the assent or authority or judicial decision of some person or persons. It may be divided into three classes, according as the judgement is supported by religious sanction, by the common practice of mankind, or by some special act of approval. A judgement has *religious sanction* if it has been rendered by judges under oath in accordance with law. A judgement rests on the *common practice of mankind* if all men in general have approved of it or have followed it, as for example, rising out of respect to elders, or pitying suppliants. A *special act of approval* is a case in which there was doubt as to how an event was to be regarded and men have settled it by an authoritative vote; for example, the Roman people approved the acts of the elder Gracchus by electing him consul after his censorship because during his censorship he had performed no act without the knowledge of

49 his colleague.[b] Lastly, probability which depends on *comparison* involves a certain principle of similarity running through diverse material. It has three subdivisions, similitude, parallel, example. A *similitude* is a passage setting forth a likeness of individuals or characters. A *parallel* is a passage putting one thing beside another on the basis of their resemblances. An *example* supports or weakens a case by appeal to precedent or experience, citing

confirmat aut infirmat. Horum exempla et descriptiones in praeceptis elocutionis cognoscentur.

Ac fons quidem confirmationis, ut facultas tulit, apertus est nec minus dilucide quam rei natura ferebat demonstratus est; quemadmodum autem quaeque constitutio et pars constitutionis et omnis controversia, sive in ratione sive in scripto versabitur, tractari debeat et quae in quamque argumentationes conveniant, singillatim in secundo libro de uno quoque genere dicemus. In praesentia tantummodo numeros et modos et partes argumentandi confuse et permixtim dispersimus; post discripte et electe in genus quodque causae, quid cuique conveniat, ex hac copia digeremus.

50   Atque inveniri quidem omnis ex his locis argumentatio poterit: inventa exornari et certas in partes distingui et suavissimum est et summe necessarium et ab artis scriptoribus maxime neglectum. Quare et de ea praeceptione nobis et in hoc loco dicendum visum est, ut ad inventionem argumentandi ratio [1] adiungeretur. Et magna cum cura et diligentia locus hic omnis considerandus est, quod rei non solum magna utilitas est, sed praecipiendi quoque summa difficultas.

---

[1] argumentandi ratio *u*: ratio argumentandi *v₇*: argumentandi *J*: argumenti *M*.

---

[a] *Infra*, §§ 79 ff.
[b] Or rhythms and melodies, *cf.* Horace, *Epist.* II, 2, 144: *verae numerosque modosque ediscere vitae.*

some person or historical event. Instances and descriptions of these principles will be given with the rules for style.[a]

Now the sources of confirmatory arguments have been revealed as the occasion offered, and explained as clearly as the nature of the subject required. But in the second book we shall discuss in connexion with each class individually what treatment is to be given to each issue or subdivision of an issue or to the whole controversy, whether it depends on general reasoning or on written documents, and also what forms of argumentation are appropriate for each issue. For the present we have merely scattered in an irregular and random manner the categories, rules,[b] and classes of argumentation. Later we shall choose and arrange, and from this material we shall explain in order what is appropriate to each kind of case.

50   Furthermore every kind of argument can be discovered under these headings: but it is the embellishment of the argument once it has been discovered, and the arrangement of it in definite divisions, which make the speech attractive to the audience; this elaboration of the argument is necessary to the highest degree, and yet has been greatly neglected by writers on the art of rhetoric. For that reason it seemed to us necessary to speak about the rules for this and to do so at this point so that the subject of invention of arguments may be combined with the theory of argumentation. This topic must be considered with great care and diligence not only because it is extremely useful, but also because there is great difficulty in formulating rules.

51   XXXI. Omnis igitur argumentatio aut per inductionem tractanda est aut per ratiocinationem.

Inductio est oratio quae rebus non dubiis captat assensiones eius quicum instituta est; quibus assensionibus facit ut illi dubia quaedam res propter similitudinem earum rerum quibus assensit probetur; velut apud Socraticum Aeschinen demonstrat Socrates cum Xenophontis uxore et cum ipso Xenophonte Aspasiam locutam : " Dic mihi, quaeso, Xenophontis uxor, si vicina tua melius habeat aurum quam tu habes, utrum illudne an tuum malis ? " " Illud," inquit. " Quid si vestem aut ceterum ornatum muliebrem preti maioris habeat quam tu habes, tuumne an illius malis ? " Respondit : " Illius vero." " Age sis," inquit, "quid si virum illa meliorem habeat
52 quam tu habes, utrumne tuum malis an illius ? " Hic mulier erubuit. Aspasia autem sermonem cum ipso Xenophonte instituit. "Quaeso," inquit, "Xenophon, si vicinus tuus equum meliorem habeat quam tuus est, tuumne equum malis an illius ? " " Illius," inquit. " Quid si fundum meliorem habeat quam tu habes, utrum tandem fundum habere malis ? " " Illum," inquit, " meliorem scilicet." " Quid si uxorem meliorem habeat quam tu habes, utrum tuamne an [1] illius malis ? " Atque hic Xenophon quoque ipse tacuit. Post Aspasia : " Quoniam uterque vestrum," inquit, " id mihi solum non respondit quod ego solum audire

[1] tuamne an *added by* v_2.

---

[a] I have kept the traditional terms, induction and deduction, but it should be understood that Cicero was describing a rhetorical, not a logical, kind of reasoning, and that his use of such terms is loose and, at times, careless. The process

51 XXXI. All argumentation, then, is to be carried on either by induction or by deduction.[a]

Induction is a form of argument which leads the person with whom one is arguing to give assent to certain undisputed facts; through this assent it wins his approval of a doubtful proposition because this resembles the facts to which he has assented. For instance, in a dialogue by Aeschines Socraticus Socrates reveals that Aspasia reasoned thus with Xenophon's wife and with Xenophon himself: "Please tell me, madam, if your neighbour had a better gold ornament than you have, would you prefer that one or your own?" "That one," she replied. "Now, if she had dresses and other feminine finery more expensive than you have, would you prefer yours or hers?" "Hers, of course," she replied. "Well now, if she had a better husband than you have, would you prefer your husband or 52 hers?" At this the woman blushed. But Aspasia then began to speak to Xenophon. "I wish you would tell me, Xenophon," she said, "if your neighbour had a better horse than yours, would you prefer your horse or his?" "His," was his answer. "And if he had a better farm than you have, which farm would you prefer to have?" "The better farm, naturally," he said. "Now, if he had a better wife than you have, would you prefer yours or his?" And at this Xenophon, too, himself was silent. Then Aspasia: "Since both of you have failed to tell me the only thing I wished to hear, I myself will tell you

which he calls induction might more accurately be described as analogy, and under deduction he describes not the syllogism of Aristotle, but the enthymeme or epicheireme, a rhetorical adaptation of the syllogism. *Cf.* p. 104, note *a*.

volueram, egomet dicam quid uterque cogitet. Nam
et tu, mulier, optimum virum vis habere et tu,
Xenophon, uxorem habere lectissimam maxime vis.
Quare, nisi hoc perfeceritis, ut neque vir melior neque
femina lectior in terris sit, profecto semper id quod
optimum putabitis esse, multo maxime requiretis ut
et tu maritus sis quam optimae et haec quam optimo
viro nupta sit.[1]   Hic cum rebus non dubiis assensum
est, factum est propter similitudinem, ut etiam illud
quod dubium videretur, si qui separatim quaereret,
id pro certo propter rationem rogandi concederetur.
53 Hoc modo sermonis plurimum Socrates usus est
propterea quod nihil ipse afferre ad persuadendum
volebat, sed ex eo quod sibi ille dederat quicum
disputabat, aliquid conficere malebat, quod ille ex
eo quod iam concessisset necessario approbare de-
beret.

XXXII. Hoc in genere praecipiendum nobis videtur primum, ut illud quod inducemus per similitudinem eiusmodi sit ut sit necesse concedere. Nam ex
quo postulabimus nobis illud quod dubium sit concedi,
dubium esse id ipsum non oportebit.   Deinde illud
cuius confirmandi causa fiet inductio, videndum est,
ut simile eis rebus sit quas res quasi non dubias ante
induxerimus, nam aliquid ante concessum nobis esse
nihil proderit si ei dissimile erit id cuius causa illud
concedi primum voluerimus ; deinde ne intellegat
quo spectent illae primae inductiones et ad quem sint

---

[1] ut . . . sit *bracketed by Weidner and Ströbel.*

---

[a] *Aesch. Socr. Rel.* (Krauss).   *Cf.* for a discussion of the
content of this dialogue, Natorp in *Philologus* li (1892), pp.
489–500.

what you both are thinking. That is, you, madam, wish to have the best husband, and you, Xenophon, desire above all things to have the finest wife. Therefore unless you can contrive that there be no better man or finer woman on earth you will certainly always be in dire want of what you consider best, namely, that you be the husband of the very best of wives, and that she be wedded to the very best of men." [a] In this instance, because assent has been given to undisputed statements, the result is that the point which would appear doubtful if asked by itself is through analogy conceded as certain, and this is due to the method employed in putting the question. Socrates used this conversational method a good deal, because he wished to present no arguments himself, but preferred to get a result from the material which the interlocutor had given him—a result which the interlocutor was bound to approve as following necessarily from what he had already granted.

XXXII. In argumentation of this kind I think the first rule to lay down is that the statement which we introduce as a basis for analogy ought to be of such a kind that its truth must be granted. For a statement on the strength of which we expect a doubtful point to be conceded, ought not itself to be doubtful. In the second place, one must make sure that the statement to be proved by the induction resembles those statements which we have presented previously as indisputable, for something granted to us previously will be no help if it is unlike the statement for the proof of which we wished the first point to be conceded. In the next place the interlocutor must not perceive what is the aim of those first examples

54 exitum perventurae. Nam qui videt, si ei rei quam
primo rogetur recte assenserit, illam quoque rem
quae sibi displiceat esse necessario concedendam,
plerumque aut non respondendo aut male respondendo longius rogationem procedere non sinit; quare
ratione rogationis imprudens ab eo quod concessit
ad id quod non vult concedere deducendus est.
Extremum autem aut taceatur oportet aut concedatur
aut negetur. Si negabitur, aut ostendenda similitudo
est earum rerum quae ante concessae sunt aut alia
utendum inductione. Si concedetur, concludenda est
argumentatio. Si tacebitur, elicienda responsio est
aut, quoniam taciturnitas imitatur confessionem, pro
eo ac si concessum sit concludere oportebit argumentationem. Ita fit hoc genus argumentandi triperti-
tum: prima pars ex similitudine constat una pluribusve; altera ex eo quod concedi volumus cuius causa
similitudines adhibitae sunt; tertia ex conclusione,
quae aut confirmat concessionem aut quid ex ea conficiatur ostendit.

55 XXXIII. Sed quia non satis alicui videbitur dilucide
demonstratum, nisi quid ex civili causarum genere
exempli subiecerimus, videtur eiusmodi quoque
utendum exemplo, non quo praeceptio differat aut
aliter hoc in sermone atque in dicendo sit utendum,
sed ut eorum voluntati satis fiat qui id quod aliquo in
loco viderunt, alio in loco, nisi monstratum est,
nequeunt cognoscere. Ergo in hac causa, quae apud
Graecos est pervagata, cum Epaminondas, Thebano-

54 or to what conclusion they will lead. For one who sees that if he gives the proper answer to the first question that he is asked, he will be compelled to grant also a proposition which is displeasing to him, will generally put a stop to further questioning by not answering or by answering incorrectly. Therefore by careful direction of the questions he must be led without his knowing it from the statement which he has granted to that which he does not wish to grant. Finally, he must either refuse to answer, or concede your point or deny it. If he denies it, you must show that it resembles the points which have previously been conceded, or use another induction. If he concedes the point, the argument must be brought to a close. If he refuses to answer, he must be lured into giving an answer, or since " silence gives consent " you must finish the argument just as if he had conceded your point. Thus this style of argument is threefold : the first part consists of one or more similar cases, the second of the point which we wish to have conceded, for the sake of which the similar cases have been cited; the third is the conclusion which reinforces the concession or shows what results follow from it.

55 XXXIII. But because some may think the demonstration is not sufficiently clear unless we add an example from the field of public issues, it seems desirable to give an example of this sort also, not that the principle is different or that it is used differently in conversation and in a speech, but to satisfy the desire of those who after seeing something in one place cannot recognize it in another unless it is pointed out. Therefore let us take the case, well known among the Greeks, of Epaminondas

rum imperator, ei [1] qui sibi ex lege praetor successerat
exercitum non tradidit et, cum paucos ipse dies contra
legem exercitum tenuisset, Lacedaemonios funditus
vicit, poterit accusator argumentatione uti per inductionem, cum scriptum legis contra sententiam defen-
56 det, ad hunc modum : " Si, iudices, id quod Epaminondas ait legis scriptorem sensisse ascribat ad legem
et addat hanc exceptionem : extra quam si quis rei
publicae causa exercitum non tradiderit, patiemini ?
Non opinor. Quid si vosmet ipsi, quod a vestra
religione et a sapientia remotissimum est, istius
honoris causa hanc eandem exceptionem iniussu
populi ad legem ascribi iubeatis, populus Thebanus id
patieturne fieri ? Profecto non patietur. Quod ergo
ascribi ad legem nefas est, id sequi, quasi ascriptum
sit, rectum vobis videatur ? Novi vestram intellegentiam ; non potest ita videri, iudices. Quodsi litteris
corrigi neque ab illo neque a vobis scriptoris voluntas
potest, videte, ne multo indignius sit id re et iudicio
vestro mutari quod ne verbo quidem commutari
potest."

Ac de inductione quidem satis in praesentia dictum
57 videtur. Nunc deinceps ratiocinationis vim et
naturam consideremus.

XXXIV. Ratiocinatio est oratio ex ipsa re probabile
aliquid eliciens quod expositum et per se cognitum

---

[1] ei *J* : quod ei *M*, *Ströbel.*

---

[a] For a discussion of this trial *v.* Bonner and Smith in *Cl.
Phil.* xl (1945), pp. 18, 19.

the Theban general. He did not hand over the
army to the officer who had legally succeeded him
as commander, and keeping the army under his
own command for a few days contrary to law, won a
decisive victory over the Lacedaemonians. The
prosecutor will be able to use the argument by
analogy in defending the letter of the law against
56 the intent, in the following way : " If, gentlemen
of the jury, Epaminondas should add to the law what
he says the author of the law intended, and should
subjoin this proviso, ' except in the case that a
commander shall for the common weal refuse to
hand over his army,' will you permit it ? I think not.
Or again, if you yourselves—though this is decidedly
out of keeping with your wisdom and punctiliousness
—if you yourselves without consulting the people
should out of respect to him order this same proviso
to be added to the law, will the people of Thebes
permit this ? Most assuredly not. Would it then
seem right to you to follow a principle as if it were a
part of the law, though it is wrong to make it a part
of the law ? I know your intelligence. It cannot
seem right to you, gentlemen of the jury. Therefore
if the intent of the law-maker cannot be amended in
writing either by him or by you, beware lest it be
much worse to alter in deed, *i.e.*, by your judicial act,
what cannot be changed even in word." [a]

Enough has been said, I think, for the present
57 about induction. In the next place let us consider
the essence and nature of the syllogism.

XXXIV. *Deduction* or syllogistic reasoning is a
form of argument which draws a probable conclusion
from the fact under consideration itself ; when this
probable conclusion is set forth and recognized by

sua se vi et ratione confirmet. Hoc de genere qui diligentius considerandum putaverunt, cum idem in usu dicendi sequerentur, paululum in praecipiendi ratione dissenserunt. Nam partim quinque eius partes esse dixerunt, partim non plus quam in tres partes posse distribui putaverunt. Eorum controversiam non incommodum videtur cum utrorumque ratione exponere. Nam et brevis est et non eiusmodi ut alteri prorsus nihil dicere putentur, et locus hic nobis in dicendo minime neglegendus videtur.

58 Qui putant in quinque tribui partes oportere, aiunt primum convenire exponere summam argumentationis, ad hunc modum: " Melius accurantur quae consilio geruntur quam quae sine consilio administrantur." Hanc primam partem numerant; eam deinceps rationibus variis et quam copiosissimis verbis approbari putant oportere, hoc modo: " Domus ea quae ratione regitur omnibus est instructior rebus et apparatior quam ea quae temere et nullo consilio administratur. Exercitus is cui praepositus est sapiens et callidus imperator omnibus partibus commodius regitur quam is qui stultitia et temeritate alicuius administratur. Eadem navigi ratio est. Nam navis optime cursum conficit ea quae scientis59 simo gubernatore utitur." Cum propositio sit hoc pacto approbata et duae partes transierint ratiocina-

---

^a This is description rather than definition. *Cf.* note on p. 92.

^b Or possibly, reading *docendo*, in teaching.

^c *Cf.* Cicero, *de Natura Deorum*, II, 85, as an example of the way in which this form of argument is given a more artistic expression. The argument, common with the Stoics, derives from Plato, *Timaeus*.

itself it proves itself by its own import and reasoning.[a]
Those who have thought this form of argument
worthy of a very careful consideration differ somewhat in their formulation of rules, although they
follow the same principles in the actual practice of
speaking. For some have said that it has five parts
and others have thought that it could be divided into
not more than three parts. I think it will not be out
of place to explain this controversy and give the
reason on both sides. For it will not take long and
is not of such a nature as to produce the impression
that either side is talking nonsense, and we think
that this topic is by no means to be neglected in
speaking.[b]

58   Those who think that the syllogism ought to be
divided into five parts say that first one should state
the basis of the argument in this way : " Things that
are done by design are managed better than those
which are governed without design." This they
count as the first part. Then they think it should
be supported by a variety of reasons and the greatest
possible fullness of expression, in the following
manner : " The house that is managed in accordance
with a reasoned plan, is in every respect better
equipped and furnished than one which is governed
in a haphazard way with a total lack of design. The
army that is commanded by a wise and shrewd
general is guided in all ways more advantageously
than one which is governed by someone's folly and
rashness. The same line of reasoning is applicable
to navigation, for the ship which has the services of
the most expert pilot makes the most successful
59 voyage."[c] When the major premise has been proved
in this fashion and two parts of the syllogism have

tionis, tertia in parte aiunt, quod ostendere velis, id
ex vi propositionis oportere adsumere, hoc pacto:
" Nihil autem omnium rerum melius, quam omnis
mundus, administratur." Huius assumptionis quarto
in loco aliam porro inducunt approbationem, hoc
modo : " Nam et signorum ortus et obitus definitum
quendam ordinem servant et annuae commutationes
non modo quadam ex necessitudine semper eodem
modo fiunt, verum ad utilitates quoque rerum
omnium accommodate, et diurnae nocturnaeque
vicissitudines nulla in re unquam mutatae quicquam
nocuerunt." Quae signo sunt omnia non mediocri
quodam consilio naturam mundi administrari. Quinto
inducunt loco complexionem eam quae aut id infert
solum quod ex omnibus partibus cogitur, hoc modo :
" Consilio igitur mundus administratur," aut unum
in locum cum conduxerit breviter propositionem et
assumptionem, adiungit quid ex his conficiatur, ad
hunc modum : " Quodsi melius geruntur ea quae
consilio quam quae sine consilio administrantur, nihil
autem omnium rerum melius administratur quam
omnis mundus, consilio igitur mundus administratur."
Quinquepertitam igitur hoc pacto putant esse argumentationem.

60   XXXV. Qui autem tripertitam putant esse, ei non
aliter tractari putant oportere argumentationem, sed
partitionem horum reprehendunt. Negant enim
neque a propositione neque ab assumptione appro-
bationes earum separari oportere, neque propositionem absolutam neque assumptionem sibi perfectam

---

ᵃ *Cf.* the discussion of this problem by Quintilian, V, xiv,
5 ff.

been completed, in the third part they say you should state as a minor premise what you wish to show, this being in line with the thought of the major premise; the following will be an example: "Of all things nothing is better governed than the universe." And then in the fourth place they introduce another proof, that is of this minor premise, in this way: "For the risings and the settings of the constellations keep a fixed order, and the changes of the seasons not only proceed in the same way by a fixed law but are also adapted to the advantage of all nature, and the alternation of night and day has never through any variations done any harm." All these points are proof that the nature of the world is governed by no ordinary intelligence. In the fifth place they put the conclusion, which either merely states the necessary deduction from all the parts, as follows: "Therefore the universe is administered by design," or after bringing the major premise and the minor premise together in one brief statement adds what follows from them, after this fashion: "Therefore if those things are administered better which are governed by design than those which are administered without design, and nothing is governed better than the universe, then the universe is governed by design." This is the way in which they think the argument is expressed in five parts.[a]

60　　XXXV. Those, however, who think that it is three-fold, hold that the argumentation should be treated in the same way, but criticize the division into five parts. For they say that the proofs ought not to be separated from the major premise and the minor premise, and that a major premise does not seem to them finished nor a minor premise complete which is

videri quae approbatione confirmata non sit. Quare
quas illi duas partes numerent, propositionem et
approbationem, sibi unam partem videri, propositionem; quae si approbata non sit, propositio non sit
argumentationis. Item, quae ab illis assumptio et
assumptionis approbatio dicatur, eandem sibi assumptionem solam videri. Ita fit ut eadem ratione
argumentatio tractata aliis tripertita, aliis quinquepertita videatur. Quare evenit ut res non tam ad
usum dicendi pertineat quam ad rationem praecep-
tionis.

61 Nobis autem commodior illa partitio videtur esse
quae in quinque partes tributa est, quam omnes ab
Aristotele et Theophrasto profecti maxime secuti
sunt. Nam quemadmodum illud superius genus
argumentandi quod per inductionem sumitur maxime
Socrates et Socratici tractarunt, sic hoc quod per
ratiocinationem expolitur summe est ab Aristotele
atque a Peripateticis[1] et Theophrasto frequentatum,
deinde a rhetoribus eis qui elegantissimi atque
artificiosissimi putati sunt. Quare autem nobis illa
magis partitio probetur dicendum videtur, ne temere
secuti putemur; et breviter dicendum, ne in huiusmodi rebus diutius quam ratio praecipiendi postulat
commoremur.

62 XXXVI. Si quadam in argumentatione satis est
uti propositione et non oportet adiungere appro-

---

[1] atque a Peripateticis *bracketed by Linsmayer and Kayser.*

---

[a] Cicero is in error here. The Peripatetic syllogism had
only three parts. The fivefold arrangement must derive
from the rhetorical adaptation of syllogistic reasoning, perhaps the work of Hermagoras. The rhetorician used an
adaptation of the logical syllogism either in the form of the

not supported by proof. Therefore major premise and proof, which the other group count as two parts, seem to them to be one, namely major premise; if this is not proved, it could not be the major premise of the argument. Likewise, what is called by the other group minor premise and proof, seems to them merely minor premise. The result is that an argument treated in the same way seems to one group threefold and to another fivefold. Consequently the subject is not so important for the actual practice of oratory as it is for methods of instruction.

61   The division into five parts would seem to us to be more suitable. This has been adopted particularly by the followers of Aristotle and Theophrastus.[a] For just as that earlier form of argument which proceeds by induction was practised particularly by Socrates and the Socratics, so this which is elaborated in the form of a syllogism, was most largely used by Aristotle and by the Peripatetics and Theophrastus, and then was taken up by the teachers of rhetoric who have been regarded as most precise and accomplished in their art. But I think that I should explain why I favour this division so that I may not be thought to have followed it without due cause: and the explanation should be brief so that we may not linger on matters of this sort longer than our plan of instruction requires.

62   XXXVI. If in a given argument it is sufficient to use the major premise and is not necessary to add the

---

enthymeme, a syllogism in which the major premise is only probable, or one in which one term is omitted, or the epicheireme, which is the technical term for the fivefold division here presented by Cicero. *Cf.* Thiele, *Hermagoras*, pp. 131–137, and *ad Her.* II, xviii, 27.

bationem propositionis, quadam autem in argumentatione infirma est propositio, nisi adiuncta sit approbatio, separatum est quiddam a propositione approbatio. Quod enim et adiungi et separari ab aliquo potest, id non potest idem esse quod est id ad quod adiungitur et a quo separatur. Est autem quaedam argumentatio in qua propositio non indiget approbationis, et quaedam in qua nihil valet sine approbatione, ut ostendemus. Separata igitur est a propositione approbatio. Ostendetur autem id, quod polliciti sumus, hoc modo: Quae propositio in se quiddam continet perspicuum et quod stare inter omnes necesse est, hanc velle approbare et firmare

63 nihil attinet. Ea est huiusmodi: "Si, quo die ista caedes Romae facta est, ego Athenis eo die fui, in caede interesse non potui." Hoc quia perspicue verum est, nihil attinet approbari. Quare assumi statim oportet, hoc modo: "Fui autem Athenis eo die." Hoc si non constat, indiget approbationis; qua inducta complexio consequetur. Est igitur quaedam propositio quae non indiget approbatione. Nam esse quidem quandam quae indigeat, quid attinet ostendere, quod cuivis facile perspicuum est? Quodsi ita est, ex hoc et ex eo quod proposueramus hoc conficitur, separatum esse quiddam a propositione approbationem. Sin autem ita est, falsum est non esse plus quam tripertitam argumentationem.

64 Simili modo liquet alteram quoque approbationem separatam esse ab assumptione. Si quadam in argumentatione satis est uti assumptione et non oportet adiungere approbationem assumptioni, quadam autem

proof of the premise, but on the other hand in another argument the major premise is weak unless the proof be added, then the proof is something separate from the major premise. For what can be added to something and separated from it cannot be the same as that to which it is added and from which it is separated. There is, moreover, a form of argument in which the major premise does not require proof, and one in which it has no validity without proof as we shall show below. Proof is therefore separate from major premise. What we promised will be shown in the following way. There is no point in requiring proof or demonstration of a premise which contains a plain statement which must be granted by 63 everyone. The following is an example: "If I was in Athens on the day on which the murder was committed at Rome, I could not have been present at the murder." Because this is obviously true there is no point in having it proved. Therefore we should pass immediately to the minor premise, as follows: "But I was at Athens on that day." If this is not granted, it needs proof, after which the conclusion follows. There is, therefore, a kind of major premise which does not need proof. What, then, is the point of showing that there *is* a premise which does need proof, for that can easily be seen by anyone? But if this is so, it follows from this statement and from my previous statement that proof is a thing separate from premise. And if this is so, it is untrue that an argument can have no more than three points.

64 In a similar way it is clear that the second proof may also be separated from the minor premise. If in a certain argument it is sufficient to use the minor premise and it is not necessary to add the proof to

in argumentatione infirma est assumptio, nisi adiuncta
sit approbatio, separatum quiddam extra assumptionem est approbatio. Est autem argumentatio
quaedam in qua assumptio non indiget approbationis,
quaedam autem in qua nihil valet sine approbatione,
ut ostendemus. Separata igitur est ab assumptione
approbatio. Ostendemus autem quod polliciti sumus
65 hoc modo: Quae perspicuam omnibus veritatem
continet assumptio, nihil indiget approbationis. Ea
est huiusmodi: " Si oportet velle sapere, dare operam
philosophiae convenit." Haec propositio indiget
approbationis; non enim perspicua est neque constat
inter omnes propterea quod multi nihil prodesse
philosophiam, plerique etiam obesse arbitrantur.
Assumptio perspicua; est enim haec : " Oportet autem
velle sapere." Hoc quia ipsum ex se perspicitur et
verum esse intellegitur, nihil attinet approbari.
Quare statim concludenda est argumentatio. Est
ergo assumptio quaedam, quae approbationis non
indiget; nam quandam indigere perspicuum est.
Separata est igitur ab assumptione approbatio.
Falsum ergo est non esse plus quam tripertitam
66 argumentationem. XXXVII. Atque ex his illud
iam perspicuum est, esse quandam argumentationem
in qua neque propositio neque assumptio indigeat
approbationis, huiusmodi, ut certum quiddam et
breve exempli causa ponamus: " Si summo opere
sapientia petenda est, summo opere stultitia vitanda
est: summo autem opere sapientia petenda est:
summo igitur opere stultitia vitanda est." Hic et
propositio et assumptio perspicua est; quare neutra
quoque indiget approbatione. Ex hisce omnibus

the premise, but in another argument the premise is weak unless the proof be added, then the proof is something different from the premise. There is, however, an argument in which the premise does not need proof and another in which it has no validity without the proof, as we shall show below. Therefore the proof is separate from the minor premise. We 65 shall show what we promised in this way: a minor premise which contains a truth plain to all does not need proof. Such an argument is of this nature: " If one ought to desire wisdom, it is proper to study philosophy." Here the major premise needs proof; for it is not plain nor agreed upon by everyone; for many think that philosophy is no help and not a few think it is a positive disadvantage. The minor premise, however, is clear; it is as follows: " One should desire wisdom." Because this is clear by itself and is known to be true, there is no point in proving it. Therefore the argument should be brought to a conclusion immediately. There is then a minor premise that does not need proof, and it is clear that some do need proof. Therefore proof is different from minor premise. It is, therefore, untrue that an argument cannot have more than 66 three parts. XXXVII. And from this it is now clear that there is a certain form of argument in which neither the major nor the minor premise needs proof of this sort (to give a brief and definite instance as illustration): " If wisdom is to be sought above all things, then folly is to be avoided above all things; but wisdom *is* to be sought above all things, therefore folly is to be avoided above all things." Here both the major and minor premise are clear, therefore neither needs proof. From all this it is clear that

illud perspicuum est approbationem tum adiungi,
tum non adiungi. Ex quo cognoscitur neque in
propositione neque in assumptione contineri approbationem, sed utramque suo loco positam vim suam
tanquam certam et propriam obtinere. Quodsi ita
est, commode partiti sunt illi qui in quinque partes
tribuerunt argumentationem.

67 Quinque igitur partes sunt eius argumentationis
quae per ratiocinationem tractatur : Propositio, per
quam locus is breviter exponitur, ex quo vis omnis
oportet emanet ratiocinationis ; approbatio, per quam
id quod breviter expositum est rationibus affirmatum
probabilius et apertius fit ; assumptio, per quam id
quod ex propositione ad ostendendum pertinet
assumitur ; assumptionis approbatio, per quam id
quod assumptum est rationibus firmatur ; complexio,
per quam id quod conficitur ex omni argumentatione
breviter exponitur. Quae plurimas habet argumentatio partes, ea constat ex his quinque partibus ;
secunda est quadripertita ; tertia tripertita ; dein
bipertita ; quod in controversia est. De una quoque
parte potest alicui videri posse consistere. XXXVIII.
68 Eorum igitur quae constant exempla ponemus,
horum quae dubia sunt rationes afferemus.

Quinquepertita argumentatio est huiusmodi :
" Omnes leges, iudices, ad commodum rei publicae
referre oportet et eas ex utilitate communi, non ex
scriptione quae in litteris est interpretari. Ea enim
virtute et sapientia maiores nostri fuerunt ut in

sometimes the proof is added and sometimes not. From this it can be recognized that the proof is not contained in a major premise nor in a minor premise but that each occupying its own place has its own character which is, as I may say, definite and proper to itself. Therefore, if this is so, those have made a suitable arrangement who have divided this form of argument into five parts.

67   There are, then, five parts of an argument by deductive or syllogistic reasoning: *major premise* which sets forth briefly the principle from which springs the whole force and meaning of the syllogism; *proof* by which the brief statement of the major premise is supported by reasons and made plainer and more plausible; the *minor premise* in which is premised the point which on the basis of the major premise is pertinent to proving the case; the *proof* of the minor premise, by which what has been premised is established by reasons; the *conclusion* in which there is stated briefly what is proved by the whole deduction. The form of the syllogism that has the largest number of parts consists of these five; the second has four, the third three, the next two, but this is disputed; it is possible that some may 68 think that it can have only one part. XXXVIII. We shall give examples of those on which there is general agreement, and bring forward reasons for those which are in doubt.

   The following is an example of a fivefold argument: " It is right, gentlemen of the jury, to relate all laws to the advantage of the state and to interpret them with an eye to the public good and not according to their literal expression. For such was the uprightness and wisdom of our ancestors that in framing

legibus scribendis nihil sibi aliud nisi salutem atque
utilitatem rei publicae proponerent. Neque enim
ipsi quod obesset scribere volebant, et, si scripsissent,
cum esset intellectum, repudiatum iri legem intellege-
bant. Nemo enim leges legum causa salvas esse
vult, sed rei publicae, quod ex legibus omnes rem
publicam optime putant administrari. Quam ob
rem igitur leges servari oportet, ad eam causam
scripta omnia interpretari convenit : hoc est, quoniam
rei publicae servimus, ex rei publicae commodo atque
utilitate interpretemur. Nam ut ex medicina nihil
oportet putare proficisci, nisi quod ad corporis utilitatem spectet, quoniam eius causa est instituta, sic a
legibus nihil convenit arbitrari, nisi quod rei publicae
conducat, proficisci, quoniam eius causa sunt com-
69 paratae. Ergo in hoc quoque iudicio desinite litteras
legis perscrutari et legem, ut aequum est, ex utilitate
rei publicae considerate. Quid magis utile fuit
Thebanis quam Lacedaemonios opprimi ? Cui magis
Epaminondam, Thebanorum imperatorem, quam
victoriae Thebanorum consulere decuit ? Quid hunc
tanta Thebanorum gloria, tam claro atque exornato
tropaeo carius aut antiquius habere convenit ? Scripto
videlicet legis omisso scriptoris sententiam considerare
debebat. At hoc quidem satis consideratum est,
nullam esse legem nisi rei publicae causa scriptam.

laws they had no object in view except the safety and welfare of the state. They did not themselves intend to write a law which would prove harmful, and they knew that if they did pass such a law, it would be repealed when the defect was recognized. For no one wishes laws to be upheld merely for their own sake, but for the sake of the state, because everyone believes that the state is best governed when administered according to law. All written laws ought, then, to be interpreted in relation to the object for which laws ought to be observed: that is, since we are servants of the community, let us interpret the laws with an eye to the advantage and profit of the community. For as it is right to think that the art of medicine produces nothing except what looks to the health of the body, since it is for this purpose that medicine was founded, so we should believe that nothing comes from the laws except what conduces to the welfare of the state,
69 since the laws were made for this purpose. Therefore in this trial also, cease to search the letter of the law and rather, as is just, examine the law in relation to the public welfare. What was more useful to Thebes than the defeat of Sparta? What should Epaminondas, the Theban commander, have had in mind more than the victory of Thebes? What should he have regarded as dearer or more precious than such a glorious exploit of the Thebans, than a trophy so honourable, so magnificent? It is obvious that he was bound to forget the letter of the law and to consider the intent of the law-maker. But certainly this point has been examined and established beyond a doubt, that no law has been passed except for the good of the state. He thought it, therefore,

Summam igitur amentiam esse existimabat, quod scriptum esset rei publicae salutis causa, id non ex rei publicae salute interpretari. Quodsi leges omnes ad utilitatem rei publicae referri convenit, hic autem saluti rei publicae profuit, profecto non potest eodem facto et communibus fortunis consuluisse et legibus non obtemperasse."

70   XXXIX. Quattuor autem partibus constat argumentatio, cum aut proponimus aut assumimus sine approbatione. Id facere oportet, cum aut propositio ex se intellegitur aut assumptio perspicua est et nullius approbationis indiget. Propositionis approbatione praeterita quattuor ex partibus argumentatio tractatur, ad hunc modum: "Iudices, qui ex lege iurati iudicatis, obtemperare legibus debetis. Obtemperare autem legibus non potestis, nisi id quod scriptum est in lege sequimini. Quod enim certius legis scriptor testimonium voluntatis suae relinquere potuit quam quod ipse magna cum cura atque diligentia scripsit? Quodsi litterae non exstarent, magno opere eas requireremus, ut ex eis scriptoris voluntas cognosceretur; nec tamen Epaminondae permitteremus, ne si extra iudicium quidem esset, ut is nobis sententiam legis interpretaretur, nedum nunc istum patiamur, cum praesto lex sit, non ex eo quod apertissime scriptum est, sed ex eo quod suae causae convenit, scriptoris voluntatem interpretari. Quodsi vos, iudices, legibus obtemperare debetis et id facere non potestis, nisi id quod scriptum est in lege sequamini, quin istum contra legem fecisse iudicatis?"

ᵃ Preiswerk in his dissertation, *De inventione orationum Ciceronianarum* (Basel, 1905), p. 101, cites the following cases of the use of this form of argument in the orations of Cicero: *pro Archia*, 18–19; *pro Caecina*, 41–43; *pro Murena* 3–5; *pro Quinctio*, 48–50; *pro Rabirio perd.* 29, 30; *pro Tullio*, 41, 42.

stark madness not to interpret a law with an eye to the safety of the state when that law had been passed for the safety of the state. In view of this, if all laws ought to be related to the advantage of the state, and Epaminondas contributed to the safety of the state, surely he cannot by the same act have promoted the common interest and have failed to obey the laws." [a]

70 XXXIX. An argument consists of four parts when we state a premise, either major or minor, without giving the proof. This should be done either when the major premise is self-intelligible or when the minor premise is an obvious statement needing no proof. An argument in four parts with the proof of the major premise omitted is handled in this fashion : " Gentlemen of the jury, you, who have sworn to decide according to the law, ought to obey the laws. But you cannot obey the laws unless you follow what is written in the law. What more certain proof of his intent could the author of the law have left than the statement which he wrote himself with great care and pains? Therefore, if there were no written documents we should be in sad need of them to learn from them the intent of the law-giver; nevertheless we should not permit Epaminondas even if he were not under the jurisdiction of the court to interpret to us the meaning of the law; much less, since we have the law before us, should we suffer him to interpret the intent of the law-maker, not by what is quite plainly written, but by what suits his case. Hence, gentlemen of the jury, if you ought to obey the laws, and you cannot do this unless you follow what is written in the law, why not decide that he acted contrary to law ? "

71 Assumptionis autem approbatione praeterita quadripertita sic fiet argumentatio: " Qui saepenumero
nos per fidem fefellerunt, eorum orationi fidem habere
non debemus. Si quid enim perfidia illorum detri-
menti acceperimus, nemo erit praeter nosmet ipsos
quem iure accusare possimus. Ac primo quidem
decipi incommodum est; iterum, stultum; tertio,
turpe. Karthaginienses autem persaepe iam nos
fefellerunt. Summa igitur amentia est in eorum
fide spem habere quorum perfidia totiens deceptus
sis."

72 Utraque approbatione praeterita tripertita fit hoc
pacto: "Aut metuamus Karthaginienses oportet si
incolumes eos reliquerimus, aut eorum urbem diruatu-
mus. At metuere quidem non oportet. Restat
igitur ut urbem diruamus."

XL. Sunt autem qui putant nonnunquam posse
complexione supersederi, cum id perspicuum sit quod
conficiatur ex ratiocinatione; quod si fiat, bipertitam
quoque fieri argumentationem, hoc modo: " Si peperit, virgo non est: peperit autem." Hic satis esse
proponere et assumere: quod conficiatur quoniam perspicuum sit, complexionis rem non indigere. Nobis
autem videtur et omnis ratiocinatio concludenda esse
et illud vitium quod illis displicet magno opere
vitandum, ne quod perspicuum sit, id in complexion-
73 em inferamus. Hoc autem fieri poterit si com-
plexionum genera intellegentur. Nam aut ita com-

71   And an argument in four parts can be made as follows, with the proof of the minor premise omitted: "We ought not to trust the statements of those who have often deceived us by false promises. For if we are harmed by their treachery, we shall have no right to blame anyone except ourselves. To be deceived once is annoying, it is foolish to be deceived twice; the third time it is a disgrace. Now the Carthaginians have deceived us many times in the past. It is therefore the height of folly to place confidence in the promises of those by whose treachery you have so often been deceived."

72   If the proof of both premises is omitted, the argument becomes threefold; for example: "We must either live in fear of the Carthaginians if we leave them with their power undiminished, or we must destroy their city. But we certainly should not live in fear. The alternative is, then, to destroy their city."

XL. There are, moreover, those who think that one may at times dispense with the conclusion when the result of the reasoning is perfectly clear; in this case the argument may also have only two parts, as follows: "If she has borne a child, she is not a virgin; but she has borne a child." Here, they say, it is sufficient to state the major and minor premises; since the deduction is perfectly plain, there is no need of a conclusion. We, on the other hand, think that every reasoning should have a formal conclusion, and also that the fault which they dislike should be avoided by all means, lest we put into the conclusion

73 a statement that is perfectly plain. This result may be secured if the different varieties of conclusion are understood. That is to say, we shall state a conclusion

117

plectemur, ut in unum conducamus propositionem et
assumptionem, hoc modo: " Quodsi leges omnes ad
utilitatem rei publicae referri convenit, hic autem
saluti rei publicae profuit, profecto non potest eodem
facto et saluti communi consuluisse et legibus non
obtemperasse." Aut ita, ut ex contrario sententia
conficiatur, hoc modo: " Summa igitur amentia est
in eorum fide spem habere, quorum perfidia totiens
deceptus sis." Aut ita, ut id solum quod conficitur
inferatur, ad hunc modum: " Urbem igitur diruamus." Aut, ut id quod eam rem quae conficitur
sequatur necesse est. Id est huiusmodi: " Si peperit,
cum viro concubuit: peperit autem." Conficitur
hoc: "Concubuit igitur cum viro." Hoc si nolis inferre
et inferas id quod sequitur: " Fecit igitur incestum,"
et concluseris argumentationem et perspicuam fugeris
74 complexionem. Quare in longis argumentationibus
aut ex conductionibus aut ex contrario complecti
oportet, in brevibus id solum quod conficitur exponere,
in eis in quibus exitus perspicuus est consecutione uti.

Si qui autem ex una quoque parte putabunt con-
stare argumentationem, poterunt dicere saepe satis
esse hoc modo argumentationem facere: " Quoniam
peperit, cum viro concubuit." Nam hoc nullius neque
approbationis neque complexionis indigere. Sed
nobis ambiguitate nominis videntur errare. Nam
argumentatio nomine uno res duas significat, ideo

---

a The " contrariness " consists in making an affirmative
statement " to place confidence " qualified by " the height
of folly " rather than saying in the negative form, " We
should not place confidence."

in one way by combining major and minor in one sentence, as, " If, then, all laws should be related to the advantage of the state, and he contributed to the safety of the state, he certainly cannot by one and the same act have had regard for the common safety and have disobeyed the laws." Or in another way by making a contrary statement, for example: " It is therefore the height of folly to place confidence in the promises of those by whose treachery you have so often been deceived." *a* Or again, it may be done by stating merely the deduction, after this fashion: " Let us therefore destroy the city," or by stating what is the necessary consequence of the deduction, of which the following is an example: " If she has borne a child, she has lain with a man; but she has borne a child." The deduction is, " Therefore she has lain with a man." If you do not wish to state the conclusion in that way, and state the next logical step: " Therefore she is unchaste," you will round out the argument and avoid stating a conclusion

74 which is perfectly obvious. Therefore, in long arguments one ought to state the conclusion by bringing major and minor together, or by a contrary statement, in short ones to state only the deduction, and in those in which the outcome is perfectly plain to state the consequence.

If any think that an argument may also consist of only one part, they will be able to assert that often it is sufficient to present an argument in the following form : " Since she has borne a child, she has lain with a man." For this needs no proof or conclusion. But they seem to be led astray by an ambiguity in the use of a word. For the one word " argument " has two meanings, because a thought on any matter that is

quod et inventum aliquam in rem probabile aut
necessarium argumentatio vocatur et eius inventi
75 artificiosa expolitio. Cum igitur proferent aliquid
huiusmodi : "Quoniam peperit, cum viro concubuit,"
inventum proferent, non expolitionem ; nos autem de
expolitionis partibus loquimur.

XLI. Nihil igitur ad hanc rem ratio illa pertinebit ;
atque hac distinctione alia quoque quae videbuntur
officere huic partitioni propulsabimus, si quis aut
assumptionem aliquando tolli posse putet aut propositionem. Quae si quid habet probabile aut necessarium, quoquo modo commoveat auditorem necesse
est. Quod si solum spectaretur ac nihil, quo pacto
tractaretur id quod esset excogitatum referret,
nequaquam tantum inter summos oratores et me-
76 diocres interesse existimaretur. Variare autem
orationem magno opere oportebit ; nam omnibus
in rebus similitudo mater est satietatis. Id fieri
poterit, si non similiter semper ingrediamur in argumentationem. Nam primum omnium generibus
ipsis distinguere convenit, hoc est, tum inductione
uti, tum ratiocinatione, deinde in ipsa argumentatione non semper a propositione incipere nec
semper quinque partibus abuti neque eadem partes
ratione expolire, sed tum ab assumptione incipere,
tum approbatione alterutra, tum utraque, tum hoc,
tum illo genere complexionis uti. Id ut perspici-

either probable or certain is called an argument, and the same term is applied to the artistic embellishment 75 of this thought. Therefore, when they offer a statement of this sort: " Since she has borne a child, she has lain with a man," they offer a thought, not embellishment. But we are talking about the methods of embellishment.

XLI. Their line of reasoning, then, will not affect this matter; and by this distinction we shall repel other attacks which will seem to be damaging to this division of the argument into five parts; for example, if anyone should think that either the minor or the major premise may sometimes be omitted. And if this idea has any probability or cogency, it must have some sort of effect on the auditor. But if the bare statement of the argument were the only object, and it were of no consequence how the thought is developed and expanded, we should certainly not think that there is such a difference between the 76 greatest orators and the ordinary ones. Variety in the treatment of the speech will be the great necessity. For in everything monotony is the mother of boredom. Variety can be secured if we do not always approach the argument in the same way. For first of all it is desirable to produce diversity merely by using different kinds of arguments, that is, to use induction at one time and deduction at another; and again, in the deductive argument not to begin in every case with the major premise nor always employ all five possible parts nor embellish the parts in the same fashion, but sometimes to begin with the minor premise, sometimes use one of the two proofs, sometimes both, and finally, use now this and now that form of conclusion. That this may be

atur, scribamus; in quolibet exemplo de eis quae
proposita sunt hoc idem exerceamus, ut quam facile
factu sit periclitari licet.[1]

77 Ac de partibus quidem argumentationis satis nobis
dictum videtur. Illud autem volumus intellegi nos
probe tenere aliis quoque rationibus tractari argumentationes in philosophia multis et obscuris, de
quibus certum est artificium constitutum. Verum
illa nobis abhorrere ab usu oratoris visa sunt. Quae
pertinere autem ad dicendum putamus, ea nos commodius quam ceteros attendisse non affirmamus; per-
quisitius et diligentius conscripsisse pollicemur. Nunc,
ut statuimus, proficisci ordine ad reliqua pergemus.

78 XLII. Reprehensio est per quam argumentando
adversariorum confirmatio diluitur aut infirmatur aut
elevatur. Haec fonte inventionis eodem utetur quo
utitur confirmatio, propterea quod, quibus ex locis
aliqua res confirmari potest, isdem potest ex locis
infirmari. Nihil enim considerandum est in his
omnibus inventionibus nisi id quod personis aut
negotiis attributum est. Quare inventionem et
argumentationum expolitionem ex illis quae ante
praecepta sunt hanc quoque in partem orationis transferri oportebit. Verumtamen, ut quaedam praeceptio detur huius quoque partis, exponemus modos
reprehensionis; quos qui observabunt, facilius ea
quae contra dicentur diluere aut infirmare poterunt.

---

[1] *The sentence is probably corrupt; Ströbel marks a lacuna
after* scribamus, *at which point* M *gives* scribamus, J *aut*
scribamus aut, *and* Weidner *reads* scribamus oportet aut, *and
brackets* hoc . . . ut, *which is omitted by* M.

made perfectly plain, we should try writing rhetorical
exercises. In any of the examples given above let
us practice this same exercise that one may prove
how easy it is to do.

77   Enough has, I think, been said about the parts and
divisions of deductive reasoning. I should, however,
like it to be understood that I am well aware that in
philosophy deductive reasoning is treated in many
other forms too; in fact they are intricate and
involved, and a precise system has been formulated.
But they seem to me to be quite unfit for oratorical
practice. But as for the principles which are pertinent to speech, I would not claim that I have
studied them more completely than all others, but I
do assert that I have written with greater care and
accuracy. And now we shall go on in order to the
other points as originally proposed.

78   XLII. The *refutation* is that part of an oration in
which arguments are used to impair, disprove, or
weaken the confirmation or proof in our opponents'
speech. It utilizes the same sources of invention that
confirmation does, because any proposition can be
attacked by the same methods of reasoning by which
it can be supported. For nothing need be considered
in all these quests for arguments except the attributes of persons or of actions. Therefore the rules
for the invention and embellishment of arguments
may properly be transferred from what has been
said before to this part of the oration. In order,
however, that some instructions may be given about
this section too, we shall set forth the methods of
refutation. Those who follow these rules will more
easily be able to impair or disprove the arguments
made against them.

79 Omnis argumentatio reprehenditur, si aut ex eis
quae sumpta sunt non conceditur aliquid unum
plurave aut his concessis complexio ex his confici
negatur, aut si genus ipsum argumentationis vitiosum
ostenditur, aut si contra firmam argumentationem
alia aeque firma aut firmior ponitur.

Ex eis quae sumuntur aliquid non conceditur, cum
aut id quod credibile dicunt negatur esse eiusmodi,
aut, quod comparabile putant, dissimile ostenditur,
aut iudicatum aliam in partem traducitur, aut
omnino iudicium improbatur, aut, quod signum esse
adversarii dixerunt, id eiusmodi negatur esse, aut si
comprehensio[a] aut una aut utraque ex parte reprehenditur, aut enumeratio falsa ostenditur, aut simplex
conclusio falsi aliquid continere demonstratur.   Nam
omne quod sumitur ad argumentandum sive pro
probabili sive pro necessario, necesse est sumatur ex
his locis, ut ante ostendimus.[b]

80 XLIII. Quod pro credibili sumptum erit, id infirmabitur si aut perspicue falsum erit, hoc modo:
"Nemo est quin pecuniam quam sapientiam malit."
Aut ex contrario quoque credibile aliquid habebit,
hoc modo: "Quis est qui non offici cupidior quam
pecuniae sit?"   Aut erit omnino incredibile, ut si
aliquis, quem constet esse avarum, dicat alicuius mediocris offici causa se maximam pecuniam neglexisse,
aut si, quod in quibusdam rebus aut hominibus accidit,
id omnibus dicitur usu venire, hoc pacto: "Qui
pauperes sunt, eis antiquior officio pecunia est."
"Qui locus desertus est, in eo caedem factam esse

---

[a] Cicero here uses *comprehensio* for the form of argument
described as *complexio* in § 45.
[b] § 44.

79   Every argument is refuted in one of these ways: either one or more of its assumptions are not granted, or if the assumptions are granted it is denied that a conclusion follows from them, or the form of argument is shown to be fallacious, or a strong argument is met by one equally strong or stronger.

One of the assumptions of the opponents is not granted when either what they say is credible is denied to be such, or what they think is a parallel case is shown to be dissimilar, or a judicial decision is interpreted in a different sense, or decisions in general are denied validity, or what the adversaries regard as sound evidence is denied to be such, or one or both horns of a dilemma [a] are shown to be unsound, or an enumeration is demonstrated to be incomplete, or a simple conclusion is shown to contain a fallacy. For everything which is used in argumentation, either as a probable or rigorous proof, must come under one of these heads, as we have shown above.[b]

80   XLIII. A statement assumed as credible may be disproved either if it is obviously false, for example: "Everyone prefers wealth to wisdom," or if there is another credible statement to be made to the contrary, for example, "Who is there who does not desire to do his duty more than to acquire wealth?" Or the statement may be wholly incredible, as in the case of a man known by everyone to be avaricious who says that he neglected great financial returns for the sake of doing some humble duty, or if what happens in certain circumstances or to certain people is said to be universally true, after this fashion: "The poor prefer money to duty," "The murder must have been committed in a lonely spot. How could

oportet; in loco celebri homo occidi qui potuit?"
Aut si id quod raro fit fieri omnino negatur, ut Curio
pro Fulvio: "Nemo potest uno aspectu neque
praeteriens in amorem incidere."

81　　Quod autem pro signo sumetur, id ex isdem locis,
quibus confirmatur, infirmabitur. Nam in signo
primum verum esse ostendi oportet; deinde esse eius
rei signum proprium qua de agitur, ut cruorem caedis;
deinde factum esse quod non oportuerit, aut non
factum quod oportuerit; postremo scisse eum de quo
quaeritur eius rei legem et consuetudinem. Nam
eae res sunt signo attributae; quas diligentius
aperiemus, cum separatim de ipsa coniecturali constitutione dicemus. Ergo horum unum quodque in
reprehensione aut non esse signo aut parum magno
esse aut a se potius quam ab adversariis stare, aut
omnino falso dici aut in aliam quoque suspicionem
duci posse demonstrabitur.

82　　XLIV. Cum autem pro comparabili aliquid inducetur, quoniam id per similitudinem maxime tractatur,
in reprehendendo conveniet simile id negare esse
quod conferetur ei quicum conferetur. Id fieri
poterit si demonstrabitur diversum esse genere,
natura, vi, magnitudine, tempore, loco, persona,
opinione; ac si, quo in numero illud quod per
similitudinem afferetur, et quo in loco hoc cuius causa
afferetur, haberi conveniat, ostendetur. Deinde quid

---

^a *Orat. Rom. Frag.*², p. 253 (Meyer).
^b In Book II, 14–51.
^c For an expansion of this, *v.* Victorinus, *ad loc.*

a man be killed in a crowd?" Or if what rarely happens is declared never to happen at all, as for example the passage in Curio's speech *In Defence of Fulvius*: [a] "No one can fall in love at first sight, or as he is passing by."

81 What is assumed to be a "sign" will be disproved by use of the same topics by which it is supported. For in the case of a sign, first it must be shown to be true; and in the second place to be a proper sign of the thing under discussion, as, for example, blood is a sign of murder; in the third place that it indicates that something has been done which ought not to have been done, or that something has been left undone which ought to have been done; and finally that the person knew the law and custom in respect to the matter under discussion. For these matters are subject to proof by signs, and will be discussed more fully when we speak separately about the conjectural issue.[b] Therefore in the refutation it will be shown of each of these points that it is not a sign, or not an important one, or that it favours one's own side rather than the opponents', or that it is absolutely false, or that it can be shifted so as to create a suspicion in a different quarter.

82 XLIV. When something is introduced as a parallel, since this topic is largely treated by showing similarity, it will be proper in refutation to deny that the thing compared is similar to that to which it is compared. This can be done if it is shown that it differs in kind, nature, meaning, importance, time, place, person, or repute;[c] and in particular if it is shown in what class it is proper to put that which is cited as similar, and in what group to put that which the comparison is intended to illumine. In the next place we shall

res cum re differat demonstrabimus : ex quo docebimus aliud de eo quod comparabitur, et de eo quicum comparabitur existimare oportere. Huius facultatis maxime indigebimus, cum ea ipsa argumentatio quae per inductionem tractatur erit reprehendenda.

Sin iudicatum aliquod inferetur, quoniam id ex his locis maxime firmatur : laude eorum qui iudicarunt ; similitudine eius rei qua de agitur ad eam rem qua de iudicatum est ; et commemorando non modo non esse reprehensum iudicium, sed ab omnibus approbatum ; et demonstrando difficilius et maius fuisse ad iudicandum quod afferatur quam id quod instet : ex contrariis locis si res aut vera aut veri similis permittet, infirmari oportebit. Atque erit observandum diligenter ne nihil ad id quo de agatur pertineat id quod iudicatum sit ; et videndum est ne ea res proferatur in qua sit offensum ut de ipso qui iudicarit iudicium 83 fieri videatur. Oportet autem animadvertere ne, cum aliter sint multa iudicata, solitarium aliquid aut rarum iudicatum afferatur. Nam sic his rebus auctoritas iudicati maxime potest infirmari. Atque ea quidem quae quasi probabilia sumentur ad hunc modum temptari oportebit.

XLV. Quae vero sicuti necessaria dicentur, ea si forte imitabuntur modo necessariam argumentationem neque erunt eiusmodi, sic reprehendentur :

---

a Cicero's thought loses clarity from too great compression ; he means that the " topic " of " praise " involves also " blame." A judgement which is supported by praising the judge can be attacked by condemning him.

demonstrate how the one thing differs from the
other; as a result we shall prove that different
judgements should be passed on the thing compared
and on the thing to which it is to be compared. We
shall especially need the ability to do this when the
criticism is to be directed against that particular
form of argument which is handled by induction.

In case a decision or judgement is offered as an
argument, it should, if truth or plausibility permits,
be attacked by using the same topics by which it is
supported, viz. by praising those who have made
the decision,[a] by the similarity between the matter
under discussion and the matter about which judgement has been given; by stating that not only has
the judgement not been attacked but that it has
received universal approval; and by demonstrating
that the case cited was more difficult or more important to decide than the present case. And one
must watch sharply to see whether the decision is
pertinent to the case under discussion, and be careful
to observe that a case is not cited of such a nature
that objection has been made to it, so that a
judgement might seem to have been passed on him
83 who has done the judging. One ought also to notice
if a unique or extraordinary case has been cited when
many decisions have been made in the opposite tenor.
For thus by such arguments the authority of a
decision or judgement can best be weakened. Also
statements which are assumed to be probably true
ought to be assailed in the same way.

XLV. Statements which are made with the impli-
cation that they are necessarily true can be attacked
in the following way if they only imitate a rigorous
argument and are not really such: in the first place

primum comprehensio quae utrum concesseris debet
tollere, si vera est, nunquam reprehendetur; sin
falsa, duobus modis, aut conversione aut alterius
partis infirmatione; conversione,[1] hoc modo:

> Nam si veretur, quid eum accuses qui est probus?
> Sin inverecundum animi ingenium possidet,
> Quid autem accuses qui id parvi auditum aesti-
> met?

Hic, sive vereri dixeris sive non vereri, concedendum
hoc putat ut neges esse accusandum. Quod conversione sic reprehendetur: " Immo vero accusandus
est. Nam si veretur, accuses; non enim parvi audi-
tum aestimabit. Sin inverecundum animi ingenium
possidet, tamen accuses; non enim probus est."
84 Alterius autem partis infirmatione hoc modo reprehendetur: " Verum si veretur, accusatione tua
correctus ab errato recedet."

Enumeratio vitiosa intellegitur si aut praeteritum
quiddam dicimus quod velimus concedere, aut
infirmum aliquid adnumeratum quod aut contra dici
possit, aut causa non sit quare non honeste possimus
concedere. Praeteritur quiddam in eiusmodi enume-
rationibus: " Quoniam habes istum equum, aut emeris
oportet aut hereditate possideas aut munere acceperis aut domi tibi natus sit aut, si eorum nihil
est, surripueris necesse est: si [2] neque emisti neque
hereditate venit neque donatus est neque domi natus
85 est, necesse est ergo surripueris." Hoc commode

---

[1] conversione *bracketed by Linsmayer, Ströbel.*
[2] si *M* : sed *J.*

---

[a] *Trag. Rom. Frag.* Ribbeck[3], p. 302. *Remains of Old
Latin,* ii, p. 614.

the dilemma, which ought to be a decisive argument no matter which alternative you choose, if it is true, can never be answered, but if it is false, it can be answered in two ways, either by conversion or by denial of one part: by conversion in this way: " For if the man be modest, why should you attack so good a man? And if the temper of his mind be shameless, then what avails your accusation of one who recks little of such a charge? " [a] Here it is expected that whether you say he is modest or not, you will have to grant that you should not accuse him. This can be answered by conversion, thus: " On the contrary, he ought most certainly to be accused. For if he is modest you should accuse him, for he will not reck little of such a charge. But if the temper of his mind be shameless, you still should accuse him, for he is not an upright 84 man." It can be answered by denial of one alternative, as follows: " But if he is modest, he will be reformed by your accusation and abandon the error of his way."

An enumeration is recognized as faulty if we mention something that has been omitted which we should be willing to grant, or if some weak point has been included in it which can be denied, or if there is no reason why we cannot honourably grant some point. A point is omitted in enumerations of this character: " Since you are in possession of that horse, you must have bought it, or inherited it, or received it as a gift, or it must have been foaled at your farm, or if none of these is true, you must have stolen it. If you did not buy it nor inherit it nor receive it as a present, and it was not foaled on your 85 farm, then you must have stolen it." A proper

reprehenditur, si dici possit ex hostibus equus esse captus, cuius praedae sectio non venierit; quo illato infirmatur enumeratio; quoniam id sit inductum quod praeteritum sit in enumeratione. XLVI. Altero autem modo reprehendetur si aut contra aliquid dicetur, hoc est, si exempli causa, ut in eodem versemur, poterit ostendi hereditate venisse, aut si illud extremum non erit turpe concedere, ut si qui, cum dixerit adversarius : " Aut insidias facere voluisti aut amico morem gessisti aut cupiditate elatus es," amico se morem gessisse fateatur.

86 Simplex autem conclusio reprehenditur si hoc quod sequitur non videatur necessario cum eo quod antecessit cohaerere. Nam hoc quidem : " Si spiritum ducit, vivit," " Si dies est, lucet," eiusmodi est, ut cum priore necessario posterius cohaerere videatur. Hoc autem : " Si mater est, diligit," " Si aliquando peccavit, nunquam corrigetur," sic conveniet reprehendi ut demonstretur non necessario cum priore posterius cohaerere. Hoc genus et cetera necessaria et omnino omnis argumentatio et eius reprehensio maiorem quandam vim continet et latius patet quam hic exponitur; sed eius artifici cognitio eiusmodi est ut non ad huius artis partem aliquam adiungi possit, sed ipsa separatim longi temporis et magnae atque arduae cognitionis indigeat. Quare illa nobis alio tempore atque ad aliud institutum, si facultas erit,

answer is made to this if it can be said that the horse was captured from the enemy and there was no sale of this booty. When this has been stated the enumeration is rendered invalid, since a point has been noted which was omitted in the enumeration. XLVI. The second method of answering, that is, if any point can be denied, is exemplified by the following case: if, for instance (to use the same illustration) it can be shown that the horse was inherited. Or it can be answered, if, finally, it will not be dishonourable to concede a point, as in the case of the man who, when his opponents have said, "You wished to lay a plot, or to gratify a friend, or you were carried away by avarice," might confess that he gratified a friend.

86　　A simple conclusion is answered if the consequence does not seem to be necessarily consistent with what precedes. For instance the sentences, "If he is breathing, he is alive," "If it is daytime, it is light," are of such a nature that the conclusion seems to be necessarily connected with the condition; but statements of this kind, "If she is his mother, she loves him," "If he has sinned once, he will never be reformed," it is proper to answer by showing that the conclusion is not necessarily consistent with the condition. This kind and the other rigorous arguments and in fact the whole science of argumentation and rebuttal have a greater importance and wider ramifications than here set forth. But the theoretical mastery of this art is so difficult that it cannot be appended to any chapter of rhetoric, but demands for itself alone a long period of profound and arduous thought. Therefore this will be treated by us at another time and in another work, if oppor-

explicabuntur; nunc his praeceptionibus rhetorum ad usum oratorium contentos nos esse oportebit. Cum igitur ex eis quae sumentur aliquid non concedetur, sic infirmabitur.

87   XLVII. Cum autem, his concessis, complexio ex his non conficitur, haec erunt consideranda: num aliud conficiatur, aliud dicatur, hoc modo: si, cum aliquis dicat se profectum esse ad exercitum, contra eum quis velit hac uti argumentatione: "Si venisses ad exercitum, a tribunis militaribus visus esses; non es autem ab his visus: non es igitur ad exercitum profectus." Hic cum concesseris propositionem et assumptionem, complexio est infirmanda. Aliud enim, quam cogebatur, illatum est.

88   Ac nunc quidem, quo facilius res cognosceretur, perspicuo et grandi vitio praeditum posuimus exemplum; sed saepe obscurius positum vitium pro vero probatur, cum aut parum memineris quid concesseris, aut ambiguum aliquid pro certo concesseris. Ambiguum si concesseris ex ea parte quam ipse intellexeris, eam partem adversarius ad aliam partem per complexionem velit accommodare, demonstrare oportebit non ex eo quod ipse concesseris, sed ex eo quod ille sumpserit, confici complexionem, ad hunc modum: "Si indigetis pecuniae, pecuniam non habetis; si pecuniam non habetis, pauperes estis: indigetis autem pecuniae; mercaturae enim, ni ita esset, operam non daretis: pauperes igitur estis."

---

a The trick lies in confusing " set out for " with " came to."

tunity shall offer. Now we shall have to be content with these rules laid down by teachers of rhetoric for the use of speakers. When, therefore, one of the assumptions made is not granted, it may be attacked thus.

87 XLVII. When, however, these points have been admitted and a conclusion does not follow from them, one must consider whether it is not true that one result follows and a different one has been expressed, for instance, if, when one might say he had set out for the army, an opponent might wish to use against him this form of argument: "If you had come to the army you would have been seen by the military tribunes. But you were not seen by them. Therefore you did not set out for the army." Here you may grant the major and minor premises, but the conclusion must be denied. For an inference has been made which was not inevitable.[a]

88 In this case in order to make the subject plainer we have given an example containing an obvious and monstrous fallacy. But often a fallacy stated obscurely is accepted as truth, either when you do not exactly recall what you have granted or you have granted something as certain which is really doubtful. If you have conceded a doubtful point in the sense in which you understand it, and your opponent wishes to work it into a conclusion in a different sense, it will be necessary to show that the conclusion does not follow from what you have admitted but from what he has assumed. The following is an example: "If you want money, you do not have money; if you do not have money, you are poor; you do want money, for otherwise you would not engage in trade; therefore you are poor." This is answered in the following

Hoc sic reprehenditur: "Cum dicebas: Si indigetis pecuniae, pecuniam non habetis, hoc intellegebam: Si propter inopiam in egestate estis, pecuniam non habetis, et idcirco concedebam; cum autem hoc sumebas: Indigetis autem pecuniae, illud accipiebam: Vultis autem pecuniae plus habere. Ex quibus concessionibus non conficitur hoc: Pauperes igitur estis; conficeretur autem, si tibi primo quoque hoc concessissem, qui pecuniam maiorem vellet habere, 89 eum pecuniam non habere." XLVIII. Saepe autem oblitum putant quid concesseris, et idcirco id quod non conficitur, quasi conficiatur, in conclusionem infertur, hoc modo: "Si ad illum hereditas veniebat, veri simile est ab illo necatum." Deinde hoc approbant plurimis verbis. Post assumunt: "Ad illum autem hereditas veniebat." Deinde infertur: "Ille igitur occidit." Id quod ex eis, quae sumpserant, non conficitur. Quare observare diligenter oportet et quid sumatur, et quid ex his conficiatur.

Ipsum autem genus argumentationis vitiosum his de causis ostendetur, si aut in ipso vitium erit aut non ad id quod instituitur accommodabitur. Atque in ipso vitium erit, si omnino totum falsum erit, si commune, si vulgare, si leve, si remotum, si mala definitione, si controversum, si perspicuum, si non concessum, si turpe, si offensum, si contrarium, si inconstans, si adversarium.

90 Falsum est in quo perspicue mendacium est, hoc modo: "Non potest esse sapiens qui pecuniam neglegit. Socrates autem pecuniam neglegebat: non

way: "When you said, 'If you want money, you do not have money,' I understood it to mean, 'If on account of poverty you are in extreme want, you do not have money,' and therefore I granted the point; when, however, you said, 'You do want money,' I took that to mean 'You do want to have more money.'" From this admission it does not follow that you are poor. It would follow, if at first I had made this admission also, "Whoever wishes to have more money, does not have money." XLVIII. 89 Moreover, they often think that you have forgotten what you have admitted, and therefore they insert in the conclusion what does not follow, under pretence that it does; for example: "If the estate came to him, it is probable that he committed the murder." Then they prove this at considerable length. Next they state the minor: "But the estate did come to him," and then the conclusion: "Therefore he killed him." But this does not follow from their premises. Therefore one ought to watch carefully both what is premised and what is deduced from the premises.

On the other hand, the very nature of the argumentation may be shown to be faulty for the following reasons: if there is any defect in the argumentation itself or if it is not adapted to prove what we purpose to prove. To be specific, there will be a defect in the argument itself if it is wholly false, general, common, trifling, far-fetched, a bad definition, controvertible, self-evident, disputable, discreditable, offensive, "contrary," inconsistent, or adverse.

90 A false argument is one containing a statement obviously untrue, for example: "One cannot be wise who is indifferent to money. But Socrates was indifferent to money: therefore he was not wise."

igitur sapiens erat." Commune est quod nihilo minus
ab adversariis, quam a nobis facit, hoc modo: " Idcirco,
iudices, quia veram causam habebam, brevi peroravi."
Vulgare est quod ad aliquam quoque rem non
probabilem, si nunc concessum sit, transferri possit,
ut hoc: " Si causam veram non haberet, vobis se,
iudices, non commisisset." Leve est quod aut post
tempus dicitur, hoc modo: " Si in mentem venisset,
non commisisset:" aut perspicue turpem rem levi
tegere vult defensione, hoc modo:

> Cum te expetebant omnes, florentissimo
> Regno reliqui: nunc desertum ab omnibus
> Summo periclo sola ut restituam paro.

91 XLIX. Remotum est quod ultra quam satis est
petitur, huiusmodi: " Quodsi non P. Scipio Corneliam
filiam Ti. Graccho collocasset atque ex ea duos
Gracchos procreasset, tantae seditiones natae non
essent; quare hoc incommodum Scipioni ascribendum
videtur." Huiusmodi est illa quoque conquestio:

> Utinam ne in nemore Pelio securibus
> Caesae accedissent abiegnae ad terram trabes!

Longius enim repetita est quam res postulabat. Mala
definitio est cum aut communia describit, hoc modo:

ᵃ TRF³, p. 304. ROL, ii, p. 262. From the *Medus* of
Pacuvius. Tr. by Warmington.
ᵇ TRF³, p. 49. ROL, i, p. 312. From the *Medea* of
Ennius.

A general argument is one which is no less helpful to the opponents' case than to ours, for example: "Therefore, gentlemen of the jury, I have summed up in a few words because justice was on my side." A common argument is one which if granted now could be transferred to another situation not worthy of approval, as in the following sentence: "If he had not had justice on his side, gentlemen of the jury, he would not have entrusted himself to your decision." A trifling argument is one which is offered too late, as: "If he had thought, he would not have done it," or in which the pleader tries to cloak an obviously disgraceful act by a trifling defence, for example:

"When all men sought you out, while yet your throne
Did flourish greatly, I deserted you;
But now that you forsaken are by all,
In greatest peril, I alone prepare
A plan whereby I can restore you." [a]

91 XLIX. A far-fetched argument is one derived from circumstances too remote, as in this case: "If Publius Scipio had not given his daughter Cornelia in marriage to Tiberius Gracchus, and if he had not had by her the two Gracchi, so great civil strife would not have arisen. Therefore this disaster seems attributable to Scipio." The following lament is of the same nature:

"Would God no axes e'er had felled to earth
The firs in Pelion's wood." [b]

For this went farther back in the succession of events than the argument required. A bad definition is one which sets forth characteristics applicable to

139

"Seditiosus est is qui malus atque inutilis civis;"
nam hoc non magis seditiosi, quam ambitiosi, quam
calumniatoris, quam alicuius hominis improbi vim
describit; aut falsum quiddam dicit, hoc pacto:
"Sapientia est pecuniae quaerendae intellegentia;"
aut aliquid non grave nec magnum continens, sic:
"Stultitia est immensa gloriae cupiditas." Est haec
quidem stultitia, sed ex parte quadam, non ex omni
genere definita. Controversum est in quo ad dubium
demonstrandum dubia causa affertur, hoc modo:

> Eho tu, di quibus est potestas motus superum
>   atque inferum,
> Pacem inter sese conciliant, conferunt con-
>   cordiam.

92 Perspicuum est de quo non est controversia: ut si
quis, cum Orestem accuset, planum faciat ab eo
matrem esse occisam. Non concessum est, cum id
quod augetur in controversia est, ut si quis, cum
Ulixem accuset, in hoc maxime commoretur: indignum esse ab homine ignavissimo virum fortissimum
Aiacem necatum. Turpe est quod aut eo loco in quo
dicitur, aut eo homine qui dicit, aut eo tempore quo
dicitur, aut eis qui audiunt, aut ea re qua de agitur,
indignum propter inhonestam rem videtur. Offensum est quod eorum qui audiunt voluntatem laedit:
ut, si quis apud equites Romanos cupidos iudicandi
93 Caepionis legem iudiciariam laudet. L. Contrarium

---

a TRF³, p. 36. ROL, i, p. 356. From the *Thyestes* of
Ennius.
b The *lex Servilia iudiciaria* which sought to deprive the
equites of their exclusive right to serve as *iudices*. See
Hendrickson's note on *Brutus* 164, LCL.

many objects, as follows: " He is seditious who is a bad and useless citizen," for this does not describe the character of a seditious man any more than of one who is over-ambitious or a pettifogger, or any wicked person; or one which makes a false statement, in this fashion: " Wisdom is knowledge of how to acquire money; " or one which contains some small or insignificant point, like the following: " Folly is boundless greed for fame." This is folly, to be sure, but is only a partial and not a complete definition. A controvertible argument is one in which a dubious reason is given to prove a dubious case, as follows:

> " See how the gods, who rule and move
> The heavens above and shades below
> In peace and harmony together stand." [a]

92 A self-evident argument is one about which there is no dispute; for instance, if one, in accusing Orestes, should make it quite plain that he killed his mother. A disputable argument is one where the point which is being amplified is a matter of controversy; for instance, if anyone in accusing Ulysses should linger long over this point, that it is unworthy that Ajax, the bravest of men, should be killed by the most arrant coward. A discreditable argument is one which because of something dishonourable seems unworthy of the place in which it is delivered or of the speaker or of the time at which it is delivered or of the audience or of the subject under discussion. An offensive argument is one which wounds the sensibilities of the audience; for instance, if anyone speaking before the Roman *equites* who desire the privilege of serving on the jury should praise Caepio's 93 law regulating jury service.[b] L. A " contrary " argu-

est quod contra dicitur atque ei qui audiunt fecerunt :
ut si quis apud Alexandrum Macedonem dicens
contra aliquem urbis expugnatorem diceret nihil esse
crudelius quam urbes diruere, cum ipse Alexander
Thebas diruisset.   Inconstans est quod ab eodem de
eadem re diverse dicitur : ut si qui, cum dixerit, qui
virtutem habeat, eum nullius rei ad bene vivendum
indigere, neget postea sine bona valetudine posse
bene vivi ; aut, se amico adesse propter benivolentiam, sperare autem aliquid commodi ad se perven-
94 turum.   Adversarium est quod ipsi causae aliqua ex
parte officit, ut si quis hostium vim et copias et felicita-
tem augeat, cum ad pugnandum milites adhortetur.

Si non ad id quod instituitur accommodabitur aliqua
pars argumentationis, horum aliquo in vitio reperietur :
si plura pollicitus pauciora demonstrabit ; aut si, cum
totum debebit ostendere, de parte aliqua loquatur,
hoc modo : " Mulierum genus avarum est ; nam
Eriphyla auro viri vitam vendidit ; " aut si non id quod
accusabitur defendet, ut si qui, cum ambitus accusabitur, manu se fortem esse defendet ; aut ut Amphion
apud Euripidem, item apud Pacuvium,[1] qui vitu-
perata musica sapientiam laudat ; aut si res ex
hominis vitio vituperabitur, ut si qui doctrinam ex
alicuius docti vitiis reprehendat ; aut si qui, cum

---

[1] item apud Pacuvium *bracketed by Kayser, Ströbel.*

ment is one which is made against actions performed by the audience; for instance, if a person speaking before Alexander of Macedon against someone who had stormed a city should say that nothing is more cruel than to destroy cities, when Alexander himself had destroyed Thebes. An argument is inconsistent when conflicting statements are made by the same speaker on the same subject; for instance, if one after stating that the virtuous man needs nothing else to live a good life, should later deny that one can live a good life without good health; or one might say that he is helping his friend out of kindness, but expects to get some 94 profit from it. An adverse argument is one which does harm to one's own case in some respect; for instance, if a general in exhorting his soldiers to fight should magnify the strength, forces and good fortune of the enemy.

If some part of the argumentation is not adapted to its purpose, it will be found to have one of the following defects: if the speaker proves fewer points than he has promised to prove; or if when he ought to demonstrate something about a whole class, he speaks only of a part, as follows: " The race of women is avaricious, for Eriphyla sold her husband's life for gold; " or if he answers a charge which has not been brought against him, for instance, if a man accused of bribery should offer as defence that he is valiant in battle; or like Amphion in the play of Euripides, and that of Pacuvius as well, who replies to an attack on music by praising philosophy; or if a thing is criticized because of the fault of a man, for instance, if some one should blame learning because of the error of some learned man; or if wishing to

aliquem volet laudare, de felicitate eius, non de
virtute dicat; aut si rem cum re ita comparabit, ut
alteram se non putet laudare, nisi alteram vituperarit;
aut si alteram ita laudet, ut alterius non faciat
95 mentionem; aut si, cum de certa re quaereretur, de
communi instituetur oratio, ut si quis, cum aliqui
deliberent, bellum gerant an non, pacem laudet
omnino, non illud bellum inutile esse demonstret;
aut si ratio alicuius rei reddetur falsa, hoc modo:
" Pecunia bonum est, propterea quod ea maxime vitam
beatam efficit; " aut infirma, ut Plautus:

> Amicum castigare ob meritam noxiam,
> Immune est facinus; verum in aetate utile
> Et conducibile; nam ego amicum hodie meum
> Concastigabo pro commerita noxia;

aut eadem, hoc modo: " Malum est avaritia; multos
enim magnis incommodis affecit pecuniae cupiditas; "
aut parum idonea, hoc modo: " Maximum bonum est
amicitia; plurimae enim delectationes sunt in
amicitia."

96 LI. Quartus modus erit reprehensionis per quem
contra firmam argumentationem aeque firma aut
firmior ponitur. Hoc genus in deliberationibus
maxime versabitur, cum aliquid quod contra dicatur,
aequum esse concedimus, sed id quod nos defendimus,
necessarium esse demonstramus; aut cum id quod
illi defendant, utile esse fatemur, quod nos dicamus,
honestum esse demonstramus.

---

a Plautus, *Trinummus*, 23–26. Tr. Nixon, LCL.

praise some one he should speak of his good luck and not of his virtue; or if he compares one thing with another with the idea that he cannot praise one 95 without blaming the other; or if he praises one without mentioning the other; or if when a definite subject is under discussion, he addresses his speech to a common topic, for instance, if one, when some state is deliberating whether to go to war or not, should devote his speech to praise of peace in general and not prove that this particular war was useless; or if a false reason is given for something, as is illustrated in the following: "Money is good, for it is the thing which does the most to make life happy;" or the reason may be weak, as in these lines from Plautus:

> "Castigating a friend even when his offence deserves it is a thankless job, but at times it's useful and expedient. Now here am I—with a friend I mean to castigate thoroughly, as his offence thoroughly deserves." [a]

or the reason may be merely a statement of the same idea in different words, for example: "Avarice is bad, for desire for money has brought great disasters on many;" or the reason may be insufficient, for example: "Friendship is the highest good, for there are many pleasures in friendship."

96 LI. The fourth method of refutation is to counter a strong argument with one equally strong or stronger. This kind will be used particularly in speaking before a deliberative body, when we grant that something said on the other side is fair, but prove that the position we are defending is necessary; or when we acknowledge that the course of action which they defend is advantageous, but prove that ours is honourable.

Ac de reprehensione haec[1] existimavimus esse dicenda.[2]

97 Hermagoras digressionem deinde, tum postremam conclusionem ponit. In hac autem digressione ille putat oportere quandam inferri orationem a causa atque a iudicatione ipsa remotam, quae aut sui laudem aut adversari vituperationem contineat aut in aliam causam deducat ex qua conficiat aliquid confirmationis aut reprehensionis, non argumentando, sed augendo per quandam amplificationem. Hanc si qui partem putabit esse orationis, sequatur licebit. Nam et augendi et laudandi et vituperandi praecepta a nobis partim data sunt, partim suo loco dabuntur.[3] Nobis autem non placuit hanc partem[4] in numerum reponi, quod de causa digredi nisi per locum communem displicet; quo de genere posterius est dicendum. Laudes autem et vituperationes non separatim placet tractari, sed in ipsis argumentationibus esse implicatas. Nunc de conclusione dicemus.

98 LII. Conclusio est exitus et determinatio totius orationis. Haec habet partes tres: enumerationem, indignationem, conquestionem.

Enumeratio est per quam res disperse et diffuse dictae unum in locum coguntur et reminiscendi causa unum sub aspectum subiciuntur. Haec si semper eodem modo tractabitur, perspicue ab omnibus arti-

---

[1] haec *Weidner*: haec quidem *Mi*: quidem haec *Jω*.

[2] *After* dicenda *the MSS. have* Deinceps nunc de conclusione ponemus. (We shall now in the next place treat the peroration.) *Bracketed by Oudendorp.*

[3] Nam . . . dabuntur *bracketed by Kayser.*

[4] hanc partem *bracketed by Weidner, Friedrich, Ströbel.*

This is what we have thought it necessary to say about refutation.

97 Hermagoras puts the digression next, and then finally the peroration. In this digression he thinks a passage should be introduced unconnected with the case and the actual point to be decided; it might contain praise of oneself or abuse of the opponent, or lead to some other case which may supply confirmation or refutation not by argument but by adding emphasis by means of some amplification. If anyone thinks this is a proper division of a speech, he may follow Hermagoras' rule. For some of the rules for amplification and praise and vituperation have already been given, and the rest will be given in the proper place. But we do not think that this should be listed among the regular parts of the speech, because we disapprove of digressing from the main subject except in case of " commonplaces "; and this topic is to be discussed later. Moreover, I am of the opinion that praise and vituperation should not be made a separate part, but should be closely interwoven with the argumentation itself. Now we shall discuss the peroration.

98 LII. The peroration is the end and conclusion of the whole speech; it has three parts, the summing-up, the *indignatio* or exciting of indignation or ill-will against the opponent, and the *conquestio* or the arousing of pity and sympathy.

The summing-up is a passage in which matters that have been discussed in different places here and there throughout the speech are brought together in one place and arranged so as to be seen at a glance in order to refresh the memory of the audience. If this is always treated in the same manner, it will be

ficio quodam tractari intellegetur; sin varie fiet, et hanc suspicionem et satietatem vitare poterit. Quare tum oportebit ita facere, ut plerique faciunt propter facilitatem, singillatim unam quamque rem attingere et ita omnes transire breviter argumentationes; tum autem, id quod difficilius est, dicere quas partes exposueris in partitione de quibus te pollicitus sis dicturum, et reducere in memoriam quibus rationibus unam quamque partem confirmaris; hoc modo: " Illud docuimus, illud planum fecimus," tum ab eis qui audiunt quaerere quid sit quod sibi velle debeant demonstrari. Ita simul et in memoriam redibit auditor et putabit nihil esse praeterea quod debeat desiderare.

99   Atque in his generibus, ut ante dictum est, tum tuas argumentationes transire separatim, tum, id quod artificiosius est, cum tuis contrarias coniungere; et cum tuam dixeris argumentationem, tum, contra eam quod afferatur, quemadmodum dilueris, osten- dere. Ita per brevem comparationem auditoris memoria et de confirmatione et de reprehensione redintegrabitur. Atque haec aliis actionis quoque modis variare oportebit. Nam tum ex tua persona enumerare possis, ut quid et quo quidque loco dixeris admoneas; tum vero personam aut rem aliquam inducere et enumerationem ei totam attribuere.

perfectly evident to everyone that it is being handled according to some rule or system. But if it is managed in different ways it will be possible to avoid both this suspicion and the boredom which comes from repetition. Therefore it will be proper at times to sum up in the manner which the majority of speakers employ, because it is easy, *i.e.* to touch on each single point and so to run briefly over all the arguments. At times, however, it is well to take the harder course and state the topics which you have set out in the partition and promised to discuss, and to recall to mind the lines of reasoning by which you have proved each point, in this fashion: "We have demonstrated this, we have made this plain." At times one may inquire of the audience what they might rightly wish to have proved to them. Thus the auditor will refresh his memory and think that there is nothing more that he ought to desire.

99   Furthermore, in the summing-up, as has been said above, you should at times run over your own arguments one by one, and at times combine the opposing arguments with yours, which requires greater artistry; and after stating your argument, show how you have refuted the argument which has been made against it. Thus by this brief comparison the memory of the audience is refreshed in regard to both the confirmation and the refutation. It may also be advisable to produce variety by changing the method of presentation. That is to say, at times you can sum up in your own person, reminding the audience of what you have said and in what order each point was discussed; but at other times you can bring on the stage some person or thing and let this actor sum up the whole argument. The following

Personam hoc modo: " Nam si legis scriptor exsistat
et quaerat sic id a vobis quid dubitetis, quid possitis
dicere, cum vobis hoc et hoc sit demonstratum.''
Atque hic, item ut in nostra persona, licebit alias
singillatim transire omnes argumentationes, alias ad
partitionis singula genera referre, alias ab auditore
quid desideret quaerere, alias haec facere per comparationem suarum et contrariarum argumentationum.

100   Res autem inducetur, si alicui rei huiusmodi, legi,
loco, urbi, monumento oratio attribuetur per enumerationem, hoc modo: " Quid, si leges loqui possent?
Nonne haec apud vos quererentur? Quidnam am-
plius desideratis, iudices, cum vobis hoc et hoc planum
factum sit? '' In hoc quoque genere omnibus isdem
modis uti licebit. Commune autem praeceptum hoc
datur ad enumerationem, ut ex una quaque argumentatione, quoniam tota iterum dici non potest, id
eligatur quod erit gravissimum, et unum quidque
quam brevissime transeatur, ut memoria, non oratio
renovata videatur.

LIII. Indignatio est oratio per quam conficitur ut
in aliquem hominem magnum odium aut in rem gravis
offensio concitetur. In hoc genere illud primum
intellegi volumus, posse omnibus ex locis eis quos in
confirmationis praeceptis posuimus tractari indignationem. Nam ex eis rebus quae personis aut quae
negotiis sunt attributae quaevis amplificationes et
indignationes nasci possunt, sed tamen ea quae

is an example of the use of a person: " If the author of the law should appear and ask why you hesitate, what, pray, could you say, since this and this has been proved to you? " And here, as when speaking in one's own proper person, the orator may at one time run over all the arguments singly, at another, refer to each topic in the partition, or again, inquire of the auditor what he desires, or again, sum up by comparing his own and the opposing arguments.

100 A thing is brought on the stage if in the enumeration the words are given to something of this sort, a law, a place, a city, or a monument; for example, " What if the laws could speak? Would they not make this complaint to you: 'What more do you desire, gentlemen of the jury, when this and this has been made plain to you?' " In this kind of summing up as well, one may use all the same methods. As a general principle for summing up, it is laid down that since the whole of any argument cannot be given a second time, the most important point of each be selected, and that every argument be touched on as briefly as possible, so that it may appear to be a refreshing of the memory of the audience, rather than a repetition of the speech.

LIII. The *indignatio* is a passage which results in arousing great hatred against some person, or violent offence at some action. In discussing this topic we wish it to be understood at the beginning that *indignatio* is used in connexion with all the topics which we laid out when giving rules for confirmation. In other words, all the attributes of persons and things can give occasion for any use of amplification that may be desired, or any method of arousing

separatim de indignatione praecipi possunt consideremus.

101 Primus locus sumitur ab auctoritate, cum commemoramus, quantae curae res ea fuerit eis quorum auctoritas gravissima debeat esse : diis immortalibus, qui locus sumetur ex sortibus, ex oraculis, vatibus, ostentis, prodigiis, responsis, similibus rebus; item maioribus nostris, regibus, civitatibus, gentibus, hominibus sapientissimis, senatui, populo, legum scriptoribus. Secundus locus est per quem illa res ad quos pertineat, cum amplificatione per indignationem ostenditur, aut ad omnes aut ad maiorem partem, quod atrocissimum est, aut ad superiores, quales sunt ei quorum ex auctoritate indignatio sumitur, quod indignissimum est; aut ad pares animo, fortuna, corpore, quod iniquissimum est; aut ad inferiores, quod superbissimum est. Tertius locus est per quem quaerimus quidnam sit eventurum si idem ceteri faciant; et simul ostendimus, huic si concessum sit, multos aemulos eiusdem audaciae futuros; ex quo

102 quid mali sit eventurum demonstrabimus. Quartus locus est per quem demonstramus multos alacres exspectare quid statuatur, ut ex eo quod uni concessum sit, sibi quoque tali de re quid liceat, intellegere possint. Quintus locus est per quem ostendimus ceteras res perperam constitutas intellecta veritate commutatas corrigi posse; hanc esse rem quae si sit semel iudicata, neque alio commutari iudicio neque

---

a Of the fifteen topics enumerated in the following passage, the first ten are given in *ad Her*. ii, 48 ff.

b *Ad Her*. ii, 48.

c *Ad Her*. ii, 48.

d *Ad Her*. ii, 48.

e *Ad Her*. ii, 48.

enmity; still we should consider what particular and separate rules can be given about *indignatio.*[a]

101   The first topic is derived from authority when we relate how much care and interest has been devoted to the subject under discussion by those whose authority ought to have the greatest weight, namely, the immortal gods (and the material on this topic will be derived from the casting of lots, from oracles, soothsayers, portents, prodigies, responses and the like); also our forefathers, kings, states, nations, men of supreme wisdom, the senate, the people and authors of laws.[b] The second topic is the one in which it is shown, with a display of passion emphasized by amplification, who is affected by this act which we are denouncing; the act may affect all or a great majority (which is most dreadful) or one's superiors, such as those whose authority gives ground for *indignatio* (which is most unbecoming), or one's equals in spirit, fortune or physique (which is most unjust) or one's inferiors (which is most arrogant).[c] The third topic is one in which we inquire what would happen if everybody else should act in the same way, and at the same time show that if he is permitted this licence, many will emulate the same career of crime; and we shall prove what evil

102 will result from this.[d] Under the fourth topic we prove that many are eagerly awaiting the decision so that from the licence which is granted to one they can know what they too may do in a similar case.[e] The fifth topic is one in which we show that in other cases a false decision has been changed when the truth was learned, and the wrong has been righted; but in this case, once the decision has been made it cannot be changed by any judicial body, nor can any

ulla potestate corrigi possit. Sextus locus est per quem consulto et de industria factum demonstratur et illud adiungitur, voluntario maleficio veniam dari non oportere, imprudentiae concedi nonnunquam convenire. Septimus locus est per quem indignamur quod taetrum, crudele, nefarium, tyrannicum factum esse dicamus, per vim, manum, opulentiam ; quae res ab legibus et ab aequabili iure remotissima sit. LIV.

103 Octavus locus est per quem demonstramus non vulgare neque factitatum esse ne ab audacissimis quidem hominibus id maleficium de quo agatur ; atque id a feris quoque hominibus et a barbaris gentibus et immanibus bestiis esse remotum. Haec erunt quae in parentes, liberos, coniuges, consanguineos, supplices crudeliter facta dicentur, et deinceps si qua proferantur in maiores natu, in hospites, in vicinos, in amicos, in eos quibuscum vitam egeris, in eos apud quos educatus sis, in eos a quibus eruditus, in mortuos, in miseros et misericordia dignos, in homines claros, nobiles et honore usos, in eos qui neque laedere alium nec se defendere potuerunt, ut in pueros, senes, mulieres ; quibus ex omnibus acriter excitata indignatio summum in eum qui violarit horum aliquid

104 odium commovere poterit. Nonus locus est per quem cum aliis peccatis, quae constat esse peccata, hoc quo de quaestio est comparatur, et ita per contentionem, quanto atrocius et indignius sit illud de quo agitur ostenditur. Decimus locus est per quem omnia quae

---

ᵃ *Ad Her.* ii, 48.   ᵇ *Ad Her.* ii, 49.   ᶜ *Ad Her.* ii, 49.
ᵈ *Ad Her.* ii, 49.   ᵉ *Ad Her.* ii, 49.

power right the wrong.[a] In the sixth topic it is shown that the deed was done purposely and intentionally and the remark is added that voluntary misdeeds should not be pardoned, but that sometimes inadvertent acts may be forgiven.[b] The seventh topic is used when we express our indignation, saying that a foul, cruel, nefarious and tyrannical deed has been done by force and violence or by the influence of riches, and that such an act is utterly at variance with law and equity.[c] LIV. Under the eighth topic we show that the crime which is under discussion is no ordinary one, nor has it been frequently committed even by the boldest of men; that it is unknown even among savages, barbarous tribes, and wild beasts. Such will be acts of cruelty which may be said to have been committed against parents, children, wives, kinsmen, or suppliants; and in the second place if any acts of injustice should be cited against elders, guests, neighbours, friends, against those with whom you have lived, those in whose home you have been reared or by whom you have been educated, against the dead, the wretched or pitiable, against famous men of renown and position, against those who can neither harm another nor defend themselves, such as children, old men, and women. By all of these circumstances violent indignation is aroused and this can produce the greatest hatred of one who has violated any of these sacred relationships.[d] The ninth topic involves a comparison of the deed in question with other crimes which are by common consent regarded as crimes, and so by contrast it is shown how much more horrible and shameful is the offence now before the court.[e] The tenth topic is that in which we bring together all the circumstances,

in negotio gerundo acta sunt quaeque post negotium
consecuta sunt, cum unius cuiusque indignatione et
criminatione colligimus et rem verbis quam maxime
ante oculos eius apud quem dicitur ponimus, ut id
quod indignum est proinde illi videatur indignum ac
si ipse interfuerit ac praesens viderit. Undecimus
locus est per quem ostendimus ab eo factum a quo
minime oportuerit, et a quo, si alius faceret, prohiberi
convenerit. Duodecimus locus est per quem indignamur, quod nobis hoc primis acciderit neque alicui
105 unquam usu venerit. Tertius decimus locus est si
cum iniuria contumelia iuncta demonstratur, per quem
locum in superbiam et arrogantiam odium concitatur.
Quartus decimus locus est per quem petimus ab eis qui
audiunt, ut ad suas res nostras iniurias referant; si ad
pueros pertinebit, de liberis suis cogitent; si ad
mulieres, de uxoribus; si ad senes, de patribus aut
parentibus. Quintus decimus locus est per quem
dicimus, inimicis quoque et hostibus ea quae nobis
acciderint indigna videri solere. Et indignatio
quidem his fere de locis gravissime sumetur.[1]
106   LV. Conquestio est oratio auditorum misericordiam captans. In hac primum animum auditoris
mitem et misericordem conficere oportet, quo
facilius conquestione commoveri possit. Id locis
communibus efficere oportebit, per quos fortunae
vis in omnes et hominum infirmitas ostenditur;
qua oratione habita graviter et sententiose
maxime demittitur animus hominum et ad miseri-

---

[1] *After* sumetur *the MSS. have* Conquestionis autem huiusmodi de rebus partes petere oportebit. (Moreover the various
kinds of *conquestio* should be sought from topics of this kind.)
Bracketed by Schuetz.

---

[a] *Ad Her.* ii, 49.

both what was done during the performance of the deed and what followed after it, accompanying the narration with reproaches and violent denunciations of each act, and by our language bring the action as vividly as possible before the eyes of the judge before whom we are pleading, so that a shameful act may seem as shameful as if he had himself been present and seen it in person.*a* The eleventh topic is one in which we show that the act was committed by one who least of all should have done it and who would have been expected to prevent it if done by another. The twelfth topic is that in which we express our indignation that this has happened to us first and has

105 never befallen anyone else. Under the thirteenth topic it is shown that insult has been added to injury; in this topic resentment is aroused against haughtiness and arrogance. Under the fourteenth topic we ask the audience to consider our injuries as their own; if it affects children let them think of their own children, if women, let them think of their wives, if the aged, let them think of their fathers or parents. Under the fifteenth topic we say that even foes and enemies are regarded as unworthy of the treatment that we have received. *Indignatio* will be derived most effectively from these topics.

106 LV. *Conquestio* (lament or complaint) is a passage seeking to arouse the pity of the audience. In this the first necessity is to make the auditor's spirit gentle and merciful that he may be more easily moved by the *conquestio*. This ought to be done by the use of " commonplaces " which set forth the power of fortune over all men and the weakness of the human race. When such a passage is delivered gravely and sententiously, the spirit of man is greatly abased and

cordiam comparatur, cum in alieno malo suam
107 infirmitatem considerabit. Deinde primus locus est
misericordiae per quem quibus in bonis fuerint et
nunc [1] quibus in malis sint ostenditur. Secundus,
qui in tempora tribuitur, per quem quibus in
malis fuerint et sint et futuri sint demonstratur.
Tertius, per quem unum quodque deploratur incommodum, ut in morte fili pueritiae delectatio, amor,
spes, solatium, educatio et, si qua simili in genere
quolibet de incommodo per conquestionem dici
poterunt. Quartus, per quem res turpes et humiles
et illiberales proferuntur et indigna esse aetate,
genere, fortuna pristina, honore, beneficiis quae passi
perpessurive sint. Quintus, per quem omnia ante
oculos singillatim incommoda ponuntur, ut videatur is
qui audit videre et re quoque ipsa quasi adsit non
108 verbis solum ad misericordiam ducatur. Sextus, per
quem praeter spem in miseriis demonstratur esse, et,
cum aliquid exspectaret, non modo id non adeptus
esse, sed in summas miserias incidisse. Septimus,
per quem ad ipsos qui audiunt [2] convertimus et
petimus, ut de suis liberis aut parentibus aut
aliquo, qui illis carus debeat esse, nos cum videant,
recordentur. Octavus, per quem aliquid dicitur
esse factum quod non oportuerit, aut non factum
quod oportuerit, hoc modo : " Non adfui, non vidi,
non postremam vocem eius audivi, non extremum
spiritum eius excepi." Item: " Inimicorum in

---

[1] per quem *repeated after* nunc *by* M.
[2] *After* audiunt M *reads* similem in causam, J similem
causam.

prepared for pity, for in viewing the misfortune of another he will contemplate his own weakness. 107 After that the first topic with which to evoke pity is that by which it is shown what prosperity they once enjoyed and from what evils they now suffer. The second employs a division according to time, and shows in what troubles they have been, still are, and are destined to be. The third, in which each separate phase of misfortune is deplored; for example, in lamenting the death of a son, one might mention the delight that his father took in his childhood, his love, his hope for the boy's future, the comfort he derived from him, the careful training, and whatever in a similar case can be said in bewailing any misfortune. The fourth, in which one recounts shameful, mean, and ignoble acts and what they have suffered or are likely to suffer that is unworthy of their age, race, former fortune, position or preferment. The fifth, in which all the misfortunes are presented to view one by one, so that the auditor may seem to see them, and may be moved to pity by the actual occurrence, as if he 108 were present, and not by words alone. The sixth, in which it is shown that one is in distress contrary to all expectation, and when he looked forward to receiving some benefit, he not only did not gain it, but fell into the greatest distress. The seventh, in which we turn to the audience and ask them when they look at us to think of their children or parents or some one who ought to be dear to them. The eighth, in which something is said to have happened which ought not, or that something did not happen which ought to have happened: for example, " I was not present, I did not see him, I did not hear his last words, I did not catch his last breath."

manibus mortuus est, hostili in terra turpiter iacuit insepultus, a feris diu vexatus, communi quoque honore in morte caruit." Nonus, per quem oratio ad mutas et expertes animi res referetur, ut si ad equum, domum, vestem sermonem alicuius accommodes, quibus animus eorum qui audiunt et aliquem dilexerunt vehementer commovetur. Decimus, per quem inopia, infirmitas, solitudo demonstratur. Undecimus, per quem liberorum aut parentum aut sui corporis sepeliendi aut alicuius eiusmodi rei commendatio fit. Duodecimus, per quem disiunctio deploratur ab aliquo, cum diducaris ab eo quicum libentissime vixeris, ut a parente filio, a fratre familiari. Tertius decimus, per quem cum indignatione conquerimur, quod ab eis a quibus minime conveniat, male tractemur, propinquis, amicis, quibus benigne fecerimus, quos adiutores fore putarimus, aut a quibus indignum est, ut servis, libertis, clientibus, supplicibus. LVI. Quartus decimus, qui per obsecrationem sumitur; in quo orantur modo illi qui audiunt humili et supplici oratione, ut misereantur. Quintus decimus, per quem non nostras, sed eorum qui cari nobis debent esse fortunas conqueri nos demonstramus. Sextus decimus, per quem animum nostrum in alios misericordem esse ostendimus et tamen amplum et excelsum et patientem incommodorum esse et futurum esse, si quid acciderit, demonstramus. Nam saepe virtus et magnificentia, in quo gravitas et auctoritas est, plus proficit ad misericordiam commovendam quam humilitas et obsecratio.

---

^a Cf. ad Her. iv, 66.

Similarly : " He died among the enemy, in a hostile land he lay shamefully unburied, long torn by wild beasts, and in death he was deprived even of the honour due to all mankind." The ninth, in which a discourse is addressed to mute and inanimate objects, for example : if you should represent one as speaking to a horse, a house, or a garment, by which the mind of the audience who have loved something is greatly affected.[a] The tenth, in which one's helplessness and weakness and loneliness are revealed. The eleventh, in which the speaker commends to the audience his children, his parents, the task of burying him, or some such duty. The twelfth, in which separation from some one is deplored, when you are torn away from one with whom you have lived with the greatest pleasure, for example a father, son, brother, or intimate friend. The thirteenth, in which with anger we complain because we are being badly treated by those whom such conduct least becomes, relatives, friends whom we have treated kindly, whom we expected to help us, or by those to whom such conduct is a disgrace, namely slaves, freedmen, clients, or suppliants. LVI. The fourteenth, which is devoted to entreaty : here the only thing is to implore the audience in humble and submissive language to have mercy. The fifteenth, in which we show that it is not our ill fortune which we bemoan but that of our dear ones. The sixteenth, in which we show that our soul is full of mercy for others, but still is noble, lofty, and patient of misfortune and will be so whatever may befall. For often virtue and highmindedness in which there is naturally influence and authority does more to arouse pity than humility and entreaty.

Commotis autem animis diutius in conquestione morari non oportebit. Quemadmodum enim dixit rhetor Apollonius, lacrima nihil citius arescit.

Sed quoniam satis, ut videmur, de omnibus orationis partibus diximus et huius voluminis magnitudo longius processit, quae sequuntur deinceps in secundo libro dicemus.

But when the emotions have been aroused it will be advisable not to linger over the *conquestio*. For as the rhetorician Apollonius said, " Nothing dries more quickly than tears." [a]

Now since I have said enough, I think, about all the divisions of the speech, and this volume has grown too long, what follows I shall include in the second book.

[a] On this proverb compare G. D. Kellogg in *Amer. Journal of Phil.* xxviii (1907), pp. 301–310. Apollonius is probably the rhetorician surnamed Molon who was later Cicero's teacher.

BOOK II

M. TULLI CICERONIS

RHETORICI LIBRI DUO

QUI VOCANTUR DE INVENTIONE

LIBER SECUNDUS

1   I. CROTONIATAE quondam, cum florerent omnibus
copiis et in Italia cum primis beati numerarentur,
templum Iunonis, quod religiosissime colebant,
egregiis picturis locupletare voluerunt. Itaque
Heracleotem Zeuxim, qui tum longe ceteris excellere
pictoribus existimabatur, magno pretio conductum
adhibuerunt. Is et ceteras complures tabulas pinxit,
quarum nonnulla pars usque ad nostram memoriam
propter fani religionem remansit, et, ut excellentem
muliebris formae pulcritudinem muta in se imago
contineret, Helenae pingere simulacrum velle dixit;
quod Crotoniatae, qui eum muliebri in corpore
pingendo plurimum aliis praestare saepe accepissent,
libenter audierunt. Putaverunt enim, si, quo in
genere plurimum posset, in eo magno opere elabor-
asset, egregium sibi opus illo in fano relicturum.
2 Neque tum eos illa opinio fefellit. Nam Zeuxis
ilico quaesivit ab eis quasnam virgines formosas
haberent. Illi autem statim hominem deduxerunt
in palaestram atque ei pueros ostenderunt multos,
166

MARCUS TULLIUS CICERO

TWO BOOKS ON RHETORIC

COMMONLY CALLED ON INVENTION

BOOK II

1   I. The citizens of Croton, once upon a time, when
they had abundant wealth and were numbered among
the most prosperous in Italy, desired to enrich with
distinguished paintings the temple of Juno, which
they held in the deepest veneration. They, therefore, paid a large fee to Zeuxis of Heraclea who was
considered at that time to excel all other artists, and
secured his services for their project. He painted
many panels, some of which have been preserved
to the present by the sanctity of the shrine; he also
said that he wished to paint a picture of Helen so
that the portrait though silent and lifeless might
embody the surpassing beauty of womanhood. This
delighted the Crotoniats, who had often heard that
he surpassed all others in the portrayal of women.
For they thought that if he exerted himself in the
genre in which he was supreme, he would leave
2 an outstanding work of art in that temple. Nor
were they mistaken in this opinion. For Zeuxis
immediately asked them what girls they had of
surpassing beauty. They took him directly to the
wrestling school and showed him many very handsome

magna praeditos dignitate. Etenim quodam tempore Crotoniatae multum omnibus corporum viribus et dignitatibus antisteterunt atque honestissimas ex gymnico certamine victorias domum cum laude maxima rettulerunt. Cum puerorum igitur formas et corpora magno hic opere miraretur: " Horum," inquiunt illi, " sorores sunt apud nos virgines. Quare qua sint illae dignitate potes ex his suspicari." " Praebete igitur mihi, quaeso," inquit, " ex istis virginibus formosissimas dum pingo id quod pollicitus sum vobis, ut mutum in simulacrum

3 ex animali exemplo veritas transferatur." Tum Crotoniatae publico de consilio virgines unum in locum conduxerunt et pictori quam vellet eligendi potestatem dederunt. Ille autem quinque delegit; quarum nomina multi poëtae memoriae prodiderunt quod eius essent iudicio probatae qui pulcritudinis habere verissimum debuisset. Neque enim putavit omnia, quae quaereret ad venustatem, uno se in corpore reperire posse ideo quod nihil simplici in genere omnibus ex partibus perfectum natura expolivit. Itaque, tamquam ceteris non sit habitura quod largiatur, si uni cuncta concesserit, aliud alii commodi aliquo adiuncto incommodo muneratur.

4 II. Quod quoniam nobis quoque voluntatis accidit ut artem dicendi perscriberemus, non unum aliquod proposuimus exemplum cuius omnes partes, quocumque essent in genere, exprimendae nobis necessarie viderentur; sed, omnibus unum in locum coactis scriptoribus, quod quisque commodissime praecipere

young men. For at one time the men of Croton excelled all in strength and beauty of body, and brought home the most glorious victories in athletic contests with the greatest distinction. As he was greatly admiring the handsome bodies, they said, "There are in our city the sisters of these men; you may get an idea of their beauty from these youths." "Please send me then the most beautiful of these girls, while I am painting the picture that I have promised, so that the true beauty may be transferred 3 from the living model to the mute likeness." Then the citizens of Croton by a public decree assembled the girls in one place and allowed the painter to choose whom he wished. He selected five, whose names many poets recorded because they were approved by the judgement of him who must have been the supreme judge of beauty. He chose five because he did not think all the qualities which he sought to combine in a portrayal of beauty could be found in one person, because in no single case has Nature made anything perfect and finished in every part. Therefore, as if she would have no bounty to lavish on the others if she gave everything to one, she bestows some advantage on one and some on another, but always joins with it some defect.

4 II. In a similar fashion when the inclination arose in my mind to write a text-book of rhetoric, I did not set before myself some one model which I thought necessary to reproduce in all details, of whatever sort they might be, but after collecting all the works on the subject I excerpted what seemed the most suitable precepts from each, and so culled the flower of many minds. For each of the writers who are worthy of

CICERO

videbatur excerpsimus et ex variis ingeniis excel-
lentissima quaeque libavimus. Ex eis enim qui
nomine et memoria digni sunt nec nihil optime nec
omnia praeclarissime quisquam dicere nobis videbatur. Quapropter stultitia visa est aut a bene
inventis alicuius recedere si quo in vitio eius offen-
deremur, aut ad vitia eius quoque accedere cuius
5 aliquo bene praecepto duceremur. Quodsi in ceteris
quoque studiis a multis eligere homines commodis-
simum quodque quam sese uni alicui certe vellent
addicere, minus in arrogantiam offenderent, non
tanto opere in vitiis perseverarent, aliquanto levius
ex inscientia laborarent. Ac si par in nobis huius
artis atque in illo picturae scientia fuisset, fortasse
magis hoc in suo genere opus nostrum, quam ille [1]
in sua [2] pictura nobilis eniteret. Ex maiore enim
copia nobis quam illi fuit exemplorum eligendi
potestas. Ille una ex urbe et ex eo numero virginum
quae tum erant eligere potuit; nobis omnium
quicumque fuerunt ab ultimo principio huius praecep-
tionis usque ad hoc tempus, expositis copiis, quod-
cumque placeret eligendi potestas fuit.

6 Ac veteres quidem scriptores artis usque a prin-
cipe illo atque inventore Tisia repetitos unum in
locum conduxit Aristoteles et nominatim cuiusque
praecepta magna conquisita cura perspicue con-
scripsit atque enodata diligenter exposuit; ac
tantum inventoribus ipsis suavitate et brevitate
dicendi praestitit ut nemo illorum praecepta ex
ipsorum libris cognoscat, sed omnes qui quod illi
praecipiant velint intellegere ad hunc quasi ad

---

[1] ille C : illius Lambinus.
[2] sua C : suo Ernesti : pictura ille P.

fame and reputation seemed to say something better
than anyone else, but not to attain pre-eminence in all
points. It seemed folly therefore, either to refuse to
follow the good ideas of any author, merely because I
was offended by some fault in his work, or to follow the
mistakes of a writer who had attracted me by some
5 correct precept. And it is also true of other pursuits
that if men would choose the most appropriate con-
tributions from many sources rather than devote
themselves unreservedly to one leader only, they would
offend less by arrogance, they would not be so obstinate in wrong courses, and would suffer somewhat less
from ignorance. And if my knowledge of the art of
rhetoric had equalled his knowledge of painting,
perhaps this work of mine might be more famous in
its class than he is in his painting. For I had a
larger number of models to choose from than he had.
He could choose from one city and from the group of
girls who were alive at that time, but I was able to
set out before me the store of wisdom of all who
had written from the very beginning of instruction
in rhetoric down to the present time, and choose
whatever was acceptable.

6 Aristotle collected the early books on rhetoric,
even going back as far as Tisias, well known as the
originator and inventor of the art; he made a careful
examination of the rules of each author and wrote
them out in plain language, giving the author's
name, and finally gave a painstaking explanation
of the difficult parts. And he so surpassed the
original authorities in charm and brevity that no one
becomes acquainted with their ideas from their own
books, but everyone who wishes to know what their
doctrines are, turns to Aristotle, believing him to

quendam multo commodiorem explicatorem rever-
7 tantur. Atque hic quidem ipse et sese ipsum nobis
et eos, qui ante fuerunt, in medio posuit, ut ceteros
et se ipsum per se cognosceremus: ab hoc autem
qui profecti sunt, quamquam in maximis philosophiae partibus operae plurimum consumpserunt,
sicuti ipse cuius instituta sequebantur fecerat, tamen
permulta nobis praecepta dicendi reliquerunt.

Atque alii quoque alio ex fonte praeceptores
dicendi emanaverunt, qui item permultum ad dicendum, si quid ars proficit, opitulati sunt. Nam fuit
tempore eodem, quo Aristoteles, magnus et nobilis
rhetor Isocrates; cuius ipsius quam constet esse
8 artem non invenimus. Discipulorum autem atque
eorum, qui protinus ab hac sunt disciplina profecti,
multa de arte praecepta reperimus. III. Ex his
duabus diversis sicuti familiis, quarum altera cum
versaretur in philosophia, nonnullam rhetoricae
quoque artis sibi curam assumebat, altera vero
omnis in dicendi erat studio et praeceptione occupata,
unum quoddam est conflatum genus a posterioribus,
qui ab utrisque ea quae commode dici videbantur
in suas artes contulerunt; quos ipsos simul atque
illos superiores nos nobis omnes, quoad facultas
tulit, proposuimus et ex nostro quoque nonnihil in
9 commune contulimus. Quodsi ea quae in his libris
exponuntur tanto opere eligenda fuerunt quanto
studio electa sunt, profecto neque nos neque alios
industriae nostrae paenitebit. Sin autem temere
aliquid alicuius praeterisse aut non satis eleganter

ᵃ The reference is to the Συναγωγὴ Τεχνῶν of Aristotle, a
work now lost.

7 give a much more convenient exposition.[a] He, then, published his own works and those of his predecessors, and as a result we became acquainted with him and the others as well through his work. His successors, although they devoted most of their attention to the noblest parts of philosophy, as the master whose principles they followed had done, nevertheless left us much instruction in rhetoric.

From another fountain head has come a stream of teachers of rhetoric who have also done much to improve oratory, as far at least as rules of art can accomplish anything. For in Aristotle's day there was a great and famous teacher of oratory named Isocrates; there is known to be a textbook from his

8 hand, but I have not seen it. I have, however, found many treatises on the art by his pupils and by those who carried on his doctrines. III. These two opposing sects (as we may call them), one busy with philosophy, but devoting some attention to the art of rhetoric as well, the other entirely devoted to the study and teaching of oratory, were fused into one group by later teachers who took into their own books from both sources what they thought was correct.[b] All of these as well as the earlier authorities I have had before me as far as possible, and have contributed

9 some ideas of my own to the common store. Therefore if the value of the principles set forth in these volumes is equal to the enthusiasm with which they were chosen, certainly neither I nor anyone else will regret my industry. But if it shall prove that I have been too rash in passing over some point in an author

[b] It is impossible to identify these sources more accurately. Hermagoras, Philo, Antiochus may be intended. *v.* Hubbell, *The Influence of Isocrates on Cicero*, p. 40.

secuti videbimur, docti ab aliquo facile et libenter
sententiam commutabimus. Non enim parum cog-
nosse, sed in parum cognito stulte et diu perse-
verasse turpe est, propterea quod alterum communi
hominum infirmitati, alterum singulari cuiusque
10 vitio est attributum. Quare nos quidem sine ulla
affirmatione simul quaerentes dubitanter unum
quidque dicemus, ne, dum parvulum hoc [1] con-
sequamur, ut satis haec commode perscripsisse
videamur, illud amittamus quod maximum est ut
ne cui rei temere atque arroganter assenserimus.
Verum hoc quidem nos et in hoc tempore et in
omni vita studiose, quoad facultas feret, conse-
quemur. Nunc autem, ne longius oratio progressa
videatur, de reliquis quae praecipienda videntur
esse dicemus.

11 Igitur primus liber, exposito genere huius artis
et officio et fine et materia et partibus, genera
controversiarum et inventiones et constitutiones [2] continebat, deinde partes orationis et in
eas omnes omnia praecepta. Quare cum in eo
ceteris de rebus distinctius dictum sit, disperse
autem de confirmatione et de reprehensione, nunc
certos confirmandi et reprehendendi in singula
causarum genera locos tradendos arbitramur. Et
quia, quo pacto tractari conveniret argumentationes,
in libro primo non indiligenter expositum est, hic
tantum ipsa inventa unam quamque in rem exponen-
tur simpliciter sine ulla exornatione, ut ex hoc

---

[1] hoc parvulum *or* parvulum hoc *J* : hoc *omitted by Ströbel* :
bracketed by Weidner, Friedrich.
[2] *After* constitutiones *a few late MSS. read* et iudicationes
(and the points for the judge's decision).

or have not followed him with sufficient discrimination, I shall, when someone points out my error, readily and gladly change my opinion. For disgrace lies not in imperfect knowledge but in foolish and obstinate continuance in a state of imperfect knowledge; for ignorance is attributed to the infirmity common to the human race, but obstinacy to a man's own fault.

10 Therefore without affirming anything positively, I shall proceed with an inquiring mind and make each statement with a degree of hesitation, lest in gaining the small point of having written an apparently useful book, I fall short of the chief goal, not to be rash and hasty in giving my approval to any item. This principle I shall of course pursue both now and in all my life as zealously as possible; now, however, that this introduction may not seem to run on too long, I shall state the topics which remain to be elucidated.

11 The first book, after discussing the nature of this art, its function, end, materials and divisions,[a] took up the kinds of controversies, the methods of invention and the determination of the issue,[b] and finally the division of a speech and all the rules for all of them.[c] Since the first book then treated all topics definitely and clearly except confirmation and refutation, of which the treatment was in somewhat general terms, now I think I ought to give concrete examples of arguments to be used in confirmation or refutation in each kind of case. And because in the first book the manner of developing argumentations was explained with some care, in the second book I shall present only the invented arguments or ideas involved in each case without any literary adornment,

[a] § 5. [b] §§ 10–19. [c] §§ 19–109.

inventa ipsa, ex superiore autem expolitio inventorum petatur. Quare haec quae nunc praecipientur ad confirmationis et reprehensionis partes referre oportebit.

12   IV. Omnis et demonstrativa et deliberativa et iudicialis causa necesse est in aliquo eorum quae ante exposita sunt constitutionis genere, uno pluribusve, versetur. Hoc quamquam ita est, tamen cum communiter quaedam de omnibus praecipi possint, separatim quoque aliae sunt cuiusque generis diversae praeceptiones. Aliud enim laus, aliud vituperatio, aliud sententiae dictio, aliud accusatio aut recusatio conficere debet. In iudiciis quid aequum sit quaeritur, in demonstrationibus quid honestum, in deliberationibus, ut nos arbitramur, quid honestum sit et quid utile. Nam ceteri utilitatis modo finem in suadendo et in dissuadendo

13   exponi oportere arbitrati sunt. Quorum igitur generum fines et exitus diversi sunt, eorum praecepta eadem esse non possunt. Neque nunc hoc dicimus, non easdem incidere constitutiones, verumtamen oratio quaedam ex ipso fine et ex genere causae nascitur, quae pertineat ad vitae alicuius demonstrationem aut ad sententiae dictionem. Quare nunc in exponendis controversiis [1] in iudiciali genere causarum et praeceptorum versabimur, ex quo pleraque in cetera quoque causarum genera simili implicata controversia nulla cum difficultate transferuntur; post autem separatim de reliquis dicemus.

[1] in exponendis controversiis *bracketed by Weidner and Ströbel.*

so that in this book one may look for the ideas, but in the former book for the embellishment of the ideas. Therefore the reader should regard the suggestions which follow as applying to confirmation and refutation.

12 IV. Every speech whether epideictic, deliberative or forensic must turn on one or more of the " issues " described in the first book.[a] Although this is true, nevertheless, in spite of there being many rules common to all, there are also other and different rules applicable to each kind of speech. For one object should be attained by praise, another by censure, another by an expression of opinion and another by accusation or defence. In trials the inquiry is about what is just, in an epideictic speech, about what is honourable, in speeches before deliberative bodies, as I think, about what is honourable and what is advantageous. Other writers, however, have thought that advantage alone should be proposed as an object

13 in urging or opposing a political measure. Those kinds of speeches, then, which have different ends and purposes cannot have the same rules. I am not saying now that the same " issues " do not arise, but that an oration which is aimed at portraying someone's life or at expressing an opinion on a political subject, arises out of its very purpose and the nature of its subject. Therefore at present I shall concern myself in explaining controversies with the class of speech delivered in courts of law and the rules applying to them; many of these rules can with no difficulty be transferred to other kinds of speeches, too, which involve a similar controversy. Later I shall speak separately of the others.

[a] §§ 10–19.

14   Nunc ab coniecturali constitutione proficiscamur;
cuius exemplum sit hoc expositum: In itinere
quidam proficiscentem ad mercatum quendam et
secum aliquantum nummorum ferentem est comitatus.
Cum hoc, ut fere fit, in via sermonem contulit; ex
quo factum est ut illud iter familiarius facere vellent.
Quare cum in eandem tabernam divertissent, simul
cenare et in eodem loco somnum capere voluerunt.
Cenati discubuerunt ibidem. Copo autem—nam
ita dicitur post inventum, cum in alio maleficio
deprehensus est—cum illum alterum, videlicet qui
nummos haberet, animum advertisset, noctu postquam illos artius iam ut ex lassitudine dormire
sensit, accessit et alterius eorum qui sine nummis
erat, gladium propter appositum e vagina eduxit et
illum alterum occidit, nummos abstulit, gladium
cruentum in vaginam recondidit, ipse se in suum
lectum recepit. Ille autem cuius gladio occisio erat
facta multo ante lucem surrexit, comitem illum suum
15 inclamavit semel et saepius. Illum somno impeditum
non respondere existimavit; ipse gladium et cetera
quae secum attulerat sustulit, solus profectus est.
Copo non multum post conclamat hominem esse
occisum et cum quibusdam diversoribus illum qui
ante exierat consequitur in itinere. Hominem
comprehendit, gladium eius e vagina educit, reperit
cruentum. Homo in urbem ab illis deducitur ac
reus fit. In hac intentio est criminis: " Occidisti."
Depulsio: " Non occidi." Ex quibus constitutio

14   Now let us begin with the conjectural issue (or issue of fact), and let the following be taken as an example. On a highway a traveller joined himself to another who was on a business trip and had with him a considerable sum of money. As is natural, they fell into conversation as they went along, and the result was that they were ready to make the trip together as close friends. Therefore on stopping at the same inn, they planned to dine together and sleep in the same apartment. After dinner they went to bed in the same room. Then the inn-keeper—for it is said the truth was found out when he had been caught in another crime—who had taken note of one of the travellers, that is the one with the money, came in the dead of night when he knew that they were sleeping heavily as people do when tired, drew the sword of the one who did not have the money—it was lying by his side—killed the other man, took his money, replaced the blood-stained sword in its sheath and went back to his own bed. Long before dawn the man whose sword had been used to commit the murder, got up and called his

15 companion again and again. Deciding that he did not answer because he was sound asleep, the traveller took his sword and the rest of his belongings and set out alone. Not long afterward the innkeeper raises a cry of " murder " and with some of the guests goes down the road in pursuit of the traveller who had left earlier. He seizes him, draws the sword from its sheath and finds it stained with blood. The fellow is brought to the city and accused of the crime. In this case the charge is, " You committed murder ; " the answer is, " I did not." From this arises the *constitutio* or issue, that is the question, the same in

est, id est quaestio,[1] eadem in coniecturali[2] quae
iudicatio: Occideritne?

16   V. Nunc exponemus locos, quorum pars aliqua
in omnem coniecturalem incidit controversiam. Hoc
autem et in horum locorum expositione et in ceterorum oportebit attendere, non omnes in omnem
causam convenire. Nam ut omne nomen ex aliqui-
bus, non ex omnibus litteris, scribitur, sic omnem in
causam non omnis argumentorum copia, sed eorum
necessario pars aliqua conveniet. Omnis igitur
ex causa, ex persona, ex facto ipso coniectura
capienda est.

17   Causa tribuitur in impulsionem et in ratiocinationem. Impulsio est quae sine cogitatione per
quandam affectionem animi facere aliquid hortatur,
ut amor, iracundia, aegritudo, vinolentia et omnino
omnia in quibus animus ita videtur affectus fuisse
ut rem perspicere cum consilio et cura non potuerit
et id quod fecit impetu quodam animi potius quam
18 cogitatione fecerit. Ratiocinatio est autem diligens
et considerata faciendi aliquid aut non faciendi
excogitatio. Ea dicitur interfuisse tum, cum aliquid
faciendi aut non faciendi[3] certa de causa vitasse
aut secutus esse animus videbitur; si amicitiae quid
causa factum dicetur, si inimici ulciscendi, si metus,
si gloriae, si pecuniae, si denique, ut omnia generatim
amplectamur, alicuius retinendi, augendi adipis-
cendive commodi aut contra reiciundi, deminuendi
devitandive incommodi causa. Nam in horum genus
alterutrum illa quoque incident in quibus aut

---

[1] id est quaestio *bracketed by Ströbel.*
[2] in coniecturali *bracketed by Ernesti.*
[3] faciendum aut non faciendum *J* : *bracketed by Schuetz.*

the conjectural issue as the point for the judge's decision, " Did he commit murder? "

16   V. Now I shall explain the arguments, some of which apply to every controversy which is determined by inference. But you must note in the exposition of these arguments and of those that follow that all do not fit every case. As, for example, every word is spelled with some letters, but not with all, so the whole store of arguments will not fit every case, but, necessarily, only a part of them. Every inference, then, is based on arguments from the cause of the action, from the character of the person involved, and from the nature of the act.

17   The cause of an act falls under the heads of impulse and premeditation. An impulse is what urges a person to do something without thinking about it, because of some feeling or emotional state; examples are love, anger, grief, intoxication, and in fact every state in which the mind seems to have been so affected that it could not examine the act with care and deliberation, but did what it did from a certain mental urge rather than from reflec-

18 tion. Premeditation on the other hand is careful and thoughtful reasoning about doing or not doing something. It is said to have been present when the mind seems to have avoided or sought something to do or not to do for a definite cause; if an act is said to have been performed because of friendship, to punish an enemy, or because of fear, glory or money, or finally, to sum the matter up in general terms, if the act is done to retain, increase or acquire some advantage, or on the other hand to throw off, lessen or avoid some disadvantage. For under one or the other of these classes those cases will

incommodi aliquid maioris adipiscendi commodi
causa aut maioris vitandi incommodi suscipitur aut
aliquod commodum maioris adipiscendi commodi aut
maioris vitandi incommodi praeteritur.

19 Hic locus sicut aliquod fundamentum est huius
constitutionis. Nam nihil factum esse cuiquam
probatur, nisi aliquid quare factum sit ostenditur.
Ergo accusator, cum impulsione aliquid factum
esse dicet, illum impetum et quandam commotionem
animi affectionemque verbis et sententiis amplificare
debebit et ostendere quanta vis sit amoris, quanta
animi perturbatio ex iracundia fiat aut ex aliqua
causa earum, qua impulsum aliquem id fecisse dicet.
Hic et exemplorum commemoratione, qui simili
impulsu aliquid commiserint, et similitudinum collatione et ipsius animi affectionis explicatione
curandum est ut non mirum videatur si quod ad
facinus tali perturbatione commotus animus acces-
serit.

20 VI. Cum autem non impulsione, verum ratiocinatione aliquem commisisse quid dicet, quid
commodi sit secutus aut quid incommodi fugerit
demonstrabit et id augebit quam maxime poterit,
ut, quod eius fieri possit, idonea quam maxime
causa ad peccandum hortata videatur. Si gloriae
causa, quantam gloriam consecuturam existimarit;
item si dominationis, si pecuniae, si amicitiae, si
inimicitiarum, et omnino quicquid erit quod causae
21 fuisse dicet id summe augere debebit. Et hoc eum

fall in which some disadvantage is accepted in order to
gain a greater advantage or avoid a greater disadvantage, or some advantage is neglected in order to gain
a greater advantage or avoid a greater disadvantage.
19   This topic is what one might call the foundation or
basis of this issue. For no one can be convinced that
a deed has been done unless some reason is given
why it was done. Therefore the prosecutor when he
says that something was done on impulse, will be
under the necessity of dilating upon that passion and,
as it were, agitation and state of mind, with the full
powers of his thought and expression, and of showing
how great is the force of love, what powerful mental
agitation arises from anger or from any of the causes
by which he claims that the defendant was urged to
commit this crime. Here pains must be taken that
it may not seem strange that a mind disquieted by
such passion should undertake some crime. This
can be done by citing examples of those who have
done something under a similar impulse and by
collecting parallels and by explaining the nature of
mental disturbance.
20   VI. When, on the other hand, the prosecutor says
that the defendant did the deed not from impulse,
but deliberately, he will show what advantage was
sought or what disadvantage avoided and will
amplify this point to the best of his ability, so that,
as far as in him lies, it may be shown that a perfectly
sufficient motive prompted the crime. If it was for
glory, how great glory he expected to win; likewise
if for power or wealth, because of friendship or enmity,
and in short whatever he says the cause was, the
prosecutor must enlarge upon it most emphatically.
21 And he ought to consider very carefully not merely

magno opere considerare oportebit, non quid in
veritate modo, verum etiam vehementius quid in
opinione eius quem arguet fuerit. Nihil enim refert
non fuisse aut non esse aliquid commodi aut incommodi, si ostendi potest ei visum esse qui arguatur.
Nam opinio dupliciter fallit homines, cum aut res
alio modo est ac putatur, aut non is eventus est
quem arbitrati sunt. Res alio modo est tum, cum
aut id quod bonum est malum putant, quod malum
est, bonum, aut quod nec malum est nec bonum,
malum aut bonum, aut quod malum aut bonum est,
22 nec malum nec bonum. Hoc intellecto si qui
negabit esse ullam pecuniam fratris aut amici vita
aut denique officio suo antiquiorem aut suaviorem,
non hoc erit accusatori negandum. Nam in eum
culpa et summum odium transferetur qui id quod
tam vere et pie dicetur negabit. Verum illud dicendum est, illi ita non esse visum; quod sumi
oportet ex eis quae ad personam pertinent, de quo
23 post dicendum est. VII. Eventus autem tum
fallit, cum aliter accidit atque ei qui arguuntur
arbitrati esse dicuntur: ut, si qui dicatur alium
occidisse ac voluerit, quod aut similitudine aut
suspicione aut demonstratione falsa deceptus sit;
aut eum necasse, cuius testamento non sit heres,
quod eo testamento se heredem arbitratus sit. Non
enim ex eventu cogitationem spectari oportere, sed
qua cogitatione animus et spe ad maleficium profectus sit considerari; quo animo quid quisque
faciat, non quo casu utatur, ad rem pertinere.

what the result might really have been, but more
particularly what the result might have been in the
opinion of the man on trial. For it is no matter if
there was or is no advantage or disadvantage con
nected with the act, if it can be shown that the
defendant thought there was. For opinion deceives
men in two ways, either when some thing is different
from what it is thought to be, or when the result of
an action is not what was expected. A thing is
different when they think what is bad, good; or on
the other hand think what is good, bad; or when
they regard as good or bad what is neither, or regard
22 as neither what is really good or bad. On this understanding, if anyone denies that any wealth is dearer
or sweeter than the life of brother or friend, or even
his duty, the prosecutor should not deny this. For
he will be blamed and loathed if he denies a statement so true and so expressive of our sentiments of
devotion. But he should say that the defendant did
not think so: and this statement should be based on
the traits of personality, which are to be discussed
23 later. VII. The result is deceptive when the matter
turns out differently from what the defendants are
said to have expected; for example, if one be said
to have killed a person other than he wished to kill
because he was misled by resemblance, or suspicion,
or false description; or to have killed a man under
whose will he did not inherit, because he thought
that he would be an heir under that will; for (the
prosecutor will say) we should not judge his intent by
the result, but consider with what intent and hope
his mind set out on a career of crime; the pertinent
fact is the purpose with which anyone performs an
act, not what success he attains.

24 Hoc autem loco caput illud erit accusatoris, si demonstrare poterit alii nemini causam fuisse faciendi; secundarium, si tantam aut tam idoneam nemini. Sin fuisse aliis quoque causa faciendi videbitur, aut potestas defuisse aliis demonstranda est aut facultas aut voluntas. Potestas, si aut nescisse aut non adfuisse aut conficere aliquid non potuisse dicentur. Facultas, si ratio, adiutores, adiumenta ceteraque quae ad rem pertinebunt defuisse alicui demonstrabuntur. Voluntas, si animus a talibus factis vacuus et integer esse dicetur. Postremo, quas ad defensionem rationes reo dabimus, eis accusator ad alios ex culpa eximendos abutetur. Verum id brevi faciendum est, et in unum multa sunt conducenda ut ne alterius defendendi causa hunc accusare, sed huius accusandi causa defendere alterum videatur.

25 VIII. Atque accusatori quidem haec fere sunt[1] consideranda. Defensor autem ex contrario primum impulsionem aut nullam fuisse dicet aut, si fuisse concedet, extenuabit et parvulam quandam fuisse demonstrabit aut non ex ea solere huiusmodi facta nasci docebit. Quo erit in loco demonstrandum quae vis et natura sit eius affectionis qua impulsus aliquid reus commisisse dicetur; in quo et exempla et similitudines erunt proferendae et ipsa diligenter natura eius affectionis quam levissime quietissima

---

[1] *After* sunt *J add* in causa facienda et.

24   Under this topic comes a familiar line of argument, if the prosecutor can show that no one else had a motive for committing the crime; secondly that no one had so strong or sufficient a motive. But if it seem that others, too, had a reason for the crime, it must be shown that others lacked the power, or the opportunity or the desire. The power, if it can be said that they did not know about the possibility of the crime, or were not present or were not physically able to perform some act. The opportunity, if it can be shown that any one lacked a plan, helpers, tools and all other things pertinent to the deed. The desire, if his mind can be said to be free from such crimes and unsullied. Finally, the prosecutor will use in excluding others from blame the same lines of reasoning which we shall assign to the accused for presenting his defence. But this must be done quickly, and much must be compressed into a brief space in order that he may not seem to accuse the defendant for the sake of defending another, but to defend another for the sake of accusing the defendant.

25   VIII. These are the points which the prosecutor must take into consideration. The counsel for the defence, on the contrary, will say, first, that there was no impulse, or if he grants that there was, he will make light of it and prove that it was only a weak emotion, and prove that it was not the kind from which deeds of this sort generally arise. Under this head it will be proper to point out the force and nature of the emotion which is said to have driven the defendant to the crime. In so doing he will have to offer examples and parallels, and carefully explain the nature of this emotion as calmly and quietly as

ab parte explicanda ut et res ipsa a facto crudeli
et turbulento ad quoddam mitius et tranquillius
traducatur et oratio tamen ad animum eius qui
audiet et ad animi quendam intimum sensum
accommodetur.

26   Ratiocinationis autem suspiciones infirmabit si
aut commodum nullum esse aut parvum aut aliis
maius esse aut nihilo sibi maius quam aliis, aut
incommodum sibi maius quam commodum dicet;
ut nequaquam fuerit illius commodi quod expetitum
dicatur magnitudo aut cum eo incommodo quod
acciderit, aut cum illo periculo quod subeatur
comparanda; qui omnes loci similiter in incommodi
27 quoque vitatione tractabuntur. Sin accusator dixerit
eum id esse secutum quod ei visum sit commodum,
aut id fugisse quod putarit esse incommodum,
quamquam in falsa fuerit opinione, demonstrandum
erit defensori neminem tantae esse stultitiae qui
tali in re possit veritatem ignorare. Quodsi hoc
concedatur, illud non concessum iri, ne dubitasse
quidem eum, quid eius iuris esset, et id quod falsum
fuerit sine ulla dubitatione pro falso, quod verum
pro vero [1] probasse; quia si dubitarit, summae
fuisse amentiae dubia spe impulsum certum in peri-
28 culum se committere. Quemadmodum autem accusator, cum ab aliis culpam demovebit, defensoris
locis utetur, sic eis locis qui accusatori dati sunt
utetur reus, eum in alios ab se crimen volet transferre.

IX. Ex persona autem coniectura capietur, si eae
res quae personis attributae sunt diligenter considerabuntur, quas omnes in primo libro exposuimus.

---

[1] pro vero *M* : pro falso quod verum pro vero *J* : *Ströbel
omits* pro falso quod verum.

possible so that even the crime may be changed from a violent and cruel deed to something milder and less agitating, and the discussion may still be adapted to the soul of the auditor and to the deepest emotions of his soul.

26   He will weaken the suspicion of premeditation if he says that there was little or no gain for the defendant, or greater gain for others, or no greater for him than for others, or that the loss was greater than the gain so that in no way was the size of the gain which he is said to have sought to be compared with the loss which he incurred, or with the danger which he faced.   And all these topics will be treated in the 27 same way in discussing the avoidance of loss. But if the prosecutor says that the defendant followed what seemed to him advantageous or avoided what he thought a disadvantage, although he was mistaken in his opinion, the counsel for the defence must point out that no one is stupid enough to be ignorant of the truth in such a matter; saying that if this be granted, the other point would not be; that the defendant had no doubts about his rights in the matter, and undoubtedly held what was false as false and what was true as true.   For if he was in doubt it was stark madness to rush into certain danger through 28 the lure of a doubtful hope.   Moreover, just as the prosecutor will use the topics of defence when he clears others of fault, so the defendant will use the topics which are given to the prosecutor when he wishes to shift the responsibility for the crime from himself to others.

IX. Inferences may be drawn from the person of the accused if the attributes of persons are carefully taken into account.   I explained all of these in the

CICERO

Nam et de nomine nonnunquam aliquid suspicionis nascitur—nomen autem cum dicimus, cognomen quoque intellegatur oportet; de hominis enim certo et proprio vocabulo agitur—ut si dicamus idcirco aliquem Caldum vocari quod temerario et repentino consilio sit; aut si ea re hominibus Graecis imperitis verba dederit quod Clodius aut Caecilius aut Mutius 29 vocaretur; et de natura licet aliquantum ducere suspicionis. Omnia enim haec, vir an mulier, huius an illius civitatis sit, quibus sit maioribus, quibus consanguineis, qua aetate, quo animo, quo corpore, quae naturae sunt attributa, ad aliquam coniecturam faciendam pertinebunt. Et ex victu multae trahuntur suspiciones, cum quemadmodum et apud quos et a quibus educatus et eruditus sit quaeritur, et quibuscum vivat, qua ratione vitae, quo more domestico vivat.

30 Et ex fortuna saepe argumentatio nascitur, cum servus an liber, pecuniosus an pauper, nobilis an ignobilis, felix an infelix, privatus an in potestate sit aut fuerit aut futurus sit, consideratur; aut denique aliquid eorum quaeritur quae fortunae esse attributa intelleguntur. Habitus autem, quoniam in aliqua perfecta et constanti animi aut corporis

---

ᵃ §§ 34–36.
ᵇ A Roman always had two names, and usually three or more. *E.g.* Marcus Tullius Cicero; Marcus was the *praenomen*, given to the child by his parents; Tullius, the *nomen*, borne by all the members of the *gens*; Cicero, the *cognomen* borne by the *familia*, as sub-group of the *gens*. *Cognomina* were frequently assumed by Romans because of some trait or physical characteristic, or to commemorate some exploit. The name *Caldus* cited in the text may have had the significance given there when it was originally applied, but as

first book.*a* For example, some suspicion arises at times from a name—when I say name, it should be understood that the cognomen is also included; we are talking about the fixed and proper appellation of an individual—for instance, if we should say that a man is called Caldus (Hot) because he has a quick and violent temper; or if inexperienced Greeks have been fooled because a man was called Clodius or

29 Caecilius or Mutius.*b* And one may base some suspicion on the nature of the defendant. For all the following attributes of nature are pertinent for making an inference: Is the person a man or woman, of this city or of that? Who were his ancestors, who are his kin? What is his age, temperament, physical condition? And many suspicions may be suggested by a man's way of life when the question is asked how and with whom and by whom he was reared and educated, and with whom he lives, what his plan or purpose in life is, and what his home life is like.

30 And frequently an argument can be made out of a person's fortune, when account is taken of whether he is, or has been, or will be slave or free, wealthy or poor, famous or unknown, successful or a failure, a private citizen or a public official; or finally when inquiry is made about any of the conditions which are understood to be predicated of fortune. And since habit consists of a complete and abiding con-

such names were inherited for many generations, the argumentative use here suggested would be sophistical.

The " inexperienced " Greeks were probably misled by the reference to a Roman by his *nomen* instead of the *cognomen*, which in some cases was the more usual form. It is as if some one referred to Cicero as Tullius, or Caesar as Julius. As a Greek had only one name, he might find the Roman practice disconcerting.

absolutione consistit, quo in genere est virtus,
scientia et quae contraria sunt, res ipsa, causa posita,
docebit ecquid hic quoque locus suspicionis ostendat.
Nam affectionis quidem ratio perspicuam solet
prae se gerere coniecturam, ut amor, iracundia,
molestia, propterea quod et ipsorum vis intellegitur
et quae res harum aliquam rem consequatur facile
est cognitu.

31   Studium autem quod est assidua et vehementer
aliquam ad rem applicata magna cum voluptate
occupatio, facile ex eo ducetur argumentatio quam
res ipsa desiderabit in causa. Item ex consilio
sumetur aliquid suspicionis; nam consilium est aliquid faciendi non faciendive excogitata ratio. Iam
facta et casus et orationes, quae sunt omnia, ut in
confirmationis praeceptis dictum est, in tria tempora
distributa, facile erit videre ecquid afferant ad
confirmandam coniecturam suspicionis.

32   X. Ac personis quidem res hae sunt attributae,
ex quibus omnibus unum in locum coactis accusatoris
erit improbatione hominis uti. Nam causa facti
parum firmitudinis habet, nisi animus eius qui
insimulatur in eam suspicionem adducitur uti a
tali culpa non videatur abhorruisse. Ut enim
animum alicuius improbare nihil attinet, cum causa
quare peccaret non intercessit, sic causam peccati
intercedere leve est si animus nulli minus honestae
rationi affinis ostenditur. Quare vitam eius quem
arguet ex ante factis accusator improbare debebit

---

    [a] *Suspicio*, translated here and elsewhere in the treatise
by " suspicion " really hovers in meaning between " suspicion " and " suggestion " or " hint." At times the latter
seems the more appropriate rendering.

stitution of mind or of body—under this head come strength, knowledge and their opposites—the circumstances, when the case has been fully set forth, will show whether this topic will yield any suspicions.[a] A consideration of feeling or emotion such as love, anger, annoyance usually reveals an obvious inference, because the force of these emotions is known and it is easy to note what the consequence of any of them is.

31 Interest is unremitting activity ardently devoted to some subject and accompanied by intense pleasure. From this such arguments can be drawn as the circumstances in the case require. Likewise some suspicion can be drawn from purpose; for purpose is a considered reason for doing or not doing something. Finally in the case of accomplishments, accidents and speeches, all of which, as was said in the rules for confirmation, may be considered in relation to three tenses,[b] it will be easy to see what suspicions they offer for strengthening an inference.

32 X. These are the attributes of persons, and it will be the task of the prosecutor to select arguments from all this collection to discredit the defendant. For there can be little foundation for a motive for crime unless such suspicion is cast on the character of the accused that it will seem not to be inconsistent with such a fault. For as there is no point in discrediting the character of a man where there was no motive for him to go wrong, so it is idle to allege a motive for a crime if his character is shown to be inclined to no line of conduct which is less than honourable. Therefore the prosecutor ought to discredit the life of the accused on the basis of his past

[b] Book I. 36.

et ostendere, si quo in pari ante peccato convictus
sit; si id non poterit, si quam in similem ante
suspicionem venerit, ac maxime, si fieri poterit,
simili quo in genere eiusdemmodi causa aliqua
commotum peccasse aut in aeque magna re aut
in maiore aut in minore, ut si qui quem pecunia
dicat inductum fecisse possit demonstrare aliqua
in re eius aliquod factum avarum.

33   Item in omni causa naturam aut victum aut
studium aut fortunam aut aliquid eorum quae
personis attributa sunt ad eam causam qua commotum peccasse dicet adiungere atque ex dispari
quoque genere culparum, si ex pari sumendi facultas
non erit, improbare animum adversari oportebit:
si avaritia inductum arguas fecisse, et avarum eum
quem accuses demonstrare non possis, aliis affinem
vitiis esse doceas, et ex ea re non esse mirandum,
qui in illa re turpis aut cupidus aut petulans fuerit,
hac quoque in re eum deliquisse. Quantum enim
de honestate et auctoritate eius qui arguitur de-
tractum est, tantundem de facultate eius totius
est defensionis deminutum.

34   Si nulli affinis poterit vitio reus ante admisso
demonstrari, locus inducetur ille per quem hortandi
iudices erunt ut veterem famam hominis nihil ad
rem putent pertinere. Nam eum ante celasse,
nunc manifesto teneri; quare non oportere hanc
rem ex superiore vita spectari, sed superiorem vitam

acts, and to point it out if he has previously been convicted of any crime equally serious. If this is impossible, he should prove that the defendant has been under suspicion of similar crime before, and particularly, if possible, that in similar circumstances he committed an offence because under the influence of some motive of the same kind, either in a matter of equal, or greater or less importance; an example would be a case in which a prosecutor could prove that the man who he alleges acted from desire for money, has acted avariciously on some other occasion.

33 Likewise in every case he should show the connexion between the motive by which he says the defendant was led to the crime and his nature, manner of life, interests or fortune or any of the attributes of persons, and discredit his character by reference to crimes of a different nature if there is no chance to cite those of a similar kind. If you charge that the man whom you accuse acted from avarice and cannot prove that he is avaricious, you should show that other vices are not foreign to his nature, and that it is no wonder if one who in that other affair acted basely, passionately and wantonly should have transgressed in this case also. For everything that detracts from the defendant's honour and repute, lessens in so far his chance for a complete defence.

34 If it cannot be shown that the accused has ever been implicated in any fault, the argument will be brought in by which the judges are to be urged to think that the long-standing reputation of the man has nothing to do with the case. For he has been concealing his true character before, and has now been caught red-handed; therefore this act should not be judged in view of his past life, but his past life

ex hac re improbari, et aut potestatem ante peccandi non fuisse aut causam; aut si haec dici non
poterunt, dicendum erit illud extremum, non esse
mirum, si nunc primum deliquerit; nam necesse esse
eum qui velit peccare aliquando primum delinquere.
Sin vita ante acta ignorabitur, hoc loco praeterito
et cur praetereatur demonstrato, argumentis accusationem statim confirmare oportebit.

35   XI. Defensor autem primum, si poterit, debebit
vitam eius qui insimulabitur quam honestissimam
demonstrare. Id faciet, si ostendet aliqua eius
nota et communia officia; quod genus in parentes,
cognatos, amicos, affines, necessarios; etiam quae
magis rara et eximia sunt, si ab eo cum magno
aliquid labore aut periculo aut utraque re, cum
necesse non esset, offici causa aut in rem publicam
aut in parentes aut in aliquos eorum qui modo
expositi sunt factum esse dicet; denique si nihil
deliquisse, nulla cupiditate impeditum ab officio
recessisse. Quod eo confirmatius erit si, cum
potestas impune aliquid faciendi minus honeste
fuisse dicetur, voluntas a faciendo demonstrabitur
36 afuisse. Hoc autem ipsum genus erit eo firmius
si eo ipso in genere quo arguetur integer ante fuisse
demonstrabitur: ut si, cum avaritiae causa fecisse
arguatur, minime omni in vita pecuniae cupidus
fuisse doceatur. Hic illa magna cum gravitate

should be discredited by this act; that previously
he had no power or motive to commit the crime.
And if none of these statements can be made, one
should have recourse to the last possible argument,
that it is no wonder that he has now for the first time
committed a crime; for one who wishes to sin, must
have a first offence. But if his past life is unknown,
it will be fitting to pass over this topic and after
showing why it is passed over, proceed to support
the accusation by arguments.

35 XI. The counsel for the defence, on the other
hand, will have to show first, if he can, that the life
of the accused has been upright in the highest degree.
He will do this if he can point to some services well
known to everyone: for example, how the defendant
has treated his parents, his kin by blood or marriage,
his friends and connexions; likewise, though this
opportunity is rarer and more unusual, if he can say
that the defendant has performed some service to the
state, his parents or some of those just mentioned,
though he was not compelled to do so but acted
merely from a sense of duty, and the act was very
difficult or dangerous or both; finally, if he can prove
that the defendant has never committed any offence
and has never been led by passion to fail in his duty.
This argument will be strengthened if it can be shown
that when he had an opportunity of doing a dishonest
deed with impunity he had no desire to do so. This
36 statement will be stronger if it can be shown that he
has previously been innocent of the kind of crime of
which he is accused: for example, if when a man is
accused of having acted through avarice, it is shown
that in his whole life he has been anything but eager
for money. At this point a passage expressing

inducetur indignatio, iuncta conquestioni, per quam
miserum facinus esse et indignum demonstrabitur,
cum animus in vita fuerit omni a vitiis remotis-
simus, eam causam putare, quae homines audaces
in fraudem rapere soleat, castissimum quoque
hominem ad peccandum potuisse impellere ; aut :
iniquum esse et optimo cuique perniciosissimum non
vitam honeste actam tali in tempore quam plurimum
prodesse, sed subita ex criminatione, quae confingi
quamvis false possit, non ex ante acta vita, quae
neque ad tempus fingi neque ullo modo mutari
possit, facere iudicium.

37   Sin autem in ante acta vita aliquae turpitudines
erunt, aut falso venisse in eam existimationem
dicetur ex aliquorum invidia aut obtrectatione aut
falsa opinione ; aut imprudentiae, necessitudini,
persuasioni, adulescentiae aut alicui non malitiosae
animi affectioni attribuentur ; aut dissimili in genere
vitiorum esse ostendentur,[1] ut animus non omnino
integer, sed ab tali culpa remotus esse videatur.
At si nullo modo vitae turpitudo aut infamia leniri
poterit oratione, negare oportebit de vita eius et
de moribus quaeri, sed de eo crimine quo de arguatur ;
quare, ante factis omissis, illud quod instet id agi
oportere.

---

[1] esse ostendentur *supplied exempli gratia by Ströbel.*

resentment coupled with one of complaint can be
introduced with great effect; [a] in this it will be
pointed out that when his character has been
throughout his life utterly foreign to wrongdoing,
it is miserable and unworthy treatment to suppose
that the motive which often hurries audacious men
into guilt could have induced the purest of men to
commit a crime. Or the argument may be handled
in this way: it is unfair and injurious to every good
man that one's honourable life in the past should
not be of the greatest possible help to him at such
a time, but that judgement should be given on the
basis of a sudden charge which can be made up out
of whole cloth rather than on the basis of his past
life, which cannot be made up for the occasion nor
changed in any way.

37   But if there are some discreditable phases in the
defendant's past life, it may be alleged that he got
this reputation wrongly through the envy of a few
people, or back-biting, or false opinion. Or these
acts may be attributed to folly, necessity, persuasion,
youth or some trait of character that is not malicious;
or they may be shown to be vices of a different kind
so that his character, though not perfect in all
respects, may seem to have no connexion with such a
crime as is now charged against him. But if a
speech can do nothing to relieve the shame and baseness of his life, the counsel will have to say that the
defendant's life and character are not under investigation, but only the crime of which he is accused; that,
therefore, his past deeds should be left out of the
discussion, and only the present case should be
debated.

[a] For this, cf. I. 98, 100, 106.

38   XII. Ex facto autem ipso suspiciones ducentur, si totius administratio negoti ex omnibus partibus pertemptabitur; atque eae suspiciones partim ex negotio separatim, partim communiter ex personis atque ex negotio proficiscentur. Ex negotio duci poterunt, si eas res quae negotiis attributae sunt diligenter considerabimus. Ex eis igitur in hanc constitutionem convenire videntur genera earum

39 omnia, partes generum pleraeque. Videre igitur primum oportebit, quae sint continentia cum ipso negotio, hoc est, quae ab re separari non possint. Quo in loco satis erit diligenter considerasse, quid sit ante rem factum ex quo spes perficiendi nata et faciendi facultas quaesita videatur; quid in ipsa re gerenda, quid postea consecutum sit.

Deinde ipsius est negoti gestio pertractanda. Nam hoc genus earum rerum quae negotio sunt attributae secundo in loco nobis est expositum.

40 Hoc ergo in genere spectabitur locus, tempus, occasio, facultas; quorum unius cuiusque vis diligenter in confirmationis praeceptis explicata est. Quare, ne aut hic non admonuisse aut ne eadem iterum dixisse videamur, breviter iniciemus, quid quaque in parte considerari oporteat. In loco igitur opportunitas, in tempore longinquitas, in occasione commoditas ad faciendum idonea, in facultate copia et potestas earum rerum propter quas aliquid facilius fit aut quibus sine omnino confici non potest, consideranda est.

38   XII. Suspicions may be derived from the act itself, if one explores the whole course of the affair from all angles, and these suspicions may proceed in part from the act considered separately, and in part from the persons and the act taken together. They can be discovered in the action if we consider carefully the attributes of actions.[a] All the main classes of these seem to fit this issue and most of the sub-

39 divisions. It will be necessary to see first what is coherent with the action itself, that is, what cannot be separated from it. Under this head it will be sufficient to examine with care what occurred before the act from which it seems that hope of success was aroused or an opportunity to perform it was sought, what was actually done in carrying out the act, and what followed after it.

   Next, the actual performance of the act should be considered. For this kind of attribute of the action

40 was put by us in the second place. Under this head we look into the place, time, occasion and facilities. The meaning of each of these was carefully explained in the rules for confirmation.[b] We shall therefore insert here a discussion of what should be looked for under each head, in order that we may not seem to have omitted it here, but we shall be brief in order that we may not seem to repeat. In reference to place one should consider the opportunity which it afforded for the act, and in reference to time, length or duration, in reference to occasion, any circumstances lending themselves to the doing of the act, and under " facilities " the supply of, and access to, the means which make an act easier to perform or without which it cannot be done at all.

---

    [a] *Cf.* Book I. 36–43.   [b] Book I. 38–41.

41   Deinde videndum est quid adiunctum sit negotio, hoc est, quid maius, quid minus, quid aeque magnum sit, quid simile; ex quibus coniectura quaedam ducitur, si, quemadmodum res maiores, minores, aeque magnae, similes agi soleant, diligenter considerabitur.   Quo in genere eventus quoque videndus erit; hoc est, quid ex quaque re soleat evenire magno opere considerandum est, ut metus, laetitia, 42 titubatio, audacia.   Quarta autem pars rebus erat ex eis quas negotiis dicebamus esse attributas, consecutio. In ea quaeruntur ea quae gestum negotium confestim aut intervallo consequuntur. In quo videbimus ecqua consuetudo sit, ecqua lex, ecqua pactio, ecquod eius rei artificium aut usus aut exercitatio, hominum aut approbatio aut offensio, ex quibus nonnunquam elicitur aliquid suspicionis.

    XIII. Sunt autem aliae suspiciones, quae communiter et ex negotiorum et ex personarum attributionibus sumuntur.   Nam et ex fortuna et ex natura et ex victu, studio, factis, casu, orationibus, consilio et ex habitu animi aut corporis pleraque pertinent ad eas res, quae rem credibilem aut incredibilem facere possunt et cum facti suspicione iunguntur. 43 Maxime enim quaerere oportet in hac constitutione, primum potueritne aliquid fieri; deinde ecquo ab alio potuerit; deinde facultas, de qua ante diximus; deinde utrum id facinus sit quod paenitere fuerit necesse, quod spem celandi non haberet; deinde necessitudo, in qua necesse fuerit id aut fieri aut ita

41 In the next place one should examine the
"adjunct" of the affair, that is, what is larger, smaller,
of equal size, and similar; on these an inference may
be based if one considers carefully how greater events,
or lesser, those equally important or similar are wont
to occur. The result has also to be considered under
this head, that is one must particularly examine what
condition usually results from every action, as for
42 example, fear, joy, vacillation, boldness. The fourth
of our attributes of actions was consequence. Under
this head we look for things which ensue on the performance of an act, either immediately or after some
interval. In so doing we shall see whether it has
given rise to any custom, law, covenant, technique,
habit or practice, whether it has received the approval
or disapproval of mankind; from these points frequently some suspicion is brought out.

XIII. There are, moreover, other angles of attack
which derive in common from the attributes of
actions and of persons. For many things in a man's
fortune, his nature, manner of life, interests, deeds,
accidents, speeches, purposes, and in his mental and
physical characteristics are pertinent to the material
which can make a charge credible or incredible, and
are closely connected with a suspicion of crime.
43 The most important questions, indeed, in this issue
are: first, could a given act have been performed?
Second, could it have been performed by any one
else? The third point concerns facilities, about
which we spoke earlier. Next, was the crime of
such a nature that the author was bound to repent of
it, or one in which there was no hope of conceal-
ment? The next point is necessity, under which
the question is, whether this act had to be done or

fieri, quaeritur. Quorum pars ad consilium pertinet, quod personis attributum est, ut in ea causa quam exposuimus. Ante rem, quod in itinere se tam familiariter applicaverit, quod sermonis causam quaesierit, quod simul diverterit, dein cenarit. In re nox, somnus. Post rem, quod solus exierit, quod illum tam familiarem tam aequo animo reliquerit,
44 quod cruentum gladium habuerit.[1]

Rursum, utrum videatur diligenter ratio faciendi esse habita et excogitata, an ita temere, ut non veri simile sit quemquam tam temere ad maleficium accessisse. In quo quaeritur num quo alio modo commodius potuerit fieri vel a fortuna administrari. Nam saepe, si pecuniae, adiumenta, adiutores desint, facultas fuisse faciendi non videtur. Hoc modo si diligenter attendamus, apta inter se esse intellegimus haec quae negotiis, et illa quae personis sunt attributa.

Hic non facile est neque necessarium est distinguere, ut in superioribus partibus, quo pacto quidque accusatorem et quomodo defensorem tractare oporteat. Non est necessarium, propterea quod causa posita, quid in quamque conveniat, res ipsa docebit eos qui non omnia hic se inventuros putabunt, sed[2] modo quandam in commune mediocrem
45 intellegentiam conferent; non facile autem quod et infinitum est tot de rebus utramque in partem

---

[1] *After* habuerit P^2J *add* Horum pars ad consilium pertinet (some of these are related to "purpose").

[2] sed C : si sv_7, *Weidner.*

---

[a] §§ 14, 15. What follows discusses the case of the two travellers and the murder.

done in this way. Part of these have reference to purpose or intent, which is an attribute of persons, as, for example, in the case which we outlined above.[a] Pertinent circumstances before the deed are that he approached the rich man so familiarly, that he sought occasion to speak to him, that he stopped at the same inn and dined with him. The circumstances immediately connected with the deed are that it was night, and the victim was asleep. Pertinent events after the deed are that the accused left the inn alone, that he abandoned his intimate friend with such indifference, that he had a blood-stained sword.

44   Another point to be considered is whether a plan of action seems to have been carefully formed and thought out, or whether the deed was done so rashly that it seems unlikely that anyone rushed with such rashness into crime. In this connexion one may inquire whether the event could not have occurred more readily in another way, or even have been a result of chance. For often, if money, assistance and assistants are lacking, there seems to have been no possibility of acting. If we watch carefully in this way we shall find that the attributes of actions and of persons are closely connected.

    In this case it is neither easy nor necessary to distinguish, as I did in earlier sections, how the prosecutor and how the counsel for the defence should handle each argument. It is not necessary, because when the case is once stated the facts themselves will show what argument applies to each side; at least it will be plain to those who will not expect to find every detail set down in this book, but will 45 contribute only a fair grade of intelligence. It is not easy because it is an endless task to explain

singillatim de una quaque explicare et alias aliter
haec in utramque partem causae solent convenire.
XIV. Quare considerare haec quae exposuimus
oportebit. Facilius autem ad inventionem animus
incidet, si gesti negoti et suam et adversarii narrationem saepe et diligenter pertractabit et quod
quaeque pars suspicionis habebit eliciens considerabit quare, quo consilio, qua spe perficiendi
quidque factum sit; hoc cur modo potius quam illo;
cur ab hoc potius quam ab illo; cur nullo adiutore
aut cur hoc; cur nemo sit conscius aut cur sit aut
cur hic sit; cur hoc ante factum sit; cur hoc ante
factum non sit;[1] cur hoc in ipso negotio, cur hoc
post negotium, an factum de industria an rem
ipsam consecutum sit; constetne oratio aut cum
re aut ipsa secum; hoc huiusne rei sit signum an
illius, an et huius et illius et utrius potius; quid
factum sit, quod non oportuerit, aut non factum,
46 quod oportuerit. Cum animus hac intentione omnes
totius negoti partes considerabit, tum illi ipsi in
medium coacervati loci procedent, de quibus ante
dictum est; et tum ex singulis, tum ex coniunctis
argumenta certa nascentur, quorum argumentorum
pars probabili, pars necessario in genere versabitur.
Accedunt autem saepe ad coniecturam quaestiones,[a]
testimonia, rumores, quae contra omnia uterque

---

[1] cur hoc ante factum non sit *omitted by M, bracketed by*
Kayser.

---

[a] *Quaestio* here probably has the meaning of " examination under torture."

so many arguments one by one about every fact of
every case, and besides these arguments usually fit
each part of the case differently on different occasions. XIV. Therefore one should study carefully
what we have set forth. Furthermore, the mind
will more easily come upon " inventions " if one
examines frequently and carefully one's own narrative of the events and that of the opponent, and
eliciting any clues that each part may afford,
ponders why, with what intent and with what hope
of success each thing was done; why it was done
in this way rather than in that; why by this man
rather than by that; why with no helper or why
with this one; why no one knew about it, or why
some one did, and why it was this one who did; why
another act was performed earlier; why another act
was not performed earlier; why this was done in
immediate connexion with the event, and this other
thing after the event; whether this was done intentionally or followed as a natural consequence of the
event; whether what he said is consistent with the
events or with itself; whether this is a sign of this or
of that, or both of this and of that and of which the
more; what was done that ought not to have been
done, or what was left undone that ought to have
46 been done. When the mind studies so attentively
every part of the whole affair, then the topics mentioned above which are stored up will come forth of
their own accord; and then sometimes from one,
sometimes from a combination of topics definite
arguments will be produced, part of which will be
classed as probable and part as irrefutable. Inference is often assisted or supported by examinations,[a]
testimony, rumours, all of which each counsel should

simili via praeceptorum torquere ad suae causae commodum debebit. Nam et ex quaestione suspiciones et ex testimonio et ex rumore aliquo pari ratione ut ex causa et ex persona et ex facto duci oportebit.

47 Quare nobis et ei videntur errare qui hoc genus suspicionum artifici non putant indigere, et ei qui aliter hoc de genere ac de omni coniectura praecipiendum putant. Omnis enim eisdem ex locis coniectura sumenda est. Nam et eius qui in quaestione aliquid dixerit, et eius qui in testimonio, et ipsius rumoris causa et veritas ex eisdem attributionibus reperietur.

Omni autem in causa pars argumentorum est adiuncta ei causae solum quae dicitur, et ex ipsa ita ducta ut ab ea separatim in omnes eiusdem generis causas transferri non satis commode possit; pars autem est pervagatior et aut in omnes eiusdem generis aut in plerasque causas accommodata.

48 XV. Haec ergo argumenta, quae transferri in multas causas possunt, locos communes nominamus. Nam locus communis aut certae rei quandam continet amplificationem, ut si quis hoc velit ostendere, eum qui parentem necarit maximo supplicio esse dignum; quo loco, nisi perorata et probata [1] causa, non est utendum; aut dubiae, quae ex contrario quoque habeat probabiles rationes argumentandi, ut suspicionibus credi oportere, et contra, suspicionibus credi non oportere. Ac pars locorum com-

---

[1] et probata *omitted by M* : *bracketed by Schuetz, Ströbel.*

---

[a] The reference is to the division of proofs into ἔντεχνοι (subject to rules of rhetoric or logic) and ἄτεχνοι (not subject to such rules). The latter class included witnesses, documents, etc. The division is as old as Aristotle. *Cf. Rhet.* I. ii, 2, 1355 b.

twist to the advantage of his own case, making them
tell in opposite directions though he follows a similar
course of rules.   For suspicion will have to be derived
from investigation and testimony and some rumour in
like manner as from the case and from the person
and from the act.

47   Therefore those seem to me to be wrong who think
that this kind of suspicion does not need systematic
treatment by the art of rhetoric, as also do those who
think that the rules about this kind should differ
from those about inference as a whole.   For all
inference has to be based on the same forms of argument.   For the cause or motive of one who makes a
statement under torture and the truth of what he
says will be ascertained from the same attributes as
other arguments, and the same is true of one who
gives testimony, and even of rumour itself.[a]

In every case some of the arguments are related
only to the case that is being pleaded, and are so
dependent on it that they cannot advantageously be
separated from it and transferred to other cases,
while others are of a more general nature, and adapt-
able to all or most cases of the same kind.   XV.
48 These arguments which can be transferred to many
cases, we call common topics.   A common topic
either contains an amplification of an undisputed
statement—for example, if one should wish to show
that a man who has murdered his father or mother
deserves the extreme penalty (this type is to be used
only when the case has been finished and proved)—
or of a doubtful statement against which there are
also plausible lines of argument; for example, it is
right to put confidence in suspicions, and on the other
hand, it is not right.   Some common topics are used

munium per indignationem aut per conquestionem
inducitur, de quibus ante dictum est; pars per ali-
49 quam probabilem utraque ex parte rationem. Distin-
guitur autem oratio atque illustratur maxime raro
inducendis locis communibus et aliquo loco iam
certioribus illis argumentis confirmato. Nam et
tum conceditur commune quiddam dicere, cum
diligenter aliqui proprius causae locus tractatus est,
et auditoris animus aut renovatur ad ea quae restant
aut omnibus iam dictis exsuscitatur. Omnia autem
ornamenta elocutionis, in quibus et suavitatis et
gravitatis plurimum consistit, et omnia quae in
inventione rerum et sententiarum aliquid habent
50 dignitatis in communes locos conferuntur. Quare
non, ut causarum, sic oratorum quoque multorum
communes loci sunt. Nam nisi ab eis qui multa in
exercitatione magnam sibi verborum et sententiarum
copiam comparaverint, tractari non poterunt ornate
et graviter, quemadmodum natura ipsa eorum
desiderat.

Atque hoc sit nobis dictum communiter de omni
genere locorum communium. XVI. Nunc exponemus, in coniecturalem constitutionem qui loci
communes incidere soleant: suspicionibus credi
oportere et non oportere; rumoribus credi oportere
et non oportere; testibus credi oportere et non
oportere; quaestionibus credi oportere et non
oportere; vitam ante actam spectari oportere et
non oportere; eiusdem esse, qui in illa re peccarit,
hoc quoque admisisse, et non esse eiusdem; causam
maxime spectari oportere et non oportere. Atque

in connexion with resentment and complaint, which
have been explained above,[a] and part in supporting
49 some probable line of reasoning on either side. A
speech, however, is occasionally rendered distinguished or brilliant by introducing common topics
and some topic backed up by arguments when the
audience is already convinced. In fact that is
certainly the moment when it is permissible to
say something " common ", when some passage
peculiar to the case has been developed with great
care, and the spirit of the audience is being refreshed
for what is to come, or is being roused to passion now
that the argument has been concluded. Moreover,
all the ornaments of style, which lend charm and
dignity, are lavished on common topics, as well as
everything which in the invention of matter or
50 thought contributes to weight and grandeur. Therefore, though these are topics " common " to many
cases, they are not common to many orators. For
they cannot be treated with elegance and dignity, as
their very nature requires, except by those who
through long practice have acquired a vast store of
words and ideas.

This is enough to say in general about every kind
of common topic. XVI. Now I shall set down what
common topics usually fit the issue of fact : one
should and should not put confidence in suspicions, in
rumours, in witnesses, in examinations under torture ;
one should and should not take into consideration a
man's past life ; it is and is not natural for the same
man to commit that offence and this crime also ; one
should and should not give especial consideration to
the motive. These and any other similar common

[a] I. 100–109.

hi quidem et si qui eiusmodi ex proprio argumento communes loci nascentur, in contrarias partes diducuntur.

51 Certus autem locus est accusatoris, per quem auget facti atrocitatem, et alter, per quem negat malorum misereri oportere : defensoris, per quem calumnia accusatorum cum indignatione ostenditur et per quem cum conquestione misericordia captatur. Hi et ceteri loci omnes communes ex eisdem praeceptis sumuntur quibus ceterae argumentationes ; sed illae tenuius et subtilius et acutius tractantur, hi autem gravius et ornatius et cum verbis tum etiam sententiis excellentibus. In illis enim finis est ut id quod dicitur verum esse videatur, in his, tametsi hoc quoque videri oportet, tamen finis est amplitudo. Nunc ad aliam constitutionem transeamus.

52 XVII. Cum est nominis controversia, quia vis vocabuli definienda verbis est, constitutio definitiva dicitur. Eius generis exemplo nobis posita sit haec causa : C. Flaminius, is qui consul rem male gessit bello Punico secundo, cum tribunus plebis esset, invito senatu et omnino contra voluntatem omnium optimatium per seditionem ad populum legem agrariam ferebat. Hunc pater suus concilium plebis habentem de templo deduxit ; arcessitur maiestatis. Intentio est : " Maiestatem minuisti, quod tribunum plebis de templo deduxisti." Depulsio est : " Non

---

a Gaius Flaminius proposed to divide the territory of Picenum and Cisalpine Gaul among needy citizens. He met his death at the battle of Lake Trasimenus in 217 B.C. Another version of the story (in *Valerius Maximus*, V, iv, 5) makes the father use only moral suasion.

topics which may spring out of an argument peculiar to the case in hand, are applicable to both sides.

51   There is, however, a common topic belonging to the prosecutor alone, in which he makes much of the atrocity of the crime, and another in which he asserts that malefactors should not be pitied, and one for the counsel for the defence in which the malice of the prosecution is indignantly denounced, and another in which he bemoans the lot of the defendant and pleads for mercy. These and other common topics are subject to the same rules as are other arguments. But the others are treated with greater restraint, simplicity and acumen, while the common topics are developed with greater emphasis and embellishment, and with lofty language and thought. For in arguments the end is to give what is said the appearance of truth; in common topics, although this should also be an object, still the chief end is amplification. Now let us pass to another issue.

52   XVII. When there is a dispute about the name by which an act is described, the issue is known as the *constitutio definitiva* (or issue of definition) because the meaning of the word must be defined; we may take the following case as an example of this class: Gaius Flaminius [a]—the one who as consul conducted an unsuccessful campaign in the Second Punic War—when tribune of the people seditiously proposed an agrarian law to the people against the wishes of the senate and in general contrary to the desires of all the upper classes. As he was haranguing the popular assembly his father dragged him from the rostrum, and was charged with lese-majesty. The charge is, " You committed lese-majesty in that you dragged a tribune of the people from the rostrum." The

minui maiestatem." Quaestio est: Maiestatemne
minuerit? Ratio: "In filium enim quam habebam
potestatem, ea sum usus." Rationis infirmatio:
"At enim, qui patria potestate, hoc est privata
quadam, tribuniciam potestatem, hoc est populi
potestatem infirmat, minuit maiestatem." Iudicatio est: Minuatne is maiestatem qui in tribuniciam potestatem patria potestate utatur? Ad
hanc iudicationem argumentationes omnes afferre
oportebit.

53 Ac ne qui forte arbitretur nos non intellegere
aliam quoque incidere constitutionem in hanc
causam, eam nos partem solam sumimus in quam
praecepta nobis danda sunt. Omnibus autem
partibus hoc in libro explicatis, quivis omni in causa,
si diligenter attendet, omnes videbit constitutiones
et earum partes et controversias si quae forte in
eas incident. Nam de omnibus praescribemus.

Primus ergo accusatoris locus est eius nominis
cuius de vi quaeritur brevis et aperta et ex opinione
hominum definitio, hoc modo: Maiestatem minuere
est de dignitate aut amplitudine aut potestate populi
aut eorum quibus populus potestatem dedit aliquid
derogare. Hoc sic breviter expositum pluribus
verbis est et rationibus confirmandum et ita esse
ut descripseris ostendendum. Postea ad id quod
definieris factum eius qui accusabitur adiungere
oportebit et ex eo quod ostenderis esse verbi causa

---

^a In Roman law a father had full authority—even of life
or death—over his children, no matter how old they might be.

^b The case might presumably be argued under the *con-
stitutio generalis* by pleading that he was carrying out the
order of the Senate in restraining a seditious person (*remotio*

answer is : " I did not commit lese-majesty." The question is, " Did he commit lese-majesty ? " The excuse is, " I used the authority which I had over my son." [a] The denial of the excuse, " On the contrary, one who uses the authority belonging to him as a father—that is private authority—to lessen the authority of a tribune—that is, the authority of the people—is guilty of lese-majesty." The point for the judge's decision is, " Would he be guilty of lese-majesty, who used his authority as father against the authority of a tribune ? " All arguments must be directed to this point.

53 And lest any one happen to think that we are not aware that another issue arises in this case, we shall say that we are taking up only the part for which we must at this time give rules and principles.[b] When all facts have been discussed in this book, any one in any case will, if he pays careful attention, find all the issues and their facts and the disputes, whatever they are, which may arise : for we shall give directions about all of them.

The first topic in the prosecutor's argument is a brief, clear and conventional definition of the word whose meaning is sought, as follows : Lese-majesty is a lessening of the dignity or high estate or authority of the people or of those to whom the people have given authority. This brief exposition must be supported by a lengthy discussion of reasons, and shown to be as you have outlined it. Then it will be necessary to show the connexion between the act of the accused and your definition, and on the basis of what you have shown to be the meaning of lese-

criminis), or that the act was committed for the sake of a greater good (*comparatio*). *Cf.* Book I. 15.

maiestatem minuere, docere adversarium maiestatem
minuisse et hunc totum locum communi loco confirmare, per quem ipsius facti atrocitas aut indignitas
aut omnino culpa cum indignatione augeatur. Post
54 erit infirmanda adversariorum descriptio. Ea autem
infirmabitur, si falsa demonstrabitur. Hoc ex
opinione hominum sumetur, cum quemadmodum
et quibus in rebus homines in consuetudine scribendi
aut sermocinandi eo verbo uti soleant, considerabitur.
Item infirmabitur, si turpis aut inutilis esse ostenditur eius descriptionis approbatio et, quae incommoda consecutura sint, eo concesso ostendetur—id
autem ex honestatis et ex utilitatis partibus sumetur,
de quibus in deliberationis praeceptis exponemus—
et si cum definitione nostra adversariorum definitionem conferemus et nostram veram, honestam,
55 utilem esse demonstrabimus, illorum contra. Quaere-
mus autem res aut maiore aut minore aut pari in
negotio similes, ex quibus affirmetur nostra descriptio.

XVIII. Iam si res plures erunt definiendae : ut,
si quaeratur, fur sit an sacrilegus, qui vasa ex privato
sacra surripuerit, erit utendum pluribus definitionibus ; deinde simili ratione causa tractanda. Locus
autem communis in eius malitiam, qui non modo
rerum, verum etiam verborum potestatem sibi
arrogare conatus et faciat quod velit, et id quod
fecerit quo velit nomine appellet.

majesty as far as words are concerned, to demonstrate that your opponent committed lese-majesty, and then to support the whole argument by a common topic in which you magnify and inveigh against the enormity of the deed itself, its heinousness or at least its guilt. After that the definition of the 54 opposing counsel must be invalidated; this can be done if it is shown to be false. Such an argument will be based on common belief when one considers how and in what connexion people are accustomed to use such a word in ordinary writing or speech. The definition of the opponents may also be attacked if we show that to approve it is dishonourable and inexpedient, and point out what disadvantages will follow if their definition is accepted (this is based on the concepts of honour and advantage which we shall expound in giving the rules for speeches before deliberative bodies);[a] and if we compare our definition with that of our opponents and prove that ours is 55 true, honourable and expedient, and theirs the opposite. Furthermore, we shall search for similar cases of greater or less or of equal seriousness to support our definition.

XVIII. In a case in which several words have to be defined—for example, when the question is whether it is theft or sacrilege to steal sacred vessels from a private house—one must make use of several definitions and then proceed to treat the case in the manner already laid down. Another common topic attacks the villainy of a man who, attempting to arrogate to himself the control not only of acts but also of words, both does what he pleases and calls his deed by whatever name he pleases.

[a] §§ 157–176.

CICERO

Deinde defensoris primus locus est item nominis
brevis et aperta et ex opinione hominum descriptio,
hoc modo: Maiestatem minuere est aliquid de re
publica, cum potestatem non habeas, administrare.
Deinde huius confirmatio similibus et exemplis et
rationibus,[1] postea sui facti ab illa definitione
separatio. Deinde locus communis, per quem
56 facti utilitas aut honestas adaugetur. Deinde
sequitur adversariorum definitionis reprehensio, quae
eisdem ex locis omnibus quos accusatori praescrip-
simus conficitur; et cetera post eadem praeter
communem locum inducentur. Locus autem communis erit defensoris is per quem indignabitur accusatorem sui periculi causa non res solum convertere,
verum etiam verba commutare conari. Nam illi
quidem communes loci, aut qui calumniae accusatorum demonstrandae aut misericordiae captandae
aut facti indignandi aut a misericordia deterrendi
causa sumuntur, ex periculi magnitudine, non ex
causae genere ducuntur. Quare non in omnem
causam, sed in omne causae genus incidunt. Eorum
mentionem in coniecturali constitutione fecimus.
Inductione [2] autem, cum causa postulabit, utemur.

57 XIX. Cum autem actio translationis aut commutationis indigere videtur, quod non aut is agit quem
oportet, aut cum eo quicum oportet, aut apud quos,
qua lege, qua poena, quo crimine, quo tempore

---

[1] similibus et exemplis et rationibus, *bracketed by Kayser,
Friedrich, Ströbel.*
[2] *For* inductione *Phillipson suggests* indignatione.

---

[a] *Cf.* I. 51.

The first topic for the defence is likewise a brief, clear and conventional definition of the word, as follows: " Lese-majesty consists in doing some public business without authority." Then follows the confirmation of this definition by examples and arguments similar to those used by the prosecution. After this it can be shown that the act does not square with the definition. Then a common topic enlarging on the advantage and honour arising from the act.

56 Then follows the invalidation of the definition given by the opposing counsel, which is accomplished by using all the same lines of argument that we have prescribed for the prosecutor. And after this all the other arguments used by the prosecution may be employed except the common topic. The common topic available for the defendant is one in which he expresses his indignation that the prosecutor attempts to put him in jeopardy not only by distorting facts but even by altering the meaning of the language. For the common topics which are used to demonstrate the ill-will of the prosecutors or to arouse pity, or to denounce a crime or to deter the judges from showing mercy, arise out of the magnitude of the peril, not out of the kind of case. Therefore they are not incidental to every case, but to every kind of case. We mentioned them in connexion with the issue of fact. Induction is another thing that we shall use when the case requires.[a]

57 XIX. When it seems necessary to transfer the action to another court, or to make a change in procedure because the proper person does not bring the action, or it is not brought against the proper person or before the proper court, or under the proper statute, or with a proper request for penalty, or with

oportet, constitutio translativa appellatur. Eius
nobis exempla permulta opus sint, si singula trans-
lationum genera quaeramus; sed quia ratio praeceptorum similis est, exemplorum multitudine supersedendum est. Atque in nostra quidem consuetudine
multis de causis fit ut rarius incidant translationes.
Nam et praetoris exceptionibus multae excluduntur
actiones et ita ius civile habemus constitutum,
ut causa cadat is qui non quemadmodum oportet
58 egerit. Quare in iure plerumque versantur. Ibi
enim et exceptiones postulantur et agendi [1] potestas
datur et omnis conceptio privatorum iudiciorum
constituitur. In ipsis autem iudiciis rarius incidunt
et tamen, si quando incidunt, eiusmodi sunt ut per
se minus habeant firmitudinis, confirmentur autem
assumpta alia aliqua constitutione: ut in quodam
iudicio, cum venefici cuiusdam nomen esset delatum
et, quia parricidi causa subscripta esset, extra
ordinem esset acceptum, cum in accusatione autem
alia quaedam crimina testibus et argumentis con-
firmarentur, parricidi autem mentio solum facta
esset, defensor in hoc ipso multum oportet et diu
consistat: cum de nece parentis nihil demonstratum
esset, indignum facinus esse ea poena afficere reum
qua parricidae afficiuntur; id autem, si damnaretur,
fieri necesse esse, quoniam et id causae subscriptum
59 et ea re nomen extra ordinem sit acceptum. Ea
igitur poena si affici reum non oporteat, damnari

---

[1] et agendi et quonammodo agendi *M* : et agendi *erased
in P* : *deleted in SL* : et quodammodo agendi *Ju* : de modo
agendi *Victorinus*.

---

[a] *I.e.* the crime was so heinous that it was brought up
immediately before a special court.

the proper accusation, or at the proper time, the issue
is called translative (or procedural). We should need
very many examples if we should look for every kind
of transfer or change; but because the principle of
all the rules is the same, we must dispense with a
multitude of examples. In legal procedure at Rome
there are many reasons why speeches involving
transfers rarely are made. For many actions are
excluded by the *exceptiones* (counter-pleas) granted
by the praetor, and the provisions of our civil law
are such that one who does not bring his action in
58 the proper form loses his suit. Therefore such
questions generally are disposed of *in iure* (before
the praetor). For it is there that exceptions are
requested and right of action is granted, and the
complete formula for the guidance of the trial of
private (or civil) actions is drawn up. Pleas for
transfer rarely come up in the actual trial and if
they do they are of such a nature that they have
little force in themselves, but are supported by
the aid of some other issue : for instance, in a
certain trial a man was accused of poisoning, and
because the indictment signed by the prosecutor
alleged parricide, the case was accepted out of turn,[a]
but at the trial certain other crimes were proved by
testimony and arguments, and parricide was barely
mentioned. The counsel for the defence should dwell
long and emphatically on this very point : that since
no proof has been given of the murder of a parent
it is an outrage to inflict on the defendant the penalty
inflicted on parricides; but if he is convicted, this
must necessarily follow, for this was in the signed
indictment and for this reason the case was accepted
59 out of turn. If, then, this penalty ought not to be

quoque non oportere, quoniam ea poena damnationem necessario consequatur. Hic defensor poenae commutationem ex translativo genere inducendo totam infirmabit accusationem. Verumtamen ceteris quoque criminibus defendendis coniecturali constitutione translationem confirmabit.

XX. Exemplum autem translationis in causa positum nobis sit huiusmodi: Cum ad vim faciendam quidam armati venissent, armati contra praesto fuerunt, et cuidam equiti Romano quidam ex armatis resistenti gladio manum praecidit. Agit is cui manus praecisa est iniuriarum. Postulat is quicum agitur a praetore exceptionem: Extra quam in
60 reum capitis praeiudicium fiat. Hic is qui agit iudicium purum postulat; ille quicum agitur exceptionem addi ait oportere. Quaestio est: Excipiendum sit an non. Ratio: " Non enim oportet in recuperatorio iudicio eius malefici, de quo inter sicarios quaeritur, praeiudicium fieri." Infirmatio rationis: " Eiusmodi sunt iniuriae, ut de eis indignum sit non primo quoque tempore iudicari." Iudicatio: Atrocitas iniuriarum satisne causae sit, quare, dum de ea iudicatur, de aliquo maiore maleficio, de quo iudicium comparatum sit, praeiudicetur? Atque exemplum quidem hoc est. In omni autem causa ab utroque quaeri oportebit a quo et per quos

---

a A board of three or five persons appointed for summary trial.

inflicted on the defendant, he should not be convicted either, because the penalty necessarily follows
conviction. Here the counsel for the defence by
bringing a change of penalty into the speech, by
using the translative issue, will invalidate the whole
accusation. Nevertheless, there will be a defence
against the other charges, too, on the issue of fact,
and that will fortify his plea for a change of procedure.

XX. As an example of *translatio* (transfer) in a
case at law let us take the following : Some armed
men had come with the intent to do violence, and
other armed men were ready to meet them. A
Roman knight resisted and one of the armed band
cut off his hand with a sword. The man whose hand
had been cut off brings action for *iniuriae* (personal
injury). The defendant claims an exception from
the praetor in these words : " Provided that pre-
judgement shall not be given against the defendant
60 on a capital charge." Here the complainant asks
for a trial on a simple fact ; the defendant says that
the exception should be added. The question is :
" Should the exception be granted or not ? " The
supporting argument for the defendant's counter-
plea is : " In a trial before *recuperatores* [a] the defendant should not be pre-judged of a crime which belongs
to the court trying assassination." The reply to his
plea is : " The wrong is so serious that it is improper
not to try the case at the earliest opportunity."
The point for the judge's decision is : " Is the seriousness of the wrong sufficient reason why, in passing
judgement upon it, a greater crime, for which a court
is assigned, should be pre-judged ? " This is an
example. But in every case it will be proper for
both sides to consider by whom and through whom

et quo modo et quo tempore aut agi aut iudicari aut
61 quid statui de ea re conveniat. Id ex partibus iuris,
de quibus post dicendum est, sumi oportebit et
ratiocinari quid in similibus rebus fieri soleat, et
videre, utrum malitia aliud agatur, aliud simuletur,
an stultitia, an necessitudine, quod alio modo agere
non possit, an occasione agendi sic sit iudicium aut
actio constituta, an recte sine ulla re eiusmodi res
agatur.

Locus autem communis contra eum qui translationem inducet: fugere iudicium ac poenam, quia
causae diffidat. A translatione autem: omnium
fore perturbationem, si non ita res agantur et in
iudicium veniant quo pacto oporteat; hoc est, si
aut eum eo agatur quocum non oporteat, aut alia
poena, alio crimine, alio tempore; atque hanc
rationem ad perturbationem iudiciorum omnium
pertinere.

Tres igitur haec constitutiones, quae partes non
habent, ad hunc modum tractabuntur. Nunc generalem constitutionem et partes eius consideremus.
62 XXI. Cum et facto et facti nomine concesso
neque ulla actionis illata controversia, vis et natura
et genus ipsius negoti quaeritur, constitutionem
generalem appellamus. Huius primas esse partes
duas nobis videri diximus, negotialem et iuridicialem.

---

^a For a full discussion of the legal proceedings involved
in *translatio* v. Greenidge, *The Legal Procedure of Cicero's
Time*, pp. 132–81; Buckland, *The Main Institutions of Roman
Private Law*, chaps. XIX, XX; Buckland, *A Text-Book of
Roman Law from Augustus to Justinian*, 2nd ed. (1932),
chap. XIII; Girard, *Manuel Élémentaire de Droit Romain*,
8th ed., pp. 1061–99.

and how and at what time it is fitting that action be
brought or judgement given or any decision made
61 about this case.[a]   One must base this on the principles of the civil law which we are to discuss later,[b]
and study what is generally done in similar cases,
and see whether through malice one thing is actually
being done while another is pretended, or whether
the trial is conducted and the action set up in this
way through stupidity or through necessity because
the action can be brought in no other way, or for the
sake of some convenience in hurrying the case,
or whether the action is properly brought without
any circumstance of this kind.

The common topic to be used against the one who
proposes a change of procedure : that he refuses to
face trial and punishment, because he has no confidence in his case ; in defence of change of procedure : that there will be a general confusion if
cases are not tried and brought to judgement in the
proper way, *i.e.* if the action is brought against the
wrong person, or with a wrong penalty, or charge, or
at a wrong time ; and that such a course of action
tends to a confusion of the whole judicial process.

These three issues, which have no subdivisions,
will be treated in this way. Now let us consider
the qualitative issue and its subdivisions.

62   XXI. When it is agreed that an act has been performed and by what name it shall be called and there
is no dispute about procedure, and the question is
simply about the import, the nature and the essence
of the occurrence, we call the issue qualitative. We
have said [c] that we think there are two divisions of
it, legal and equitable.

<hr />

[b] Below, §§ 65–68.   [c] I. 14.

CICERO

Negotialis est quae in ipso negotio iuris civilis habet implicatam controversiam. Ea est huiusmodi: Quidam pupillum heredem fecit; pupillus autem ante mortuus est, quam in suam tutelam venit. De hereditate ea quae pupillo venit, inter eos qui patris pupilli heredes secundi sunt et inter agnatos pupilli controversia est. Possessio heredum secundorum est. Intentio est agnatorum: " Nostra pecunia est, de qua is cuius agnati sumus testatus non est." Depulsio est: " Immo nostra qui heredes testamento patris sumus." Quaestio est: Utrorum sit? Ratio: " Pater enim et sibi et filio testamentum scripsit, dum is pupillus esset. Quare, quae fili fuerunt, testamento patris nostra fiant necesse est." Infirmatio rationis: " Immo pater sibi scripsit et secundum heredem non filio, sed sibi iussit esse. Quare, praeterquam quod ipsius fuit, testamento illius vestrum esse non potest." Iudicatio: Possitne quisquam de fili pupilli re testari; an heredes secundi ipsius patrisfamilias, non fili quoque eius pupilli heredes sint?

---

^a That is, next of kin on the male side, who would take the inheritance in default of a will.

^b Cf. the similar case cited in *Brutus*, 194–98, and *de Oratore* I. 180. Such cases seem to have been resolved in

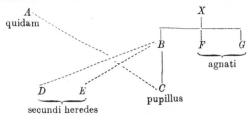

A legal issue is one which has a dispute involving only a point of civil law. The following is an example: A certain man made a ward his heir; the ward, however, died before coming of age. A dispute arises between the reversionary heirs of the father of the ward and the agnates [a] of the ward over the property which the ward had inherited. The reversionary heirs have possession. The complaint of the agnates is: "We should have the property concerning which he, whose agnates we are, left no will." The answer is: "On the other hand, it belongs to us who are the heirs under the father's will." The question is: "Who takes?" The plaintiff's argument is: "The father made a will for himself and for his son as long as he should be a ward; therefore the property of the son must be ours according to the father's will." The reply to the argument is: "On the other hand, the father made his will for himself, and named reversionary heirs for himself, but not for his son; therefore nothing except what belonged to the father can come to you by his will." The point for the judge's decision is: "Can anyone bequeath property of a son who becomes a ward? Or are the reversionary heirs heirs of the father only, and not of his minor son also?" [b]

---

later law, at least, in favour of the reversionary heir. *Cf.* Girard, *Manuel Élémentaire de Droit Romain*, 8th ed., pp. 881–85; Buckland, *A Text-Book of Roman Law*, 2nd ed., p. 302. The diagram may elucidate the case.

There was no dispute over the property which *C* inherited from *B*; that went to *D* and *E* under *B*'s will. The question is about the inheritance of property inherited by *C* from *A* after *B*'s death.

63 Atque hoc non alienum est, quod ad multa pertineat, ne aut nusquam aut usquequaque dicatur,
hic admonere. Sunt causae quae plures habent
rationes in simplici constitutione; quod fit, cum id
quod factum est aut quod defenditur, pluribus de
causis rectum aut probabile videri potest, ut in hac
ipsa causa. Supponatur enim ab heredibus haec
ratio: " Unius enim pecuniae plures dissimilibus
de causis heredes esse non possunt, nec unquam
factum est, ut eiusdem pecuniae alius testamento,
64 alius lege heres esset." Infirmatio autem haec
erit: " Non est una pecunia, propterea quod altera
pupilli iam erat adventicia; cuius heres non illo
in testamento quisquam scriptus erat, si quid pupillo
accidisset; et de altera patris etiamnunc mortui
voluntas plurimum valebat, quae iam mortuo pupillo
suis heredibus concedebat." Iudicatio est: Unane
pecunia fuerit; aut si hac erunt usi infirmatione:
Posse plures esse unius heredes pecuniae dissimilibus de causis et de eo ipso esse controversiam,
iudicatio nascitur: Possintne eiusdem pecuniae
plures dissimilibus generibus heredes esse? XXII.
Ergo una in constitutione intellectum est quomodo
et rationes et rationum infirmationes et propterea
iudicationes plures fiant.

65 Nunc huius generis praecepta videamus. Utrisque
aut etiam omnibus, si plures ambigent, ius ex quibus
rebus constet, considerandum est. Initium ergo
eius ab natura ductum videtur; quaedam autem
ex utilitatis ratione aut perspicua nobis aut obscura

63 A warning applicable to many cases may not be amiss at this point, that it may not be omitted altogether or repeated everywhere. There are cases that have several supporting arguments for one issue. This occurs when what has been done or what is defended can seem right or probable from several causes, as in this very case. For suppose that the heirs offer this argument: " There cannot be several heirs of one property for different reasons, nor was there ever a case in which one person inherited property by will and another inherited the same 64 property by law." The answer is as follows: " It is not *one* property, because part of the minor's property at the time of his death was adventitious, and there was no statement in that will that anyone was to inherit property which might have fallen to the minor; and about the other part the wish of the father now dead was perfectly valid, which bequeathed the property to his heirs when once the minor was dead." The point for decision is: " Was there one property ? " Or if they use this reply: that there can be several heirs of one property for different reasons, and that the dispute is about this very question, the point for decision arises: " Can there be several heirs of the same property for different reasons ? " XXII. And so it has been shown how there can be several arguments and replies and points for decision in connexion with one issue.

65 Now let us look at the rules governing this issue. Both parties (or all parties if there are more than two concerned in the litigation) must consider the sources from which law arises. Its origin seems to be in nature. Certain principles either obvious or obscure to us have by reason of advantage passed into custom;

in consuetudinem venisse; post autem approbata
quaedam a consuetudine aut vero utilia visa legibus
esse firmata; ac naturae quidem ius esse, quod
nobis non opinio, sed quaedam innata vis adferat,
ut religionem, pietatem, gratiam, vindicationem,
66 observantiam, veritatem. Religionem eam quae
in metu et caerimonia deorum sit appellant; pietatem, quae erga patriam aut parentes aut alios
sanguine coniunctos officium conservare moneat;
gratiam, quae in memoria et remuneratione officiorum
et honoris et amicitiarum observantiam teneat;
vindicationem, per quam vim et contumeliam
defendendo aut ulciscendo propulsamus a nobis et
nostris, qui nobis cari esse debent, et per quam
peccata punimur; observantiam, per quam aetate
aut sapientia aut honore aut aliqua dignitate antecedentes veremur et colimus; veritatem, per quam
damus operam, ne quid aliter quam confirmaverimus
67 fiat aut factum aut futurum sit. Ac naturae quidem
iura minus ipsa quaeruntur ad hanc controversiam,
quod neque in hoc civili iure versantur et a vulgari
intellegentia remotiora sunt; ad similitudinem vero
aliquam aut ad rem amplificandam saepe sunt
inferenda.

Consuetudine autem ius esse putatur id quod
voluntate omnium sine lege vetustas comprobarit.
In ea autem quaedam sunt iura ipsa iam certa
propter vetustatem. Quo in genere et alia sunt
multa et eorum multo maxima pars quae praetores
edicere consuerunt. Quaedam autem genera iuris

---

[a] On taking office the praetor published the rules for legal
procedure by which he would be governed during his term. In
the course of time these came to be more and more a repetition
of the practice of the past, and developed into a code of civil law.

afterward certain principles approved by custom
or deemed to be really advantageous have been
confirmed by statute. And the law of nature is
something which is implanted in us not by opinion,
but by a kind of innate instinct; it includes religion,
duty, gratitude, revenge, reverence, and truth.
66 Religion is the term applied to the fear and worship
of the gods. Duty warns us to keep our obligations
to our country or parents or other kin. Gratitude
has regard for remembering and returning services,
honour, and acts of friendship. Revenge is the act
through which by defending or avenging we repel
violence and insult from ourselves and from those
who ought to be dear to us, and by which we punish
offences. Reverence is the act by which we show
respect to and cherish our superiors in age or wisdom
or honour or any high position. Truth is the
quality by which we endeavour to avoid any dis-
crepancy between our statements and facts, past,
67 present or future. The rights of nature themselves
are, however, relatively unimportant for this sort of
controversy because they are not involved in the civil
law and are somewhat remote from the understanding of the vulgar; they may, however, frequently be
brought in for a comparison or to enlarge on some
topic.

Customary law is thought to be that which lapse
of time has approved by the common consent of all
without the sanction of statute. In it there are
certain principles of law which through lapse of time
have become absolutely fixed. Among the many
others in this class are by far the largest part of
those which the praetors have been accustomed to
embody in their edicts.[a] Moreover, certain ideas of

iam certa consuetudine facta sunt; quod genus
68 pactum, par, iudicatum. Pactum est quod inter
quos convenit ita iustum putatur ut iure praestare
dicatur. Par, quod in omnes aequabile est. Iudicatum, de quo iam ante sententia alicuius aut aliquorum constitutum est. Iam iura legitima ex legibus
cognosci oportebit. His ergo ex partibus iuris,
quod cuique aut ex ipsa re aut ex simili aut maiore
minoreve nasci videbitur, attendere atque elicere
pertemptando unamquamque iuris partem oportebit.

Locorum autem communium quoniam, ut ante
dictum est, duo genera sunt, quorum alterum dubiae
rei, alterum certae continet amplificationem, quid
ipsa causa det, et quid augeri per communem locum
possit et oporteat, considerabitur. Nam certi qui
in omnes incidant loci praescribi non possunt; in
plerisque fortasse ab auctoritate iuris consultorum
et contra auctoritatem dici oportebit. Attendendum
est autem et in hac et in omnibus num quos locos
communes praeter eos quos nos exponimus ipsa res
ostendat.

Nunc iuridiciale genus et partes consideremus.
69 XXIII. Iuridicialis est in qua aequi et iniqui natura
et praemi aut poenae ratio quaeritur. Huius partes
sunt duae, quarum alteram absolutam, assumptivam
alteram nominamus. Absoluta est quae ipsa in se,
non ut negotialis implicite et abscondite, sed patentius
et expeditius recti et non recti quaestionem continet.

---

^a Or, to be manifest in principles of justice.
^b II. 48.

law have now become fixed by custom; among these
68 are covenants, equity and decisions. A covenant is a
compact which is regarded as so binding between the
contracting parties that it is said to take priority in
law.[a] Equity is what is just and fair to all. A
decision is something determined previously by the
opinion of some person or persons. Statute law
must be learned from the statutes. Using these
divisions of the law the speaker must study what
seems to develop in each case either from the case
itself or from a similar case or one of greater or less
importance, and bring out the proper argument by
a careful examination of each division of the law.

As for common topics, since, as has been said
before,[b] there are two kinds, one of which contains
an amplification of a doubtful statement, the other,
of an undisputed fact, one will consider what the
case offers, and what can and should be amplified by
a common topic. For definite common topics cannot be prescribed to fit all cases; it is likely that in
many cases it will be necessary to speak for and
against the authority of jurisconsults. Moreover, it is
necessary to consider in this issue, and in all, whether
the facts of the case themselves do not suggest other
common topics than those which we propose.

Now let us consider the division of the qualitative
issue which is known as equitable, and its sub-
69 divisions. XXIII. The term equitable covers cases
in which there is a question of the nature of justice
and of the principles of reward or punishment.
There are two subdivisions, absolute and assumptive. The absolute contains in itself the question
of right and wrong, not confusedly and obscurely,
as in the legal, but more clearly and obviously.

Ea est huiuscemodi: Cum Thebani Lacedaemonios
bello superavissent et fere mos esset Graiis, cum
inter se bellum gessissent, ut ei qui vicissent tropaeum aliquod in finibus statuerent victoriae modo
in praesentiam declarandae causa, non ut in perpetuum belli memoria maneret, aëneum statuerunt
tropaeum. Accusantur apud Amphictyonas id est
70 apud commune Graeciae consilium.[1] Intentio est:
"Non oportuit." Depulsio est: "Oportuit."
Quaestio est: Oportueritne? Ratio est: "Eam
enim ex bello gloriam virtute peperimus, ut eius
aeterna insignia posteris nostris relinquere velle-
mus." Infirmatio est: "At tamen aeternum inimicitiarum monumentum Graios de Graiis statuere
non oportet." Iudicatio est: Cum summae virtutis
concelebrandae causa Graii de Graiis aeternum
inimicitiarum monumentum statuerunt, rectene an
contra fecerint? Hanc ideo rationem subiecimus,
ut hoc causae genus ipsum de quo agimus cognosceretur. Nam si eam supposuissemus qua fortasse
usi sunt: "Non enim iuste neque pie bellum ges-
sistis," in relationem criminis delaberemur, de qua
post loquemur. Utrumque autem causae genus
in hanc causam incidere perspicuum est. In hanc
argumentationes ex isdem locis sumendae sunt
atque in causam negotialem, qua de ante dictum est.
71 Locos autem communes et ex causa ipsa, si quid

---

[1] id . . . consilium *bracketed by Schuetz, Ströbel.*

---

[a] §§ 65–68.

It is illustrated by the following case: It was a nearly universal custom among the Greeks when they had fought with one another that the victors should set up a trophy in the country to commemorate the victory, but only for the time being, not that the record of the war might remain forever. The Thebans, having defeated the Lacedaemonians in battle, set up a trophy of bronze. They were accused before the Amphictyons, that is, before 70 the common council of Greece. The charge is: "It was not right." The reply is: "It was right." The question is: "Was it right?" The defendants' reason is: "By our valour we won such glory in war that we wished to leave a perpetual memorial of it to our descendants." The counter-argument is: "Still it is not right for Greeks to set up a permanent memorial of their quarrels with Greeks." The point for the judge's decision is: "Granted that Greeks in order to publish abroad their consummate valour have set up a permanent memorial of their quarrels with Greeks, did they do right or wrong?" We have given this as the defendant's reason in order to make clear the essential nature of this kind of case which we are discussing. For if we had given this reason, which perhaps they actually used: "You made war contrary to the dictates of justice and religion," we should be going over to *relatio criminis* (retort of the accusation) of which we shall speak later. It is clear that either kind of issue fits this case. Arguments for it must be drawn from the same topics as in the legal issue 71 which was discussed above.[a] It will be permissible and right to take many weighty common topics both from the case itself if it contains any grounds

inerit indignationis aut conquestionis, et ex iuris utilitate et natura multos et graves sumere licebit et oportebit, si causae dignitas videbitur postulare.

XXIV. Nunc assumptivam partem iuridicialis consideremus. Assumptiva igitur tum dicitur, cum ipsum ex se factum probari non potest, aliquo autem foris adiuncto argumento defenditur. Eius partes sunt quattuor: comparatio, relatio criminis, remotio criminis, concessio.

72 Comparatio est cum aliquid factum quod ipsum non sit probandum ex eo cuius id causa factum est defenditur. Ea est huiusmodi: Quidam imperator, cum ab hostibus circumsederetur neque effugere ullo modo posset, depectus est cum eis ut arma et impedimenta relinqueret, milites educeret; itaque fecit; armis et impedimentis amissis praeter spem milites conservavit. Accusatur maiestatis. Incurrit huc definitio. Sed nos hunc locum de quo agimus 73 consideremus. Intentio est: "Non oportuit arma et impedimenta relinquere." Depulsio est: "Oportuit." Quaestio est: Oportueritne? Ratio est: "Milites enim omnes perissent." Infirmatio est aut coniecturalis: "Non perissent;" aut altera coniecturalis: "Non ideo fecisti." Ex quibus iudicatio est: Perissentne? et: Ideone fecerit? [1]

---

[1] *Weidner, Friedrich, and Ströbel bracket* Ex . . . fecerit.

---

[a] In *Auctor ad Herennium*, I. 25 the commander is said to have been Gaius Popilius: the incident occurred in the war against the Tigurini, 107 B.C. (Livy, *Epit.* LXV). Orosius, V. 15, 24, says that he also gave hostages.

for the use of resentment or complaint, and from the nature and expediency of law if the importance of the case seems to require it.

XXIV. Now let us consider the assumptive branch of the equitable issue. The issue is said to be assumptive when the act taken by itself cannot be approved, but is defended by some argument from extraneous circumstances. There are four subdivisions: *comparatio* (comparison), *relatio criminis* (retort of the accusation), *remotio criminis* (shifting the charge), *concessio* (confession and avoidance).

72 *Comparatio* (comparison) is the case where some act which cannot be approved by itself, is defended by reference to the end for which it was done. It is of this sort: A certain commander, being surrounded by the enemy and unable to escape in any way, made an agreement with them to surrender the arms and baggage, and withdraw with his men. The agreement was carried out. He lost the arms and baggage but saved the soldiers from a hopeless situation. He is accused of lese-majesty.[a] Here an issue of definition confronts us, but let us examine
73 only the topic that we are discussing. The charge is: " It was not right to abandon the arms and baggage." The answer is: " It was right." The question is: " Was it right? " The reason is: " I did it because otherwise all the soldiers would have perished." The denial is either concerned with fact: " They would not have perished," or another concerned with fact: " That was not the reason why you did it," (from which the point for decision becomes, " Would they have perished? " or " Was that the reason why he did it? ") or this

237

aut haec comparativa, cuius nunc indigemus: " At
enim satius fuit amittere milites quam arma et
impedimenta concedere hostibus." Ex qua iudicatio nascitur: Cum omnes perituri milites essent,
nisi ad hanc pactionem venissent, utrum satius
fuerit amittere milites, an ad hanc condicionem
venire?

74 Hoc causae genus ex suis locis tractare oportebit et adhibere ceterarum quoque constitutionum
rationem atque praecepta; ac maxime coniecturis
faciendis infirmare illud quod cum eo quod crimini
dabitur ei qui accusabuntur comparabunt. Id fiet,
si aut id quod dicent defensores futurum fuisse
nisi id factum esset, de quo facto iudicium est,
futurum fuisse negabitur; aut si alia ratione et
aliam ob causam ac dicet reus se fecisse demonstrabitur esse factum. Eius rei confirmatio et item
contraria de parte infirmatio ex coniecturali constitutione sumetur. Sin autem certo nomine malefici vocabitur in iudicium, sicut in hac causa—nam
maiestatis arcessitur—definitione et praeceptis definitionis uti oportebit. XXV. Atque haec quidem
plerumque in hoc genere accidunt ut et coniectura et
definitione utendum sit. Sin aliud quoque aliquod
genus incidet, eius generis praecepta licebit huc
pari ratione transferre. Nam accusatori maxime
est in hoc elaborandum ut id ipsum factum propter
quod sibi reus concedi putet oportere quam plurimis

one involving comparison which we want for our present discussion: " But surely it was better to lose the soldiers than to surrender the arms and baggage to the enemy." From this arises the point for the judge's decision: " Granted that all the soldiers were going to perish unless they had come to this agreement, was it better to lose the soldiers or to come to these terms? "

74 One should treat this kind of case by topics peculiar to itself and also adapt the principles and rules which apply in the other issues. And in particular by making inferences one should attack the comparison which the accused will make with the act of which he is accused. This will be done, if it is denied that the result would have followed which the counsel for the defence say would have followed if the act now before the court for judgement had not been performed; or if it is shown to have been done in a different fashion or for a reason other than that alleged by the defendant. Arguments in support of this statement of the defence and likewise arguments used by the opponents to demolish it will be derived from the conjectural issue. Furthermore, if the defendant is brought to trial for a definite crime, as in this case—for he is accused of lese-majesty—one should employ definition and the rules for its use. XXV. And it frequently happens in this kind of case that one must use both inference and definition; and if any other issue applies it will be permissible to transfer its rules to the case in hand in a similar way. For the chief task of the prosecutor is to attack by all possible means the act because of which the defendant thinks that some concession should be made

infirmet rationibus. Quod facile est, si quam
plurimis constitutionibus aggredietur id improbare.
75 Ipsa autem comparatio separata a ceteris generibus controversiarum sic ex sua vi considerabitur, si
illud quod comparabitur aut non honestum aut non
utile aut non necessarium fuisse aut non tantopere
utile aut non tantopere honestum aut non tantopere necessarium fuisse demonstrabitur. Deinde
oportet accusatorem illud quod ipse arguat ab eo
quod defensor comparat separare. Id autem faciet,
si demonstrabit non ita fieri solere neque oportere neque esse rationem quare hoc propter hoc
fiat, ut propter salutem militum ea quae salutis
causa comparata sunt hostibus tradantur. Postea
comparare oportet cum beneficio maleficium et
omnino id quod arguitur cum eo quod factum ab
defensore laudatur aut faciendum fuisse demonstratur contendere et hoc extenuando malefici
magnitudinem simul adaugere. Id fieri poterit,
si demonstrabitur honestius, utilius, magis necessarium fuisse illud quod vitarit reus quam illud quod
76 fecerit. Honesti autem et utilis et necessarii vis
et natura in deliberationis praeceptis cognoscetur.[a]
Deinde oportebit ipsam illam comparativam iudicationem exponere tamquam causam deliberativam
et de ea ex deliberationis praeceptis dicere. Sit
enim haec iudicatio quam ante exposuimus: Cum
omnes perituri milites essent, nisi ad hanc pactionem
venissent, utrum satius fuerit perire milites an ad

---

to him. This is easy if he proceeds to invalidate it by using as many issues as possible.

75 But comparison itself separated from the other kinds of dispute will be considered on its own merits, if the act which is compared is shown not to have been honourable or advantageous or necessary, or not advantageous or honourable or necessary to such a degree. In the second place the prosecutor should separate the crime which he charges from the act which the counsel for the defence brings in for comparison. He will accomplish this if he shows that it is not usual or right for events to move in this way and that there is no reason why *this* should be done for *that*, as for example that for the safety of the soldiers the instruments provided for their safety should be surrendered to the enemy. Then he should compare the harm with the advantage and in general contrast the crime with the act which is praised by the counsel for the defence, or is shown to have been necessary to do, and by belittling this act should magnify the enormity of the wrong. This can be done, if it is shown that the action which the defendant avoided is more honourable, more advantageous or more necessary than that which 76 he performed. But the essence and nature of honour, advantage and necessity will be investigated in connexion with the rules for deliberative speeches.[a] Then it will be necessary to expound this whole question of comparison as if it were a deliberative case and to discuss it in the light of the rules for deliberative speeches. Take, for instance, this problem which we stated above: " Granted that all the soldiers were going to perish unless they had come to this agreement, was it better to let the soldiers perish

hanc pactionem venire? Hoc ex locis deliberationis, quasi aliquam in consultationem res veniat,
tractari oportebit. XXVI. Defensor autem, quibus
in locis ab accusatore aliae constitutiones erunt
inductae, in eis ipse quoque ex isdem constitutionibus defensionem comparabit; ceteros autem omnes
locos qui ad ipsam comparationem pertinebunt
ex contrario tractabit.

77 Loci communes autem erunt: accusatoris, in
eum qui, cum de facto turpi aliquo aut inutili aut
utroque fateatur, quaerat tamen aliquam defensionem, et facti inutilitatem aut turpitudinem cum
indignatione proferre;[1] defensoris est, nullum factum
inutile neque turpe neque item utile neque honestum
putari oportere, nisi quo animo, quo tempore, qua
de causa factum sit intellegatur; qui locus ita communis est ut bene tractatus in hac causa magno
ad persuadendum momento futurus sit; et alter
locus, per quem magna cum amplificatione benefici
magnitudo ex utilitate aut honestate aut facti
78 necessitudine demonstratur; et tertius, per quem
res expressa verbis ante oculos eorum qui audiunt
ponitur, ut ipsi se quoque idem facturos fuisse
arbitrentur, si sibi illa res atque ea faciendi causa
per idem tempus accidisset.

Relatio criminis est cum reus id quod arguitur
confessus, alterius se inductum peccato, iure fecisse

---

[1] et facti . . . proferre *bracketed by Weidner.*

or to come to this agreement?" This should be treated along the lines of a deliberative speech, just as if the matter were to come up for an inquiry about policy. XXVI. In the places where the prosecutor has brought in other forms of the issue, the counsel for the defence likewise will work up his defence on the basis of these issues; but all the other topics which pertain exclusively to comparison he will discuss so as to turn them against the prosecutor.

77 The common topics will be: of the prosecutor, to inveigh against a man who when he confesses to a deed that is base or disadvantageous or both, yet seeks some defence, and to bring out the inexpediency or the baseness of the deed with great indignation; of the counsel for the defence, that no deed should be judged inexpedient or base, or for that matter advantageous or honourable unless it is known with what intent, at what time and for what reason it was done. This topic is so general in its application that if well handled it will have great persuasive force in such a case. And a second common topic is that in which the magnitude of the service performed is demonstrated and enlarged upon by reference to the advantage or honour or necessity 78 of the deed; and a third, in which by a vivid verbal picture the event is brought before the eyes of the audience, so that they will think that they too would have done the same if they had been confronted with the same situation and the same cause for action at the same time.

A retort of the charge occurs when the defendant admits the act of which he is accused but shows that he was justified in doing it because he was influenced

demonstrat. Ea est huiusmodi: Horatius occisis tribus Curiatiis et duobus amissis fratribus domum se victor recepit. Is animadvertit sororem suam de fratrum morte non laborantem, sponsi autem nomen appellantem identidem Curiatii cum gemitu⁻ et lamentatione. Indigne passus virginem occidit.

79 Accusatur. Intentio est: "Iniuria sororem occidisti." Depulsio est: "Iure occidi." Quaestio est: Iurene occiderit? Ratio est: "Illa enim hostium mortem lugebat, fratrum neglegebat; me et populum Romanum vicisse moleste ferebat." Infirmatio est: "Tamen a fratre indamnatam necari non oportuit." Ex quo iudicatio fit: Cum Horatia fratrum mortem neglegeret, hostium lugeret, fratris et populi Romani victoria non gauderet, oportueritne eam a fratre indamnatam necari?

XXVII. Hoc in genere causae primum, si quid ex ceteris dabitur constitutionibus, sumi oportebit, sicuti in comparatione praeceptum est; postea, si qua facultas erit, per aliquam constitutionem illum in
80 quem crimen transferetur defendere; deinde, levius esse illud quod in alterum peccatum reus transferat quam quod ipse susceperit; postea translationis partibus uti et ostendere a quo et per quos et quo modo et quo tempore aut agi aut iudicari aut statui

---

by an offence committed by the other party. The following is an example: Horatius after killing the Curiatii and losing his two brothers returned home in triumph. He noticed his sister not distressed by the death of her brothers, but repeatedly calling on the name of Curiatius, her betrothed, with groans 79 and tears. Filled with rage he killed the girl. He is brought to trial. The charge is: "You killed your sister without warrant." The answer is: "I was justified in killing her." The question is: "Was he justified in killing her?" The defendant's reason is: "For she was distressed at the death of our enemies; she was unmoved by the fall of her brothers; she was grieved that I and the Roman people were victorious." The prosecutor's answer is: "Nevertheless she ought not to have been killed by her brother uncondemned." From this the point for decision arises: "Granted that Horatia was unmoved by the death of her brothers, and was distressed at the death of our enemies and did not rejoice over the victory of her brother and the Roman people, ought she to have been killed by her brother without condemnation?"

XXVII. In this kind of case it will be proper first to take from the other issues what assistance they may offer, as was directed in connexion with "comparison," [a] then, if there shall be opportunity, one may use some issue to defend the person to whom 80 the guilt is transferred; then one may show that the offence which the defendant imputes to the other party is less serious than that with which he himself is charged. Next one may use the forms of *translatio* (transfer) and show by whom and through whom and how and at what time it was proper that action

de ea re convenerit; ac simul ostendere non oportuisse ante supplicium quam iudicium interponere.
Tum leges quoque et iudicia demonstranda sunt,
per quae potuerit id peccatum quod sponte sua reus
poenitus sit moribus et iudicio vindicari. Deinde
negare audire oportere id quod in eum criminis
conferatur, de quo is ipse qui conferat iudicium
fieri noluerit, et id quod iudicatum non sit pro infecto
81 habere oportere; postea impudentiam demonstrare eorum qui eum nunc apud iudices accusent
quem sine iudicibus ipsi condemnarint, et de eo
iudicium faciant de quo iam ipsi supplicium sump-
serint; postea perturbationem iudici futuram dicemus et iudices longius quam potestatem habeant
progressuros, si simul et de reo et de eo quem reus
arguat iudicarint; deinde, si hoc constitutum sit,
ut peccata homines peccatis et iniurias iniuriis
ulciscantur, quantum incommodorum consequatur;
ac si idem facere ipse qui nunc accusat voluisset, ne
hoc quidem ipso quicquam opus fuisse iudicio; si
vero ceteri quoque idem faciant, omnino iudicium
82 nullum futurum. Postea demonstrabitur, ne si
iudicio quidem illa damnata esset in quam id crimen
ab reo conferatur, potuisse hunc ipsum de illa supplicium sumere; quare esse indignum eum qui ne

---

^a *I.e.* a court has never decided that Horatia mourned for
Curiatius, therefore her mourning is not admissible as evidence.

should be brought and the case adjudged and decided; and at the same time one may point out that punishment should not be inflicted before judgement is given. Then one should also point to the laws and courts of justice by which the crime which the defendant avenged on his own authority, could have been punished in accordance with custom and judicial process. Then the prosecutor should deny that it is right to listen to the charge which the defendant brings against the other party, which he himself, the very man who brings it, was unwilling to submit to a court of law, and then claim that an act which has not been passed upon by a court should be 81 regarded as not done.[a] After that he should call attention to the shamelessness of those who now accuse before a jury one whom they themselves have condemned without a jury, and are now trying an offence which they have already punished with their own hands. After that he should argue that the judicial process will be disturbed, and that the judges will go beyond their authority if they pass judgement at the same time on the defendant and the person whom the defendant accuses; then he should point out what disastrous results will follow if it is established that men may avenge crimes with crimes and injuries with injuries; and if the prosecutor had been willing to do the same there would have been no need of this trial either; and if everyone should act in the same way there would be no 82 trials at all. After that it will be pointed out that even if she had been condemned whom the defendant blames for his offence, he himself could not have inflicted the punishment on her; therefore it is intolerable that he who could not with his own

de damnata quidem poenas sumere ipse potuisset
de ea supplicium sumpsisse quae ne adducta quidem
sit in iudicium. Deinde postulabit, ut legem, qua
lege fecerit, proferat. Deinde quemadmodum in
comparatione praecipiebamus, ut illud quod compararetur extenuaretur ab accusatore quam maxime,
sic in hoc genere oportebit illius culpam in quem
crimen transferatur cum huius maleficio qui se iure
fecisse dicat comparare. Postea demonstrandum est
non esse illud eiusmodi ut ob id hoc fieri convenerit.
Extrema est, ut in comparatione, assumptio iudicationis et de ea per amplificationem ex deliberationis
praeceptis dictio.

83   XXVIII. Defensor autem, quae per alias constitutiones inducentur, ex eis locis qui traditi sunt
infirmabit; ipsam autem relationem comprobabit,
primum augendo eius in quem referet crimen
culpam et audaciam, et quam maxime per indignationem, si res feret, iuncta conquestione ante
oculos ponendo; postea levius demonstrando se
poenitum quam sit illius promeritum, et suum
supplicium cum illius iniuria conferendo. Deinde
oportebit eos locos qui ita erunt ab accusatore trac-
tati ut refelli et contrariam in partem converti

---

a Above, § 76.
b The construction of the sentence is changed as if " defendant " had been the subject, rather than " counsel for
the defence."

hand have exacted the penalty from her even if she had been condemned, should have inflicted punishment on one who has not even been brought to trial. Then he will demand that the defendant produce the law under which he acted. Then, just as we suggested in the case of comparison that the prosecutor should disparage as much as possible the deed which is cited by way of comparison, so in this case he should compare the fault of the person to whom the blame is transferred with the crime of him who says that he was justified in committing it; afterward it should be pointed out that the one act is not of such a nature that because of it the other should have been done. Finally, as in case of comparison, the point for decision is taken up and dilated upon in accordance with the rules for a deliberative speech.[a]

83   XXVIII. The counsel for the defence will answer the arguments which will be brought in from other issues by using the topics which have already been set forth; he will support his attempt to lay the blame on some one else, first, by magnifying the culpability and audacity of the person on whom he lays the blame, and by placing the scene vividly before the eyes of the jury with an intense display of indignation, if opportunity presents, coupled with vehement complaint; secondly, by proving that he punished the offence more lightly than the offender deserved, and by comparing the punishment which he inflicted with the crime that she had committed.[b]   In the next place he should attack by contrary reasoning the arguments which have been presented by the prosecutor in such a way that they can be refuted and turned to the advantage

possint, quo in genere sunt tres extremi, contrariis
84 rationibus infirmare. Illa autem acerrima accusatorum criminatio, per quam perturbationem fore
omnium iudiciorum demonstrant, si de indamnato
supplici sumendi potestas data sit, levabitur, primum
si eiusmodi demonstrabitur iniuria, ut non modo
viro bono, verum omnino homini libero videatur non
fuisse toleranda; deinde ita perspicua, ut ne ab
ipso quidem, qui fecisset, in dubium vocaretur;
deinde eiusmodi, ut in eam is maxime debuerit
animadvertere qui animadverterit;[1] ut non tam
rectum, non tam fuerit honestum in iudicium illam
rem pervenire quam eo modo atque ab eo vindicari
quo modo et ab quo sit vindicata; postea sic rem
fuisse apertam ut iudicium de ea re fieri nihil atti-
85 nuerit. Atque hic demonstrandum est rationibus
et similibus rebus permultas ita atroces et perspicuas
res esse ut de his non modo non necesse sit, sed ne
utile quidem, quam mox iudicium fiat exspectare.

Locus communis accusatoris in eum qui, cum id
quod arguitur negare non possit tamen aliquid
sibi spei comparet ex iudiciorum perturbatione.
Atque hic utilitatis iudiciorum demonstratio et de eo
conquestio qui supplicium dederit indamnatus; in
eius autem qui sumpserit audaciam et crudelitatem
86 indignatio. Ab defensore, in eius, quem ultus sit
audaciam ⟨cum⟩ sui conquestione; rem non ex

---

[1] animadvertit *Ströbel.*

---

[a] In the Latin, " counsel for the defence." *Cf.* the confusion in § 83.

of the opposing side; the last three are of this kind.
84 But the force of the severest attack of the prosecutors, by which they point out that the whole
judicial process will be thrown into confusion if
privilege is given of punishing offences without
convicting the criminal, will be lessened, in the
first place if it is demonstrated that the offence was
of such a nature that it would seem intolerable not
only to a good man, but to any sort of free man at
all; in the second place that it was so manifest that
it could not be questioned even by the offender;
then that it was of such a nature that he who punished
it was in duty bound to punish it; that it was not
so right or so honourable for the offence to be brought
before a court as to have it avenged in the manner
in which it was and by the person by whom it was;
then that the case was so clear that there was no
85 point in having a court pass upon it. And here it
must be made plain by arguments and similar means
that there are many offences so foul and undisputed
that it is not only unnecessary but even inexpedient
to wait for the trial to take place.

The prosecutor will use the common topic against
the man who when he cannot deny the crime with
which he is charged, nevertheless raises some hope
for himself by disturbing the due course of the law.
This is the place for showing the advantages of
orderly trials and for complaining about the fate
of one who was punished without being convicted,
and for denouncing the audacity and cruelty of him
86 who inflicted the punishment. The defendant[a]
will speak against the audacity of the criminal on
whom he took revenge, and lament his own lot,
saying that a deed should be judged not by the name

nomine ipsius negoti, sed ex consilio eius qui fecerit
et causa et tempore considerari oportere; quid mali
futurum sit aut ex iniuria aut scelere alicuius, nisi
tanta et tam perspicua audacia ab eo ad cuius
famam aut ad parentes aut ad liberos pertineret aut
ad aliquam rem quam caram esse omnibus aut
necesse est aut oportet esse, vindicata.

XXIX. Remotio criminis est cum eius intentio
facti quod ab adversario infertur in alium aut
in aliud demovetur. Id fit bipertito: nam tum
87 causa, tum res ipsa removetur. Causae remotionis
hoc nobis exemplo sit: Rhodii quosdam legarunt
Athenas. Legatis quaestores sumptum, quem oportebat dari, non dederunt. Legati profecti non sunt.
Accusantur. Intentio est: "Proficisci oportuit."
Depulsio est: "Non oportuit." Quaestio est:
Oportueritne? Ratio est: "Sumptus enim, qui de
publico dare solet, is ab quaestore non est datus."
Infirmatio est: "Vos tamen id, quod publice vobis
erat negoti datum, conficere oportebat." Iudicatio
est: Cum eis qui legati erant sumptus qui debebatur
de publico non daretur, oportueritne eos conficere
nihilo minus legationem?

Hoc in genere primum, sicut in ceteris, si quid aut
ex coniecturali aut ex alia constitutione sumi possit,
videri oportebit. Deinde pleraque et ex compara-

attached to it, but in the light of the intent of the
person who performed it, and of the cause and of
the time; showing what ill results will follow from
someone's wrongdoing or crime unless such wanton
and manifest audacity were avenged by him whose
reputation, parents, children or something which
must and ought to be dear to all men, is affected by
such conduct.

XXIX. *Remotio criminis* (shifting of the charge)
occurs when the accusation for the offence which is
alleged by the prosecutor is shifted to another
person or thing. It is done in two ways: sometimes
the responsibility is shifted and sometimes the act
87 itself. Let us take the following as an example
of the shifting of the responsibility: The Rhodians
appointed certain men as ambassadors to Athens.
The treasury board did not give them the money
for travelling expenses which should have been given.
The ambassadors did not set out. They are accused.
The charge is: "They should have set out." The
answer is: "They should not." The question is:
"Should they?" The defendant's reason is: "The
money for expenses which is regularly paid from the
public funds, was not paid by the treasurer." The
refutation is: "Nevertheless you should have
performed the task assigned to you by the state."
The point for the judge's decision is: "Granted
that the money which was due the ambassadors
from the public funds was not paid to them, should
they nonetheless have discharged their duties?"

In this kind of case, as in the other, the first
requisite is to see if any help can be got from the
issue of fact or from any other issue. In the
second place many arguments used in comparison

tione et ex relatione criminis in hanc quoque causam
convenire poterunt.

88   Accusator autem illum cuius culpa id factum reus
dicet primum defendet, si poterit; sin minus poterit,
negabit ad hoc iudicium illius, sed huius quem
ipse accuset culpam pertinere. Postea dicet suo
quemque officio consulere oportere; nec, si ille
peccasset, hunc oportuisse peccare; deinde, si ille
deliquerit, separatim illum sicut hunc accusari
oportere et non cum huius defensione coniungi illius
accusationem.

Defensor autem cum cetera, si qua ex aliis incident
constitutionibus, pertractarit, de ipsa remotione sic
89 argumentabitur: Primum, cuius acciderit culpa,
demonstrabit; deinde, cum id aliena culpa accidisset,
ostendet se aut non potuisse aut non debuisse id
facere quod accusator dicat oportuisse; quid potuerit,
ex utilitatis partibus, in quibus est necessitudinis
vis implicata, demonstrabit; quid debuerit, ex
honestate considerabitur. De utroque distinctius in
deliberativo genere dicetur. Deinde omnia facta
esse ab reo quae in ipsius fuerint potestate; quod
minus quam convenerit factum sit, culpa id alterius
90 accidisse. Deinde alterius culpa exponenda demonstrandum est, quantum voluntatis et studi fuerit
in ipso; et id signis confirmandum huiusmodi:
ex cetera diligentia, ex ante factis aut dictis; atque

---

[a] In the Latin, " counsel for defence." *Cf.* §§ 83, 85.
[b] Below, §§ 157–76.

and in retort of the charge can be adapted to this case also.

88 The prosecutor will first defend, if he can, the person who the defendant says was responsible for the act. If he cannot do this, he will say that this court is not concerned with the fault of that other person, but only with the fault of the man whom he is accusing. Then he will say that each man should think of his own duty; that if one official has done wrong, that is no reason why the other should; finally, if the treasurer has been delinquent he ought to be accused separately, as the ambassador is, and that the accusation of the treasurer should not be joined with the defence of the ambassador.

The defendant,[a] after treating the other points which arise from other issues, will argue as follows
89 about the actual shifting of the charge: first, he will show by whose fault the event happened; then since it happened through another's fault, he will show that it was not possible or obligatory for him to do what the prosecutor says he should have done. What was possible will be examined with reference to the principles of advantage, in which an element of necessity is involved; what was obligatory, with reference to honour. Both these topics will be treated more precisely under deliberative oratory.[b] In the next place counsel will assert that the defendant did everything in his power; it was due to another's fault that less was
90 done than was proper. Then, in pointing out the other's fault, it will be necessary to show what good will and devotion the defendant exhibited, and to support this statement by evidence like the following: his diligence in other offices, his previous acts

hoc ipsi utile fuisse facere, inutile autem non facere, et cum cetera vita fuisse hoc magis consentaneum quam quod propter alterius culpam non fecerit. XXX. Si autem non in hominem certum, sed in rem aliquam causa demovebitur, ut in hac eadem re, si quaestor mortuus esset et idcirco legatis pecunia data non esset, accusatione alterius et culpae depulsione dempta ceteris similiter uti locis oportebit et ex concessionis partibus, quae convenient assumere; de quibus nobis dicendum erit.

91　Loci autem communes idem utrisque fere qui in superioribus assumptivis, incident; hi tamen certissime: accusatoris, facti indignatio; defensoris, cum in alio culpa sit, in ipso non sit, supplicio se affici non oportere.

Ipsius autem rei fit remotio, cum id quod datur crimini negat neque ad se neque ad officium suum reus pertinuisse; nec, si quid in eo sit delictum, sibi attribui oportere. Id causae genus est huiusmodi: In eo foedere quod factum est quondam cum Samnitibus quidam adulescens nobilis porcum sustinuit iussu imperatoris. Foedere autem ab senatu improbato et imperatore Samnitibus dedito, quidam in senatu eum quoque dicit qui porcum tenuerit, dedi

---

[a] Below, §§ 94–109.

[b] Above, § 71 ff.

[c] The reference is to the treaty concluded with Samnites by the consuls, Postumius and Veturius, after the disastrous defeat of the Romans at the Caudine Forks, 321 B.C. The incident given here is not recorded elsewhere and is undoubtedly a fiction of the rhetorical schools. In fact the whole story of the rejection of the treaty by the Senate is probably an invention of Roman historians. For the

and words; and that it was advantageous to him to
do it, and disadvantageous not to, and that doing
it was more consistent with his past life than to fail
to do it through the fault of another. XXX. But
if the blame is shifted not to a definite person but
to some circumstance, as, for instance, in this same
case, if the treasurer had died, and for that reason
the ambassadors did not receive the money, then
as there is no opportunity to accuse another or to
avoid responsibility, it will be proper to use all the
other arguments without change, and to take such
arguments as may fit from the topics of *concessio*
(confession and avoidance) which we must discuss
presently.[a]

91   Both sides will have available about the same
common topics as in the divisions of " assumptive "
issue already discussed.[b] But the following will
most assuredly be used: the prosecutor will arouse
indignation at the deed; the defendant will claim
that he ought not to be punished since the fault is
in another and not in himself.

The act itself is shifted when the defendant
denies that the act imputed to him concerned him
or his duty, and says that if there was any criminality
in the act, it should not be attributed to him. This
kind of case is illustrated as follows: In ratifying
the treaty which was made once upon a time with
Samnites, a youth of noble birth held the sacrificial
pig as ordered by his general.[c] The treaty, however,
was disavowed by the Senate and the commander
was surrendered to the Samnites, whereupon some
one in the Senate said that the youth also, who held

sacrifice of a pig in concluding a treaty, see the full description
in Livy I. 24.

92 oportere. Intentio est: "Dedi oportet." Depulsio est: "Non oportet." Quaestio est: Oporteatne? Ratio est: "Non enim meum fuit officium nec mea potestas, cum et id aetatis [1] et privatus essem et esset summa cum auctoritate et potestate imperator, qui videret ut satis honestum foedus feriretur." Infirmatio est: "At enim quoniam particeps tu factus es in turpissimo foedere summae religionis, dedi te convenit." Iudicatio est: Cum is qui potestatis nihil habuerit iussu imperatoris in foedere et in tanta religione interfuerit, dedendusne sit hostibus necne? Hoc genus causae cum superiore hoc differt, quod in illo concedit se reus oportuisse facere id quod fieri dicat accusator oportuisse, sed alicui rei aut homini causam attribuit quae voluntati suae fuerit impedimento sine concessionis partibus; nam earum maior quaedam vis est, quod

93 paulo post intellegetur. In hoc autem non accusare alterum nec culpam in alium transferre debet, sed demonstrare eam rem nihil ad se nec ad potestatem neque ad officium suum pertinuisse aut pertinere. Atque in hoc genere hoc accidit novi, quod accusator quoque saepe ex remotione criminationem conficit, ut, si quis eum accuset qui, cum praetor esset, in expeditionem ad arma populum vocarit, cum consules essent. [2] Nam ut in superiore exemplo reus ab suo

---

[1] *After* id aetatis *HS and Alcuin add* non habui.
[2] essent *M* : adessent *J* : ibi essent *P³*.

ᵃ This case is stated as it would be in a deliberative speech. Before a court it would run: Charge: "You were guilty of lese-majesty." Answer: "I was not." Question: "Was he guilty of lese-majesty?" etc.

ᵇ In view of the last sentence in § 90, it may be that we should read with Weidner, *non sine*, not without pleas etc.

92 the pig, ought to be surrendered. The charge is:
"He ought to be surrendered." The answer is:
"He ought not." The question is: "Ought he to
be surrendered?"[a] The defendant's reason is:
"It was not my duty nor was it in my power, since
I was so young and a private soldier, and there was
a commander with supreme power and authority
to see that an honourable treaty was made." The
prosecutor's reply is: "But since you had a part
in a most infamous treaty sanctioned by solemn
religious rites, you ought to be surrendered." The
point for decision is: "Granted that he who had
no authority took part in making the treaty and in
performing the holy rites, should he be surrendered
to the enemy or not?" This kind of case differs
from the former in that in the former the defendant
grants that he ought to have done what the prosecutor says ought to have been done, but attributes
to some thing or person the cause which interfered
with his desires, without pleas of confession and
avoidance.[b] For these pleas have a greater influence
93 as will be recognized presently. But in this case
he must not accuse the other party nor transfer
the blame to another but prove that this act did
not and does not bear any relation to himself, his
powers or his duty. And in this case there is this
new point, that even the prosecutor often makes
his accusation by shifting the responsibility as
in the case of one who accuses a man who while
praetor called the people to arms for a campaign,
when there were consuls in office.[c] For just as in

[c] Both praetors and consuls had the *imperium*, *i.e.* the
right among other things to call out the troops, but the
consul held higher rank than the praetor.

officio et a potestate factum demovebat, sic in hoc ab
eius officio ac potestate qui accusatur ipse accusator
factum removendo hac ipsa ratione confirmat ac-
94 cusationem. In hac ab utroque ex omnibus partibus honestatis et ex omnibus utilitatis partibus,
exemplis, signis, ratiocinando, quid cuiusque offici,
iuris, potestatis sit, quaeri oportebit et fueritne ei
quo de agetur id iuris, offici, potestatis attributum
necne.

Locos autem communes ex ipsa re, si quid indignationis aut conquestionis habebit, sumi oportebit.

XXXI. Concessio est per quam non factum ipsum
probatur ab reo, sed ut ignoscatur, id petitur. Cuius
partes sunt duae: purgatio et deprecatio. Purgatio
est per quam eius qui accusatur non factum ipsum,
sed voluntas defenditur. Ea habet partes tres:
imprudentiam, casum, necessitudinem.

95 Imprudentia est, cum scisse aliquid is qui arguitur
negatur; ut apud quosdam lex erat: Ne quis
Dianae vitulum immolaret. Nautae quidam cum
adversa tempestate in alto iactarentur, voverunt
si eo portu quem conspiciebant potiti essent, ei
deo qui ibi esset se vitulum immolaturos. Casu
erat in eo portu fanum Dianae eius, cui vitulum
immolare non licebat. Imprudentes legis, cum
exissent, vitulum immolaverunt. Accusantur. Intentio est: " Vitulum immolastis ei deo cui non

---

the former instance the defendant denied any connexion between the act and his duty or powers, so in this case the prosecutor by denying that the act is connected with the duty or power of the accused man, supports his accusation by this very 94 line of reasoning. In this case both sides ought to use all the principles of honour and advantage, historical parallels, evidence and reasoning from analogy to inquire what is each one's duty, right and power, and whether such right, duty or power has, or has not been given to the man on trial.

Common topics ought to be suggested by the circumstances of the case, if it affords grounds for denunciation or complaint.

XXXI. *Concessio* (confession and avoidance) is the plea in which the defendant does not as a matter of fact approve of the deed itself, but asks that it be pardoned. It has two forms, *purgatio* and *deprecatio.*[a] *Purgatio* is the plea by which the intent of the accused is defended but not his act. It has three forms, ignorance, accident, necessity.

95 It is a plea of ignorance when the accused claims that he was not aware of something. For instance, a certain people had a law that prohibited the sacrifice of a bull-calf to Diana. Some sailors tossed on the deep by a terrible storm vowed that if they could gain the harbour which was in sight, they would sacrifice a bull-calf to the divinity whose temple stood there. It so happened that in that port there was a shrine of that Diana to whom it was unlawful to sacrifice a bull-calf. Ignorant of the law they landed and sacrificed a bull-calf. They are brought to trial. The charge is: " You sacrificed a bull-calf to the divinity to whom it was

licebat." Depulsio est in concessione posita. Ratio
est: "Nescivi non licere." Infirmatio est: "Tamen, quoniam fecisti quod non licebat ex lege,
supplicio dignus es." Iudicatio est: Cum id fecerit
quod non oportuerit, et id non oportere nescierit,
sitne supplicio dignus?

96 Casus autem inferetur in concessionem, cum
demonstratur aliqua fortunae vis voluntati obstitisse,
ut in hac: Cum Lacedaemoniis lex esset ut, hostias
nisi ad sacrificium quoddam redemptor praebuisset,
capital esset, hostias is qui redemerat cum sacri-
fici dies instaret, in urbem ex agro coepit agere.
Tum subito magnis commotis tempestatibus fluvius
Eurotas, is qui praeter Lacedaemonem fluit, ita
magnus et vehemens factus est ut ea traduci victimae
97 nullo modo possent. Redemptor suae voluntatis
ostendendae causa hostias constituit omnes in litore,
ut qui trans flumen essent videre possent. Cum
omnes studio eius subitam fluminis magnitudinem
scirent fuisse impedimento, tamen quidam capitis
arcesserunt. Intentio est: "Hostiae quas debuisti
ad sacrificium praesto non fuerunt." Depulsio est [1]
concessio. Ratio: "Flumen enim subito accrevit et
ea re traduci non potuerunt." Infirmatio: "Tamen,
quoniam quod lex iubet factum non est, supplicio
dignus es." Iudicatio est: Cum in ea re contra

---

[1] est *LRJ* : *omitted by Ströbel.*

unlawful." The answer consists in confession and avoidance. The reason is: "I did not know that it was unlawful." The prosecutor's reply is: "Nevertheless, since you have done what was unlawful, you deserve punishment." The point for the judge's decision is: "Granted that he did what he ought not, and did not know that he ought not, does he deserve punishment?"

96 Chance will be brought into the plea of avoidance when it is shown that the defendant's intention was thwarted by some act of Fortune, as in the following case: The Lacedaemonians had a law that visited capital punishment on a contractor who did not furnish the animals for a certain sacrifice. When the day for the sacrifice was at hand, the man who had taken the contract began to drive the animals from the country to the city. Then suddenly a great storm came up, and the river Eurotas which flows by Lacedaemon became so high and rapid that the victims could not by any possibility be driven across at that point. 97 The contractor to show his intent placed all the animals on the bank so as to be seen by those across the river. Although every one knew that his efforts had been thwarted by the sudden rise of the river, nevertheless some citizens put him on trial for his life. The charge is: "The animals which you were bound to furnish for the sacrifice were not at hand." The answer is confession and avoidance. The reason is: "The river rose suddenly and for that reason they could not be driven across." The prosecutor's reply is: "Nevertheless since the provisions of the law were not carried out, you deserve punishment." The point for the judge's decision is: "Granted that the contractor acted

legem redemptor aliquid fecerit, qua in re studio
eius subita fluminis obstiterit magnitudo, supplicio
dignusne sit?

98   XXXII. Necessitudo autem infertur, cum vi
quadam reus id quod fecerit fecisse defenditur, hoc
modo: Lex est apud Rhodios ut si qua rostrata in
portu navis deprehensa sit, publicetur. Cum magna
in alto tempestas esset, vis ventorum invitis nautis
in Rhodiorum portum navem coëgit. Quaestor
navem populi vocat, navis dominus negat oportere
publicari. Intentio est: " Rostrata navis in portu
deprehensa est." Depulsio est [1] concessio. Ratio:
" Vi et necessario sumus in portum coacti." Infirmatio est: " Navem ex lege tamen populi esse
oportet." Iudicatio est: Cum rostratam navem
in portu deprehensam lex publicarit cumque haec
navis invitis nautis vi tempestatis in portum coniecta
sit, oporteatne eam publicari?

99   Horum trium generum idcirco in unum locum
contulimus exempla, quod similis in ea praeceptio
argumentorum traditur. Nam in his omnibus,
primum si quid res ipsa dabit facultatis, coniecturam
induci ab accusatore oportebit, ut id quod voluntate
factum negabitur consulto factum suspicione aliqua
demonstretur; deinde inducere definitionem necessitudinis aut casus aut imprudentiae et exempla
ad eam definitionem adiungere in quibus imprudentia

---

[1] est *SRi* : *omitted by Ströbel.*

---

[a] *Quaestor* is probably a translation of the Greek ταμίας, a
financial officer with rather broad powers in most Greek states.

contrary to law in this case in which his efforts were thwarted by the sudden rise of the river, does he deserve punishment?"

98   XXXII. Necessity is brought in when the accused is defended as having done what he did because of some force beyond his control, as follows: There is a law at Rhodes that if any ship with a ram is caught in the harbour it is confiscated. There was a violent storm at sea, and the force of the wind compelled the sailors against their will to put into the harbour of Rhodes. The treasurer [a] claims the ship as public property, the master of the vessel denies that it ought to be confiscated. The charge is: " A ship with a ram has been caught in the harbour." The answer is confession and avoidance. The reason is: " We were driven into the harbour by force and necessity." The prosecutor's reply is: " Nevertheless the ship ought to be confiscated according to law." The point for the judge's decision is: " Granted that the law confiscates a ship with a ram caught in the harbour, and that this ship was driven into port by the force of the storm against the desire of the crew, should it be confiscated?"

99   We have placed the examples of these three varieties together because similar rules for argument are given for them. For in all of these, first the prosecutor should, if the facts of the case provide any opportunity, introduce the argument from conjecture, so as to prove by some inference that the act which, it will be asserted, was performed involuntarily, was really done intentionally. Then he should introduce a definition of necessity or chance or ignorance and accompany the definition by examples in which ignorance or accident or

fuisse videatur aut casus aut necessitudo et ab his id
quod reus inferat separare, id est ostendere dissimile,
quod [1] non ignorabile, non fortuitum, non necessarium
fuerit; postea demonstrare potuisse vitari: aut
ratione [2] provideri potuisse, si hoc aut illud fecisset,
aut, nisi [3] fecisset, praecaveri; et definitionibus
ostendere non hanc imprudentiam aut casum aut
necessitudinem, sed inertiam, neglegentiam, fatuita-
100 tem nominari oportere. Ac si qua necessitudo turpitudinem videbitur habere, oportebit per locorum communium implicationem redarguentem demonstrare
quidvis perpeti, mori denique satius fuisse quam
eiusmodi necessitudini obtemperare. Atque tum
ex eis locis de quibus in negotiali parte dictum est
iuris et aequitatis naturam oportebit quaerere et
quasi in absoluta iuridiciali per se hoc ipsum ab rebus
omnibus separatim considerare. Atque hoc in loco,
si facultas erit, exemplis uti oportebit, quibus in
simili excusatione non sit ignotum, et contentione,
magis illis ignoscendum fuisse, et deliberationis
partibus, turpe aut inutile esse concedi eam rem,
quae ab adversario commissa sit; permagnum esse
et magno futurum detrimento, si ea res ab eis qui
potestatem habent vindicandi neglecta sit.

101   XXXIII. Defensor autem conversis omnibus his
partibus poterit uti; maxime autem in voluntate

---

[1] *After* quod *J has* levius facilius, *M,* lenius facilius:
bracketed by Kayser.
[2] et hac ratione *J* : hac ratione *M, Ströbel* : aut ratione
Weidner.
[3] nisi *Mi* : ne sic *P* : ni sic *or* nisi sic *i.*

---

[a] Above, §§ 65–8.   [b] Above, §§ 69–71.

necessity seem to have played a part, and separate
the defendant's story from these, that is to show
the dissimilarity between the cases, because the
matter was such that it could not be unknown,
fortuitous or necessary. After that he should show
that it could have been avoided, or by the use of
reason could have been foreseen if he had done
thus and so, or could have been guarded against if
he had not done thus and so. Furthermore he may
show by definitions that this should not be called
ignorance or chance or necessity, but laziness, care-
100 lessness or folly. And if in any case yielding to
necessity seems to involve an act of baseness he
should weave in common topics and prove in rebuttal
that it was better to endure any fate, even death,
rather than yield to such a necessity. And then
by use of the topics described under legal issue [a] he
should inquire into the nature of law and equity
and as if it were a case under the " absolute " section
of the issue of equity [b] consider this point by itself
without reference to other things. At this point, if
opportunity offers, he should cite examples of those
who have not been pardoned though offering a
similar excuse, and argue that they were by comparison more worthy of pardon, and adopt the
arguments of a deliberative speech, that it is base
and inexpedient to condone the act which has been
committed by the opponent; saying that this is a
serious case and that great harm will ensue if this
act is overlooked by those who have the power to
punish it.

101 XXXIII. The defendant, on the other hand, will
be able to turn all these arguments about and use
them for a different conclusion; in particular,

defendenda commorabitur et in ea re adaugenda, quae voluntati fuerit impedimento; et se plus, quam fecerit, facere non potuisse; et in omnibus rebus voluntatem spectari oportere; et se convinci non posse, quod absit a culpa; suo nomine communem hominum infirmitatem posse damnari. Deinde nihil esse indignius quam eum qui culpa careat supplicio non carere.

Loci autem sunt communes: accusatoris in confessionem, et quanta potestas peccandi relinquatur, si semel institutum sit ut non de facto, sed de facti 102 causa quaeratur; defensoris conquestio est calamitatis eius, quae non culpa, sed vi maiore quadam acciderit, et de fortunae potestate et hominum infirmitate et uti suum animum, non eventum considerent. In quibus omnibus conquestionem suarum aerumnarum et crudelitatis adversariorum indignationem inesse oportebit.

Ac neminem mirari conveniet, si aut in his aut in aliis exemplis scripti quoque controversiam adiunctam videbit. Quo de genere post erit nobis separatim dicendum, propterea quod quaedam genera causarum simpliciter ex sua vi considerantur, quaedam autem sibi aliud quoque aliquod contro- 103 versiae genus assumunt. Quare omnibus cognitis, non erit difficile in unam quamque causam transferre quod ex eo quoque genere convenit; ut in his exemplis concessionis inest omnibus scripti contro-

---

a I.e. the dispute over the letter of the law.

however, he will spend some time in defending his good intentions and in magnifying the circumstances which thwarted his purpose; saying that it was impossible to do more than he did, that in all things one should regard the intent and that he cannot be convicted because he is free of guilt, and that under his name the weakness common to all men may be condemned; finally, that nothing is more shocking than that he who is free of guilt should not be free of punishment.

Now for the common topics: the prosecutor will attack the plea of confession and avoidance and point out what a chance is offered for transgression if it is once established that the thing to be inquired 102 into is not the act but the excuse for the act. The defendant may lament the misfortune which has befallen one not because of his fault but from *force majeure*, enlarge on the power of fortune and the infirmity of mankind, and beg the jury to consider his intent and not the result. With all of which there should be combined a lament over his own tribulations and a denunciation of the cruelty of his opponents.

No one should be surprised if he sees in these or in other examples a dispute over the letter of the law also. We shall have to speak separately about this question because certain kinds of cases are considered straightforwardly on their own merits, while others involve some other form of dispute. 103 Therefore when all forms have been studied, it will not be hard to transfer to each case anything in this form,[a] too, which shall be appropriate; as in all these examples of confession and avoidance there is involved a dispute about the letter of the

versia, ea quae ex scripto et sententia nominatur;
sed, quia de concessione loquebamur, in eam praecepta dedimus, alio autem loco de scripto et de
sententia dicemus.

Nunc ut [1] alteram concessionis partem considere-
104 mus [2] iam contendemus.[3] XXXIV. Deprecatio est
in qua non defensio facti, sed ignoscendi postulatio
continetur. Hoc genus vix in iudicio probari potest,
ideo quod concesso peccato difficile est ab eo, qui
peccatorum vindex esse debet, ut ignoscat, impetrare.
Quare parte eius generis, cum causam non in eo
constitueris, uti licebit; ut si [4] pro aliquo claro aut
forti viro, cuius in rem publicam multa sunt beneficia, dicens [5] possis, cum videaris non uti deprecatione, uti tamen, ad hunc modum: " Quodsi,
iudices, hic pro suis beneficiis, pro suo studio, quod
in vos semper habuit, tali suo tempore multorum
suorum recte factorum causa uni delicto ut ignosce-
retis postularet, tamen dignum vestra mansuetudine,
dignum virtute huius esset, iudices, a vobis hanc rem
hoc postulante impetrari." Deinde augere beneficia
licebit et iudices per locum communem ad ignoscendi
105 voluntatem ducere. Quare hoc genus, quamquam
in iudiciis non versatur nisi quadam ex parte, tamen,
quia et pars haec ipsa inducenda nonnunquam est
et in senatu aut in consilio saepe omni in genere
tractanda, in id quoque praecepta ponemus. Nam

---

[1] ut *Weidner*: in *MP*: *erased by P*[2]: *omitted by R.*
[2] consideremus *M, Weidner*: considerationem *J.*
[3] iam contendemus *Friedrich*: iam intendemus *Ströbel*:
intendemus *Jω*: la contendemus *HS*: iam tendamus *PL*:
iam contendimus *R.*
[4] si *omitted by H, Weidner.*
[5] dicens *Kayser*: dicere *M*: dixeris *J.*

law, which goes by the name of the letter and the intent. But because we were speaking of confession and avoidance we gave the rules for that; in another place [a] we shall discuss the letter and the intent.

Now we shall go about the consideration of the 104 second form of confession and avoidance. XXXIV. *Deprecatio* (plea for pardon) is the designation of the plea which contains no defence of the deed but only a request for pardon. This form can hardly be recommended in a trial because when the offence is admitted, it is difficult to demand pardon from him whose duty it is to punish offences. Therefore it will be admissible to make partial use of this form, although you do not rest your case upon it. For instance, if you are speaking on behalf of a brave or distinguished man who has performed many services for the state you might plead for pardon without seeming to in this way: "Therefore, gentlemen of the jury, if this man in return for his services, in return for the devotion which he has always shown to you, at such a critical moment for him asked you to pardon one error for the sake of his many good deeds, it would be only what is due to your reputation for clemency and to his virtue that he should obtain from you this favour that he requests." Then it will be right to magnify his services and to lead the jury by a common topic to a mood of forgiveness. 105 Therefore, although this form is not used commonly in trials except in part, nevertheless because this very part has to be brought in occasionally and is often adopted exclusively in the Senate and Council, we shall give rules for it too. For instance, there

[a] Below, §§ 121–43.

et in senatu aut in consilio [1] de Syphace diu deli-
beratum est, et de Q. Numitorio Pullo apud L.
Opimium et eius consilium diu dictum est, et magis
in hoc quidem ignoscendi quam cognoscendi postulatio
valuit. Nam semper animo bono se in populum
Romanum fuisse non tam facile probabat cum
coniecturali constitutione uteretur quam ut propter
posterius beneficium sibi ignosceretur cum depre-
cationis partes adiungeret.

106   XXXV. Oportebit igitur eum qui sibi ut ignoscatur postulabit commemorare si qua sua poterit
beneficia et, si poterit, ostendere ea maiora esse
quam haec quae deliquerit, ut plus ab eo boni quam
mali profectum esse videatur; deinde maiorum
suorum beneficia, si qua exstabunt, proferre; deinde
ostendere non odio neque crudelitate fecisse quod
fecerit, sed aut stultitia aut impulsu alicuius aut
aliqua honesta aut probabili causa; postea polliceri
et confirmare se et hoc peccato doctum et beneficio
eorum, qui sibi ignoverint, confirmatum, omni tempore a tali ratione afuturum; deinde spem ostendere aliquo se in loco magno eis qui sibi concesse-
107   rint usui futurum; postea, si facultas erit, se aut
consanguineum magnis et principibus viris [2] aut

---

[1] aut in consilio *omitted by Victorinus, bracketed by Kayser.*
[2] magnis et principibus viris *added by Kayser from Victorinus.*

---

[a] An African prince, alternately allied to the Romans
and the Carthaginians in the Second Punic War. Livy
(XXX. 17) records that on his arrival in Italy as a captive
the Senate debated his case, and decided to imprison him
at Alba. There are conflicting stories about his death.
[b] In 125 B.C. Pullus betrayed his native town, Fregellae,

was a long deliberation in the Senate or in the
Council about Syphax [a] and long speeches were
made about Quintus Numitorius Pullus [b] before
Lucius Opimius and his council; and in this case
the plea for mercy prevailed over the demand for
judicial action. For he did not find it as easy to
prove that he had always been well affected towards
the Roman people when he was using the issue of
fact, as to urge that he should be pardoned for his
subsequent services while adding the plea for pardon
to his defence.

106 XXXV. One who requests that he be pardoned
will, therefore, have to recount whatever good deeds
of his own he can, and if possible to show that they
are of greater weight than these present mistakes,
so that he may seem to have been the source of
more good than harm. Then he should mention
the good deeds of his ancestors if there are any
such; then show that he did what he did, not out
of hatred or cruelty, but through folly or the instiga-
tion of some one, or from some honourable or
plausible reason. After that he should promise
and affirm that, taught by this error and strengthened
by the kindness of those who have pardoned him,
he will forever after refrain from such a course of
conduct. Then he may hold out the hope that
at some great crisis he will be able to help those
107 who have done him this favour. After that, if facts
permit, he may show that he is kin to great and
leading men of the state or that from the earliest

to the Roman commander, Lucius Opimius. The incident
in the text, which is not found elsewhere, obviously involved
the decision whether Pullus should be punished as a rebel
or pardoned for his services as a traitor.

iam a maioribus imprimis amicum esse [1] demonstrabit et amplitudinem suae voluntatis, nobilitatem generis, eorum qui se salvum velint dignitatem ostendere, et cetera ea quae personis ad honestatem et amplitudinem sunt attributa cum conquestione, sine arrogantia, in se esse demonstrabit [1] ut honore potius aliquo quam ullo supplicio dignus esse videatur; deinde ceteros proferre, quibus maiora delicta concessa sint. Ac multum proficiet, si se misericordem in potestate, propensum ad ignoscendum fuisse ostendet. Atque ipsum illud peccatum erit extenuandum, ut quam minimum obfuisse videatur, et aut turpe aut inutile demonstrandum tali de 108 homine supplicium sumere. Deinde locis communibus misericordiam captare oportebit ex eis praeceptis quae in primo libro sunt exposita.

XXXVI. Adversarius autem malefacta augebit: nihil imprudenter, sed omnia ex crudelitate et malitia facta dicet; ipsum immisericordem, superbum fuisse; et, si poterit, ostendet semper inimicum fuisse et amicum fieri nullo modo posse. Si beneficia proferet, aut aliqua de causa facta, non propter benivolentiam demonstrabit, aut post ea odium esse acre susceptum, aut illa omnia maleficiis esse deleta, aut leviora beneficia quam maleficia, aut, cum beneficiis honos habitus sit, pro maleficio poenam 109 sumi oportere. Deinde turpe esse aut inutile ignosci. Deinde, de quo ut potestas esset saepe

---

[1] *After esse the MSS. have* demonstrabit: *bracketed by Lindemann.*

---

times his family have been friends to them, and set forth the earnestness of his good will, the nobility of his family and the high position of those who wish him to be saved, and in sorrow rather than in arrogance show that he possesses all the other qualities which are regarded as making for honour and greatness of character, so that he may seem to deserve some honour rather than any punishment. Then he should cite the example of the others who have had graver errors pardoned. Furthermore, it will help his case greatly if he shows that he has been merciful when in authority, and prone to forgiveness. He should also make light of the offence so that it may appear that very little harm resulted from it, and prove that it is shameful or inexpedient 108 to inflict punishment on such a man. Then he ought to try to arouse pity by using common topics in accordance with the rules that were set forth in the first book.[a]

XXXVI. The opponent, on the other hand, will magnify the offences; he will say that nothing was done inadvertently, but everything out of cruelty and ill-will; that the defendant has been merciless and overbearing; and if possible, he will show that the defendant has always been unfriendly and can by no possibility become a friend. If he mentions any good acts he will prove that they were done from some ulterior motive and not out of good-will, or that later the defendant conceived a violent hatred, or that all those good deeds were outweighed by the bad, or that the offence should be punished 109 because the good deeds have been rewarded. Then that it is base or inexpedient to pardon; then that it is the height of folly not to use the opportunity

optarint, in eum oblata potestate [1] non uti summam esse stultitiam; cogitare oportere quem
animum in eum et quod odium habuerint.

Locus autem communis erit indignatio malefici
et alter eorum misereri oportere, qui propter fortunam, non propter malitiam in miseriis sint.

Quoniam ergo in generali constitutione tamdiu
propter eius partium multitudinem commoramur,
ne forte varietate et dissimilitudine rerum diductus
alicuius animus in quendam errorem deferatur, quid
etiam nobis ex eo genere restet et quare restet ad-
monendum videtur.

Iuridicialem causam esse dicebamus, in qua
aequi et iniqui natura et praemi aut poenae ratio
quaereretur. Eas causas, in quibus de aequo et
110 iniquo quaeritur, exposuimus. XXXVII. Restat
nunc ut de praemio et de poena explicemus. Sunt
enim multae causae quae ex praemi alicuius petitione
constant. Nam et apud iudices de praemio saepe
accusatorum quaeritur et a senatu aut a consilio
aliquod praemium saepe petitur. Ac neminem
conveniet arbitrari nos, cum aliquod exemplum
ponamus, quod in senatu agatur, ab iudiciali genere
exemplorum recedere. Quicquid enim de homine
probando aut improbando dicitur, cum ad eam
dictionem sententiarum quoque ratio accommodetur,
id non, si per sententiae dictionem agitur, delibera-

---

[1] oblata potestate *A, Klotz*: ob potestatem *HS¹, Ströbel
with sign of lacuna*: potestatem *PL, bl*: potestate *RJ.*

that is offered to punish him whom they have often prayed to have the opportunity to punish; finally that they ought to remember what feelings, nay, what hatred they have had toward him.

A common topic will be denunciation of crime and for the other side that those should be pitied who are in misery through ill fortune and not through wickedness.

Now then, since I have lingered so long over the qualitative issue because of the great number of its subdivisions, it seems necessary to remind the reader of what remains to be said about this issue and why anything is left, in order that his mind may not by chance be distracted by the variety and difference in the subject matter, and so be led astray.

We said that equitable was the term applied to a case in which there was a question of the nature of justice and injustice and of the principles of reward or punishment. We have expounded the cases in which there is a question of justice and injustice. 110 XXXVII. It now remains to explain about reward and punishment. There are, as a matter of fact, many speeches which consist of a request for some reward. For example, one often raises before a court the question of rewarding the prosecutors, and often some reward is requested from Senate or Council. And no one should think that in citing some instance of a case to come up in the Senate, we are abandoning our principle of referring to trials in court. For whatever is said in approval or disapproval of a person, even though the speech is classified under the advocacy of policy, is not a deliberative speech for all that it is presented as a declaration of policy, but it is to be regarded as

tivum est; sed quia de homine statuitur, iudiciale est habendum. Omnino autem qui diligenter omnium causarum vim et naturam cognoverit, genere et prima conformatione eas intelleget dissidere, ceteris autem partibus aptas inter se omnes et aliam in alia implicatam videbit.

111 Nunc de praemiis consideremus. L. Licinius Crassus consul quosdam in citeriore Gallia nullo illustri neque certo duce neque eo nomine neque numero praeditos uti digni essent qui hostes populi Romani esse dicerentur, qui tamen excursionibus et latrociniis infestam provinciam redderent, consectatus est et confecit. Romam redit: triumphum ab senatu postulat. Hic et in deprecatione nihil ad nos attinet rationibus et infirmationibus rationum supponendis ad iudicationem pervenire, propterea quod, nisi alia quoque incidet constitutio aut pars constitutionis, simplex erit iudicatio et in quaestione ipsa continebitur in deprecatione huiusmodi: Oporteatne poena affici? in hac, huiusmodi: Oporteatne dari praemium?

112 Nunc ad praemi quaestionem appositos locos exponemus. XXXVIII. Ratio igitur praemi quattuor est in partes distributa: in beneficia, in hominem, in praemi genus, in facultates.

Beneficia ex sua vi, ex tempore, ex animo eius qui fecit, ex casu considerantur. Ex sua vi quaerentur hoc modo: magna an parva, facilia an diffi-

---

a The distinguished orator, consul 95 B.C.

a judicial or forensic speech because a decision is sought about a person. But in general, one who diligently studies the function and character of all speeches will find that they differ in a large way and in general arrangement, but will see that they are all connected and related one to another as far as the smaller divisions of the speech are concerned.

11 Now let us consider rewards. Lucius Licinius Crassus *a* when consul ran down and destroyed some bands in Cisalpine Gaul. They had no distinguished or even regular leader, nor were they so famous or numerous that they deserved to be called enemies of the Roman people, yet by their plundering raids they had made the province unsafe. Crassus returns to Rome and demands that the Senate grant him a triumph. In such a case and in a plea for pardon we are not interested in reaching the point for decision by supplying reasons and rebuttals of reasons, because unless some other issue or part of an issue comes into the case the point for the judge's decision is simple and is wholly contained in the question. In a plea for pardon, it is: "Should he be punished?" In this case it is: "Should he receive a reward?"

12 Now I shall give topics apposite to the question of reward. XXXVIII. The matter of reward has four heads: the services to be rewarded, the person to receive it, the kind of reward, and the ability to give it.

Services are examined with reference to their character, the time at which they were performed, the intent of the person who rendered them, and chance. They are examined with reference to their character as follows: Are they great or small, easy

279

cilia, singularia sint an vulgaria, vera an falsa quadam exornatione honestentur; ex tempore autem, si tum, cum indigeremus, cum ceteri non possent aut nollent opitulari, si tum, cum spes deseruisset; ex animo, si non sui commodi causa, si eo consilio fecit omnia, ut hoc conficere posset; ex casu, si non fortuna, sed industria factum videbitur aut si industriae fortuna obstitisse.

113   In hominem autem, quibus rationibus vixerit, quid sumptus in eam rem aut laboris insumpserit; ecquid aliquando tale fecerit; num alieni laboris aut deorum bonitatis praemium sibi postulet; num aliquando ipse talem ob causam aliquem praemio affici negarit oportere; aut num iam satis pro eo quod fecerit honos habitus sit; aut num necesse fuerit ei facere id quod fecerit; aut num eiusmodi sit factum, ut, nisi fecisset, supplicio dignus esset, non, quia fecerit, praemio; ut num ante tempus praemium petat, et spem incertam certo venditet pretio; aut num, quod supplicium aliquod vitet, eo praemium postulet, uti de se praeiudicium factum esse videatur.

XXXIX. In praemi autem genere, quid et quantum et quamobrem postuletur et quo et quanto quaeque res praemio digna sit, considerabitur;

or difficult, unique or common, esteemed and honoured for their merit or only on false pretences? With reference to the time when the services were performed: Was it at a time when we were in need, when others could not or would not succour us, when hope had been abandoned? With reference to the intent, it is asked whether he did not do it for his own advantage, and if he did everything with the intent of accomplishing this result. With reference to chance, if it seems to have been done intentionally rather than accidentally, or if an accident seems to have thwarted his intention.

113   Under the heading person one considers in what manner he lived, what expense or effort he devoted to this service; whether he has ever done anything like it at any other time; whether he is demanding for himself the reward for another's labour or for the blessings sent by the gods; whether at any time he himself denied that a reward should be granted for similar services; whether he has already received sufficient honour for what he did; whether he was obliged to do what he did; or whether the act was such that he would have deserved punishment for not performing it rather than reward for its accomplishment; whether he is seeking a reward before the proper time, and bartering a vague hope for a definite price; or whether he claims a reward because he is trying to avoid punishment so that the case may seem to have already been decided in his favour.

XXXIX. Under the heading, "kind of reward," consideration will be given to what and how much is demanded and why, and what and how great a reward each act deserves; then one inquires what

deinde, apud maiores quibus hominibus et quibus
de causis talis honos habitus sit, quaeretur; deinde,
114 ne is honos nimium pervulgetur. Atque hic eius
qui contra aliquem praemium postulantem dicet
locus erit communis: Praemia virtutis et offici
sancta et casta esse oportere neque ea aut cum
improbis communicari aut in mediocribus hominibus
pervulgari; et alter: Minus homines virtutis cupidos
fore virtutis praemio pervulgato; quae enim rara
et ardua sint, ea experiendo pulchra et iucunda
hominibus videri; et tertius: Si exsistant, qui apud
maiores nostros ob egregiam virtutem tali honore
dignati sunt, nonne de sua gloria, cum pari praemio
tales homines affici videant, delibari putent? et eorum enumeratio et cum eis, quos contra dicas, comparatio. Eius autem qui praemium petet facti sui
amplificatio, eorum qui praemio affecti sunt cum
115 suis factis contentio. Deinde ceteros a virtutis
studio repulsum iri, si ipse praemio non sit affectus.

Facultates autem considerantur, cum aliquod
pecuniarum praemium postulatur; in quo, utrum
copiane sit agri, vectigalium, pecuniae, an penuria,
consideratur. Loci communes: Facultates augere,
non minuere oportere; et, impudentem esse qui
pro beneficio non gratiam, verum mercedem postulet;
contra autem de pecunia ratiocinari sordidum esse,

men received such honour in the time of our forefathers, and for what reasons; then it will be urged
that such an honour should not be made too common.

114 Here one who is opposing the demand for a reward
will use the common topic: that the rewards for
heroism and devotion to duty ought to be considered sacred and holy and should not be shared
with inferior men nor made common by being
bestowed on men of no distinction; a second: men
will be less eager to be virtuous if the reward of
virtue is made common; that it is the rare and
difficult which seems fair and pleasant for men to
attain; and a third: if those should rise from the
dead who in our forefathers' day were deemed
worthy of such honour because of their outstanding
heroism, would they not think that their glory was
lessened, when they see such men receiving an equal
reward? Then these men of the past can be named
over and compared with those whom you are opposing. The common topic for one seeking a reward
is to magnify his own act and compare the deeds
of those who have received a reward with his own.

115 Then he will urge that others will be deterred from
the pursuit of virtue if he himself does not receive
a reward.

Ability to give is taken into consideration when
a demand is made for some valuable reward. In
this case one considers whether there is a plenty
or scarcity of land, revenues and money. The
common topics: the national resources should be
increased, rather than diminished; and that he is
a shameless man who demands wages for his service
to the state rather than gratitude. On the other
hand it may be urged that it is mean to haggle over

cum de gratia referenda deliberetur; et, se pretium non pro facto, sed honorem ita ut factitatum sit pro beneficio postulare.

Ac de constitutionibus quidem satis dictum est; nunc de eis controversiis quae in scripto versantur dicendum videtur.

116 XL. In scripto versatur controversia cum ex scriptionis ratione aliquid dubii nascitur. Id fit ex ambiguo, ex scripto et sentential, ex contrariis legibus, ex ratiocinatione, ex definitione.

Ex ambiguo autem nascitur controversia cum quid senserit scriptor obscurum est, quod scriptum duas pluresve res significat, ad hunc modum: Paterfamilias, cum filium heredem faceret, vasorum argenteorum pondo centum [1] uxori suae sic legavit: heres meus uxori meae vasorum argenteorum pondo centum, quae volet, dato. Post mortem eius vasa magnifica et pretiose caelata petit a filio mater. Ille se, quae ipse vellet, debere dicit.[a]

Primum, si fieri poterit, demonstrandum est non esse ambigue scriptum, propterea quod omnes in consuetudine sermonis sic uti solent eo verbo uno pluribusve in eam sententiam in quam is qui dicet
117 accipiendum esse demonstrabit. Deinde ex superiore et ex inferiore scriptura docendum id quod quaeratur fieri perspicuum. Quare si ipsa separatim ex se verba considerentur, omnia aut pleraque ambigua visum iri; quae autem ex omni considerata scriptura perspicua fiant, haec ambigua non oportere existi-

[1] pondo centum P^2J: centum pondo S^3i, *Ströbel*: centum pondus *M*.

---

[a] Literally as (he *or* she) wishes. The ambiguity arises from the nature of the Latin verb, which may have a pronominal subject understood but not expressed.

money when debating about showing gratitude; and that he does not ask for pay for his work but the customary honour for his good services.

Enough has now been said about the " issues "; now I think we should discuss the controversies which turn upon written documents.

116   XL. A controversy turns upon written documents when some doubt arises from the nature of writing. This comes about from ambiguity, from the letter and intent, from conflict of laws, from reasoning by analogy, from definition.

A controversy arises from ambiguity when there is doubt as to what the writer meant, because the written statement has two or more meanings, after this fashion: A father, in making his son his principal heir bequeathed to his wife a hundred pounds of silver plate in the following terms: " Let my heir give to my wife a hundred pounds of silver plate as desired." [a] After his death the mother asks her son for some magnificent examples of plate with costly chasing. He says that he is obligated to give her only what *he* desires.

In the first place it should be shown, if possible, that there is no ambiguity in the statement, because in ordinary conversation everyone is accustomed to use this single word or phrase in the sense in which the speaker will prove that it should be taken.

117 In the second place it must be shown that from what precedes or follows in the document the doubtful point becomes plain. Therefore, if words are to be considered separately by themselves, every word, or at least many words, would seem ambiguous; but it is not right to regard as ambiguous what becomes plain on consideration of the whole context.

mare. Deinde, qua in sententia scriptor fuerit ex
ceteris eius scriptis et ex factis, dictis, animo atque
vita eius sumi oportebit, et eam ipsam scripturam,
in qua inerit illud ambiguum de quo quaeretur totam
omnibus ex partibus pertemptare, si quid aut ad id
appositum sit quod nos interpretemur, aut ei quod
adversarius intellegat, adversetur. Nam facile, quid
veri simile sit eum voluisse qui scripsit ex omni
scriptura et ex persona scriptoris atque eis rebus
quae personis attributae sunt considerabitur.

118   Deinde erit demonstrandum, si quid ex re ipsa
dabitur facultatis, id quod adversarius intellegat
multo minus commode fieri posse quam id quod nos
accipimus, quod illius rei neque administratio neque
exitus ullus exstet; nos quod dicamus, facile et
commode transigi posse; ut in hac lege—nihil
enim prohibet fictam exempli loco ponere, quo
facilius res intellegatur—: meretrix coronam auream
ne habeto; si habuerit, publica esto, contra eum
qui meretricem publicari dicat ex lege oportere
possit dici neque administrationem esse ullam
publicae meretricis neque exitum legis in mere-
trice publicanda, at in auro publicando et administrationem et exitum facilem esse et incommodi
nihil inesse.

119   XLI. Ac diligenter illud quoque attendere oportebit, num, illo probato quod adversarius intellegat,

---

[a] Again the ambiguity arises from a peculiarity of the Latin
language : a confusion of real and grammatical gender. Both
meretrix (prostitute) and *corona* (crown) are feminine in
gender, and the adjective *publica* might modify either. The
instance is, however, far-fetched, and could hardly arise in
actual practice.

In the next place, one ought to estimate what the writer meant from his other writings, acts, words, disposition and in fact his whole life, and to examine the whole document which contains the ambiguity in question in all its parts, to see if any thing is apposite to our interpretation or opposed to the sense in which our opponent understands it. For it is easy to estimate what it is likely that the writer intended from the complete context and from the character of the writer, and from the qualities which are associated with certain characters.

118   In the next place it should be pointed out, if opportunity presents, that the interpretation which our opponent favours can be followed with much less convenience than the one which we take, because there is no way of carrying out or complying with his interpretation, whereas what we propose can be easily and conveniently managed. For example, in the following law—there is no reason for not using an imaginary case for illustration in order to make the problem more intelligible : " A prostitute shall not wear a crown of gold ; if she does, the penalty shall be confiscation as public property" [a] —against a litigant who argues that the prostitute should be seized as public property in accordance with the law, it can be urged that there is no way to manage a prostitute as state property nor can one comply with the law by seizing a prostitute, but that it is easy to administer and comply with the law by seizing gold, and that it causes no inconvenience.

119   XLI. Another point which will deserve careful attention is whether it will not appear if we accept the interpretation proposed by our opponent, that

CICERO

res utilior aut honestior aut magis necessaria ab
scriptore neglecta videatur. Id fiet, si id quod nos
demonstrabimus honestum aut utile aut necessarium demonstrabimus, et si id quod ab adversariis
dicetur minime eiusmodi esse dicemus. Deinde si
in lege erit ex ambiguo controversia, dare operam
oportebit ut de eo quod adversarius intellegat
120 alia in [1] lege cautum esse doceatur. Permultum
autem proficiet illud demonstrare, quemadmodum
scripsisset, si id quod adversarius accipiat fieri aut
intellegi voluisset ut in hac causa in qua de vasis
argenteis quaeritur possit mulier dicere, nihil atti-
nuisse ascribi, quae volet, si heredis voluntati per-
mitteret. Eo enim non ascripto nihil esse dubita-
tionis, quin heres, quae ipse vellet, daret. Amentiae
igitur fuisse, cum heredi vellet cavere, id ascribere,
quo non ascripto nihilominus heredi caveretur.
121 Quare hoc genere magno opere talibus in causis uti
oportebit: "Hoc modo scripsisset, isto verbo usus
non esset, non isto loco verbum istud collocasset."
Nam ex his sententia scriptoris maxime perspicitur.
Deinde quo tempore scriptum sit quaerendum est,
ut quid eum voluisse in eiusmodi tempore veri simile
sit intellegatur. Post ex deliberationis partibus,
quid utilius et quid honestius et illi ad scribendum
et his ad comprobandum sit, demonstrandum; et
ex his, si quid amplificationis dabitur, communibus
utrimque locis uti oportebit.

[1] *After* in *HP have* re.

the writer neglected something more expedient, more honourable or more necessary. This can be brought about by saying that the interpretation which we make is honourable, expedient and necessary, and that of the opposition by no means of such a nature. Then if the controversy arises over an ambiguity in a law, we must try to make it appear that the interpretation which our opponent offers is dealt with 120 in another law. It will help greatly to show how he would have written if he had wished the opponent's interpretation to be carried out or adopted. For instance, in this case which deals with the silver plate, the woman could say that there was no point in adding the words " as desired " if the testator was leaving the choice to his heir. For with these words omitted there is no doubt that the heir was to give what he himself wished. It was therefore stark madness, if he wished to provide for the interest of his heir, to add the words the omission of which would not prejudice the heir's interest. 121 Therefore in such cases it will be necessary to make use of this kind of argument: " He would have written it in this way," " He would not have used that word," " He would not have put that word in that place." For these considerations particularly reveal the intention of the writer. Then one might ask when it was written, so that it may be known what he was likely to write at such a time. Finally, by the topics of deliberative oratory we must show what was more expedient and more honourable both for the testator to write and for our opponents to sanction; and on the basis of these statements if there is any chance for amplification, both sides may use common topics.

CICERO

XLII. Ex scripto et sententia controversia consistit, cum alter verbis ipsis quae scripta sunt utitur, alter ad id quod scriptorem sensisse dicet omnem adiungit 122 dictionem. Scriptoris autem sententia ab eo qui sententia se defendet tum semper ad idem spectare et idem velle demonstrabitur; tum ex facto aut ex eventu aliquo ad tempus id quod instituit accommodabitur. Semper ad idem spectare, hoc modo: Paterfamilias cum liberorum haberet nihil, uxorem autem haberet, in testamento ita scripsit: si mihi filius genitur unus pluresve, is mihi heres esto. Deinde quae assolent. Postea: si filius ante moritur, quam in tutelam suam venerit, tum mihi dicet [1] heres esto. Filius natus non est. Ambigunt agnati cum eo qui est heres si filius ante quam in suam 123 tutelam veniat mortuus sit. In hoc genere non potest hoc dici, ad tempus et ad eventum aliquem sententiam scriptoris oportere accommodari, propterea quod ea sola esse demonstratur, qua fretus ille, qui contra scriptum dicit, suam esse hereditatem defendit. Aliud autem genus est eorum, qui sententiam inducunt, in quo non simplex voluntas scriptoris ostenditur, quae in omne tempus et in omne factum idem valeat; sed ex quodam facto aut eventu ad tempus interpretanda dicitur. Ea partibus iuridicialis assumptivae maxime sustinetur. Nam tum inducitur

---

[1] dicet *M* : dicebat secundus *J*.

---

[a] *Cf.* above, II. 62 for a slightly different statement of this case.

XLII. A controversy over the letter and the intent occurs when one party follows the exact words that are written, and the other directs his whole pleading 122 to what he says the writer meant. The one who bases his defence on the intent will sometimes show that the intent of the writer always had the same end in view and desired the same result, at other times he will show that the writer's purpose has to be modified to fit the occasion as a result of some act or event. He may be proved to have always had the same end in view in the following way: A head of a family, having a wife but no children, drew his will as follows: " If one or more sons are born to me, he or they are to inherit my estate." Then follow the usual phrases. Then comes, " If my son dies before coming of age, then So-and-So is to be my heir." No son was born. The agnates dispute with the man who was to be the reversionary 123 heir in case the son died before coming of age.[a] In this kind of case it cannot be said that the intent of the writer ought to be made to fit some time or some event, because the only possible meaning is shown to be that on which the litigant who opposes the literal interpretation of the will defends his own right to inherit. But there is another kind of argument brought forward by advocates of the intent in which the wish of the writer is shown not to be absolute, *i.e.* having the same weight for every occasion and for every action, but it is argued that his wishes ought to be interpreted to fit the occasion in the light of some act or some event. This argument will be supported largely by topics under the assumptive branch of the issue of equity. For example, sometimes *comparatio* (com-

comparatio, ut in eo qui, cum lex aperiri portas noctu vetaret, aperuit quodam in bello et auxilia quaedam in oppidum recepit, ne ab hostibus opprimerentur, si
124 foris essent, quod prope muros hostes castra haberent; tum relatio criminis, ut in eo milite qui, cum communis lex omnium hominem occidere vetaret, tribunum militum,[1] qui vim sibi afferre conaretur, occidit; tum remotio criminis, ut in eo qui, cum lex quibus diebus in legationem proficisceretur praestituerat, quia sumptum quaestor non dedit, profectus non est; tum concessio per purgationem et per imprudentiam, ut in vituli immolatione, et per vim, ut in nave rostrata, et per casum, ut in Eurotae magnitudine. Quare aut ita sententia inducetur, ut unum quiddam voluisse scriptor demonstretur; aut sic, ut in eiusmodi re et tempore hoc voluisse doceatur.

125 XLIII. Ergo is qui scriptum defendet his locis plerumque omnibus, maiore autem parte semper poterit uti: primum scriptoris collaudatione et loco communi, nihil eos qui iudicent nisi id quod scriptum[2] spectare oportere; et hoc eo magis, si legitimum scriptum proferetur, id est, aut lex ipsa aut aliquid ex lege; postea, quod vehementissimum est, facti aut intentionis adversariorum cum ipso scripto

---

[1] *After* militum *the MSS. have* suum: *bracketed by Friedrich.*

[2] *After* scriptum *SP²Ri insert* est: *J* sit.

---

[a] The case is stated more explicitly in the speech *In Defence of Milo*, 9.

[b] Above, §§ 87–98.

parison) is used, as in the case of the man who, though the law forbade opening the gates at night, opened them in a certain war and let certain auxiliary forces into the town in order that they might not be wiped out by the enemy if left outside, for the enemy was encamped near the walls.

124 Sometimes *relatio criminis* (retort of accusation) is used; an example is the case of the soldier who killed a military tribune who offered him violence,[a] although the universal law of the human race forbids killing a man. Again *remotio criminis* (shifting of the charge) may be used; an instance is the case of the ambassador who although the law set a certain date for him to proceed on his embassy did not set out because the Treasurer did not supply funds. Again one may use *concessio* (confession and avoidance) in the form of *purgatio*, by a plea of ignorance as in the case of the sacrifice of the bull-calf, or of *force majeure*, as in the case of the warship, or of accident, as in the case of the flood of the Eurotas.[b] To sum up, intent will be presented so as to show that the writer desired one definite thing, or to prove that he desired this in such circumstances and at such a time.

125 XLIII. An advocate who will defend the letter will be able to use all of the following topics most of the time, and the greater part of them on every occasion; first, high praise of the writer, and a common topic that the judges should regard nothing except what is written; and this may be made more emphatic if some statutory document is offered, *i.e.* either a whole law or some part of it; after that one may use the most effective argument, a comparison of the action and purpose of the op-

contentione, quid scriptum sit, quid factum, quid
iuratus iudex; quem locum multis modis variare
oportebit, tum ipsum secum admirantem quidnam
contra dici possit, tum ad iudicis officium rever-
tentem et ab eo quaerentem, quid praeterea audire
aut exspectare debeat; tum ipsum adversarium
quasi in testis loco producendo hoc est inter-
rogandum utrum scriptum neget esse eo modo,
an ab se contra factum esse aut contra contendi
neget; utrum negare ausus sit, se dicere desiturum.

126 Si neutrum neget et contra tamen dicat: nihil esse
quo hominem impudentiorem quisquam se visurum
arbitretur. In hoc ita commorari conveniet, quasi
nihil praeterea dicendum sit et quasi contra dici
nihil possit, saepe id quod scriptum est recitando,
saepe cum scripto factum adversarii confligendo
atque interdum acriter ad iudicem ipsum revertendo.
Quo in loco iudici demonstrandum est quid iuratus
sit, quid sequi debeat: duabus de causis iudicem
dubitare oportere, si aut scriptum sit obscure aut

127 neget aliquid adversarius; XLIV. cum et scriptum
aperte sit et adversarius omnia confiteatur, tum
iudicem legi parere, non interpretari legem oportere.

Hoc loco confirmato tum diluere ea quae contra
dici poterunt oportebit. Contra autem dicetur si
aut prorsus aliud sensisse scriptor et scripsisse aliud
demonstrabitur; ut in illa de testamento, quam

ponents with the letter of the law, showing what
was written, what was done, what the judge has
sworn to do. And it will be well to vary this topic
in many ways, first expressing wonder in his own
mind as to what can possibly be said on the other
side, then turning to the judge's duty and asking
what more he can think it necessary to hear or
expect. Then one may bring in the opponent
himself like a witness, that is ask him whether he
denies that the law is so written, or denies that he
has acted contrary to it or endeavoured so to do,
and offer to stop speaking if he dares deny either.
126 But if he denies neither statement and still con-
tinues to dispute, say that there is no reason why
any one should think that he will ever see a more
shameless man. It will be wise to linger over this
point as if it were unnecessary and impossible to
say anything more, often reading the document,
often comparing the act of the opponent with the
letter of the law, and often turning sharply to the
judge. In this connexion one should point out to
the judge what oath he has taken, and what course
he is bound to follow, saying that there are two
reasons why a judge should hesitate: if the document is obscurely drawn, or if the accused denies
127 any allegation. XLIV. That when the document is
plain and the accused confesses everything, then the
judge ought to comply with the law and not interpret
it.

When this point has been established it will be
time to attack the arguments which can be made
on the other side. Arguments will be made in
reply to either of two positions, that is, if it is shown
definitely that the writer meant one thing and

posuimus, controversia, aut causa assumptiva inferetur quamobrem scripto non potuerit aut non oportuerit obtemperari.

128 Si aliud sensisse scriptor, aliud scripsisse dicetur, is qui scripto utetur haec dicet: non oportere de eius voluntate nos argumentari, qui, ne id facere possemus, indicium nobis relinquerit suae voluntatis; multa incommoda consequi, si instituatur ut ab scripto recedatur. Nam et eos qui aliquid scribant non existimaturos id quod scripserint ratum futurum; et eos qui iudicent certum quod sequantur nihil habituros si semel ab scripto recedere consueverint. Quod si voluntas scriptoris conservanda sit, se, non adversarios, a voluntate eius stare. Nam multo propius accedere ad scriptoris voluntatem eum qui ex ipsius eam litteris interpretetur quam illum qui sententiam scriptoris non ex ipsius scripto spectet, quod ille suae voluntatis quasi imaginem reliquerit, sed domesticis suspicionibus perscrutetur.

129 Sin causam afferet is qui a sententia stabit, primum erit contra dicendum: quam absurdum non negare contra legem fecisse, sed, quare fecerit, causam aliquam invenire; deinde, conversa esse omnia: ante solitos esse accusatores iudicibus persuadere, affinem esse alicuius culpae eum qui accusaretur, causam proferre quae eum ad peccan-

wrote another, as in the controversy which we
have cited about the will, or if an assumptive argument is introduced to show why it was impossible
or undesirable to comply with the written word.

128   If the writer is alleged to have meant one thing
and written another, the advocate who follows the
letter will say: It is not right for us to argue about
the intent of one who left us a clear indication of
his intent in order that we might not be able to dispute it; that much inconvenience would result if
it should be established as a principle that we may
depart from the written word. For those who draw
up a written document will not feel that what they
have written will be fixed and unalterable, and
judges will have no sure guide to follow if once
they become accustomed to depart from the written
word. Therefore if the object is to carry out the
wish of the writer, counsel will urge that it is he
rather than the opponents who adhere to the writer's
wishes; for one gets much closer to a writer's intent
if one interprets it from the writer's own words
than one who does not learn the writer's intention
from his own written document which he has left
as a picture, one might say, of his own desires, but
makes one's own inferences.

129   If the litigant who adheres to the writer's intent
adduces a reason or excuse, the rebuttal should take
the following form: first, how absurd it is not to
deny that he broke the law, but to invent some
reason for breaking it; in the second place that the
whole world is turned upside down. Formerly
prosecutors used to persuade the judges that the
accused was implicated in a crime, and offer a
reason which impelled him to offend; now the

dum impulisset; nunc ipsum reum causam afferre
130 quare deliquerit. Deinde hanc inducere partitionem, cuius in singulas partes multae convenient
argumentationes: primum, nulla in lege ullam
causam contra scriptum accipi convenire; deinde, si
in ceteris legibus conveniat, hanc esse eiusmodi legem
ut in ea non oporteat; postremo, si in hac quoque
lege oporteat, hanc quidem causam accipi minime
oportere. XLV. Prima pars his fere locis con-
firmabitur: scriptori neque ingenium neque operam
neque ullam facultatem defuisse quo minus aperte
posset perscribere id quod cogitaret; non fuisse ei
grave nec difficile eam causam excipere quam
adversarii proferant si quicquam excipiendum
putasset: consuesse eos qui leges scribant exceptio-
131 nibus uti. Deinde oportet recitare leges cum
exceptionibus scriptas et maxime videre, ecquae in
ea ipsa lege, qua de agatur, sit exceptio aliquo in
capite aut apud eundem legis scriptorem, quo magis
probetur eum fuisse excepturum, si quid excipiendum putaret; et ostendere causam accipere nihil
aliud esse nisi legem tollere; ideo quod, cum semel
causa consideretur, nihil attineat eam ex lege considerare, quippe quae in lege scripta non sit. Quod
si sit institutum, omnibus dari causam et potestatem
peccandi, cum intellexerint vos ex ingenio eius qui
contra legem fecerit non ex lege, in quam iurati

---

a Note the sudden change to direct discourse. Cicero is
no longer listing arguments proper to the topic, but is ad-
dressing a jury (" You "). This is a quotation from a
rhetorical exercise. The same phenomenon recurs at § 139.

defendant himself offers the reason for his delin-
130 quency. Then he should introduce the following
partition, each head of which will have many suitable
arguments: first, under no law should a reason or
excuse be accepted contrary to the letter of the
law; secondly, if such a course is permissible under
other laws, this is not the kind of law under which
it should be done; finally, even if such a course is
permissible under this law, this excuse at least
should by no means be accepted. XLV. The first
topic will be supported by arguments like these:
the author of the law did not lack the intelligence,
diligence or opportunity to write plainly what he
intended; it was not hard or difficult to make an
exception of the excuse which the opposing advocates
offer, if he had thought that any exception ought to
be made. The law-makers are accustomed to make
131 exceptions. Then it will be in point to read laws
that include exceptions and in particular to see if
there is any exception in any chapter of the law in
question or in laws by the same law-maker, in order
that it may be better established that he would
have made an exception if he had thought one ought
to be made. Furthermore, one should show that
accepting an excuse is nothing more than repealing
the law, because when once an excuse is taken
into consideration there is no point in weighing it
with reference to the law, seeing that it is not
written in the law. And if this principle is set up,
all men will be given a reason and opportunity for
violating the law, when they know that you are
deciding the case by the character of the man who
broke the law rather than by the law which you are
sworn to uphold.[a] Again he may show that all

sitis, rem iudicare; deinde et ipsis iudicibus iudicandi
et ceteris civibus vivendi rationes perturbatum iri,
132 si semel ab legibus recessum sit; nam et iudices
neque quid sequantur habituros si ab eo quod
scriptum sit recedant, neque quo pacto aliis probare
possint quod contra legem iudicarint; et ceteros
cives quid agant ignoraturos si ex suo quisque
consilio et ex ea ratione quae in mentem aut in
libidinem venerit, non ex communi praescripto
civitatis unam quamque rem administrabit; postea
quaerere ab iudicibus ipsis quare in alienis detine-
antur negotiis; cur rei publicae munere impediantur,
quo setius suis rebus et commodis servire possint;
cur in certa verba iurent; cur certo tempore conveniant, cur certo discedant, nihil quisquam afferat
causae, quo minus frequenter operam rei publicae
det, nisi quae causa in lege excepta sit; an se legibus obstrictos in tantis molestiis esse aequum cen-
seant, adversarios nostros leges neglegere conce-
133 dant;[a] deinde item quaerere ab iudicibus, si eius rei
propter quam se reus contra legem fecisse dicat,
exceptionem ipse in lege ascribat, passurine sint;
hoc[1] quod faciat indignius et impudentius esse
quam si ascribat; age porro, quid, si ipsi vellent
iudices ascribere, passurusne sit populus? atque hoc
esse indignius, quam rem verbo et litteris mutare
non possint, eam re ipsa et iudicio maximo commu-
134 tare; deinde indignum esse de lege aliquid derogari

---

[1] Before hoc the *MSS.* have postea; *bracketed by Kayser.*

---

[a] I translate *concedant* as if it were *concedere*, which would
make a more logical sentence.

principles which enable judges to give judgement
and the rest of the citizens to live will be unsettled
132 if once they depart from the law; for the judges
will have no rule to follow if they depart from the
letter of the law, nor will they have any means of
winning the approval of others to their decision
which has been made contrary to the law, and other
citizens will not know what to do if every one
regulates all his affairs according to his own ideas
or any whim that strikes his mind or fancy, and not
according to the ordinances common to the whole
state. And then he may make an appeal to the
judges' own interest, asking them why they spend
their time over other people's business; why they
let public duties prevent them from serving their
own interest and advantage; why they swear a
precise and definite oath; why they assemble at a
fixed time and leave at a fixed time, and no one offers
any excuse for not serving the state frequently
except such excuse as is particularly stated in the
law. Do they think it fair that they should be
bound by law in so many annoying details, and
133 allow [a] our opponents to violate the laws? Then he
might ask the judges another question, whether
they would permit the defendant to write into the
law as an exception the excuse for which he says
he acted contrary to law; and that what he is doing
is bolder and more shameful than adding to the
law. Or to go one step further, if the judges
should desire to add a provision to the law on their
own authority, would the people permit it? But
it is bolder to alter actually by the weight of their
decision what they cannot alter by changing the
134 written words of the law. Then it may be urged

aut legem abrogari aut aliqua ex parte commutari,
cum populo cognoscendi et probandi aut impro-
bandi potestas nulla fiat; hoc ipsis iudicibus invi-
diosissimum futurum; non hunc locum esse neque
hoc tempus legum corrigendarum; apud populum
haec et per populum agi convenire; quodsi nunc
id agant, velle se scire qui lator sit, qui sint accep-
turi; se factiones videre et dissuadere velle; quodsi
haec cum summe inutilia tum multo turpissima sint,
legem, cuicuimodi sit, in praesentia conservari ab
iudicibus, post, si displiceat, a populo corrigi con_
venire; deinde, si scriptum non exstaret, magno
opere quaereremus neque isti, ne si extra periculum
quidem esset, crederemus; nunc cum scriptum sit,
amentiam esse eius qui [1] peccarit potius quam legis
ipsius verba cognoscere. His et huiusmodi rationibus
ostenditur causam extra scriptum accipi non oportere.

135   XLVI. Secunda pars est, in qua est ostendendum,
si in ceteris legibus oporteat, in hac non oportere.
Hoc demonstrabitur, si lex aut ad res maximas,
utilissimas, honestissimas, religiosissimas videbitur
pertinere; aut inutile aut turpe aut nefas esse tali
in re non diligentissime legi obtemperare; aut ita

---

[1] eius rei C.

that it is improper to repeal a law in part or in whole
or to change any provision when the people have
no opportunity to examine the matter and approve
or disapprove; that such conduct is certain to bring
the judges into ill repute; that this is not the place
nor the time to correct the laws; such action should
be taken before the people and by the people;
that if they are trying to do that now, he would
like to know who is proposing the amendment,
and what body is going to accept it; that he sees
party strife arising and wishes to resist it. In view
of this, he will urge that if the proposals of the
opposing counsel are not only highly disadvantageous
but also very scandalous, the judges ought for the
present to leave the law unchanged, whatever its
character may be, and that later it may properly
be amended by the people if they disapprove of it.
Besides, if there were no written document we
should be at great pains to get one, and we should
not believe the defendant even if he were not in
peril; but now since there is a written law it is silly
to accept the argument of the man who has broken
it rather than the plain words of the law. By these
and similar arguments it is shown that an excuse
ought not to be accepted contrary to the letter of
the law.

135   XLVI. The second head is that under which it is
made plain that departure from the letter of the law
though permissible under other laws, is not permissible in this case. This may be done if it is
made to appear that the law has to do with matters
of the highest importance, advantage, honour and
sanctity; that it is inexpedient, or base or criminal
not to follow the law most exactly in such a case. Or

303

lex diligenter perscripta demonstrabitur, ita cautum una quaque de re, ita quod oportuerit exceptum, ut minime conveniat quicquam in tam diligenti scriptura praeteritum arbitrari.

Tertius est locus ei qui pro scripto dicet maxime necessarius, per quem oportet ostendat, si conveniat causam contra scriptum accipi, eam tamen mimine 136 oportere quae ab adversariis afferatur. Qui locus idcirco est huic necessarius, quod semper is qui contra scriptum dicet aequitatis aliquid afferat oportet. Nam summa impudentia sit eum qui contra quam scriptum sit aliquid probare velit non aequitatis praesidio id facere conari. Si quid igitur ex hac ipsa [1] accusator derogat, omnibus partibus iustius et probabilius accusare videatur. Nam superior oratio hoc omnis faciebat ut, iudices etiamsi nollent, necesse esset; haec autem, etiamsi 137 necesse non esset, ut vellent contra iudicare. Id autem fiet, si, quibus ex locis culpa demonstrabitur esse in eo qui comparatione aut remotione aut relatione criminis aut concessionis partibus se defendet —de quibus ante, ut potuimus, diligenter perscripsimus—ex eis locis,[2] quae res postulabit ad causam adversariorum improbandam transferemus, aut causae et rationes afferentur quare et quo consilio ita sit in lege aut in testamento scriptum, ut sententia quoque et voluntate scriptoris, non ipsa solum scrip-

[1] ipsa quippiam *J*.
[2] ex eis locis *Weidner*: si de his *i*: si his *M*: de his *J*: si de iis *Ströbel*.

---

[a] II. 72-109.

it may be shown that the law was so carefully framed, that such provision was made for every situation and proper exceptions made, that it is not at all fitting to think that anything was omitted from a document drawn up with such care.

The third head is highly important for one who is speaking in favour of the letter; in this he should show that, if it is proper to accept an excuse contrary to the letter of the law, the excuse offered by the opponents should by no means be admitted. 136 This topic is indispensable for him because one who is speaking against the letter ought always to adduce some principle of equity. For it would be the height of impudence for one who wishes to gain approval for some act contrary to the letter of the law, not to attempt to gain his point with the help of equity. If, then, the prosecutor can weaken this argument at all, his accusation would seem in every way more just and plausible. For all the earlier part of his speech was devoted to making conviction necessary even if the judges were unwilling: but this, to making them willing to convict even if it 137 is unnecessary. This will be done if the topics which prove that guilt attaches to someone who defends himself by the arguments of comparison, or shifting the charge or retort of the accusation or confession and avoidance concerning which we have given rules as carefully as we could above,[a]—if such of these topics as the case demands are taken over to attack the excuse offered by our opponents. Or if causes and reasons are given why and with what design it was so written in the law or the will, in order that our case may seem to be supported by the intent and wish of the writer and not merely

CICERO

tura causa confirmata esse videatur, aut aliis quoque
constitutionibus factum coarguetur.

138 XLVII. Contra scriptum autem qui dicet, primum
inducet eum locum per quem aequitas causae
demonstretur; aut ostendet quo animo, quo consilio,
qua de causa fecerit; et, quamcumque causam
assumet, assumptionis partibus se defendet de quibus
ante dictum est. Atque in hoc loco cum diutius
commoratus sui facti rationem et aequitatem causae
exornaverit, tum ex his locis fere contra adversarios
dicet oportere causas accipi. Demonstrabit nullam
esse legem quae aliquam rem inutilem aut iniquam
fieri velit; omnia supplicia quae ab legibus proficiscantur culpae ac malitiae vindicandae causa
139 constituta esse; scriptorem ipsum, si exsistat, factum hoc probaturum et idem ipsum, si ei talis res
accidisset, facturum fuisse; ea re legis scriptorem
certo ex ordine iudices certa aetate praeditos
constituisse, ut essent, non qui scriptum suum
recitarent, quod quivis puer facere posset, sed
qui cogitatione assequi possent et voluntatem interpretari; deinde illum scriptorem, si scripta sua
stultis hominibus et barbaris iudicibus committeret,
omnia summa diligentia perscripturum fuisse; nunc
vero, quod intellegeret quales viri res iudicaturi
essent, idcirco eum quae perspicua videret esse non
ascripsisse; neque enim vos scripti sui recitatores,
sed voluntatis interpretes fore putavit.

---

^a §§ 71–109.
^b With this sudden change from indirect to direct state-
ment compare § 131 and note.

by the written word. Or if the crime is proved without a doubt by the use of other issues.

138   XLVII. On the other hand the speaker who is attacking the letter will first of all present the argument to prove the equity of making an excuse; or he will show with what intention or design he did what he did, and for what reason; and whatever excuse he adopts he will make his defence with the assumptive arguments which we have discussed above.[a] When he has spent some time on this topic and put a fair front on the reason for his act and the justice of his excuse, he will then use the following arguments against his opponents to prove that excuses ought to be accepted. He will point out that there is no law which requires the performance of any inexpedient or unjust act; that all penalties provided by law were established to punish wickedness and

139   vice; that the author of the law himself, if he should rise from the dead, would approve this act, and would have done the same if he had been in a similar situation; that the reason why the author of the law provided for judges from a certain class and of a certain age was that there might be a judicial body able not only to read his law, which any child could do, but to comprehend it with the mind and interpret his intentions; again, that if the law-maker had been giving his law to ignorant men and barbarous judges, he would have written everything out in precise detail; but as he knew the quality of the men who were to judge the cases, he did not add what he saw was perfectly plain. For he did not think of you as clerks to read his law aloud in court, but as interpreters of his wishes.[b]

140 Postea quaeret [1] ab adversariis: Quid, si hoc
fecisset? Quid, si hoc accidisset? Eorum aliquid,
in quibus aut causa sit honestissima aut necessitudo certissima, tamenne accusaretis? Atqui lex [2]
nusquam excepit; non ergo omnia scriptis, sed
quaedam, quae perspicua sint, tacitis exceptionibus
caveri; deinde nullam rem neque legibus neque
scriptura ulla, denique ne in sermone quidem coti-
diano atque imperiis domesticis recte posse administrari si unus quisque velit verba spectare et non
ad voluntatem eius qui ea verba habuerit accedere;

141 XLVIII. deinde ex utilitatis et honestatis partibus
ostendere quam inutile aut quam turpe sit id quod
adversarii dicant fieri oportuisse aut oportere, et id
quod nos fecerimus aut postulemus, quam utile aut
quam honestum sit; deinde leges nobis caras esse
non propter litteras, quae tenues et obscurae notae
sint voluntatis, sed propter earum rerum quibus de
scriptum est utilitatem et eorum qui scripserint
sapientiam et diligentiam; postea, quid sit lex
describere, ut ea videatur in sententiis, non in verbis
consistere; et iudex is videatur legi obtemperare
qui sententiam eius, non qui scripturam sequatur;
deinde quam indignum sit eodem affici supplicio
eum qui propter aliquod scelus et audaciam contra
leges fecerit, et eum qui honesta aut necessaria de
causa non ab sententia, sed ab litteris legis recesserit;

[1] quaeret *Schuetz*: quaerere *C.*
[2] hoc lex *J.*

140 After that he will ask his opponents: " Suppose that I had done so and so; suppose that so and so had happened—mentioning any of those acts for which there is a most honourable excuse or a certain plea of necessity—would you still accuse me? " But the law makes no exception. Therefore all cases are not covered by exceptions expressed in writing, but some that are self-evident are covered by exceptions understood but not expressed. Then it may be urged that nothing at all could be done either with laws or with any instrument in writing, or even about our every day conversation and the orders issued in our own homes, if every one wished to consider only the literal meaning of the words and not to follow the intentions of the speaker.

141 XLVIII. Then from the principles of advantage and honour he may show how inexpedient and base is the course of conduct which the opponents say we were or are bound to follow, and how advantageous and honourable is our act or request. Then, that we value the laws not because of the words, which are but faint and feeble indications of intention, but because of the advantage of the principles which they embody, and the wisdom and care of the law-makers. Next he may set forth the true nature of law, that it may be shown to consist of meanings, not of words, and that the judge who follows the meaning may seem to comply with law more than one who follows the letter. Again, how harsh it is to visit the same punishment on one who from criminal audacity has violated the laws, and on one who from some honourable and necessary cause has departed from the letter but not from the intent of the law. By these and similar arguments he will prove that on

atque his et huiusmodi rationibus et accipi causam
et in hac lege accipi et eam causam quam ipse afferat
oportere accipi demonstrabit.

142   Et quemadmodum ei dicebamus qui ab scripto
diceret hoc fore utilissimum, si quid de aequitate
ea quae cum adversario staret derogasset, sic huic
qui contra scriptum dicet plurimum proderit, ex
ipsa scriptura aliquid ad suam causam convertere
aut ambigue aliquid scriptum ostendere; deinde
ex illo ambiguo eam partem quae sibi prosit defendere
aut verbi definitionem inducere et illius verbi vim
quo urgueri videatur ad suae causae commodum
traducere aut ex scripto non scriptum aliquid inducere
143 per ratiocinationem, de qua post dicemus. Quacumque autem in re, quamvis leviter probabili, scripto
ipso defenderit, cum aequitate causa abundabit,
necessario multum proficiet, ideo quod, si id quo
nititur adversariorum causa subduxerit, omnem eius
illam vim et acrimoniam lenierit ac diluerit.

Loci autem communes ceteris ex assumptionis
partibus in utramque partem convenient. Praeterea
autem eius qui a scripto dicet: leges ex se, non ex
eius qui contra commiserit utilitate spectari oportere
et legibus antiquius haberi nihil oportere. Contra

---

^a §§ 148–53.

general principles an excuse ought sometimes to be accepted, that it ought to be accepted under this law, and that the excuse which he offers for his own actions ought to be accepted.

142 And just as we said that the speaker who is upholding the letter of the law would find it most useful to lessen in some degree the justice or equity which supports his opponent's claim, so the speaker who opposes the letter will profit greatly by converting something in the written document to his own case or by showing that it contains some ambiguity; then on the basis of that ambiguity he may defend the passage which helps his case, or introduce a definition of some word and interpret the meaning of the word which seems to bear hard upon him, so as to support his own case, or develop from the written word something that is not expressed; this is the method of reasoning from

143 analogy, which we shall discuss below.[a] In a word, in whatever way, however slightly plausible it may be, he can defend himself by appealing to the letter of the law, when his case is amply supported by abstract justice, he will profit greatly, because if he can remove the foundation on which his opponents' case rests, he will lessen and mitigate all its force and effectiveness.

Common topics from the other parts of the assumptive issue will suit both sides. In addition, however, the speaker who defends the letter of the law may use the following: laws ought to be judged with reference to their own intrinsic merits and not to the advantage of the transgressor; and that nothing should be esteemed more highly than the laws. Against the letter of the law: the value of

scriptum : leges in consilio scriptoris et utilitate communi, non in verbis consistere; quam indignum sit aequitatem litteris urgueri, quae voluntate eius qui scripserit defendatur.

144 XLIX. Ex contrariis autem legibus controversia nascitur cum inter se duae videntur leges aut plures discrepare, hoc modo: Lex: Qui tyrannum occiderit, Olympionicarum praemia capito et quam volet sibi rem a magistratu deposcito et magistratus ei concedito. Et altera lex: Tyranno occiso quinque eius proximos cognatione magistratus necato. Alexandrum, qui apud Pheraeos in Thessalia tyrannidem occuparat, uxor sua, cui Thebe nomen fuit, noctu, cum simul cubaret, occidit. Haec filium suum, quem ex tyranno habebat, sibi in praemi loco deposcit. Sunt qui ex lege occidi puerum dicant oportere. Res in iudicio est.

In hoc genere utramque in partem idem loci atque eadem praecepta convenient, ideo quod uterque suam legem confirmare, contrariam infirmare debebit. Primum igitur leges oportet contendere considerando, utra lex ad maiores, hoc est, ad utiliores, ad honestiores ac magis necessarias res pertineat; ex quo conficitur, ut, si leges duae aut si plures erunt, quotquot erunt,[1] conservari non possint, quia discrepent inter se, sed[2] ea maxime conservanda putetur, quae ad maximas res

[1] quotquot erunt R : aut quotquot erunt C.
[2] se sed M : se tamen P[3] : se J.

[a] According to Xenophon, Hell. VI. iv, 35-37, Alexander was killed by his wife's brothers with her connivance, and she

law depends on the intention of the legislator and on the common weal, not on words: how unfair it is that justice and equity, which it is the intention of the legislator to protect, should be hindered by words.

144   XLIX. A controversy arises from a conflict of laws when two or more laws seem to disagree; the following is an example. Law: A tyrannicide shall receive the reward commonly given to victors at the Olympic games and he shall ask the magistrate for whatever he wishes, and the magistrate shall give it to him. Another law: When a tyrant has been slain the magistrate shall execute his five nearest blood-relations. Alexander, who had set himself up as tyrant at Pherae in Thessaly, was killed by his wife, named Thebe, at night, when he was in bed with her. She demands as a reward her son whom she had by the tyrant. Some say that the boy ought to be executed according to law. The case is brought before a court.[a]

In this kind of case the same topics and the same rules will suit each side because each litigant will be under the necessity of supporting his own law 145 and attacking the one that conflicts. In the first place, then, one should compare the laws by considering which one deals with the most important matters, that is, the most expedient, honourable or necessary. The conclusion from this is that if two laws (or whatever number there may be if more than two) cannot be kept because they are at variance, the one is thought to have the greatest claim to be upheld which has reference to the greatest matters.

had no son. History has been altered to make a good illustration for the rhetorician.

pertinere videatur; deinde, utra lex posterius lata
sit; nam postrema quaeque gravissima est; deinde,
utra lex iubeat aliquid, utra permittat; nam id
quod imperatur, necessarium, illud quod permittitur,
voluntarium est; deinde, in utra lege, si non ob-
temporatum sit, poena adiciatur aut in utra maior
146 poena statuatur; nam maxime conservanda est ea
quae diligentissime sancta est; deinde, utra lex
iubeat, utra vetet; nam saepe ea quae vetat, quasi
exceptione quadam corrigere videtur [1] illam quae
iubet; deinde, utra lex de genere omni, utra de
parte quadam; utra communiter in plures, utra
in aliquam certam rem scripta videatur; nam quae
in partem aliquam et quae in certam quandam rem
scripta est, propius ad causam accedere videtur
et ad iudicium magis pertinere; deinde, ex lege
utrum statim fieri necesse sit, utrum habeat aliquam
moram et sustentationem; nam id quod statim
147 faciendum sit perfici prius oportet; deinde operam
dare, ut sua lex ipso scripto videatur niti, contraria
autem aut per ambiguum aut per ratiocinationem
aut per definitionem induci, cum [2] sanctius et
firmius id videatur esse quod apertius scriptum sit;
deinde suae legis ad scriptum ipsum sententiam
quoque adiungere, contrariam legem item ad aliam
sententiam transducere, ut, si fieri poterit, ne
discrepare quidem videantur inter se; postremo
facere, si causa facultatem dabit, ut nostra ratione

---

[1] videtur *PRi*: videatur *C*.
[2] cum *added by Stroux*.

In the second place, he should consider which law
was passed last, for the latest law is always the most
important; then which law enjoins some action
and which permits, for that which is commanded
is necessary, that which is permitted is optional;
then in which law a penalty is prescribed for non-
compliance or which law has the greater penalty,
146 for that law has the highest claim to be upheld in
which the penalties are most carefully prescribed;
then which law enjoins and which prohibits, for
frequently the law that prohibits seems to have
amended the law that enjoins by making an exception; then, which law applies to a whole class, and
which to a subdivision; which seems to have been
framed with reference to many cases in common,
and which to one certain case, for the law that is
framed to apply to some part or to some particular situation seems to get closer to the case
and have a closer relation to the trial; whether
in one case the law enjoins immediate action,
and in the other admits of some postponement or
delay, for what must be done immediately should
147 be done first. Again, the litigant should be at some
pains to show that his law rests on the precise
language in which it is drawn, whereas the contradictory law is brought in through an ambiguity or
by reasoning by analogy, or by definition, since what
is plainly stated seems to be stronger and more
binding. Again, he should show that in his law the
intent is at one with the letter, and then prove that
the other law has a different intent, so that, if
possible, it may appear that the two do not even
disagree. Finally, if the circumstances of the
case permit, we should make it clear that on

utraque lex conservari videatur, adversariorum
ratione altera sit necessario neglegenda.

Locos autem communes et quos ipsa causa det
videre oportebit et ex utilitatis et ex honestatis
amplissimis partibus sumere demonstrantem per
amplificationem ad utram potius legem accedere
oporteat.

148 L. Ex ratiocinatione nascitur controversia cum
ex eo quod uspiam est ad id quod nusquam scriptum est venitur, hoc pacto: Lex: Si furiosus est,
agnatum gentiliumque in eo pecuniaque eius potestas esto. Et lex: Paterfamilias uti super familia
pecuniaque sua legassit, ita ius esto. Et lex: Si
paterfamilias intestato moritur, familia pecuniaque
149 eius agnatum gentiliumque esto. Quidam iudicatus
est parentem occidisse et statim, quod effugiendi
potestas non fuit, ligneae soleae in pedes inditae
sunt; os autem obvolutum est folliculo et praeliga-
tum; deinde est in carcerem deductus, ut ibi esset
tantisper, dum culleus, in quem coniectus in pro-
fluentem deferretur, compararetur. Interea quidam eius familiares in carcerem tabulas afferunt et
testes adducunt; heredes, quos ipse iubet, scribunt;
tabulae obsignantur. De illo post supplicium sumitur. Inter eos qui heredes in tabulis scripti sunt,
et inter agnatos de hereditate controversia est.

---

[a] Literally, ratiocination or reasoning. The method of
stretching a statute to cover an analogous case is common
in modern law, but there seems to be no technical term to
denote it. A lawyer would probably say that the case
" comes within the purview of the statute."

[b] Agnates are near kin on the male side, gentiles all those
bearing the same " gentile " name, *e.g.* Cornelius, Julius.

[c] " Household " here means slaves, and " property "
inanimate objects.

our principles both laws are upheld, and on the opponents' one must be disregarded.

It will be well to consider the common topics offered by the case itself and to borrow some from the most general topics of advantage and honour, pointing out in passages of amplification to which law adherence should be given.

148 L. A controversy arises from reasoning from analogy [a] when from a statement written somewhere one arrives at a principle which is written nowhere after this fashion: there is a law, If a man is mad, his agnates and gentiles [b] shall have power over him and his property; and another law: In whatever way a head of a household has made a will concerning his household and property,[c] so let it be; and another law: If a head of a household dies intestate, his household and property shall 149 go to the agnates and gentiles. A certain man was convicted of murdering a parent,[d] and because there was no chance of his avoiding the penalty, the wooden sandals were immediately put on his feet, his head was covered and tied up with a bag and he was then taken to prison to stay there until they could get ready the sack into which he was to be placed before being thrown into the river.[e] Meanwhile some of his friends bring tablets and witnesses to the prison, they write a will naming as heirs those whom he wished; the tablets are sealed. Later he was executed. A controversy about succession arose between the heirs that were

---

[d] *Auctor ad Her.* in citing the same case (I. 23) says that he killed his mother.

[e] The parricide was sewn in a sack with a dog, a cock, a viper and a monkey, and thrown into the river, or sea.

Hic certa lex, quae testamenti faciendi eis qui in eo loco sint adimat potestatem, nulla profertur. Ex ceteris legibus et quae hunc ipsum supplicio eiusmodi afficiunt et quae ad testamenti faciendi potestatem pertinent, per ratiocinationem veniendum est ad eiusmodi rationem, ut quaeratur, habueritne testamenti faciendi potestatem.

150 Locos autem communes in hoc genere argumentandi hos et huiusmodi quosdam esse arbitramur: primum eius scripti quod proferas laudationem et confirmationem; deinde eius rei qua de quaeratur cum eo de quo constet collationem eiusmodi, ut id de quo quaeritur ei, de qua constet, simile esse videatur; postea admirationem per contentionem, qui fieri possit ut qui hoc aequum esse concedat illud neget, quod aut aequius aut eodem sit in genere; deinde idcirco de hac re nihil esse scriptum quod, cum de illa esset scriptum, de hac is qui scribebat dubitaturum neminem arbitratus sit; 151 postea multis in legibus multa praeterita esse, quae idcirco praeterita nemo arbitretur, quod ex ceteris de quibus scriptum sit intellegi possint; deinde aequitas rei demonstranda est, ut in iuridiciali absoluta.

Contra autem qui dicet, similitudinem infirmare debebit; quod faciet, si demonstrabit illud, quod

named in the will, and the agnates. In this case no law is offered which definitely deprives those in such a situation of testamentary capacity. But on the basis of other laws, both those which visit a penalty of this sort on the man, and those which relate to testamentary capacity, one must come by reasoning from analogy to a consideration of the question whether or not he possessed testamentary capacity.

150 As for topics, we are of the opinion that in this style of argument the following and others of similar nature are used: first, praise and support of the law which you quote; then a comparison of the circumstances in question with the accepted principles of the law in order to show the similarity between the circumstances in question and the established principle; then comparing the two cases the speaker will wonder how it can be that one who grants that one is fair, should deny that the other is, which as a matter of fact is just as fair or fairer. Then he may argue that no rule was laid down for this case, because when the rule was made for the other, the author of the law thought that no one would 151 have any hesitation about this case; furthermore, that many provisions have been omitted in many laws, but nobody thinks that they have been omitted, because they can be inferred from the other cases about which rules have been laid down. Finally, he should point out the fairness of his position, as is done in the absolute subdivision of the equitable issue.

The litigant who is opposing the extension of the law will have to attack the similarity of the two cases, which he will do if he points out that the cases

conferatur, diversum esse genere, natura, vi, magnitudine, tempore, loco, persona, opinione; si, quo
in numero illud quod per similitudinem afferetur,
et quo in loco illud cuius causa afferetur, haberi
conveniat, ostendetur; deinde, quid res cum re
differat, demonstrabitur, ut non idem videatur de
152 utraque existimari oportere. Ac, si ipse quoque
poterit ratiocinationibus uti, isdem rationibus, quibus ante praedictum est, utetur; si non poterit,
negabit oportere quicquam, nisi quod scriptum sit,
considerare; multas de similibus rebus et in unam
quamque rem tamen singulas esse leges; omnia
posse inter se vel similia vel dissimilia demonstrari.

Loci communes: a ratiocinatione, oportere coniectura ex eo quod scriptum sit ad id quod non sit
scriptum pervenire; et neminem posse omnes res
per scripturam amplecti, sed eum commodissime
scribere qui curet ut quaedam ex quibusdam in-
153 tellegantur; contra ratiocinationem huiusmodi:
coniecturam divinationem esse et stulti scriptoris
esse non posse omnibus de rebus cavere quibus
velit.

LI. Definitio est cum in scripto verbum aliquod
est positum cuius de vi quaeritur, hoc modo: Lex:
Qui in adversa tempestate navem reliquerint, omnia
amittunto; eorum navis et onera sunto qui in nave
remanserint. Duo quidam, cum iam in alto navi-
garent, et cum eorum alterius navis, alterius onus
esset, naufragum quendam natantem et manus ad
se tendentem animum adverterunt; misericordia
commoti navem ad eum applicarunt, hominem ad

---

^a *Cf.* I. 82 note *c*.

compared differ in kind, nature, meaning, importance, time, place, person or repute,[a] and in particular, if it is shown in what class it is proper to put that which is cited as similar, and in what group to put that which the comparison is intended to illumine so that it may seem that it is not proper to take the same position in regard to both. And if he too can 152 use reasoning by analogy, he may adopt the same arguments that have been set forth above; if he cannot, he will deny that anything should be considered except the letter of the law; saying that there are many laws about similar cases, but only one law applicable to any one case; and that all things can be proved to be like or unlike.

Common topics: in favour of reasoning by analogy, that it is proper to proceed by inference from what is written to what is not written, and that no one can include every case in one statute but that he makes the most suitable law who takes care that some things may be understood from certain others. 153 Against reasoning by analogy as follows: that inference is no better than divination, and that it is a stupid lawmaker who cannot provide for every case that he desires.

LI. Definition is used in a case in which a document contains some word the meaning of which is questioned. The following is an instance. Law: "Whoever abandons ship in time of storm, shall lose everything; the ship and the cargo shall belong to those who have remained on the ship." Two men were sailing on the high seas; one owned the ship, the other, the cargo. They caught sight of a shipwrecked mariner swimming and begging for help. Taking pity on him they brought the ship

154 se sustulerunt. Postea aliquanto ipsos quoque tempestas vehementius iactare coepit, usque adeo, ut dominus navis, cum idem gubernator esset, in scapham confugeret et inde funiculo qui a puppi religatus scapham annexam trahebat navi quoad posset moderaretur, ille autem cuius merces erant in gladium in navi ibidem incumberet. Hic ille naufragus ad gubernaculum accessit et navi, quod potuit, est opitulatus. Sedatis autem fluctibus et tempestate iam commutata navis in portum pervehitur. Ille autem, qui in gladium incubuerat, leviter saucius facile ex vulnere est recreatus. Navem cum onere horum trium suam quisque esse dicit. Hic omnes scripto ad causam accedunt et ex nominis vi nascitur controversia. Nam et relinquere navem et remanere in navi, denique navis ipsa quid sit, definitionibus quaeretur. Isdem autem ex locis omnibus quibus definitiva constitutio tractabitur.

155 Nunc expositis eis argumentationibus quae in iudiciale causarum genus accommodantur, deinceps in deliberativum genus et demonstrativum argumentandi locos et praecepta dabimus, non quo non in aliqua constitutione omnis semper causa versetur, sed quia proprii tamen harum causarum quidam loci sunt, non a constitutione separati, sed ad fines

156 horum generum accommodati. Nam placet in iudiciali genere finem esse aequitatem, hoc est,

---

a This case smells of scholastic rhetoric. It is ingeniously constructed to make decision difficult; almost too ingeniously. What good could the man in the dinghy do by pulling on the tow line? The parallel case in *ad Herennium* I, 19 is simpler; there all abandon ship except one who is too ill to leave. The ship is saved by accident and is claimed by the sailor who did not leave because he could not. There

154 alongside and took him on board. Shortly afterward, they too, began to be tossed about by a violent storm, so violent in fact that the owner of the ship who was also the pilot, took refuge in the skiff, and from there guided the ship, as far as he could, by the line by which the skiff was towed from the stern of the vessel. The owner of the cargo then and there fell on his sword on the ship. The shipwrecked sailor took the helm and did what he could to save the ship. When the weather changed and the sea went down the ship got into port. The merchant who had fallen on his sword proved to have only a slight wound and made a quick recovery. Each of the three claims the ship and cargo.[a] In this instance all come into court relying on the letter of the law, and the controversy arises over the meaning of words. For they will seek to define " abandon ship " and " remain on ship " and finally " ship " itself. The case will be argued by using the same topics that apply to the issue of definition.[b]

155 Now that I have explained the forms of argumentation that fit the forensic type of speech, I shall next give the topics and the rules for the presentation of arguments in the deliberative and epideictic types. It is not that every speech does not always turn on some *constitutio* (or issue), but there are certain topics that are peculiar to these speeches; they are not distinct from the " issues," but are particularly appropriate to the ends proposed for

156 these types of speech. For example, it is generally agreed that the end in the forensic type is equity,

is another variant form of the story in *Hermogenes* (II, 141, 11 Sp.).

[b] Above, §§ 52-6.

partem quandam honestatis. In deliberativo autem
Aristoteli placet utilitatem, nobis et honestatem
et utilitatem; in demonstrativo, honestatem. Quare
in [1] quoque genere causae quaedam argumentationes communiter ac similiter tractabuntur,
quaedam separatius ad finem quo referri omnem
orationem oportet adiungentur. Atque unius
cuiusque constitutionis exemplum supponere non
gravaremur, nisi illud videremus, quemadmodum
res obscurae dicendo fierent apertiores sic res apertas
obscuriores fieri oratione.

Nunc ad deliberationis praecepta pergamus.
157 LII. Rerum expetendarum tria genera sunt; par
autem numerus vitandarum ex contraria parte.
Nam est quiddam quod sua vi nos alliciat ad sese,
non emolumento captans aliquo, sed trahens sua
dignitate, quod genus virtus, scientia, veritas. Est
aliud autem non propter suam vim et naturam, sed
propter fructum atque utilitatem petendum; quod
genus pecunia est. Est porro quiddam ex horum
partibus iunctum, quod et sua vi et dignitate nos
illectos ducit et prae se quandam gerit utilitatem,
quo magis expetatur, ut amicitia, bona existimatio.
Atque ex his horum contraria facile, tacentibus
158 nobis, intellegentur. Sed ut expeditius ratio trada-
tur, ea quae posuimus brevi nominabuntur. Nam
in primo genere quae sunt honesta appellabuntur;
quae autem in secundo, utilia. Haec autem tertia,

---

[1] *After* in *the MSS. have* hoc: *bracketed by Lambinus.*

i.e. a subdivision of the larger topic of "honour." In the deliberative type, however, Aristotle accepts advantage as the end, but I prefer both honour and advantage. In the epideictic speech it is honour alone. Therefore certain forms of argument will be handled in the same way that is common to every kind of speech, but others will have a distinct reference to the end to which the whole speech should tend. And I should not hesitate to give an example of each " issue " if I did not see that just as obscure problems are cleared up by discussion, so plain cases can be obscured by too much language.

157 Now let us proceed to the rules for deliberative oratory. LII. There are three kinds of things to be sought, and on the opposite side an equal number to be avoided. There is, namely, something which draws us to it by its intrinsic merit, not winning us by any prospect of gain, but attracting us by its own worth; to this class belong virtue, knowledge and truth. But there is something else that is to be sought not because of its own merit and natural goodness, but because of some profit or advantage to be derived from it. Money is in this class. There is, furthermore, something which unites qualities from both these classes; by its own merit and worth it entices us and leads us on, and also holds out to us a prospect of some advantage to induce us to seek it more eagerly. Examples are friendship and a good reputation. And these will easily suggest their opposites without our saying more.

158 But that the principle may be stated more concisely, we shall give them names in a few words. The things in the first class will be called honourable, those in the second, advantageous. Because the

quia partem honestatis continent et quia maior est vis honestatis, iuncta esse omnino et duplici genere intelleguntur, sed in meliorem partem vocabuli conferuntur et honesta nominentur. Ex his illud conficitur ut petendarum rerum partes sint honestas et utilitas, vitandarum turpitudo et inutilitas. His igitur duabus rebus res duae grandes sunt attributae, necessitudo et affectio; quarum altera ex vi, altera ex re et personis consideratur. De utraque post apertius perscribemus; nunc honestatis rationes primum explicemus.

159   LIII. Quod aut totum aut aliqua ex parte propter se petitur, honestum nominabimus. Quare, cum eius duae partes sint, quarum altera simplex, altera iuncta sit, simplicem prius consideremus. Est igitur in eo genere omnes res una vi atque uno nomine amplexa virtus. Nam virtus est animi habitus naturae modo atque rationi consentaneus. Quamobrem omnibus eius partibus cognitis tota vis erit simplicis honestatis considerata. Habet igitur partes quattuor: prudentiam, iustitiam, fortitudinem, temperantiam.

160   Prudentia est rerum bonarum et malarum neutrarumque scientia. Partes eius: memoria, intellegentia, providentia. Memoria est per quam animus repetit illa quae fuerunt; intellegentia, per quam ea perspicit quae sunt; providentia, per quam futurum aliquid videtur ante quam factum est.

---

[a] " Affection " is used in the older philosophical meaning of " a temporary or non-essential state, condition or relation of anything."

[b] Below, §§ 170–5.

[c] Here, as in many other passages, *honestum* is used to translate the Greek καλόν, and denotes " honour " in a broad sense; " moral beauty " might be a more exact rendering.

third group possesses some of the characteristics of honour, and because honour is a higher quality, we may apply the better term to them and call them honourable, although it is understood that they are undoubtedly complex and belong to both groups. From this it follows that honour and advantage are the qualities of things to be sought, and baseness and disadvantage, of things to be avoided. These two classes—things to be sought and things to be avoided—are related to two important circumstances—necessity and affection.[a] Necessity is considered with reference to force, and affection with reference to events and persons. We shall write at length with somewhat more detail about both later in the book.[b] Now let us explain the nature of what is honourable.

159 LIII. We shall call honourable [c] anything that is sought wholly or partly for its own sake. Now, since it has two divisions, one simple and the other complex, let us consider the simple one first. Everything in this class is embraced in one meaning and under one name, virtue. Virtue may be defined as a habit of mind in harmony with reason and the order of nature. Therefore when we have become acquainted with all its parts we shall have considered the full scope of honour, pure and simple. It has four parts: wisdom, justice, courage, temperance.

160 Wisdom is the knowledge of what is good, what is bad and what is neither good nor bad. Its parts are memory, intelligence, and foresight. Memory is the faculty by which the mind recalls what has happened. Intelligence is the faculty by which it ascertains what is. Foresight is the faculty by which it is seen that something is going to occur before it occurs.

Iustitia est habitus animi communi utilitate
conservata suam cuique tribuens dignitatem. Eius
initium est ab natura profectum; deinde quaedam
in consuetudinem ex utilitatis ratione venerunt;
postea res et ab natura profectas et ab consuetudine
161 probatas legum metus et religio sanxit. Naturae ius
est quod non opinio genuit, sed quaedam in natura
vis insevit, ut religionem, pietatem, gratiam, vindicationem, observantiam, veritatem. Religio est,
quae superioris cuiusdam naturae, quam divinam
vocant, curam caerimoniamque affert; pietas, per
quam sanguine coniunctis patriaeque benivolum
officium et diligens tribuitur cultus; gratia, in qua
amicitiarum et officiorum alterius memoria et
remunerandi voluntas continetur; vindicatio, per
quam vis aut iniuria et omnino omne, quod obfu-
turum est, defendendo aut ulciscendo propulsatur;
observantia, per quam homines aliqua dignitate
antecedentes cultu quodam et honore dignantur;
veritas, per quam immutata ea quae sunt aut ante
fuerunt aut futura sunt dicuntur.

162   LIV. Consuetudine ius est, quod aut leviter a
natura tractum aluit et maius fecit usus, ut religionem; aut si quid eorum quae ante diximus ab
natura profectum maius factum propter consuetudinem videmus, aut quod in morem vetustas vulgi
approbatione perduxit; quod genus pactum est,

---

a With these definitions compare the similar but variant
version given above, §§ 65–7.

Justice is a habit of mind which gives every man his desert while preserving the common advantage. Its first principles proceed from nature, then certain rules of conduct became customary by reason of their advantage; later still both the principles that proceeded from nature and those that had been approved by custom received the support of religion 161 and the fear of the law. The law of nature is that which is not born of opinion, but implanted in us by a kind of innate instinct: it includes religion, duty, gratitude, revenge, reverence and truth. Religion is that which brings men to serve and worship a higher order of nature which they call divine. Duty is the feeling which renders kind offices and loving service to one's kin and country. Gratitude embraces the memory of friendships and of services rendered by another, and the desire to requite these benefits. Revenge is the act of defending or avenging ourselves and so warding off violence, injury or anything which is likely to be prejudicial. Reverence is the feeling by which men of distinguished position are held worthy of respect and honour. Truth is the quality by which events in the past, present or future are referred to without alteration of material fact.[a]

162 LIV. Customary law is either a principle that is derived only in a slight degree from nature and has been fed and strengthened by usage—religion, for example—or any of the laws that we have mentioned before which we see proceed from nature but which have been strengthened by custom, or any principle which lapse of time and public approval have made the habit or usage of the community. Among these are covenants, equity and decisions. A

par, iudicatum. Pactum est quod inter aliquos convenit; par, quod in omnes aequabile est; iudicatum, de quo alicuius aut aliquorum iam sententiis constitutum est. Lege ius est, quod in eo scripto, quod populo expositum est, ut observet, continetur.

163 Fortitudo est considerata periculorum susceptio et laborum perpessio. Eius partes magnificentia, fidentia, patientia, perseverantia. Magnificentia est rerum magnarum et excelsarum cum animi ampla quadam et splendida propositione cogitatio atque administratio; fidentia est per quam magnis et honestis in rebus multum ipse animus in se fiduciae certa cum spe collocavit; patientia est honestatis aut utilitatis causa rerum arduarum ac difficilium

164 voluntaria ac diuturna perpessio; perseverantia est in ratione bene considerata stabilis et perpetua permansio.

Temperantia est rationis in libidinem atque in alios non rectos impetus animi firma et moderata dominatio. Eius partes continentia, clementia, modestia. Continentia est per quam cupiditas consili gubernatione regitur; clementia, per quam animi temere in odium alicuius inferioris [1] concitati comitate retinentur; modestia, per quam pudor honesti curam et stabilem comparat auctoritatem. Atque haec omnia propter se solum, ut nihil adiungatur emolumenti, petenda sunt. Quod ut demonstretur neque ad hoc nostrum institutum pertinet et

---

[1] inferioris *Lambinus*: iniectionis *M*: invectionis *P³J*.

---

[a] The text is corrupt and the meaning uncertain. The restoration and translation which I have given is suggested

covenant is an agreement between some persons.
Equity is what is just and fair to all. A decision is
something determined previously by the opinion
of some person or persons. Statute law is what is
contained in a written document which is published
for the people to observe.

163 Courage is the quality by which one undertakes
dangerous tasks and endures hardships. Its parts
are highmindedness, confidence, patience, perseverance. Highmindedness consists in the con-
templation and execution of great and sublime
projects with a certain grandeur and magnificence
of imagination. Confidence is the quality by which
in important and honourable undertakings the spirit
has placed great trust in itself with a resolute hope
of success. Patience is a willing and sustained
endurance of difficult and arduous tasks for a noble
164 and useful end. Perseverance is a firm and abiding
persistence in a well-considered plan of action.

Temperance is a firm and well-considered control
exercised by the reason over lust and other improper
impulses of the mind. Its parts are continence,
clemency, and modesty. Continence is the control
of desire by the guidance of wisdom. Clemency
is a kindly and gentle restraint of spirits that have
been provoked to dislike of a person of inferior
rank.[a] Modesty is a sense of shame or decency
which secures observance and firm authority for
what is honourable. All these qualities are desirable
for their own sake, though no profit be connected
with them. To prove this is not pertinent to our
present purpose nor is it consistent with the brevity

by a definition in Seneca *de Clementia*, 2, 31. Clemency is
gentleness of a superior to an inferior.

165 a brevitate praecipiendi remotum est. Propter se
autem vitanda sunt non ea modo quae his contraria
sunt, ut fortitudini ignavia et iustitiae iniustitia,
verum etiam illa quae propinqua videntur et finitima
esse, absunt autem longissime; quod genus, fidentiae
contrarium est diffidentia et ea re vitium est;
audacia non contrarium, sed appositum est ac
propinquum et tamen vitium est. Sic uni cuique
virtuti finitimum vitium reperietur, aut certo iam
nomine appellatum, ut audacia, quae fidentiae,
pertinacia, quae perseverantiae finitima est, super-
stitio, quae religioni propinqua est, aut sine ullo
certo nomine. Quae omnia item uti contraria rerum
bonarum in rebus vitandis reponentur.

Ac de eo quidem genere honestatis quod omni ex
166 parte propter se petitur, satis dictum est. LV.
Nunc de eo in quo utilitas quoque adiungitur, quod
tamen honestum vocamus, dicendum videtur. Sunt
igitur multa quae nos cum dignitate tum quoque
fructu suo ducunt; quo in genere est gloria, dignitas,
amplitudo, amicitia. Gloria est frequens de aliquo
fama cum laude; dignitas est alicuius honesta et
cultu et honore et verecundia digna auctoritas;
amplitudo potentiae aut maiestatis aut aliquarum
copiarum magna abundantia; amicitia voluntas erga
aliquem rerum bonarum illius ipsius causa quem

165 required in a text-book. On the other side the qualities to be avoided for their own sake are not only the opposites of these—as, for example, cowardice is the opposite of courage, and injustice of justice—but also those qualities which seem akin and close to these but are really far removed from them. To illustrate, diffidence is the opposite of confidence, and is therefore a vice; temerity is not opposite to courage, but borders on it and is akin to it, and yet is a vice. In a similar way each virtue will be found to have a vice bordering upon it, either one to which a definite name has become attached, as temerity which borders on courage, or stubbornness, which borders on perseverance, or superstition which is akin to religion; or one without any definite name. All of these as well as the opposites of good qualities will be classed among things to be avoided.

Enough has been said about the kind of honourable thing that is sought entirely for its own sake.

166 LV. Now I think I should speak of that which is also coupled with advantage; which, nevertheless, we call honourable. There are then many things that attract us not only by their intrinsic worth but also by the advantage to be derived from them; this class includes glory, rank, influence, and friendship. Glory consists in a person's having a widespread reputation accompanied by praise. Rank is the possession of a distinguished office which merits respect, honour, and reverence. Influence is a fulness of power, dignity, or resources of some sort. Friendship is a desire to do good to some one simply for the benefit of the person whom one loves, with a requital of the feeling on his

CICERO

167 diligit cum eius pari voluntate. Hic, quia de civilibus causis loquimur, fructus ad amicitiam adiungimus
ut eorum quoque causa petenda videatur; ne forte
qui nos de omni amicitia dicere existimant, repre-
hendere incipiant. Quamquam sunt qui propter
utilitatem modo petendam putant amicitiam; sunt
qui propter se solum; sunt qui propter se et utilitatem. Quorum quid verissime constituatur, alius
locus erit considerandi. Nunc hoc sic ad usum
oratorium relinquatur, utramque propter rem amici-
168 tiam esse expetendam. Amicitiarum autem ratio,
quoniam partim sunt religionibus iunctae, partim
non sunt, et quia partim veteres sunt, partim novae,
partim ab illorum, partim ab nostro beneficio profectae, partim utiliores, partim minus utiles, ex
causarum dignitatibus, ex temporum opportuni-
tatibus, ex officiis, ex religionibus, ex vetustatibus
habebitur.

LVI. Utilitas autem aut in corpore posita est aut
in extrariis rebus; quarum tamen rerum multo
maxima pars ad corporis commodum revertitur, ut
in re publica quaedam sunt quae, ut sic dicam, ad
corpus pertinent civitatis, ut agri, portus, pecunia,
classis, nautae, milites, socii, quibus rebus incolumitatem ac libertatem retinent civitates, aliae
vero, quae iam quiddam magis amplum et minus
necessarium conficiunt, ut urbis egregia exornatio
atque amplitudo, ut quaedam excellens pecuniae
magnitudo, amicitiarum ac societatum multitudo.

167 part. Since we are here discussing speeches about public issues, we associate friendship with benefits to be derived from it, so that it may seem desirable because of these as well as for its own sake. I say this that I may not perhaps be taken to task by those who think I am speaking of every kind of friendship. As a matter of fact there are some who think that friendship is to be sought solely for advantage, others, for itself alone, and others for itself and for advantage. Which opinion has the best foundation is a matter to be considered at another time. For the present let it be left thus as far as oratorical practice is concerned, that friendship is to be sought 168 for both reasons. In as much as some friendships are related to religious scruples, and some not, and some are old and some new, some arise from a kindness done to us by others, and some from our own services to them, some are more advantageous and some less, an examination of their nature will involve a consideration of the value of causes, the suitableness of times and occasion, moral obligation, religious duties, and length of time.

LVI. Advantage lies either in the body or in things outside the body. By far the largest part of external advantages, however, results in advantage of the body. For example, in the state there are some things that, so to speak, pertain to the body politic, such as fields, harbours, money, a fleet, sailors, soldiers and allies—the means by which states preserve their safety and liberty—and other things contribute something grander and less necessary, such as the great size and surpassing beauty of a city, an extraordinary amount of money and a multitude of friendships and alliances.

169 Quibus rebus non illud solum conficitur ut salvae
et incolumes, verum etiam ut amplae atque potentes
sint civitates. Quare utilitatis duae partes videntur
esse, incolumitas et potentia. Incolumitas est
salutis rata atque integra conservatio; potentia est
ad sua conservanda et alterius attenuanda idone-
arum rerum facultas. Atque in eis omnibus quae
ante dicta sunt, quid fieri et quid facile fieri possit,
oportet considerare. Facile id dicemus quod sine
magno aut sine ullo labore, sumptu, molestia quam
brevissimo tempore confici potest; posse autem fieri
quod quamquam laboris, sumptus, molestiae, longin-
quitatis indiget atque[1] omnes aut plurimas aut
maximas causas habet difficultatis, tamen, his sus-
ceptis difficultatibus, confieri atque ad exitum
perduci potest.

170 Quoniam ergo de honestate et de utilitate diximus, nunc restat ut de eis rebus quas his attributas
esse dicebamus, necessitudine et affectione, per-
scribamus. LVII. Puto igitur esse hanc necessitudinem, cui nulla vi resisti potest, quo ea setius id
quod facere potest perficiat, quae neque mutari
neque leniri potest. Atque, ut apertius hoc sit,
exemplo licet vim rei qualis et quanta sit cognosca-
mus. Uri posse flamma ligneam materiam necesse
est. Corpus mortale aliquo tempore interire necesse
est; atque ita necesse, ut vis postulat ea, quam
modo describebamus, necessitudinis.[2] Huiusmodi
necessitudines cum in dicendi rationes incident,
recte necessitudines appellabuntur; sin aliquae res
accident difficiles, in illa superiore, possitne fieri,

[1] atque *M* : atque aut *J*.
[2] Atque . . . necessitudinis *bracketed by Friedrich, Ströbel.*

---

[a] See note on § 158,

169 These things not only make states safe and secure, but
also important and powerful. Therefore, there seem
to be two parts of advantage—security and power.
Security is a reasoned and unbroken maintenance
of safety. Power is the possession of resources
sufficient for preserving one's self and weakening
another. Moreover, it is proper to inquire in connexion with all these things that have been mentioned
above, what can be done and what can easily be
done. We shall call easy anything which can be
accomplished in the shortest possible time without
great or without any exertion, expense or trouble.
A task is said to be possible which although it
requires exertion, expense, trouble or long-continued
effort and presents every reason for considering it
difficult, or at least the most or greatest reasons,
can nevertheless, if these difficulties are faced, be
accomplished and brought to an end.

170 Now that we have discussed honour and advantage
there remain to be described the qualities that go
with these, namely necessity and affection.[a] LVII.
I regard necessity as something that no force can
resist and thereby one is prevented from accomplishing some possible task; and this necessity cannot
be altered or alleviated. To make the matter plainer,
we may use an illustration to show the nature and
extent of its influence. It is necessary that anything
made of wood is capable of being consumed by fire.
It is necessary that a mortal body die at some time or
other. And it is necessary in the way that the force
of necessity, which we just now described, requires.
When necessities of this sort come up in planning
a speech, they are rightly called necessities; but
if other matters arise that are merely difficult we

171 quaestione considerabimus. Atque etiam hoc mihi
videor videre, esse quasdam cum adiunctione necessitudines, quasdam simplices et absolutas. Nam
aliter dicere solemus: "Necesse est Casilinenses
se dedere Hannibali." Aliter autem: "Necesse est
Casilinum venire in Hannibalis potestatem." Illic,
in superiore, adiunctio est haec: "Nisi si malunt
fame perire." Si enim id malunt, non est necesse;
hoc inferius non item, propterea quod, sive velint
Casilinenses se dedere sive famem perpeti atque ita
perire, necesse est Casilinum venire in Hannibalis
potestatem. Quid igitur haec perficere potest
necessitudinis distributio? Prope dicam plurimum
cum locus necessitudinis videbitur incurrere. Nam
cum simplex erit necessitudo, nihil erit quod multa
dicamus, cum eam nulla ratione lenire possimus;
172 cum autem ita necesse erit, si aliquid effugere aut
adipisci velimus, tum adiunctio illa᾿ quid habeat
utilitatis atque honestatis, erit considerandum. Nam
si velis attendere, ita tamen ut id quaeras quod
conveniat ad usum civitatis, reperias nullam esse
rem quam facere necesse sit, nisi propter aliquam
causam, quam adiunctionem nominamus; pariter
autem esse multas res necessitatis, ad quas similis
adiunctio non accedit; quod genus,[1] homines mor-
tales necesse est interire, sine adiunctione; ut cibo

---

[1] *After the MSS. have* ut: *bracketed by Ernesti.*

---

a § 169.

shall consider them under the question discussed
171 above:[a] Can it be done? Furthermore, I seem to
see that there are some necessities with qualifications
and some that are simple and absolute. For example,
we use the word in one sense when we say: " It
is necessary for the people of Casilinum to surrender
to Hannibal," but in a different sense when we
say: " It is necessary for Casilinum to fall into the
power of Hannibal." In the first case there is this
qualification: " Unless they prefer to die of starvation." For if they prefer that, it is not necessary
to surrender. But in the second statement the
case is not the same, because whether the people
of Casilinum choose to surrender or to face starvation
and so perish, it is necessary that Casilinum fall into
the power of Hannibal. What can be accomplished by such a distinction between different
kinds of necessity? I might say, a great deal,
when it seems likely that the subject of necessity
will come up. For when the necessity is simple
there is no reason for saying a great deal since it is
172 utterly impossible to modify it. When, however,
we use the word necessary meaning thereby that
an act is necessary if we wish to avoid or gain something, then we must consider to what extent that
qualification is advantageous or honourable. For if
you would observe, under condition, however, that
you seek the thing that will conduce to the advantage of the state, you would find that there is nothing
which must be done except for some reason which
we call the qualification. In the same way there are
many acts of necessity for which there is no similar
qualification. In this class is the statement that
mortal men must die, without qualification. It is not

utantur, non necesse est, nisi cum illa exceptione
173 "extra quam, si nolint fame perire." Ergo, ut dico,
illud quod adiungitur semper cuiusmodi sit erit considerandum. Nam omni tempore id pertinebit, ut
aut ad honestatem hoc modo exponenda necessitudo
sit : " Necesse est si honeste volumus vivere ; " aut ad
incolumitatem, hoc modo : " Necesse est si incolumes
volumus esse ; " aut ad commoditatem, hoc modo :
" Necesse est si sine incommodo volumus vivere."

LVIII. Ac summa quidem necessitudo videtur
esse honestatis ; huic proxima, incolumitatis ; tertia
ac levissima, commoditatis ; quae cum his nunquam
174 poterit duabus contendere. Hasce autem inter
se saepe necesse est comparari, ut, quamquam
praestet honestas incolumitati, tamen utri potissimum consulendum sit deliberetur. Cuius rei certum
quoddam praescriptum videtur in perpetuum dari
posse. Nam, qua in re fieri poterit, ut, cum incolumitati consuluerimus, quod sit in praesentia de
honestate delibatum, virtute aliquando et industria
recuperetur, incolumitatis ratio videbitur habenda ;
cum autem id non poterit, honestatis. Ita in
huiusmodi quoque re, cum incolumitati videbimur
consulere, vere poterimus dicere nos honestatis
rationem habere, quoniam sine incolumitate eam
nullo tempore possumus adipisci. Qua in re vel
concedere alteri vel ad condicionem alterius descendere vel in praesentia quiescere atque aliud
175 tempus exspectare oportebit, modo illud attendatur,
dignane causa videatur ea quae ad utilitatem pertinebit quare de magnificentia aut de honestate quiddam

necessary for them to eat, except with the qualification, "Unless they prefer to die of starvation."
173 Therefore, as I say, the nature of the qualification must always be examined. For it will always be pertinent to the extent that the necessity has to be explained either with reference to honour in this way: "It is necessary if we wish to live honourably," or with reference to security in this way, "It is necessary if we wish to be secure," or with reference to convenience in this way, "It is necessary if we wish to live without inconvenience."

LVIII. The greatest necessity is that of doing what is honourable; next to that is the necessity of security and third and last the necessity of convenience; this can never stand comparison with
174 the other two. It is often necessary to weigh these, one against the other, so that, although honour is superior to security, it may be a question which it is preferable to follow. In this matter it seems possible to give a fixed and universal rule. For one should take thought for security in a case in which though honour is lost for the moment while consulting security, it may be recovered in the future by courage and diligence. If this is not possible, one should take thought for honour. So in a case of this sort, too, when we seem to consult our security, we shall be able to say with truth that we are concerned about honour, since without security we can never attain to honour. In such circumstances it will be proper to yield to another, or to meet another's terms, or to keep quiet for the present and await
175 another opportunity, provided only that some attention is paid to the question whether this cause which conduces to our advantage is worth a loss in

derogetur. Atque in hoc loco mihi caput illud videtur esse, ut quaeramus quid sit illud quod si adipisci
aut effugere velimus, aliqua res nobis sit necessaria,
hoc est quae sit adiunctio, ut proinde, uti quaeque
res erit, elaboremus et gravissimam quamque causam
vehementissime necessariam iudicemus.

176 Affectio est quaedam ex tempore aut ex negotiorum eventu aut administratione aut hominum
studio commutatio rerum, ut non tales, quales ante
habitae sint aut plerumque haberi soleant, habendae
videantur esse; ut ad hostes transire turpe videatur
esse, at non illo animo quo Ulixes transiit; et
pecuniam in mare deicere inutile, at non eo consilio
quo Aristippus fecit. Sunt igitur res quaedam ex
tempore et ex consilio, non ex sua natura considerandae; quibus in omnibus, quid tempora petant,
quid personis dignum sit, considerandum est et non
quid, sed quo quidque animo, quicum, quo tempore,
quamdiu fiat, attendendum est. His ex partibus
ad sententiam dicendam locos sumi oportere
arbitramur.

177 LIX. Laudes autem et vituperationes ex eis locis
sumentur qui loci personis sunt attributi, de quibus
ante dictum est. Sin distributius tractare qui volet,

---

^a The reference is to Odysseus' entering Troy as a spy,
Odyssey IV, 242–264.

^b The pupil of Socrates, and founder of the Cyrenaic School
of philosophy. *Diogenes Laertius*, II, 77, tells the story :
" He was taking a sea trip once upon a time, and discovered
that he was on a pirate ship. So he took out his money and
began to count it, let it fall overboard as if by accident and
then bewailed his loss. Some say that he remarked afterward that it was better for the money to perish because of
Aristippus than for Aristippus to perish because of the
money."

glory and honour. The main thing under this head seems to me to be the question what the thing is which makes some action necessary for us if we wish to acquire or avoid it; in other words, what is the qualification—in order that we may expend our energies in harmony with the real state of affairs, and may judge the most important reason in each case to be the most overwhelmingly necessary.

176 " Affection " is a change in the aspect of things due to time, or the result of actions or their management, or to the interests and desires of men, so that it seems that things should not be regarded in the same light as they have been or have generally been regarded. For example, it is an act of baseness to go over to the enemy, but not if done with the purpose which Ulysses had.[a] It is useless to throw money into the sea, but not so if done with the purpose with which Aristippus did it.[b] There are then certain matters that must be considered with reference to time and intention and not merely by their absolute qualities. In all these matters one must think what the occasion demands and what is worthy of the persons concerned, and one must consider not what is being done but with what spirit anything is done, with what associates, at what time, and how long it has been going on. From these divisions we think the ideas should be drawn for expressing an opinion.

177 LIX. Praise and censure will be derived from the topics that are employed with respect to the attributes of persons; these have been discussed above.[c] If one wishes to treat the subject more

[c] Book I, 34-6, II, 32-4.

partiatur in animum et corpus et extraneas res
licebit. Animi est virtus cuius de partibus paulo
ante dictum est; corporis valetudo, dignitas, vires,
velocitas; extraneae honos, pecunia, affinitas, genus,
amici, patria, potentia, cetera quae simili esse in
genere intellegentur. Atque in his id quod in
omnia valere oportebit; contraria quoque, quae et
qualia sint, intellegentur.

178   Videre autem in laudando et in vituperando
oportebit non tam, quae in corpore aut in extraneis
rebus habuerit is de quo agetur, quam quo pacto
his rebus usus sit. Nam fortunam quidem et laudare
stultitia et vituperare superbia est, animi autem et
laus honesta et vituperatio vehemens est.

Nunc quoniam omne in causae genus argumentandi
ratio tradita est, de inventione, prima ac maxima
parte rhetoricae, satis dictum videtur. Quare, quoniam et una pars ad exitum hoc ac superiore libro
perducta est et hic liber non parum continet
litterarum, quae restant in reliquis dicemus.

methodically, these may be divided into mind, body and external circumstances. The virtue of the mind is that whose parts we discussed only recently.[a] The virtues of the body are health, beauty, strength, speed. Extraneous virtues are public office, money, connexions by marriage, high birth, friends, country, power, and all other things that are understood to belong to this class. And the principle ought to apply to these which applies everywhere; the opposites of these qualities and their nature will be apparent.

178   Moreover, in praise and censure it will be necessary to observe not so much what the subject of the speech possessed in bodily endowment or in extraneous goods as what use he made of them. For it is foolish to praise one's good fortune and arrogant to censure it, but praise of a man's mind is honourable and censure of it very effective.

Now that I have presented the principles on which arguments can be made in every kind of speech, enough has, I think, been said about Invention, which is the first and most important part of rhetoric. Therefore since one section has been brought to completion in this and the preceding book, and this book has grown to a great length, we shall leave the other topics for the later books.

[a] §§ 159-65.

EXCURSUS

^a In *de Inv.* I, 9, 12 Cicero objects to Hermagoras' division of the *constitutio generalis* into (*pars*) *deliberativa, demonstrativa, iuridicialis* and *negotialis*. The criticism arises because Cicero has (in I, 5, 7) divided all oratory into three classes, deliberative, demonstrative and forensic. This is the tripartite division of Aristotle, based on the difference in the *audience* to which the speech is addressed, *i.e.* the deliberative speech is addressed to a legislative body, the forensic to a court of law, and the demonstrative to a group which is gathered for entertainment or amusement.

Hermagoras, on the other hand, began his division with *subject matter*. All speeches are divided according to the subject matter into two classes : (1) θέσεις or general questions, (2) ὑποθέσεις or special cases. Special cases are subdivided into λογικὰ ζητήματα or questions involving reasoning, and νομικὰ ζητήματα or questions involving law. The questions involving reasoning are divided according to the four στάσεις or *constitutiones, coniecturalis, definitiva, generalis, translativa.* The *constitutio generalis* involved the question of right and wrong and was divided again into four parts : (1) concerning the correctness of future acts (*i.e.* deliberative); (2) concerning a person—whether he was good or bad (*i.e.* epideictic or demonstrative, covering both laudatory and vituperative speeches); (3) *iuridicialis*, dealing with principles of equity and justice as applied to a given law suit; (4) *negotialis*, which involved questions of the interpretation of laws. Naturally the classification which brought the kinds of speeches under the *constitutio generalis* did not square with Aristotle's method of classification, but the error is in Cicero's source who attempted to combine the two systems, and not in Hermagoras. There was, however, a logical fault in Hermagoras' classification. The νομικὰ ζητήματα really belong under στάσεις (*constitutiones*) and are not co-ordinate with the λογικὰ ζητήματα.

Cicero does not see that similar difficulties arise in the *constitutio coniecturalis*, where the examples of present and future time both belong to the *causa deliberativa.*

346

THE BEST KIND OF ORATOR

INTRODUCTION

THE short treatise which bears the title *de Optimo Genere Oratorum* was written by Cicero in the year 46 B.C. sometime between the publication of the *Brutus* and the composition of the *Orator*. This can be determined by internal evidence; the *Brutus* was a history of Roman Oratory, but also used that history to demonstrate the correctness of Cicero's attitude toward oratorical style, and to combat the views of the Roman Atticists who would confine the orator to the simplicity and artlessness of the early Attic orators. To Cicero in the *Brutus* and again in the present treatise Demosthenes, who could command at will all styles from the opulent to the simple, is the greatest orator of all time, and a standing rebuke to those who would confine the term "Attic" to writers such as Lysias. In the *Orator* Cicero goes one step further and seeks for the pattern of the perfect orator, for an ideal which has never been embodied in any one orator, and perhaps never will be found, but to which Demosthenes is the closest approximation. Of this advanced position there is no trace in the *de Optimo Genere Oratorum*, and it seems unlikely that if it had been written after the *Orator*, Cicero would have reverted to his earlier views.

It professes to be an introduction to a translation of Demosthenes *On the Crown*, and Aeschines *Against*

INTRODUCTION

Ctesiphon. The translation was never published and probably never made. Furthermore, the introduction was not published during Cicero's lifetime. It exhibits a roughness and at times obscurity of style which would hardly have been put forth by the fastidious author of the *Brutus* and the *Orator*; and beyond that there are two passages (12, 18) in which the confusion of thought can best be explained by assuming that the manuscript contained two drafts of the same ideas, which waited for a final revision that never came because the task was laid aside for the more ambitious *Orator*.[a]

For the constitution of the text of the *de Optimo Genere* we have two classes of manuscripts; one composed of two codices of the eleventh century, Sangallensis 818 (G) and Parisinus 7347 (P); the other comprising a number of manuscripts from the fifteenth century. As in the case of the *de Inventione* the war has prevented the translator from making his own collations. He offers, therefore, a second-hand text based on the apparatus offered by Orelli, Friedrich, Hedicke, Fossataro, Wilkins and others. Furthermore, he is embarrassed by the disagreement among previous editors as to the readings in several passages and can therefore give no assurance that even the apparatus criticus is correct.

The eleventh-century codices seem to contain many minor errors, most of which have been corrected in one or another of the later manuscripts. The more serious difficulties, however, are common to all, and

---

[a] In this preface I follow in general the theories of Professor Hendrickson in his article, "Cicero De Optimo Genere Oratorum," in the *American Journal of Philology* xlvii. (1926), pp. 109–123.

some may even derive from the peculiar circumstances of its composition and publication which have
been described above.

The manuscripts used in the apparatus with their
sigla are :

    G.   codex Sangallensis 818
    P.   codex Parisinus 7347
    C.   codices
    c.   some or all of the fifteenth-century codices
    f.   codex Vitebergensis (Halensis Yg24)
    g.   codex Gudianus 38
    O.   codex Ottobonianus 2057
    o.   codex Ottobonianus 4449
    ω.   codex Ottobonianus 1996
    r.   codex Vaticanus reginensis 1841
    T.   codex Parisinus 7704
    vulg. early editions

BIBLIOGRAPHY

Besides the complete texts of Cicero mentioned in the bibliography of the *de Inventione* (p. xv) we have text editions of :

A. S. Wilkins, M. Tulli Ciceronis Rhetorica, in two volumes. Volume II contains Brutus, Orator, De Optimo Genere Oratorum, Partitiones Oratoriae, Topica ;

and the following special editions :

Marco Biglia, M. Tullio Cicerone De Optimo Genere Oratorum : Turin 1933. A school edition.

Henri Bornecque, Orator et De Optimo Genere Oratorum. Paris 1921. Text and Translation.

Paolo Fossataro, Cicerone, Della Forma Perfetta di Eloquenza. Second edition, Citta di Castello 1914. Fossataro gives an exegetical commentary and the fullest *apparatus criticus.*

Edmund Hedicke, M. Tulli Ciceronis libellus De Optimo Genere Oratorum. Sorau 1889. Hedicke was the first to collate Parisinus 7347 (P) and Parisinus 7704 (T).

Otto Jahn, Ciceros Orator : Anhang : De Optimo Genere Oratorum. Leipzig 1851. Commentary and concise *apparatus criticus.*

L. Quicherat, Brutus et De Optimo Genere Oratorum, Paris 1900.

BIBLIOGRAPHY

There is an English translation by Charles Duke Yonge in the volume cited in the bibliography of the *de Inventione* (p. xvi); and French translations by F. Richard, Brutus et la perfection oratoire, Paris 1934; and H. Bornecque, above.

M. TULLI CICERONIS

DE OPTIMO GENERE ORATORUM

I. Oratorum genera esse dicuntur tamquam poetarum; id secus est, nam alterum est multiplex.
Poematis enim tragici, comici, epici, melici, etiam ac
dithyrambici, quod magis est tractatum a Graecis
quam a Latinis, suum cuiusque est,[1] diversum a
reliquis. Itaque et in tragoedia comicum vitiosum
est et in comoedia turpe tragicum; et in ceteris suus
est cuique[2] certus sonus et quaedam intellegentibus
nota vox. Oratorum autem si quis ita numerat plura
genera, ut alios grandis aut gravis aut copiosos, alios
tenuis aut subtilis aut brevis, alios eis interiectos et
tamquam medios putet, de hominibus dicit[3] aliquid,
de re parum. In re enim quid optimum sit quaeritur,
in homine dicitur quod est. Itaque licet dicere et
Ennium summum epicum poetam, si cui ita videtur,
et Pacuvium tragicum et Caecilium fortasse comicum.

---

[1] quod . . . cuiusque est *Pluygers, Mnemosyne* N.F. viii,
p. 367: quod c: quo *GOP*: magis *C*: rarius *Hedicke*: a Latinis
bracketed by Friedrich: suum cuiusque *Manutius*: suum
quo ius *GO*: suum cuius *P*: suumque ius *r*: suum quodvis *o*:
suum quod ius *T*.

[2] cuique *G*: cuiusque *P*.

[3] de hominibus dicit *Orelli*: hominibus deicit *GP*.

---

[a] Quintus Ennius, 239–169 B.C.; Roman poet who wrote in
many genres, but was best known for his epic of Roman
History, the *Annales*.

MARCUS TULLIUS CICERO

THE BEST KIND OF ORATOR

I. IT is said that there are various kinds of orators
as there are of poets. But the fact is otherwise, for
poetry takes many forms. That is to say, every
composition in verse, tragedy, comedy, epic, and
also melic and dithyrambic (a form more extensively
cultivated by Greeks than by Romans) has its own
individuality, distinct from the others. So in
tragedy a comic style is a blemish, and in comedy the
tragic style is unseemly; and so with the other
genres, each has its own tone and a way of speaking
2 which the scholars recognize. But in the case of
orators if one in the same way enumerates several
kinds, regarding some as grand, stately or opulent,
others as plain, restrained or concise, and others in an
intermediate position, forming as it were a mean
between the other two, he gives some information
about the men but does not tell us enough about the
art of oratory. For in an art we ask what is ideal
perfection; in a man we describe what actually is.
Therefore, one may call Ennius [a] supreme in epic, if
he thinks that is true, and Pacuvius [b] in tragedy and
3 Caecilius,[c] perhaps, in comedy. The orator I do not

[b] Marcus Pacuvius, 220–circa 132 B.C., nephew of Ennius;
his writing was confined almost entirely to tragedy.

[c] Statius Caecilius, circa 168 B.C., a contemporary of
Ennius, and the immediate predecessor of Terence. Cicero
elsewhere (cf. *ad Atticum* vii, 3, 10; *Brutus* 258) speaks
slightingly of his Latinity.

3 Oratorem genere non divido ; perfectum enim quaero.
Unum est autem genus perfecti, a quo qui absunt, non
genere differunt, ut Terentius ab Accio, sed in eodem
genere non sunt pares. Optimus est enim orator qui
dicendo animos audientium et docet et delectat et
permovet. Docere debitum est, delectare hono-
4 rarium, permovere necessarium. Haec ut alius melius
quam alius, concedendum est ; verum id fit non
genere sed gradu. Optimum quidem unum est et
proximum quod ei simillimum. Ex quo perspicuum
est, quod optimo dissimillimum sit, id esse deterri-
mum.

II. Nam quoniam eloquentia constat ex verbis et
ex sententiis, perficiendum est, ut pure et emendate
loquentes, quod est Latine, verborum praeterea et
propriorum et translatorum elegantiam persequamur :
in propriis ut lautissima eligamus, in translatis ut
similitudinem secuti verecunde utamur alienis.
5 Sententiarum autem totidem genera sunt quot dixi
esse laudum. Sunt enim docendi acutae, delectandi
quasi argutae, commovendi graves. Sed et verborum
est structura quaedam duas res efficiens, numerum
et levitatem,[1] et sententiae suam compositionem

---

[1] lenitatem c, Bentley (ad Hor. Art. Poet. 26).

---

[a] Publius Terentius Afer, circa 190–159 B.C.

[b] Lucius Accius, born 170 B.C., lived to a great age. Writer
of tragedies and of history of the Roman stage.

[c] This version takes *honorarium* in the sense of compli-
mentary gift, contrasted with debt (*debitum*) which the orators
owe in the giving of information. It may also be taken in
the sense of " winning him honour and esteem," *i.e.* securing
the audience's favour; *delectare* is in this statement of the
orator's function frequently replaced by *conciliare*, " win the
favour of the audience."

divide into types, for I am looking for the perfect example. There is only one kind of perfect orator : those who do not belong to this group do not differ in genre as Terence [a] differs from Accius,[b] but though classified with him do not equal him in attainments. The supreme orator, then, is the one whose speech instructs, delights and moves the minds of his audience. The orator is in duty bound to instruct ; giving pleasure is a free gift to the audience,[c] to 4 move them is indispensable. We must grant that one does it better than another, but the difference is in degree, not in kind. There is one best, and the next best is that which resembles it most. It is plain from this that what is most unlike the best is the worst.

II. For as eloquence consists of language and thought,[d] we must manage while keeping our diction faultless and pure—that is in good Latin—to achieve a choice of words both " proper " and figurative. Of " proper " words we should choose the most elegant, and in the case of figurative language we should be modest in our use of metaphors and careful to avoid 5 far-fetched comparisons. On the other hand, there are as many kinds of thoughts as I said above there are of styles of oratory. For exposition and explanation they should be pointed, for entertainment, bright and witty, for rousing the emotions, weighty and impressive. In addition to this, there is a way of putting words together—a structure as it were—to produce the two effects of rhythm and smoothness,

[d] The Latin *sententia* means a thought, and also the expression of it, a sentence, or if the expression is pointed, a maxim or apophthegm. All these meanings hover over this paragraph and can hardly be brought out in English.

habent, et [1] ad probandam rem accommodatum
ordinem. Sed earum omnium rerum ut aedifici-
orum [2] memoria est quasi fundamentum, lumen
actio.

6   Ea igitur omnia in quo summa erunt,[3] erit perfectissimus [4] orator; in quo media, mediocris; in quo
minima, deterrimus. Et appellabuntur omnes oratores, ut pictores appellantur etiam mali, nec
generibus inter sese, sed facultatibus different.
Itaque nemo est orator qui Demostheni se [5] similem
nolit esse; at Menander Homeri noluit; genus enim
erat aliud. Id non est in oratoribus aut, etiam si est
ut alius gravitatem sequens subtilitatem fugiat,
contra alius acutiorem se quam ornatiorem velit,
etiam si est in genere tolerabilis,[6] certe non est
optimus, si quidem, quod omnis laudes habet, id est
optimum.

7   III. Haec autem dixi brevius quidem quam res
petebat, sed ad id quod agimus non fuit dicendum
pluribus; unum enim cum sit genus, id quale sit
quaerimus. Est autem tale quale floruit Athenis;
ex quo Atticorum oratorum ipsa vis ignota est, nota
gloria. Nam alterum multi viderunt, vitiosi nihil
apud eos esse, alterum pauci, laudabilia esse multa.
Est enim vitiosum in sententia si quid absurdum aut
alienum aut non acutum aut subinsulsum est; in
verbis si inquinatum, si abiectum, si non aptum, si

---

[1] et added by Lambinus.

[2] ut aediciorum bracketed by Lambinus.

[3] erunt added by Lambinus.

[4] perfectissimus c, Lambinus: peritissimus C.

[5] se added by Aldus, c.

[6] tolerabilis . . . optimus Hendrickson, A.J.P. xlvii (1926),
p. 116: tolerabili, certe non est in optimo C: tolerabile T.

and a way of arranging the ideas and an order which is best suited to proving one's case. But all these are but parts of a building as it were; the foundation is memory; that which gives it light is delivery.

6 The man who is supreme in all these departments will be the most perfect orator; one who attains moderate success will be mediocre; he who has the least success will be the worst speaker. Still they will all be called orators, as painters are called painters, though they may be inferior, and will differ in ability, not in kind. Therefore, there is no orator who is unwilling to resemble Demosthenes, but Menander [a] did not wish to write like Homer, for he was working in a different genre. But the same is not true of orators, or, even if one in pursuit of weight and dignity avoids simplicity, and on the other hand, another prefers to be plain and to the point rather than ornate, though he is tolerable as an orator, he is not the best if it is true that the best style is that which includes all virtues.

7 III. I have made this introduction briefer than the subject deserved, but for our present purpose there was no need of a fuller statement. Since there is but one kind of oratory, we are searching for what its nature is. It is the kind that flourished at Athens. The distinction of the Attic orators in their style is well known, but their essential characteristics are unknown. Many see one side—that there was nothing in them with which to find fault—but few see the other side—that there was much to praise. For it is a fault in an idea if it is absurd, or irrelevant, or pointless, or flat; a word is faulty if it is impure, mean.

---

[a] Menander, 343/2–291/0 B.C. (both dates approximate); the leading representative of New Comedy.

8 durum, si longe petitum. Haec vitaverunt fere
omnes qui aut Attici numerantur aut dicunt Attice.
Sed qui eatenus [1] valuerunt, sani et sicci dumtaxat
habeantur, sed ita ut palaestritae; spatiari in xysto
ut liceat, non ab Olympiis coronam petant. Qui,
cum careant omni vitio, non sunt contenti quasi bona
valetudine, sed viris, lacertos, sanguinem quaerunt,[2]
quandam etiam suavitatem coloris, eos imitemur si
possumus; si minus, illos potius qui incorrupta
sanitate sunt, quod est proprium Atticorum, quam eos
quorum vitiosa abundantia est, qualis Asia multos
9 tulit. Quod cum faciemus—si modo id ipsum asse-
quemur; est enim permagnum—imitemur, si potueri-
mus, Lysiam et eius quidem tenuitatem potissimum;
est enim multis locis grandior, sed quia et privatas
ille plerasque et eas ipsas aliis [3] et parvarum rerum
causulas scripsit, videtur esse ieiunior, cum se ipse
consulto ad minutarum causarum genera limaverit.
IV. Quod qui ita faciet, ut,[4] si cupiat uberior esse,
non possit, habeatur sane orator, sed de minoribus;
magno autem oratori etiam illo modo saepe dicendum
10 est in tali genere causarum. Ita fit ut Demosthenes
certe possit summisse dicere, elate Lysias fortasse
non possit. Sed si eodem modo putant exercitu in

[1] qui eatenus *Gulielmius* : quatenus *C.*
[2] quaerunt *c* : quaerant *GP.*
[3] ipsas aliis *c* : ipsas et alias *C.*
[4] faciet ut si *c* : faciet si *GP.*

---

[a] Lysias, circa 445–circa 378 B.C. He was supreme in the
plain or unadorned style.
[b] Titus Annius Milo, accused of the murder of Clodius in
52 B.C. Cicero attempted his defence, but was unnerved by

8 inappropriate, harsh, or far-fetched. These errors have been avoided by well nigh all who are accounted Attics or who speak the Attic tongue. But those who have attained only to this may be considered sound and spare as far as that goes, but may be compared to athletes who are fit to promenade in the gymnasium, but not to seek the prize at Olympia. The prize-winners, though free from all diseases, are not content with merely good health, but seek strength, muscles, blood, and even as it were an attractive tan. Let us imitate them if we can; if not, let us imitate those whose purity is untainted—which is characteristic of the Attic writers—rather than those whose opulent style is full of faults; Asia produced this latter

9 sort in abundance. In doing this—if indeed we can accomplish even this much, for it is a very great achievement—let us imitate Lysias,[a] if possible, and his simplicity above all. He does indeed rise toward a loftier style in many passages, but because he wrote private speeches almost exclusively, and even these were for other people and concerned with trifling affairs, he seems excessively meagre, since he purposely filed down his style to match the nature of the petty suits. IV. If anyone speaks in this manner without being able to use a fuller style if he wishes, he should be regarded as an orator, but as a minor one. The great orator must often speak in that way

10 in dealing with cases of such a kind. In other words, Demosthenes could certainly speak calmly, but Lysias perhaps not with passion. But if they think that at the trial of Milo,[b] when the army was

the unusual situation described in the text. The extant oration *In Defence of Milo* was written and published after the trial.

foro et in omnibus templis, quae circum forum sunt,
collocato dici pro Milone decuisse, ut si de re privata
ad unum iudicem diceremus, vim eloquentiae sua
facultate, non rei natura metiuntur.

11   Qua re quoniam non nullorum sermo iam increbruit,
partim se ipsos Attice dicere, partim neminem
nostrum [1] dicere, alteros neglegamus; satis enim eis
res ipsa respondet, cum aut non adhibeantur [2] ad
causas aut adhibiti derideantur; nam si rideretur,[3]
esset id ipsum Atticorum.   Sed qui dici a nobis Attico
more nolunt,[4] ipsi autem se non oratores esse pro-
fitentur, si teretes auris habent intellegensque
iudicium, tamquam ad picturam probandam adhibentur etiam inscii faciendi cum aliqua sollertia iudicandi;

12   sin autem intellegentiam ponunt in audiendi fastidio
neque eos quicquam excelsum magnificumque delectat, dicant se quiddam subtile et politum velle, grande
ornatumque contemnere; id vero desinant dicere,
qui subtiliter dicant, eos solos Attice dicere, id est
quasi sicce et integre.   Et ample et ornate et copiose
cum eadem integritate Atticorum est.   Quid? dubium est utrum orationem nostram tolerabilem tantum

---

[1] nostrum *vulg.* : vestrum *GP* : nostrorum *f*.
[2] adhibeantur *Manutius alii* : adhibentur *C*.
[3] rideretur *Hendrickson, o.c.*, p. 118 : riderentur *C*.
[4] nolunt *Ofg* : volunt *GPT*.

---

[a] " They " in this sentence refers to the self-styled " Attic "
orators at Rome, who are not formally introduced until the
next paragraph.
[b] The two classes are perhaps represented by Calvus (cf.
Brutus 284) and his followers, practising orators who had
greater success than Cicero here grants them : the second

stationed in the Forum and in all the temples round about, it was fitting to defend him in the same style that we would use in pleading a private case before a single referee, they measure the power of eloquence by their own limited ability, not by the nature of the art.[a]

11   Therefore we must make an answer to the claims of certain people which have now gained some currency : one group say that they themselves speak in the Attic manner, the others that no Roman does.[b] The second group we may neglect, for they are sufficiently answered by the facts, since they are not invited to conduct trials, or if invited, they are laughed out of court ; for if it was their wit which caused the jury to laugh, this would be prime evidence that they were " Attic." But those who deny that we speak in the Attic manner, but confess that they themselves are not orators, if they have cultivated ears and an intelligent judgement, we consult them as a painter consults people invited to view a painting, who have

12 no ability to paint, but a certain skill in criticism. If, on the other hand, they make intelligence consist in fastidiousness of taste in oratory and take no pleasure in anything lofty and magnificent, let them say that they prefer a plain and refined style and despise the grand and ornate. But let them cease to claim that the plain orators are the only ones who speak in the Attic manner, that is, as they say, sparely and without fault. A grand, ornate, and copious style that is equally faultless is the mark of Attic orators. Is there any doubt whether we desire our eloquence to

group is not so easy to identify ; the most plausible conjecture is that it is composed of men like Memmius (*Brutus* 247), highly trained in letters, but only in Greek, for he scorned Latin.

an etiam admirabilem esse cupiamus? Non enim iam quaerimus quid sit Attice, sed quid sit optime dicere.
13 Ex quo intellegitur, quoniam Graecorum oratorum praestantissimi sint ei qui fuerint Athenis, eorum autem princeps facile Demosthenes, hunc si qui imitetur, cum et Attice dicturum et optime, ut,[1] quoniam Attici nobis propositi sunt ad imitandum, bene dicere id sit Attice dicere.

V. Sed cum in eo magnus error esset, quale esset id dicendi genus, putavi mihi suscipiendum laborem utilem studiosis, mihi quidem ipsi non necessarium.
14 Converti enim ex Atticis duorum eloquentissimorum nobilissimas orationes inter seque contrarias, Aeschinis et[2] Demosthenis; nec converti ut interpres, sed ut orator, sententiis isdem et earum formis tamquam figuris, verbis ad nostram consuetudinem aptis. In quibus non verbum pro verbo necesse habui reddere, sed genus omne[3] verborum vimque servavi. Non enim ea me adnumerare lectori putavi oportere, sed tam-
15 quam appendere. Hic labor meus hoc assequetur,[4] ut nostri homines quid ab illis exigant, qui se Atticos volunt, et ad quam eos quasi formulam dicendi revocent intellegant.

" Sed exorietur[5] Thucydides; eius enim quidam eloquentiam admirantur."[6] Id quidem recte; sed

[1] ut *Oo*: utrus *G*: utrum *PT*: verum *r*: cf. *Hendrickson, o.c.,* p. 119.
[2] et *added by Orelli.*
[3] omne *Hieronymus*: omnium *C.*
[4] adsequetur *Ascensius*: adsequitur *C.*
[5] exorietur *GPc*: exoritur *c.*
[6] admirantur *c*: admiratur *GP.*

[a] The *Oration against Ctesiphon* of Aeschines (circa 390–circa 315 B.C.) and *The Oration on the Crown* (or *In Defence of Ctesiphon*) by Demosthenes (384/3–322 B.C.).

be merely tolerable, or to arouse admiration as well?
For we are not inquiring what speaking in the Attic
13 manner is, but what is the best manner. It can be
inferred from this that since the most outstanding
Greek orators were those who lived at Athens, and
of these Demosthenes was easily the chief, one who
imitates him will speak in the Attic manner and in
the best manner, so that, since they set up Attic
orators as models for our imitation, speaking in the
Attic fashion means speaking well.

V. But since there was a complete misapprehen-
sion as to the nature of their style of oratory, I
thought it my duty to undertake a task which will be
useful to students, though not necessary for myself.
14 That is to say I translated the most famous orations
of the two most eloquent Attic orators, Aeschines
and Demosthenes, orations which they delivered
against each other.[a] And I did not translate them
as an interpreter, but as an orator, keeping the same
ideas and the forms, or as one might say, the
" figures " of thought, but in language which con-
forms to our usage. And in so doing, I did not hold
it necessary to render word for word, but I preserved
the general style and force of the language. For I
did not think I ought to count them out to the reader
like coins, but to pay them by weight, as it were.
15 The result of my labour will be that our Romans will
know what to demand from those who claim to be
Atticists and to what rule of speech, as it were, they
are to be held.

" But Thucydides [b] will rise up against you; for
some admire his eloquence." Right they are; but

[b] Athenian of the fifth century B.C., who wrote the history
of the Peloponnesian War.

nihil ad eum oratorem quem quaerimus. Aliud est
enim explicare res gestas narrando, aliud argumentando criminari crimenve dissolvere; aliud narrantem
tenere auditorem, aliud concitare.[1] "At loquitur
16 pulchre." Num melius quam Plato? Necesse est
tamen oratori quem quaerimus controversias explicare [2] forensis dicendi genere apto ad docendum, ad
delectandum, ad permovendum. VI. Qua re si quis
erit qui se Thucydideo genere causas in foro dicturum
esse profiteatur, is abhorrebit etiam a suspicione eius
quod [3] versatur in re civili et forensi; sin [4] Thucy-
didem laudabit, ascribat suae nostram sententiam.

17   Quin ipsum Isocratem, quem divinus auctor Plato
suum fere aequalem admirabiliter in Phaedro laudari
fecit ab Socrate quemque omnes docti summum [5]
oratorem esse dixerunt, tamen hunc in numerum non
repono.   Non enim in acie versatur nec ferro,[6] sed
quasi [7] rudibus eius eludit oratio.   A me autem, ut
cum maximis minima conferam, gladiatorum par
nobilissimum inducitur, Aeschines, tamquam Aeserninus, ut ait Lucilius, non spurcus homo, sed acer et
doctus

     cum Pacideiano hic componitur,—optimus longe
     post homines natos—.

[1] concitare o: concitantem C.
[2] explicare c : explicantem GPT.
[3] quod Ernesti : quae C.
[4] sin Orelli in apparatus: in GP : (et) qui c, Orelli in
text.
[5] docti summum c vulg.: doctissimum C.
[6] nec ferro Hammer: et ferro GP: et (in) foro c.
[7] sed quasi c: et quasi GP.

that has no bearing on the orator whom we are seeking. For it is one thing to set forth events in an historical narrative, and another to present arguments to clinch a case against an opponent, or to refute a charge. It is one thing to hold an auditor while telling a story, and another to arouse him. " But his style is beautiful." Is it better than Plato's?

16 For the orator whom we are seeking must treat cases in court in a style suitable to instruct, to delight, and to move. VI. Therefore, if there shall ever be a man who professes to plead cases in court in the style of Thucydides, he will prove that he has not the faintest notion of what goes on in political and legal life. But if he is content to praise Thucydides, let him enter my vote beside his.

17 Even Isocrates,[a] whom the divine Plato, practically his contemporary, represents as receiving high praise from Socrates in the Phaedrus,[b] and whom all scholars have cited as a consummate orator, even him I do not include in the class of perfection. For his oratory does not take part in the battle nor use steel, but plays with a wooden sword, as I may say.[c] But, to compare the magnificent with the insignificant, what I am now doing is rather introducing a famous pair of gladiators, Aeschines like Aeserninus, not a nasty fellow as Lucilius says, but bold and clever; he is matched with Pacideianus, by far the best fighter

---

[a] Greek orator, 436–338 B.C., perhaps more famous as a teacher and founder of a school and tradition of rhetoric.

[b] Plato, Phaedrus, 278E–279B.

[c] A wooden sword was used by gladiators and soldiers for practice. Isocrates, lacking nerve and a good voice, refrained from public appearances; almost all of his "speeches" were written to be read.

CICERO

Nihil enim illo oratore arbitror cogitari posse divinius.

18   Huic labori nostro duo genera reprehensionum opponuntur. Unum hoc: "Verum melius Graeci." A quo quaeratur ecquid possint ipsi[1] melius Latine? Alterum: "Quid istas potius legam quam Graecas?" Idem Andriam et Synephebos nec minus[2] Andromacham aut Antiopam aut Epigonos Latinos recipiunt.[3] Quod igitur est eorum in orationibus e Graeco[4] conversis fastidium, nullum cum sit in versibus?

19   VII. Sed adgrediamur iam quod suscepimus, si prius exposuerimus quae causa in iudicium deducta sit. Cum esset lex Athenis, NE QVIS POPVLI SCITVM FACERET VT QVISQVAM CORONA DONARETVR IN MAGISTRATV PRIVS QVAM RATIONES RETTVLISSET; et altera lex, EOS QVI A POPVLO DONARENTVR, IN CONTIONE DONARI DEBERE; QVI A SENATV,[5] IN SENATV, Demosthenes curator muris reficiendis fuit eosque refecit pecunia sua; de hoc igitur Ctesiphon scitum fecit nullis ab illo

[1] ipsi *C*: illi *G*.
[2] *After* minus *the MSS. have* Terentium et Caecilium quam Menandrum legunt nec: *bracketed by Jahn.*
[3] *After* recipiunt *the MSS. have* sed tamen Ennium et Pacuvium et Accium potius quam Euripidem et Sophoclem legunt: *bracketed by Jahn.*
[4] e Graeco *Lambinus*: a greco *C*.
[5] qui a senatu *Muretus*: quia *C*.

[a] Cicero is quoting freely from the second satire of Lucilius. The passage in full is (text and translation by E. H. Warmington, *Remains of Old Latin* iii, pp. 56, 57 (LCL)):

> Aeserninus fuit Flaccorum munere quidam
>   Samnis, spurcus homo, vita illa dignus locoque.
> Cum Pacideiano componitur, optimus multo
>   post homines natos gladiator qui fuit unus.

since the creation of man, for I think nothing can be imagined more inspired than the orator Demosthenes.[a]

18   Two sorts of objections can be raised to this undertaking of mine. The first is: "It is better in the original Greek." One might ask this critic whether they themselves can produce anything better in Latin. The second is: "Why should I read this translation of yours, rather than the Greek original?" But at the same time they accept the Andria, the Synephebi and likewise the Andromache or the Antiope or the Epigoni in Latin.[b] Why their aversion to speeches translated from the Greek when they have none to translations of poetry?

19   VII. But let us now turn to our task, after an introductory explanation of the case which was brought before the court. There was a fundamental law at Athens that no one should propose a bill to crown a citizen while he was a magistrate before he had rendered an account of his office; and another law providing that those who were rewarded by the people should receive the award in the popular assembly, and those who were rewarded by the Council should receive it in the Council chamber. Demosthenes was superintendent in charge of repairing the city walls, and repaired them at his own expense. For this service, then, Ctesiphon proposed

---

In the public show given by the Flacci was a certain Aeserninus, a Samnite, a nasty fellow, worthy of that life and station. He was matched with Pacideianus, who was by far the best of all the gladiators since the creation of man.

[b] The *Andria* of Terence; Caecilius' *Synephebi* (Companions in Youth), fragments in Warmington, ROL i, pp. 536–540; the *Andromacha* of Ennius, ROL i, pp. 244–254; the *Antiopa* of Pacuvius, ROL ii, pp. 158–170; the *Epigoni* of Accius, ROL ii, pp. 420–428.

rationibus relatis, ut corona aurea donaretur eaque
donatio fieret in theatro populo convocato, qui locus
non est contionis legitimae, atque ita praedicaretur,
EVM DONARI VIRTVTIS ERGO BENEVOLENTIAEQVE QVAM IS
20 ERGA POPVLVM ATHENIENSEM HABERET. Hunc igitur
Ctesiphontem in iudicium adduxit Aeschines quod
contra leges scripsisset, ut et rationibus non relatis
corona donaretur et ut in theatro, et quod de virtute
eius et benevolentia falsa scripsisset, cum Demosthenes nec vir bonus esset nec bene meritus de
civitate.

Causa ipsa abhorret illa quidem a formula con-
suetudinis nostrae, sed est magna. Habet enim et
legum interpretationem satis acutam in utramque
partem et meritorum in rem publicam contentionem
21 sane gravem. Itaque causa fuit Aeschini, cum ipse a
Demosthene esset capitis accusatus, quod legationem
ementitus esset, ut ulciscendi inimici causa nomine
Ctesiphontis iudicium fieret de factis famaque Demosthenis. Non enim tam multa dixit de rationibus non
relatis, quam de eo quod civis improbus ut optimus
22 laudatus esset. Hanc multam Aeschines a Ctesi-
phonte petivit quadriennio ante Philippi Macedonis
mortem; sed iudicium factum est aliquot annis post
Alexandro iam Asiam tenente; ad quod iudicium

---

a According to the spurious indictment inserted in Demosthenes, *On the Crown* (55), this last charge involved violation
of a fundamental law forbidding false statements in bills;
Cicero does not mention this law above.

b In 343 B.C. Both orations are extant.

c The complaint was lodged in 336 and the trial took place
in 330. As a matter of fact, Philip was murdered in 336
shortly after Aeschines' complaint against Ctesiphon. The
error arises from a confusion of the event here mentioned with
an earlier crowning of Demosthenes in 340.

in a bill, though Demosthenes had not rendered an
account of his office, that he should receive a crown
of gold, and that the presentation should be made in
the theatre before the assembled people, though this
was not the place for a legal assembly ; and that pro-
clamation should be made that he received the crown
for his virtue and the benevolence which he had shown
20 to the people of Athens. Aeschines then summoned
this Ctesiphon to court charging him with proposing
a bill contrary to the fundamental law in that the
crown was to be presented before Demosthenes had
rendered his account, and in that the presentation
was to be made in the theatre, and because the statement about virtue and benevolence was untrue, since
Demosthenes neither was a good man nor had deserved well of the city.[a]

This case in its very nature is far removed from the
customary procedure of our courts ; still it is important. For it involves a very nice interpretation of
the law on both sides, and a comparison of the public
services of the two orators which is extremely
21 impressive. Furthermore, as Aeschines had been
accused by Demosthenes on the capital charge of
malfeasance on an embassy,[b] he had reason to seek
vengeance on his enemy by subjecting the career and
reputation of Demosthenes to a judicial review under
the guise of an attack on Ctesiphon. Therefore, he
did not make so much of the charge that Demosthenes
had not rendered his account as he did of his having
been praised as the best of citizens when he was a
22 villain. Aeschines instituted this prosecution against
Ctesiphon four years before the death of Philip of
Macedon, but the trial was held several years later
when Alexander was now master of Asia.[c] The trial

371

concursus dicitur e tota Graecia factus esse. Quid
enim tam aut visendum aut audiendum fuit quam
summorum oratorum in gravissima causa accurata et
23 inimicitiis incensa contentio? Quorum ego[1] orationes
si, ut[2] spero, ita expressero virtutibus utens illorum
omnibus, id est sententiis et earum figuris et rerum
ordine, verba persequens eatenus, ut ea non abhor-
reant a more nostro—quae si e Graecis omnia conversa non erunt, tamen ut generis eiusdem sint,
elaboravimus—,[3] erit regula, ad quam eorum dirigan-
tur orationes qui Attice volent dicere. Sed de nobis
satis. Aliquando enim Aeschinem ipsum Latine
dicentem audiamus.

[1] ego *vulg.*: ergo *GP*.
[2] si ut *C*: sicut *Go*.
[3] elaboravimus *Hieronymus*: elaborabimus *C*.

was attended by a crowd from every part of Greece For what was so worth going to see or hear as two consummate orators engaged in a desperate struggle for which they had prepared with great effort and in which they were influenced by personal animosity ? 23 If I shall succeed in rendering their speeches, as I hope, by retaining all their virtues, that is, the thoughts, the figures of thought and the order of topics, and following the language only so far as it does not depart from our idiom—if all the words are not literal translations of the Greek, we have at least tried to keep them within the same class or type—there will be a norm by which to measure the speeches of those who may wish to speak in the Attic manner. But enough of myself. Now at last let us listen to Aeschines himself speaking in the Latin tongue.

TOPICA

INTRODUCTION

THE genesis of the *Topica* is explained fully in the opening paragraphs, nor is there any reason to doubt the essential facts of the story or to assume that it is merely a literary artifice. Trebatius had found in Cicero's library at Tusculum a copy of Aristotle's *Topica*, and had asked Cicero to explain it to him. For a while Cicero declined, but finally, while sailing from Velia to Rhegium, composed the treatise entirely from memory. This is confirmed by the letter (*ad Fam.* vii, 19) which Cicero wrote from Rhegium on July 28, 44 B.C. and sent to Trebatius with the *Topica*.

So far so good. But we are immediately confronted with the problem of what Cicero was doing, and what he thought he was doing. The work professes to be a translation or adaptation of the *Topics of Aristotle*, with illustrations and examples from Roman jurisprudence, but it bears little resemblance to this treatise. True, some of the topics presented by Cicero can be discovered in Aristotle's *Topica*; more can be found in the list given in the twenty-third chapter of the second book of Aristotle's *Rhetoric*; still others are demonstrably later, and of Stoic origin. There is a further consideration that the same topics, classified according to the same scheme, are given in the *de Oratore*, II, 162–173.

INTRODUCTION

It must also be noted that the *Topica* deals with more than topics of argumentation. At § 72 Cicero apologizes to Trebatius for going beyond his original plan. The following sections discuss testimony, and are succeeded by an enumeration of the three kinds of oratory, the parts of a speech, etc. What emerges is a miniature treatise on Invention, and it seems clear that Cicero is adapting, perhaps from memory, some late Hellenistic treatise, and that he was misled by the mention of Aristotle (§ 6) as the first writer on Topics into thinking that his source really represented Aristotle's work.

Attempts have been made to determine more precisely the author of the work which Cicero reproduces. Wallies suggested Antiochus of Ascalon, and his view was followed by Kroll; Hammer thought of Diodotus. Both suggestions are plausible, but not much more can be said for them.

Trebatius, to whom the book is dedicated, was Gaius Trebatius Testa, a jurisconsult of repute, who on Cicero's recommendation had served with Caesar in Gaul. Cicero addressed to him the letters *ad Familiares* vii, 6–22 (cf. also *ad Fam.* vii, 5, Cicero's letter commending him to Caesar), and Horace makes him a speaker in the first Satire of the second book.

OUTLINE OF CONTENTS

INTRODUCTION

9–23. The intrinsic topics are enumerated, with a brief example of each.

24. The extrinsic topics.

25. Interlude: We shall now take up the topics in detail.

26–71. The intrinsic topics are discussed again, this time with a full analysis of each.

72. Interlude: The extrinsic topics are not pertinent to jurisprudence, but will be included for the sake of completeness.

73–78. The extrinsic topics are fully treated.

79–86. There are two kinds of subjects for speeches: the general proposition and the special case. The general proposition is discussed at length in connexion with the " issues " (*status*) raised in them—of fact (*sitne*), of definition (*quid sit*), of quality (*quale sit*).

87–90. Certain topics are suited to each form of the general proposition.

91–96. Special cases are forensic, deliberative or epideictic: certain topics are appropriate to each.

97–99. The four parts of a speech—introduction, narrative, proof, peroration—and the appropriate topics.

100. Conclusion: this work has included more than was originally planned.

Bibliography

Besides the complete texts of Cicero, mentioned on pp. xv and 352, there is a text, translation and commentary by Henri Bornecque, *Cicéron, Divisions de l'art oratoire, Topiques*, Paris, 1924.

An English translation by Charles Duke Yonge

is included in the volume cited in the bibliography on p. xvi.

The following monographs and articles have been found useful:

Emilio Costa, *Cicerone Giureconsulto*. Bologna, 1927.

Wilhelm Friedrich, *Zu Ciceros Topica*. Jahrbücher für classische Philologie xxxv (1889), pp. 281–296. The fullest information about the manuscripts.

Casper Hammer, *Commentatio de Ciceronis Topicis*. Prog. Landau, 1879.

Johann Joseph Klein, *Dissertatio de Fontibus Topicorum Ciceronis*. Bonn, 1844; thinks that Cicero used Aristotle's *Rhetoric* as a source.

Thomas Stangl, *Textkritische Bemerkungen zu Ciceros rhetorischen Schriften*. Blätter für das bayerische Gymnasialschulwesen, xviii (1882), pp. 245–253.

Maximilian Wallies, *De Fontibus Topicorum Ciceronis*. Diss. Halle, 1878; thinks that Cicero used Antiochus of Ascalon who had combined Peripatetic, Academic and Stoic logic.

Text

The manuscripts fall into three classes. The first contains two codices, Ottobonianus 1406 (O) of the tenth century and the closely related *Vitebergensis* (f). These are the best evidence and in most cases their reading is to be preferred. The second group, nearly as reliable, comprises (A), Codex Vossianus 84; (B), Codex Vossianus 86; and m, Codex Marcianus 257, all three of the tenth

century. These manuscripts so frequently agree that it is convenient to cite them together as A. There remain for the third class a large number of inferior manuscripts, of which I cite only L, Codex Leidensis 90; V, Codex Vossianus 70; a, Codex Einsiedlensis 324; c, Codex Sangallensis 854. I have seen none of these except the photographic facsimile of (A), and as the reports in *apparatus critici* are sometimes contradictory, it has not always been possible to be certain about the proper reading.

O. Codex Ottobonianus 1406.
f. Codex Vitebergensis.
A. Consensus of

> (*A*) Codex Vossianus 84.
> (*B*) Codex Vossianus 86.
> m Codex Marcianus 257.

L. Codex Leidensis 90.
V. Codex Vossianus 70.
a. Codex Einsiedlensis 324.
c. Codex Sangallensis 854.
codd. Consensus of all MSS. or of those not otherwise cited.

MARCUS TULLI CICERONIS

TOPICA

I. Maiores nos res scribere ingressos, C. Trebati,
et his libris quos brevi tempore satis multos edidimus
digniores, e cursu ipso revocavit voluntas tua. Cum
enim mecum in Tusculano esses et in bibliotheca
separatim uterque nostrum ad suum studium libellos
quos vellet evolveret, incidisti in Aristotelis Topica
quaedam, quae sunt ab illo pluribus libris explicata.
Qua inscriptione commotus continuo a me librorum
2 eorum sententiam requisisti; quam cum tibi ex-
posuissem, disciplinam inveniendorum argumentorum, ut sine ullo errore ad ea [1] ratione et via [2]
perveniremus, ab Aristotele inventam illis libris
contineri, verecunde tu quidem ut omnia, sed tamen
facile ut cernerem te ardere studio, mecum ut tibi
illa traderem egisti. Cum autem ego te non tam
vitandi laboris mei causa quam quia tua id interesse
arbitrarer, vel ut eos per te ipse legeres vel ut totam
rationem a doctissimo quodam rhetore acciperes,
hortatus essem, utrumque, ut ex te audiebam, es

---

[1] ad ea *Klotz from Boethius* : ad eam *codd.*
[2] ratione et via *vulg. from Boethius* : rationem via *codd.*

---

[a] He had begun the *de Officiis*, which was interrupted
and not finished until his return from his voyage mentioned
below. He had within a year published the *Consolatio, de*

MARCUS TULLIUS CICERO

TOPICS

I. I had set out to write on a larger subject and one more in keeping with the books of which I have published enough surely in the recent past, when I was recalled from my course by your request, my dear Trebatius.[a] You will remember that when we were together in my Tusculan villa and were sitting in the library, each of us according to his fancy unrolling the volumes which he wished, you hit upon certain Topics of Aristotle which were expounded by him in several books. Excited by the title, you immediately asked me what the subject

2 of the work was. And when I had made clear to you that these books contained a system developed by Aristotle for inventing arguments so that we might come upon them by a rational system without wandering about, you begged me to teach you the subject. Your request was made with the modesty which you show in everything, yet I could easily see that you were aflame with eagerness. Not so much to avoid labour as because I thought it would be for your good, I urged you to read the books yourself, or acquire the whole system from a very learned teacher of oratory whom I named. You

Finibus, Academicae Quaestiones, de Natura Deorum, de Divinatione, de Fato, de Amicitia, de Senectute and *de Gloria.*

3 expertus. Sed a libris te obscuritas reiecit; rhetor autem ille magnus haec, ut opinor, Aristotelia se ignorare respondit. Quod quidem minime sum admiratus eum philosophum rhetori non esse cognitum, qui ab ipsis philosophis praeter admodum paucos ignoretur; quibus eo minus ignoscendum est, quod non modo rebus eis quae ab illo dictae et inventae sunt allici debuerunt, sed dicendi quoque incredibili quadam cum copia tum etiam suavitate.

4 Non potui igitur tibi saepius hoc roganti et tamen verenti ne mihi gravis esses—facile enim id cernebam —debere diutius, ne ipsi iuris interpreti fieri videretur iniuria. Etenim cum tu mihi meisque multa saepe scripsisses,[1] veritus sum ne, si ego gravarer, aut ingratum id aut superbum videretur. Sed dum fuimus una, tu optimus es testis quam fuerim occupa-

5 tus; ut autem a te discessi in Graeciam proficiscens, cum opera mea nec res publica nec amici uterentur nec honeste inter arma versari possem, ne si tuto quidem mihi id liceret, ut veni Veliam tuaque et tuos vidi, admonitus huius aeris alieni nolui deesse ne tacitae quidem flagitationi tuae. Itaque haec, cum mecum libros non haberem, memoria repetita in ipsa navigatione conscripsi tibique ex itinere misi, ut mea diligentia mandatorum tuorum te quoque, etsi admonitore non eges, ad memoriam

[1] scripsisses : cavisses *Of.*

---

a This may refer to legal opinions given for Cicero and his clients, or to books which Trebatius had dedicated to Cicero. Trebatius was the author of several works, now lost.

3 had tried both, as you told me. But you were repelled from reading the books by their obscurity; and that great teacher replied that he was not acquainted with these works, which are, as I think, by Aristotle. I am not indeed astonished in the slightest degree that the philosopher was unknown to the teacher of oratory, for he is ignored by all except a few of the professed philosophers. The philosophers deserve less excuse for their neglect, because they should have been attracted, not only by the matter which he has discovered and presented, but also by an unbelievable charm and richness in his style.

4   When you repeated your request again and again, and at the same time were afraid of annoying me— that I could easily see—I could no longer refrain from paying the debt, lest the interpreter of the law should be treated unlawfully. For taking into consideration that you had often written at great length for me and my friends,[a] I was afraid that my hesitation might be thought to be ingratitude or discourtesy. But you yourself can best testify how

5 busy I was when we were together; and when I left you, and set out on my way to Greece, since neither the state nor my friends required my services and I could not with honour live in the midst of the strife of arms, supposing that I might have done so with safety, and on reaching Velia I saw your family and your home, I was reminded of this debt, and was unwilling to refuse even your silent demand for payment. Therefore, since I had no books with me, I wrote up what I could remember on the voyage and sent it to you, in order that by my diligence in obeying your commands I might arouse you— though you need no admonition—to keep my busi-

nostrarum rerum excitarem. Sed iam tempus est
ad id quod instituimus accedere.

6   II. Cum omnis ratio diligens disserendi duas habeat
partis, unam inveniendi alteram iudicandi, utriusque
princeps, ut mihi quidem videtur, Aristoteles fuit.
Stoici autem in altera elaboraverunt; iudicandi enim
vias diligenter persecuti sunt ea scientia quam
διαλεκτικὴν appellant, inveniendi artem quae τοπικὴ
dicitur, quae et ad usum potior erat et ordine naturae
7   certe prior, totam reliquerunt. Nos autem, quoniam
in utraque summa utilitas est et utramque, si erit
otium, persequi cogitamus, ab ea quae prior est
ordiemur.   Ut igitur earum rerum quae absconditae
sunt demonstrato et notato loco facilis inventio est,
sic, cum pervestigare argumentum aliquod volumus,
locos nosse debemus; sic enim appellatae ab
Aristotele sunt eae quasi sedes, e quibus argumenta
8   promuntur. Itaque licet definire locum esse argumenti sedem, argumentum autem rationem quae rei
dubiae faciat fidem.

Sed ex his locis in quibus argumenta inclusa sunt,
alii in eo ipso de quo agitur haerent, alii assumuntur
extrinsecus.   In ipso tum ex toto, tum ex partibus
eius, tum ex nota, tum ex eis rebus quae quodam

ª Apparently Trebatius was acting in some capacity for
Cicero : the phrase here used may be compared with the
similar language of the letter which Cicero wrote to Trebatius from Velia at this time : *ad Fam.* vii, 20, 3 : Sed
valebis meaque negotia videbis (But you must keep well,
and look after my affairs).

ᵇ Greek τόπος " place " or " region " gives the adjective
τοπικός from which " topic " is derived.   Aristotle used
τόπος to denote the pigeon-hole or region in the mind where
similar arguments are stored, and secondarily the *type* of
such similar arguments.   For a fuller discussion *v.* Cope,

ness in mind.[a] But it is now time to turn to our appointed task.

6   II. Every systematic treatment of argumentation has two branches, one concerned with invention of arguments and the other with judgement of their validity; Aristotle was the founder of both in my opinion. The Stoics have worked in only one of the two fields. That is to say, they have followed diligently the ways of judgement by means of the science which they call διαλεκτική (dialectic), but they have totally neglected the art which is called τοπική (topics), an art which is both more useful

7   and certainly prior in the order of nature. For my part, I shall begin with the earlier, since both are useful in the highest degree, and I intend to follow up both, if I have leisure. A comparison may help: It is easy to find things that are hidden if the hiding place is pointed out and marked; similarly if we wish to track down some argument we ought to know the places or topics: for that is the name given by Aristotle to the " regions ", as it were, from

8   which arguments are drawn. Accordingly, we may define a topic as the region of an argument, and an argument as a course of reasoning which firmly establishes a matter about which there is some doubt.[b]

Of the topics under which arguments are included, some are inherent in the very nature of the subject which is under discussion, and others are brought in from without. Inherent in the nature of the subject are arguments derived from the whole, from its parts, from its meaning, and from the things which are in some way closely connected with the

Introduction to Aristotle's Rhetoric, pp. 124–133; Jebb, *The Rhetoric of Aristotle, a Translation*, pp. 142–144.

CICERO

modo affectae [1] sunt ad id de quo quaeritur. Extrinsecus autem ea ducuntur quae absunt longeque disiuncta sunt.

9   Sed ad id totum de quo disseritur tum definitio adhibetur, quae [2] quasi involutum evolvit [3] id de quo quaeritur; eius argumenti talis est formula: Ius civile est aequitas constituta eis qui eiusdem civitatis sunt ad res suas obtinendas; eius autem aequitatis utilis cognitio est; utilis ergo est iuris civilis scientia;

10   —tum partium enumeratio, quae tractatur hoc modo: Si neque censu nec vindicta nec testamento liber factus est, non est liber; neque ulla est earum rerum; non est igitur liber;—tum notatio, cum ex verbi vi argumentum aliquod elicitur hoc modo: Cum lex assiduo vindicem assiduum esse iubeat, locupletem iubet locupleti; is est enim assiduus, ut ait L. Aelius, appellatus ab aere dando.

[1] adfectae *codd* : adfictae *Nettleship*.
[2] quae *O* : qua *codd*.
[3] evolvit *O* : evolvitur *codd*.

---

[a] For these methods of manumission see Buckland, W. W., *A Text-Book of Roman Law from Augustus to Justinian*, 2nd ed. (1932), pp. 72–78.

[b] *I.e. assi* from *as*, gen. *assis*, a coin, and *duus* from *do*, I give. The etymology is wrong, but was the one commonly accepted at the time; *assidui* (tax-payers or freeholders) were contrasted in early times with *proletarii*.

The Aelius who is quoted as the authority for this etymology is probably Lucius Aelius Stilo Praeconinus, a noted grammarian and rhetorician, and one of Cicero's teachers; or he may be the jurist Sextus Aelius Paetus Catus, consul 198 B.C. who wrote a commentary on the Twelve Tables.

The law involved is explained in the following quotation from Buckland, *A Text-Book of Roman Law from Augustus to Justinian*, 2nd ed., p. 618 f., describing the procedure for collecting a judgement. " The process was as follows :

subject which is being investigated. Arguments from external circumstances are those that are removed and widely separated from the subject.

9 Sometimes a definition is applied to the whole subject which is under consideration; this definition unfolds what is wrapped up, as it were, in the subject which is being examined. The following is the pattern of such an argument: The civil law is a system of equity established between members of the same state for the purpose of securing to each his property rights; the knowledge of this system of equity is useful; therefore the science of civil
10 law is useful. Sometimes there is an enumeration of parts, and this is handled in the following manner: So-and-So is not a free man unless he has been set free by entry in the census roll, or by touching with the rod, or by will.[a] None of these conditions has been fulfilled, therefore he is not free. Then etymology may be employed, when some argument is derived from the force or meaning of a word, in this fashion: Since the law provides that an *assiduus* (tax-payer or freeholder) shall be *vindex* (representative) for an *assiduus,* it provides that a rich man be representative for a rich man; for that is the meaning of *assiduus,* it being derived, as Aelius says, from *aere dando* (paying money).[b]

after 30 days from the judgement or other event justifying the seizure, the claimant brought the party liable before the magistrate. . . . The defendant might not defend himself against the *manus iniectio,* but if he claimed that it was not justified, some one must appear on his behalf to prove this—a *vindex.* The effect of the intervention was that the defendant was released, and further proceedings were against the *vindex.*" *Cf.* also, Bruns, *Fontes Iuris Romani,* 7th ed., p. 18.

11 III. Ducuntur etiam argumenta ex eis rebus quae
quodam modo affectae sunt ad id de quo quaeritur.
Sed hoc genus in pluris partis distributum est.
Nam alia coniugata appellamus, alia ex genere,
alia ex forma, alia ex similitudine, alia ex differentia,
alia ex contrario, alia ex adiunctis,[1] alia ex antecedentibus, alia ex consequentibus, alia ex repugnantibus, alia ex causis, alia ex effectis, alia ex comparatione maiorum aut parium aut minorum.

12 Coniugata dicuntur quae sunt ex verbis generis
eiusdem. Eiusdem autem generis verba sunt quae
orta ab uno varie commutantur, ut sapiens sapienter
sapientia. Haec verborum coniugatio συζυγία dicitur,
ex qua huius modi est argumentum: Si compascuus
ager est, ius est compascere.

13 A genere sic ducitur: Quoniam argentum omne
mulieri legatum est, non potest ea pecunia quae
numerata domi relicta est non esse legata; forma
enim a genere, quoad suum nomen retinet, nunquam seiungitur, numerata autem pecunia nomen
argenti retinet; legata igitur videtur.

14 A forma generis, quam interdum, quo planius
accipiatur, partem licet nominare hoc modo: Si
ita Fabiae pecunia legata est a viro, si ei viro mater-
familias esset; si ea in manum non convenerat,
nihil debetur. Genus enim est uxor; eius duae
formae: una matrumfamilias, eae sunt, quae in

---

[1] adiunctis *Oc* : coniunctis *codd.*

---

[a] I have translated *compascuus* as " common " rather than
as " common pasture," because freeholders might cut wood
on it as well as use it for pasture. *Cf.* Voigt, in *Abhandlungen
der philol.-hist. Classe der K. sächischen Gesellschaft der Wis-*

11 III. Arguments are also drawn from circumstances closely connected with the subject which is under inquiry. But this class has many subdivisions. For we call some arguments " conjugate," others we derive from genus, species, similarity, difference, contraries, adjuncts, antecedents, consequents, contradictions, cause, effect, and comparison with events of greater, less or equal importance.

12 " Conjugate " is the term applied to arguments based on words of the same family. Words of the same family are those which are formed from one root but have different grammatical forms, as *wise, wisely, wisdom*. Such a " conjugation " of words is called συζυγία (syzygy), and yields an argument of this sort: If a field is " common " (*compascuus*), it is legal to use it as a common pasture (*compascere*).[a]

13 An argument is derived from genus in the following way: Since all the silver was bequeathed to the wife, the coin which was left in the house must also have been bequeathed. For the species is never separated from its genus, as long as it keeps its proper name; coin keeps the name of silver; therefore it seems to have been included in the legacy.

14 An argument is derived from the species of a genus as follows (sometimes for greater clarity we may call a species a part): If Fabia's husband has bequeathed her a sum of money on condition that she be *mater familias*, and she has not come under his *manus*, nothing is due her. For " wife " is a genus, and of this genus there are two species; one *matres familias*, that is, those who have come

senschaften X. (1888), pp. 229-233. Quintilian (V, x, 85) says that the argument is too silly to mention, except that Cicero had included it in the *Topica*.

manum convenerunt; altera earum, quae tantum
modo uxores habentur. Qua in parte cum fuerit
Fabia, legatum ei [1] non videtur.

15 A similitudine hoc modo: Si aedes eae corruerunt
vitiumve faciunt quarum usus fructus legatus est,
heres restituere non debet nec reficere, non magis
quam servum restituere, si is cuius usus fructus
legatus esset deperisset.

16 A differentia: Non, si uxori vir legavit argentum
omne quod suum esset, idcirco quae in nominibus
fuerunt legata sunt. Multum enim differt in arcane
positum sit argentum an in tabulis debeatur. [2]

17 Ex contrario autem sic: Non debet ea mulier
cui vir bonorum suorum usum fructum legavit cellis
vinariis et oleariis plenis relictis, putare id ad se
pertinere. Usus enim, non abusus, legatus est.
Ea sunt inter se contraria. [3]

18 IV. Ab adiunctis: Si ea mulier testamentum fecit
quae se capite nunquam deminuit, non videtur ex
edicto praetoris secundum eas tabulas possessio
dari. Adiungitur enim, ut secundum servorum,

---

[1] ei *omitted by* O.
[2] debeatur *bracketed by Hotman.*
[3] Ea . . . contraria *bracketed by Hammer.*

---

[a] In the primitive Roman form of marriage the woman
passed from the power of her father into that of her husband
and became a member of his agnatic family; such a wife
was called *mater familias* and said to be *in manu.* Besides
this there grew up very early another form of marriage by
which the woman remained *in patria potestate* and did not
change her family. This ultimately became the prevailing
form. *Cf.* Sohm-Mitteis-Wenger, *Institutionen, Geschichte
und System des römischen Privatrechts,* 17th ed. (1933), pp.

under *manus*; the second, those who are regarded only as wives (*uxores*). Since Fabia belonged to the second class, it is clear that no legacy was made to her.[a]

15   An argument is based on similarity or analogy in the following manner: If one has received by will the usufruct of a house, and the house has collapsed or is in disrepair, the heir (*i.e.* the remainder-man) is not bound to restore or repair it, any more than he would have been bound to replace a slave of which the usufruct had been bequeathed, if the slave had died.

16   An argument based on difference: If a man has bequeathed to his wife all the money that is his, he has not, therefore, bequeathed what is owed him; for it makes a great difference whether the money is stored in a strong-box or is on his books.

17   An argument from contraries, as follows: A woman whose husband has bequeathed her the usufruct of his property and has left full wine and oil cellars ought not to think that she has a right in these. For it is use and not consumption that was bequeathed. And these are contrary one to the other.[b]

18   IV. From adjuncts (corollaries): If a woman who has never changed her civil status makes a will, it appears that possession of the inheritance cannot be given by praetorian edict in accordance with the terms of this instrument. For the corollary is that it would appear that possession is given by praetorian

---

506–509; Corbett, P. E., *The Roman Law of Marriage*, pp. 68–106, 113.

[b] " As the usufructuary was bound to return the thing in good condition, there was no usufruct of perishables." Buckland, *A Text-Book of Roman Law*, 2nd ed., p. 271.

secundum exsulum, secundum puerorum tabulas possessio videatur ex edicto dari.

19   Ab antecedentibus autem et consequentibus et repugnantibus hoc modo; ab antecedentibus: Si viri culpa factum est divortium, etsi mulier nuntium remisit, tamen pro liberis manere nihil oportet.

20   A consequentibus: Si mulier, cum fuisset nupta cum eo quicum conubium non esset, nuntium remisit; quoniam qui nati sunt patrem non sequuntur, pro liberis manere nihil oportet.

21   A repugnantibus: Si paterfamilias uxori ancillarum usum fructum legavit a filio neque a secundo herede legavit, mortuo filio mulier usum fructum non amittet. Quod enim semel testamento alicui datum est, id ab eo invito cui datum est auferri non potest. Repugnat [1] enim recte accipere et invitum reddere.

22   Ab efficientibus rebus hoc modo: Omnibus est ius parietem directum ad parietem communem adiungere vel solidum vel fornicatum. Sed qui in pariete communi demoliendo damni infecti promiserit, non debebit praestare quod fornix viti fecerit. Non enim eius vitio qui demolitus est damnum factum est, sed eius operis vitio quod ita aedificatum est ut suspendi non posset.

---

[1] repugnat *O* : pugnat *codd.*

---

[a] Until the time of Hadrian a woman could not make a will unless she became *sui iuris* by suffering *capitis deminutio* (change of civil status) and coming under a *tutor*. *V.* Buckland, *op. cit.*, p. 288; and for *capitis deminutio*, pp. 134–141.

[b] The rule was that if a woman or her *paterfamilias* divorced her husband without due cause on his part, one-sixth of the dowry was left with the husband for each child of the marriage. (Not more than half the total dowry was so left.) *V.* Corbett, *op. cit.*, p. 192, and the authorities there cited.

edict in accordance with the terms of the wills of slaves, exiles, and minors.[a]

19 From antecedents, consequents and contradictions in the following manner. From antecedents: If a divorce occurs through an offence by the husband, although the woman has sent the letter of divorcement, still no part of the dowry should be left for the children.[b]

20 From consequents: If a woman, married to a man with whom she does not have *conubium* (right of marriage), has divorced him, inasmuch as the children who have been born do not follow the father, no part of the dowry should be left for the children.

21 From contradictions: If a *pater familias* has bequeathed to his wife the usufruct of maid-servants as a proviso in naming his son as heir, and has made no such proviso in naming a reversionary heir, on the death of the son the woman will not lose her usufruct. For what has once been given to some one by will cannot be taken from him to whom it has been given without his consent. For " receiving legally " and " surrendering unwillingly " are contradictory.

22 From efficient causes in this way: Anyone has a right to build a wall to touch a party wall at a right angle; and this new wall may be either solid or resting on arches. But a man who has given guarantees against eventual damage in demolishing a party wall will not be bound to make good the loss which is caused by an arch. For the damage was not caused by any fault of the man who demolished the party wall, but by a defect in building the arch which was so constructed that it could not be supported (without the party wall).

395

23 Ab effectis rebus hoc modo: Cum mulier viro in manum convenit, omnia quae mulieris fuerunt viri fiunt dotis nomine.

Ex comparatione autem omnia valent quae sunt huius modi: Quod in re maiore valet valeat in minore,[1] ut si in urbe fines non reguntur, nec aqua in urbe arceatur. Item contra: Quod in minore valet, valeat in maiore. Licet idem exemplum convertere. Item: Quod in re pari valet valeat in hac quae par est; ut: Quoniam usus auctoritas fundi biennium est, sit etiam aedium. At in lege aedes non appellantur et sunt ceterarum rerum omnium quarum annuus est usus. Valeat aequitas, quae paribus in causis paria iura desiderat.

24 Quae autem assumuntur extrinsecus, ea maxime ex auctoritate ducuntur. Itaque Graeci talis argumentationes ἀτέχνους vocant, id est artis expertis, ut si ita respondeas: Quoniam P. Scaevola id solum esse ambitus aedium dixerit, quod [2] parietis communis tegendi causa tectum proiceretur, ex quo

---

[1] re minore *OLV*.
[2] quod *vulg.*: quantum *OB Boethius*: quo *d*: quoad *Valla*.

---

a For the discussion of the law in such a case, *v.* Buckland, *op. cit.*, p. 107; Corbett, *op. cit.*, p. 149.

b The boundaries (*fines*) here referred to were strips of land five feet wide between estates, which could not be acquired by either neighbour through *usucapio*. The action for excluding water (actio aquae pluviae arcendae) lay against your neighbour who diverted a water-course to your land.

c In case of a farm, the vendor sells the use (*usus*) of it and warrants the possessor that he is well and duly seized of the property. This warranty (*auctoritas*) runs for two years, after which the purchaser has title by adverse pos-

23   From effects as follows: When a woman comes
under the *manus* (legal control) of her husband,
all her property goes to the husband under the
designation of dowry.[a]

All arguments from comparison are valid if they
are of the following character: What is valid in the
greater should be valid in the less, as for example
since there is no action for regulating boundaries [b]
in the city, there should be no action for excluding
water in the city. Likewise the reverse: What
is valid in the less should be valid in the greater;
the same example may be used if reversed. Likewise: What is valid in one of two equal cases should
be valid in the other; for example: Since use and
warranty run for two years in the case of a farm,
the same should be true of a (city) house. But a
(city) house is not mentioned in the law, and is
included with the other things use of which runs for
one year.[c] Equity should prevail, which requires
equal laws in equal cases.

24   Extrinsic arguments depend principally on
authority. Therefore the Greeks call such means
of argumentation ἄτεχνοι (atechnoi), that is, not
invented by the art of the orator; such would be the
case if you answered your opponent as follows: Since
Publius Scaevola [d] has said that the *ambitus* of a
house is only that space which is covered by a roof
put up to protect a party wall, from which roof the

session (*usucapio*). *V.* Th. Mommsen, *Ad legem de scribis
et viatoribus et de auctoritate commentationes duae*, Doctoral
Dissertation (1843), pp. 18-20 = *Gesammelte Schriften* III, pp.
463-464.

[d] A jurisconsult, whose opinion on a point of law would
have weight (*auctoritas*) with a jury.

tecto in eius [1] aedis qui protexisset aqua deflueret,
id ambitus [2] videri.

25 His igitur locis qui sunt expositi ad omne argumentum reperiendum [3] tamquam elementis quibusdam significatio et demonstratio [4] datur. Utrum
igitur hactenus satis est? Tibi quidem tam acuto et
tam occupato puto. V. Sed quoniam avidum hominem ad has discendi epulas recepi, sic accipiam, ut
reliquiarum sit potius aliquid quam te hinc patiar
26 non satiatum discedere. Quando ergo unus quisque
eorum locorum quos exposui sua quaedam habet
membra, ea quam subtilissime persequamur.

Et primum de ipsa definitione dicatur. Definitio
est oratio quae id quod definitur explicat quid sit.
Definitionum autem duo genera prima: unum
earum rerum quae sunt, alterum earum quae intel-
27 leguntur. Esse ea dico quae cerni tangique possunt,
ut fundum aedes, parietem stillicidium, mancipium
pecudem, supellectilem penus et cetera; quo ex
genere quaedam interdum vobis definienda sunt.
Non esse rursus ea dico quae tangi demonstrarive
non possunt, cerni tamen animo atque intellegi
possunt, ut si usus capionem, si tutelam, si gentem,

---

[1] tecto in eius *Boethius* : in tectum eius *codd.*
[2] ambitus *Parker, Hermathena* xiii (1905), p. 252 : tibi ius *C.*
[3] reperiendum *omitted by O.*
[4] *After* demonstratio *the MSS. except O have* ad reperiendum.

---

[a] There is a vagueness about the meaning of *ambitus.*
The grammarian Festus (*Paul. ex Fest.*, p. 16, Mueller) says
that " properly speaking it is a space of 2½ feet left as a
passage way between neighbouring buildings."
The passage in the text is obscure, and probably corrupt.

water flows into the home of the man who has put
up the roof, this seems to be the meaning of *ambitus.*[a]
25 Well then, the topics which I have set forth as
the rudiments so to speak for discovering any
argument, have been defined and described. Is it
enough to have gone thus far? For you, I think, yes;
you are so quick to get the point, and so busy.
V. But as I have a guest with such a ravenous
appetite for this feast of learning, I shall provide
such an abundance that there may be something
left from the banquet, rather than let you go un-
26 satisfied. Therefore, since each of the topics which
I have set forth has certain subdivisions of its
own, let us hunt them out even to the minutest
detail.

First of all, then let us take up definition itself.
A definition is a statement which explains what the
thing defined is. Of definitions there are two prime
classes, one defining things that exist, and the
other, things which are apprehended only by the
27 mind. By things that exist I mean such as can be
seen and touched: for example, farm, house, wall,
rain-water, slave, animal, furniture, food, etc.; sometimes you[b] have to define objects of this class.
On the other hand, by things which do not exist
I mean those which cannot be touched or pointed out,
but can, for all that, be perceived by the mind and
comprehended; for example, you might define
acquisition by long possession, guardianship, *gens,*[c]

The sense would be improved by bracketing *communis.* I
owe this emendation to my colleague, A. R. Bellinger.
[b] *i.e.* the jurisconsults.
[c] *Gens* included all who bore a common name, such as
Claudius, Julius.

si agnationem definias, quarum rerum nullum subest [1]
corpus, est tamen quaedam conformatio insignita et
impressa intellegentia, quam notionem voco. Ea
saepe in argumentando definitione explicanda est.

28   Atque etiam definitiones aliae sunt partitionum
aliae divisionum; partitionum, cum res ea quae
proposita est quasi in membra discerpitur, ut si quis
ius civile dicat id esse quod in legibus, senatus
consultis, rebus iudicatis, iuris peritorum auctoritate,
edictis magistratuum, more, aequitate consistat.
Divisionum autem definitio formas omnis com-
plectitur quae sub eo genere sunt quod definitur hoc
modo: Abalienatio est eius rei quae mancipi est
aut traditio alteri nexu aut in iure cessio inter quos
ea iure civili fieri possunt.

VI. Sunt etiam alia genera definitionum, sed ad
huius libri institutum illa nihil pertinent; tantum
29 est dicendum qui sit definitionis modus. Sic igitur
veteres praecipiunt: cum sumpseris ea quae sint
ei rei quam definire velis cum aliis communia, usque
eo persequi, dum proprium efficiatur, quod nullam
in aliam rem transferri possit. Ut haec: Hereditas
est pecunia. Commune adhuc; multa enim genera

---

[1] *After* subest *the MSS. have* quasi: *bracketed by Proust.*

---

[a] Relation on the father's side.
[b] *Mancipatio* (grasping by the hand) was an ancient
method of transferring " by copper and scales " in the
presence of five witnesses and a weigher, certain property
known as *res mancipi, i.e.* Italian soil, rustic servitudes
(easements) such as the right to cross land (*via, iter, actus,
aquaeductus*), slaves and beasts of draught or burden. The
second method required the intended vendee to claim the
property in court : the vendor put up no defence, and the
court gave title. *V.* Buckland, *op. cit.*, pp. 226–241. *Traditio nexu* is here equivalent to *mancipatio. V.* Pflüger, *Zur*

agnation;[a] of these things there is no body, but a clear pattern and understanding impressed on the mind, and this I call a notion. In the course of argumentation this notion frequently requires definition.

28 Secondly, definitions are made partly by enumeration and partly by analysis; by enumeration, when the thing which has been set up for definition is divided into its members as it were: for instance, if one should define the civil law as made up of statutes, decrees of the Senate, judicial decisions, opinions of those learned in the law, edicts of magistrates, custom, and equity. Definition by analysis includes all the *species* that come under the *genus* which is being defined, as follows: *Abalienatio* (transfer of property according to the forms of civil law) of a thing which is *mancipi* is either transfer with legal obligation (*mancipatio*) or cession at law (fictitious suit) between those who can do this in accordance with the civil law.[b]

VI. There are also other kinds of definition, but they have no connexion with the purpose of this book; we have only to describe the method of 29 definition. The ancients, then, lay down the rules as follows: when you have taken all the qualities which the thing you wish to define has in common with other things, you should pursue the analysis until you produce its own distinctive quality which can be transferred to no other thing. Here is an example: An inheritance is property. This is a common quality; for there are many kinds of

Lehre vom Erwerbe des Eigentums nach römischen Recht, pp. 97–110, where the extensive literature on the subject is cited. Also v. Mitteis, *Römisches Privatrecht*, pp. 136–146.

pecuniae. Adde quod sequitur: quae morte alicuius ad quempiam pervenit. Nondum est definitio; multis enim modis sine hereditate teneri pecuniae mortuorum possunt. Unum adde verbum: iure; iam a communitate res diiuncta videbitur, ut sit explicata definitio sic: Hereditas est pecunia quae morte alicuius ad quempiam pervenit iure. Nondum est satis; adde: nec ea aut legata testamento aut possessione retenta; confectum est. Itemque:[1] Gentiles sunt inter se qui eodem nomine sunt. Non est satis. Qui ab ingenuis oriundi sunt. Ne id quidem satis est. Quorum maiorum nemo servitutem servivit. Abest etiam nunc. Qui capite non sunt deminuti. Hoc fortasse satis est. Nihil enim video Scaevolam pontificem ad hanc definitionem addidisse. Atque haec ratio valet in utroque genere definitionum, sive id quod est, sive id quod intellegitur definiendum est.

30   Partitionum autem[2] et divisionum genus quale esset ostendimus, sed quid inter se differant planius dicendum est. In partitione quasi membra sunt, ut corporis, caput, umeri, manus, latera, crura, pedes et cetera. VII. In divisione formae, quas Graeci

---

[1] *After* itemque *the MSS. have* ut illud: *bracketed by Friedrich.*

[2] autem *bracketed by Lambinus.*

---

[a] " Where a *hereditas* was, or had been *iacens* (there being no *heres suus* or *necessarius*, who was in without acceptance), anyone might, by taking the property or part of it not yet possessed by the *heres*, even after acceptance, become owner by holding it (even land) for one year without good faith." Buckland, *op. cit.*, p. 244. *Gaius* II, 52.

[b] *Capitis deminutio* (loss of civil capacity) was of three degrees : *maxima*, loss of liberty, *i.e.* enslavement, involving loss of citizenship and family rights; *media* or *minor*, loss of

property. Add the following: which comes to
some one at the death of another. It is not yet a
definition; for the property of the dead can be held
in many ways without inheritance. Add one word,
" legally." By now the thing will seem to be
separated from those with which it shares qualities
in common, so that the definition has been developed
as follows: An inheritance is property which has
come to one legally at the death of another. It is
still not satisfactory. Add: and this property was
not bequeathed by will or kept by adverse possession.[a] The definition is complete. A second
example follows: " Gentiles " are those who have
the same name in common. That is not enough.
Who are sprung from freeborn ancestors. Not
even that is sufficient. None of whose ancestors
has ever been in slavery. There is still something
wanting. Who have never suffered loss of civil
capacity.[b] This is probably enough; for I see that
Scaevola the pontiff [c] added nothing to this definition.
Furthermore, the method is valid in either kind of
definition, whether we must define what exists or
what is apprehended by the mind.

30   We have explained the nature of enumeration
and analysis, but must make plainer how they differ
from one another. In an enumeration we have,
as it were, parts, as for example a body has head,
shoulders. hands, sides, legs, feet and so forth. VII.
In analysis we have classes or kinds which the

citizenship and family rights without loss of liberty; *minima*,
change of family position, *e.g.* by adoption.
 [c] Quintus Mucius Scaevola, consul 95 B.C. Pontifex
Maximus and jurisconsult. Cicero, who was his pupil,
speaks of him in *de Oratore* (i. 180) as the ablest orator in the
ranks of jurists and the ablest jurist in the ranks of orators.

εἴδη vocant, nostri, si qui haec forte tractant, species appellant, non pessime id quidem sed inutiliter ad mutandos casus in dicendo. Nolim enim, ne si Latine quidem dici possit, specierum et speciebus dicere; et saepe his casibus utendum est; at formis et formarum velim. Cum autem utroque verbo idem significetur, commoditatem in dicendo non arbitror neglegendam.

31 Genus et formam definiunt hoc modo: Genus est notio ad pluris differentias pertinens; forma est notio cuius differentia ad caput generis et quasi fontem referri potest. Notionem appello quod Graeci tum ἔννοιαν tum πρόληψιν. Ea est insita et ante [1] percepta [2] cuiusque cognitio enodationis indigens. Formae sunt igitur [3] eae in quas genus sine ullius praetermissione dividitur; ut si quis ius in legem, morem, aequitatem dividat. Formas qui putat idem esse quod partis, confundit artem et similitudine quadam conturbatus non satis acute quae 32 sunt secernenda distinguit. Saepe etiam definiunt et oratores et poetae per translationem verbi ex similitudine cum aliqua suavitate. Sed ego a vestris exemplis nisi necessario non recedam. Solebat igitur Aquilius collega et familiaris meus, cum de

---

[1] ante *C*: animo *Hammer*.
[2] percepta *codd.*: praecepta *f*.
[3] igitur *bracketed by Orelli*: *omitted by f*.

---

[a] The difficulty exists, of course, only in Latin. I shall translate Cicero's *forma* by "species."
[b] For the interpretation of this passage, *v.* Norman W. De Witt, *The Gods of Epicurus and the Canon, Transactions of the Royal Society of Canada*, 1942, Section II, p. 41.

Greeks call εἴδη (eidê), and Latin authors who have
happened to treat of the subject call *species*, not a
bad translation, to be sure, but inconvenient if we
wish to use different cases of the word in a sentence.
For even if Latin usage allowed, I should be unwilling
to say *specierum* (genitive plural) or *speciebus* (dative
or ablative plural). Still we often have to use these
cases. But I should prefer *formis* and *formarum*.
Since, however, either word has the same meaning,
I think one should not fail to use the convenient
word.[a]

31   They define genus and species as follows : a genus
is a concept which applies to several different classes ;
species is a concept whose special characteristic can
be referred to a head and source, as it were, in the
genus. By concept I mean what the Greeks call
now ἔννοια (ennoia), now πρόληψις (prolepsis). This
is an innate knowledge of anything, which has been
previously apprehended, and needs to be unfolded.[b]
The species are the classes into which the genus is
divided without omitting anything, as, for example,
if one should divide jurisprudence into statutes,
custom, and equity. If anyone thinks that species
are the same as parts, he brings confusion into the
subject, and misled by a casual resemblance fails to
distinguish sharply enough between things which
32 must be separated. Orators and poets often go so
far as to define by comparison, using metaphors
with a pleasing effect. But I, unless forced to do
so, will not use any examples except those supplied
by you jurisconsults. A case in point is Aquilius,
my colleague and intimate friend.[c] When there

----

[c] Gaius Aquilius Gallus, a distinguished jurist, was praetor
with Cicero in 66 B.C.

litoribus ageretur, quae omnia publica esse vultis, quaerentibus eis quos ad id pertinebat, quid esset litus, ita definire, qua fluctus eluderet; hoc est, quasi qui adulescentiam florem aetatis, senectutem occasum vitae velit definire; translatione enim utens discedebat a verbis propriis rerum ac suis. Quod ad definitiones attinet, hactenus; reliqua videamus.

33 VIII. Partitione tum sic utendum est, nullam ut partem relinquas; ut, si partiri velis tutelas, inscienter facias, si ullam praetermittas. At si stipulationum aut iudiciorum formulas partiare, non est vitiosum in re infinita praetermittere aliquid. Quod idem in divisione vitiosum est. Formarum enim certus est numerus quae cuique generi subiciantur; partium distributio saepe est infinitior, 34 tamquam rivorum a fonte diductio. Itaque in oratoriis artibus quaestionis genere proposito, quot eius formae sint, subiungitur absolute. At cum de ornamentis verborum sententiarumve praecipitur, quae vocant σχήματα, non fit idem. Res est enim infinitior; ut ex hoc quoque intellegatur quid velimus inter partitionem et divisionem interesse. Quamquam enim vocabula prope idem valere videbantur,[1] tamen quia res differebant, nomina rerum distare voluerunt.

[1] videbantur *Orelli* : videantur *C* : videntur *Boethius*.

was a discussion of shores, which you jurists claim
are all public property, and those who were interested
in the matter asked what a shore was, he was accustomed to define it as the place upon which the
waves play. This is as if one should choose to define
youth as the flower of a man's age or old age as the
sunset of life, for by using a metaphor he abandoned
the language proper to the object and to his profession. As for definition, this is enough; let us
now consider the other points.

33   VIII. You must at times use enumeration with
care not to omit any part. For instance, if you
wished to enumerate guardianships, you must be
stupid to pass over any. But if you were enumer-
ating the formulas for contracts and actions, it is
not wrong to pass over something in a class which
is indefinitely large. But the same procedure is
faulty in an analysis. For there is a fixed number
of species which are included in each genus. But a
division into parts is more indefinite, like drawing
34 streams of water from a fountain. And so in text-
books of rhetoric when the genus "quaestio"
(subject for debate) is under discussion, there is added
a precise statement of the number of its species.[a]
But the same method is not used when rules are
being given about the figures of style and thought
which they call σχήματα (schemata), for there is no
limit to this subject. From this, too, it may be plain
what distinction we wish to make between enumeration and analysis. For although the words seemed
to mean almost the same, it was desired that the
names of the processes should differ, because the
processes were distinct.

[a] Cf. the analysis in *de Inv.* I, 10.

35 Multa etiam ex notatione sumuntur. Ea est autem, cum ex vi nominis argumentum elicitur; quam Graeci ἐτυμολογίαν appellant, id est verbum ex verbo veriloquium; nos autem novitatem verbi non satis apti fugientes genus hoc notationem appellamus, quia sunt verba rerum notae. Itaque hoc quidem Aristoteles σύμβολον appellat, quod Latine est nota. Sed cum intellegitur quid signi-
36 ficetur, minus laborandum est de nomine. Multa igitur in disputando notatione eliciuntur ex verbo, ut cum quaeritur postliminium quid sit—non dico quae sint postlimini; nam id caderet in divisionem, quae talis est: Postliminio redeunt haec: homo, navis, mulus clitellarius, equus, equa quae frenos recipere solet—; sed cum ipsius postlimini vis quaeritur et verbum ipsum notatur; in quo Servius noster, ut opinor, nihil putat esse notandum nisi post, et liminium illud productionem esse verbi vult, ut in finitimo, legitimo, aeditimo non plus inesse
37 timum quam in meditullio tullium; Scaevola autem P. F. iunctum putat esse verbum, ut sit in eo et post et limen; ut, quae a nobis alienata, cum ad hostem pervenerint, ex suo tamquam limine exierint, hinc

---

[a] Men (or chattels) captured by the enemy lost their legal position in the Roman state, but regained it on return-ing home. In the case of citizens the right of *postliminium* was contingent on there being no disgrace in their capture by the enemy.

[b] *Meditullium* is probably from *medius* and *tullus*, an old form of *tellus* (earth). The Servius referred to is Servius Sulpicius Rufus, consul 51 B.C., a noted jurisconsult.

[c] *v.* p. 403, note *c.*

408

35 Many arguments are derived from *notatio* (etymology). This is what is used when an argument is developed out of the meaning of a word. The Greeks call this ἐτυμολογία (etymologia), and this translated word for word would be in Latin *veriloquium* (veriloquence). But to avoid using a new word that is not very suitable, we call this kind *notatio*, because words are tokens (*notae*) of things. So Aristotle uses σύμβολον (symbolon) for the idea represented by the Latin *nota*. But when the meaning is clear, we need not be so particular about the word

36 which expresses it. In debate, as I have said, many arguments are developed from a word by etymology. An example would be the question as to the meaning of *postliminium* (*reverter* or return to one's former status) [a]—I do not mean what things are subject to *postliminium*, for that would be a case for analysis, somewhat as follows: By the right of *postliminium*, the following return home: man, ship, pack-mule, stallion, mare which is customarily used with bridle ;— but when the meaning of the term *postliminium* is sought, and etymology is applied to the word itself. In this connexion our friend Servius, I think, holds that *post* is the only part which determines the meaning, and will have it that -*liminium* is merely a formative suffix, as in *finitimus* (neighbour), *legitimus* (lawful), *aeditimus* (attendant in a temple), the ending -*timus* has no more meaning than -*tullium* in *meditullium*

37 (middle).[b] But Scaevola, the son of Publius,[c] regards it as a compound word, the component parts being *post* (behind or after) and *limen* (threshold); as property of which we have lost control on its passing into the power of the enemy has departed, as it were, from its own threshold, hence when it returns

ea cum redierint post ad idem limen, postliminio redisse videantur. Quo genere etiam Mancini causa defendi potest, postliminio redisse; deditum non esse, quoniam non sit receptus; nam neque deditionem neque donationem sine acceptione intellegi posse.

38 IX. Sequitur is locus qui constat ex eis rebus quae quodam modo adfectae sunt ad id de quo ambigitur; quem modo dixi in plures partes distributum. Cuius est primus locus ex coniugatione, quam Graeci συζυγίαν vocant, finitimus notationi, de qua modo dictum est; ut, si aquam pluviam eam modo intellegeremus quam imbri collectam videremus, veniret Mucius, qui, quia coniugata [1] verba essent pluvia et pluendo, diceret omnem aquam oportere arceri quae pluendo crevisset.

39 Cum autem a genere ducetur argumentum, non erit necesse id usque a capite arcessere. Saepe etiam citra licet, dum modo supra sit quod sumitur, quam id ad quod sumitur; ut aqua pluvia ultimo genere ea est quae de caelo veniens crescit imbri, sed propiore, in quo quasi ius arcendi continetur, genus est aqua pluvia nocens: eius generis formae

---

[1] coniugata *Of*: iugata *codd.*

---

[a] Gaius Hostilius Mancinus was defeated by the army of Numantia in 136 B.C., and concluded a treaty. The Senate not only refused to accept the treaty, but delivered him to Numantia as a captive. The authorities of Numantia refused to receive him. He returned to Rome and resumed his place in the Senate, but was challenged on the ground that citizenship lost by delivery to the enemy could not be regained *postliminio*. (Cicero, *de Oratore* I, 181.) The case was settled by a special law confirming his citizenship. (*Dig.* 50. 7. 17).

[b] § 11.

afterward (*post*) to the same threshold it seems to
have returned *postliminio*. The case of Mancinus
can be defended in this style, by arguing that he
returned by right of *postliminium:* he was not surrendered by the state as a captive because he was
not accepted by the enemy. For surrender and
gift have no meaning without acceptance.[a]

38   IX. Next comes the topic embracing circumstances
which are in one way or another closely connected
with the subject under inquiry. As stated above [b]
this has many subdivisions. The first of these is
" conjugation " (words etymologically related), which
is called συζυγία (syzygia) by the Greeks, and is
near akin to etymology, which we discussed a
moment ago. For example, if we were defining
rain-water as only that which we see collect from
showers, Mucius would come to argue that because
rain-water (*pluvia*) and rain (*pluere*) are " conjugate "
words, all water which has risen because of rain
should be excluded (from a neighbour's property).[c]

39   When, however, an argument is drawn from *genus*
it will not be necessary to trace it back to its origin.
Frequently one may stop short of that point, provided that what is assumed as a genus is higher
than what is subsumed under it. For example,
rain-water in the last analysis is water which falls
from heaven and is increased by showers, but on a
nearer analysis (and the legal principle of excluding
rain-water depends on this) the genus is harmful
rain-water. Of this there are two species: one
which does damage because of a fault in the land,

---

c In certain circumstances *A* could be restrained by an
actio aquae pluviae arcendae (suit for keeping off rain-water)
from allowing rain-water to run from his land to *B*'s.

loci vitio et manu nocens, quarum altera iubetur ab
40 arbitro coerceri altera non iubetur. Commode etiam
tractatur haec argumentatio quae ex genere sumitur,
cum ex toto partis persequare hoc modo: Si dolus
malus est, cum aliud agitur aliud simulatur, enumerare licet quibus id modis fiat, deinde in eorum
aliquem id quod arguas dolo malo factum includere;
quod genus argumenti in primis firmum videri
solet.

41 X. Similitudo sequitur, quae late patet, sed
oratoribus et philosophis magis quam vobis. Etsi
enim omnes loci sunt omnium disputationum ad
argumenta suppeditanda, tamen aliis disputationibus
abundantius occurrunt aliis angustius. Itaque
genera tibi nota sint; ubi autem eis utare, quae-
42 stiones ipsae te admonebunt. Sunt enim similitudines quae ex pluribus collationibus perveniunt
quo volunt hoc modo: Si tutor fidem praestare debet,
si socius, si cui mandaris, si qui fiduciam acceperit,
debet etiam procurator. Haec ex pluribus perveniens
quo vult appellatur inductio, quae Graece ἐπαγωγὴ
nominatur, qua plurimum est usus in sermonibus
43 Socrates. Alterum similitudinis genus collatione
sumitur, cum una res uni, par pari comparatur hoc
modo: Quem ad modum, si in urbe de finibus
controversia est, quia fines magis agrorum videntur
esse quam urbis, finibus regendis adigere arbitrum
non possis, sic, si aqua pluvia in urbe nocet, quoniam

and the other because of the work of man. The
law provides that one of these shall be restrained
40 by the arbitrator, but not the other. It makes a
neat treatment of this argument from genus when
you can tell off the parts of the whole, as follows:
If " fraud " is defined as doing one thing and pre-
tending to do another, one may enumerate the
various ways in which this can be done, and include
under one of these heads the act which you allege
was fraudulently committed. This kind of argument
generally seems highly cogent.

41   X. Similarity comes next. This is an extensive
topic, but of more interest to orators and philosophers
than to you jurists. For although all topics can be
used to supply arguments in all sorts of debate, still
they occur more frequently in some debates and
more rarely in others. Well then, know the types
of argument; the case itself will instruct you when
42 to use them. For example, there are certain arguments from similarity which attain the desired proof
by several comparisons, as follows: If honesty is
required of a guardian, a partner, a bailee, and a
trustee, it is required of an agent. This form of
argument which attains the desired proof by citing
several parallels is called induction, in Greek ἐπαγωγή
(epagoge); Socrates frequently used this in his dia-
43 logues. Another kind of argument from similarity
rests on comparison, when one thing is compared to
one, equal to equal, as follows: If there is a dispute
about boundary lines in the city you could not require
arbitration for the regulation of boundaries, because
the whole matter of boundary regulation applies
to country property rather than to city; on the
same principle, if rain-water does damage in the

res tota magis agrorum est, aquae pluviae arcendae
44 adigere arbitrum non possis. Ex eodem similitudinis loco etiam exempla sumuntur, ut Crassus in
causa Curiana exemplis plurimis usus est, qui testamento sic heredes instituti,[1] ut si filius natus esset
in decem mensibus isque mortuus prius quam in
suam tutelam venisset, hereditatem obtinuissent.
Quae commemoratio exemplorum valuit, eaque vos
45 in respondendo uti multum soletis. Ficta enim
exempla similitudinis habent vim; sed ea oratoria
magis sunt quam vestra; quamquam uti etiam vos
soletis, sed hoc modo: Finge mancipio aliquem
dedisse id quod mancipio dari non potest. Num
idcirco id eius factum est qui accepit? aut num is
qui mancipio dedit ob eam rem se ulla re obligavit?
In hoc genere oratoribus et philosophis concessum
est, ut muta etiam loquantur, ut mortui ab inferis
excitentur, ut aliquid quod fieri nullo modo possit
augendae rei gratia dicatur aut minuendae, quae
ὑπερβολὴ dicitur, multa alia mirabilia. Sed latior
est campus illorum. Eisdem tamen ex locis, ut
ante dixi, et [in][2] maximis et minimis [in][3] quaestionibus argumenta ducuntur.

[1] instituti: instituisset *codd.*: qui cum . . . instituti
essent *Madvig.*
[2] in *omitted by codd.*
[3] in minimis *Of* : in *omitted by V.*

---

[a] *v.* p. 396, note 6, § 23.
[b] This is the famous *causa Curiana*, 92 B.C., in which
Lucius Licinius Crassus successfully defended the claims of
Curius, who was the reversionary heir named in the will

city you could not require arbitration for excluding
rain-water, since the whole matter applies rather
44 to country property.[a]   Under the same topic of
similarity comes also the citing of examples or
parallel cases, as Crassus in his defence of Curius
cited many cases of men who, having been named as
heirs in the event that a son was born within ten
months and died before attaining his majority, would
have taken the inheritance. Such a citation of parallel
cases carried the day, and you jurists make frequent
45 use of it in your responses.[b] In fact fictitious examples
of similarity have their value, but they belong to
oratory rather than to jurisprudence, although even
you are wont to use them, but in the following way :
Suppose some one has conveyed property by mancipa-
tion which cannot be so conveyed.[c] Does it therefore become the property of the one who has accepted
it ? Or has the one who has conveyed by manci-
pation in any way obligated himself by that act ?
Under this topic of similarity orators and philosophers
have licence to cause dumb things to talk, to call
on the dead to rise from the world below, to tell of
something which could not possibly happen, in order
to add force to an argument or lessen it : this is
called ὑπερβολή (hyperbole).   And they do many
other strange things ; but they have a wider field.
Nevertheless, as I said above,[d] whether the question
be important or trifling, the arguments for it are
derived from the same topics.

against the attack of Scaevola, counsel for one Coponius.
v. Brutus, 194-198, de Orat. I, 180, and the note on p. 226.
(de Inv. II, 62.)
    [c] On the restrictions of this form of conveyance, v. p. 400,
note b, § 28.
    [d] § 41.

46 XI. Sequitur similitudinem differentia rei maxime contraria superiori; sed est eiusdem dissimile et simile invenire. Eius generis haec sunt: Non, quem ad modum quod mulieri debeas, recte ipsi mulieri sine tutore auctore solvas, item, quod pupillo aut pupillae debeas, recte possis eodem modo solvere.

47 Deinceps locus est qui e contrario dicitur. Contrariorum autem genera plura; unum eorum quae in eodem genere plurimum differunt, ut sapientia stultitia. Eodem autem genere dicuntur quibus propositis occurrunt tamquam e regione quaedam contraria, ut celeritati tarditas, non debilitas. Ex quibus contrariis argumenta talia existunt: Si stultitiam fugimus, sapientiam sequamur, et bonitatem si malitiam. Haec quae ex eodem genere 48 contraria sunt appellantur adversa. Sunt enim alia contraria, quae privantia licet appellemus Latine, Graeci appellant στερητικά. Praeposito enim "in" privatur verbum ea vi quam haberet si "in" praepositum non fuisset, dignitas indignitas, humanitas inhumanitas, et cetera generis eiusdem, quorum tractactio est eadem quae superiorum quae adversa 49 dixi. Nam alia quoque sunt contrariorum genera, velut ea quae cum aliquo conferuntur, ut duplum simplum, multa pauca, longum breve, maius minus. Sunt etiam illa valde contraria quae appellantur negantia; ea ἀποφατικά Graece, contraria aientibus:

46 **XI.** After similarity comes difference, which is the exact opposite of the foregoing, but it is the same mental process which finds differences and similarities. The following is an example of this sort: Though you may properly pay a debt owed to a woman directly to the woman without the authorization of her tutor, you may not in the same way discharge a debt owed to a minor, whether male or female.

47 The next topic is that which is called "from contraries." But there are several sorts of contraries. One, of things which belong to the same class, but differ absolutely, as wisdom and folly. Words are said to belong to the same class if when they are uttered they are met face to face, as it were, by certain opposites. For example slowness is contrary to speed, but weakness is not. From these contraries arguments develop such as these: If we shun folly (as of course we do), let us pursue wisdom; and kindness if we shun malice. These contraries which belong to the same class are called

48 opposites. For there are other contraries which we may call *privantia* (privatives) in Latin; the Greeks call them στερητικά (steretica). For if " *in* " is prefixed, a word loses the force which it would have if " *in* " were not prefixed, such as dignity and indignity, humanity and inhumanity and others of this sort; these are handled in the same way as the former

49 class which I called " opposites." There are still other kinds of contraries, such as those which are compared with something, as double and single, many and few, long and short, greater and less. There are also those intensely contrary expressions which are called negatives, in Greek ἀποφατικά (apophatica), being contrary to affirmative, as shown

Si hoc est, illud non est. Quid enim opus exemplo est? Tantum intellegatur, in argumento quaerendo contrariis omnibus contraria non convenire.

50 Ab adiunctis autem posui equidem exemplum paulo ante, multa adiungi, quae suscipienda essent si statuissemus ex edicto secundum eas tabulas possessionem dari, quas is instituisset cui testamenti factio nulla esset. Sed locus hic magis ad coniecturales causas, quae versantur in iudiciis, valet, 'cum quaeritur quid aut sit aut evenerit aut futurum

51 sit aut quid omnino fieri possit. XII. Ac loci quidem ipsius forma talis est. Admonet autem hic locus, ut quaeratur quid ante rem, quid cum re, quid post rem evenerit. " Nihil hoc ad ius; ad Ciceronem," inquiebat Gallus noster, si quis ad eum quid tale rettulerat, ut de facto quaereretur. Tu tamen patiere nullum a me artis institutae locum praeteriri; ne, si nihil nisi quod ad te pertineat scribendum putabis, nimium te amare videare. Est igitur magna ex parte locus hic oratorius non modo non iuris consultorum, sed ne philosophorum quidem.

52 Ante rem enim quaeruntur quae talia sunt: apparatus, colloquia, locus, constitutum, convivium; cum re autem: pedum crepitus, strepitus hominum,[1] corporum umbrae et si quid eius modi; at post rem: pallor, rubor, titubatio, si qua alia signa con-

---

[1] strepitus hominum *bracketed by Friedrich*: *not used by Boethius*: pedum strepitus, crepitus hominum *O*.

---

[a] § 18.
[b] For Gallus, *v.* note *c* on p. 405.

in the following: If this is so, that is not. Need I give an example? It is sufficient to understand that in seeking an argument it is not every contrary which is suitable to be opposed to another.

50 I gave an example of argument from adjuncts (corollaries) a little while ago,[a] saying that there were many corollaries which would have to be admitted if we decided that possession of an inheritance could be given by the praetor's edict in accordance with the terms of a will made by one who did not have testamentary capacity. But this topic is of more value in conjectural issues which come up in trials, when it is a question of what is true or what has occurred, or what will happen, or 51 what can happen at all. XII. Such indeed is the bare outline of the topic. It suggests, however, that one should inquire what happened before an event, what at the same time, and what afterward. Our friend Gallus [b] used to say, "This is not a matter for the law but for Cicero" when any one brought to him a case which turned on a question of fact. You, however, will allow me to omit no part of the text-book which I have begun, lest you appear to be selfish if you think that only matters of interest to you should be included. As I was saying, this topic is of value largely to orators, and is not only not used by jurisconsults, but not even by philosophers.

52 To give examples: Circumstances before the event which are looked for are the following: preparations, conversation, the locale, a compact, a banquet; contemporary with the event: sound of feet, people shouting, shadows of bodies, and the like; after the event: pallor, a blush, trembling, and any

turbationis et conscientiae, praeterea restinctus
ignis, gladius cruentus ceteraque quae suspicionem
facti possunt movere.

53 Deinceps est locus dialecticorum proprius ex
consequentibus et antecedentibus et repugnantibus.
Nam coniuncta, de quibus paulo ante dictum est,
non semper eveniunt; consequentia autem semper.
Ea enim dico consequentia quae rem necessario
consequuntur; itemque et antecedentia et repug-
nantia. Quidquid enim sequitur quamque rem, id
cohaeret cum re necessario; et quidquid repugnat,
id eius modi est ut cohaerere nunquam possit.
XIII. Cum tripertito igitur distribuatur locus hic, in
consecutionem, antecessionem, repugnantiam, re-
periendi argumenti locus simplex est, tractandi
triplex. Nam quid interest, cum hoc sumpseris,
pecuniam numeratam mulieri deberi cui sit argentum omne legatum, utrum hoc modo concludas
argumentum: Si pecunia signata argentum est,
legata est mulieri. Est autem pecunia signata
argentum. Legata igitur est; an illo modo: Si
numerata pecunia non est legata, non est numerata
pecunia argentum. Est autem numerata pecunia
argentum; legata igitur est; an illo modo: Non et
legatum argentum est et non est legata numerata
pecunia. Legatum autem argentum est; legata
54 igitur numerata pecunia est? Appellant autem
dialectici eam conclusionem argumenti, in qua, cum
primum assumpseris, consequitur id quod annexum
est primum conclusionis modum; cum id quod

---

[a] Cf. de Inv. I, 38–41 for a fuller treatment of this topic.
[b] Cf. § 13.

other signs of agitation and a guilty conscience;
and besides, an extinguished fire, a bloody sword,
and other things which can arouse suspicions about
a crime.[a]

53   Next comes the topic which is the peculiar province
of the logicians—consequents, antecedents, and
contradictories. For conjuncts, which have just been
discussed, do not always happen, but consequents
always do. By "consequents," of course, I mean
what necessarily follows something; and the same
necessary connexion is characteristic of antecedents
and contradictories. For whatever follows something is inevitably connected with it. And whatever is contradictory has such a nature that it can
never be connected with it. XIII. Since, as I have
said, this topic is divided into three parts—consequence, antecedence and contradiction—the topic
is single as far as concerns the discovery of arguments,
but the treatment is threefold. For what difference
does it make in which way you draw a conclusion
in this assumed case—that a woman who has received
as a bequest "all the silver," is entitled to the
coin?[b] You may do it in this way: If coined
money is silver, it was bequeathed to the woman.
But coined money is silver, therefore it was bequeathed. Or in this way: If coin was not bequeathed, coin is not silver; but coin is silver;
therefore it was bequeathed. Or in this way: It
is not possible to say that silver was bequeathed,
but coin was not; but silver was bequeathed, there-
54 fore coin was bequeathed. The logicians give the
name of "first form of conclusion" to this way of
concluding an argument, in which when you have
assumed the first statement, that which is connected

annexum est negaris, ut id quoque cui fuerit annexum negandum sit, secundus is appellatur con-
cludendi modus; cum autem aliqua coniuncta
negaris et ex eis unum aut plura sumpseris, ut quod
relinquitur tollendum sit, is tertius appellatur con-
55 clusionis modus. Ex hoc illa rhetorum ex contrariis conclusa, quae ipsi ἐνθυμήματα appellant;
non quod omnis sententia proprio nomine ἐνθύμημα
non dicatur, sed, ut Homerus propter excellentiam
commune poetarum nomen efficit apud Graecos
suum, sic, cum omnis sententia ἐνθύμημα dicatur,
quia videtur ea quae ex contrariis conficitur acutis-
sima, sola proprie nomen commune possedit. Eius
generis haec sunt :

hoc metuere, alterum in metu non ponere !
eam quam nihil accusas damnas, bene quam
    meritam esse autumas

---

[a] Strangely enough in a treatise which purports to be a
translation of Aristotle, Cicero is here stating the five
ἀναπόδεικτοι συλλογισμοί as formulated by the Stoics. (In
terms of modern logic they are hypothetical and disjunctive
syllogisms.) They are set forth by Sextus Empiricus in
Πυρρώνειοι Ὑποτυπώσεις 157, as follows :

(1) If it is day, there is light. (Constructive hypothetical
    It is day,   syllogism or *modus ponendo*
    ∴ there is light.   *ponens*.)
(2) If it is day, there is light. (Destructive hypothetical
    There is no light,   syllogism or *modus tollendo*
    ∴ it is not day.   *tollens*.)
(3) It cannot be day and   (Affirmative disjunctive syl-
    night at the same time.   logism or *modus ponendo*
    It is day,   *tollens*.)
    ∴ it is not night.

with it follows as true;[a] when you deny what is connected, with the result that that statement with which it is connected must also be denied, this is called the second form; when, however, you deny that certain things are associated and assume the truth of one or more, so that the remaining statement must be excluded, this is called the third form.

55 To this belong those forms of conclusion from contraries adopted by teachers of rhetoric, to which they themselves have given the name ἐνθυμήματα (enthymemes). Not that any expression of thought is not properly called an ἐνθύμημα, but just as among the Greeks Homer by his outstanding merit has made the name of poet peculiarly his own,[b] although it is common to all poets, so although every expression of thought may be called ἐνθύμημα (enthymema), that one which is based on contraries has, because it seems the most pointed form of argument, appropriated the common name for its sole possession. The following lines will illustrate this sort of argument: Fear this, and not dread the other! You condemn the woman whom you accuse of nothing, and do you assert that the one deserves punishment whom

(4) It is either day or night.	(Affirmative disjunctive syllogism or *modus ponendo tollens*.)
It is day,	
∴ it is not night.	
(5) It is either day or night.	(Negative disjunctive syllogism or *modus tollendo ponens*.)
It is not night,	
∴ it is day.	

Cicero's sixth and seventh forms are merely re-statements of number three.

[b] "The Poet," without further qualification, meant Homer: *v.* A. M. Harmon, *The Poet* κατ᾽ ἐξοχήν, Classical Philology xviii (1923), pp. 35-47.

dicis [1] male merere?

id quod scis prodest nihil; id quod nescis obest?

56 XIV. Hoc disserendi genus attingit omnino vestras quoque in respondendo disputationes, sed philosophorum magis, quibus est cum oratoribus illa ex repugnantibus sententiis communis conclusio quae a dialecticis tertius modus, a rhetoribus ἐνθύμημα dicitur. Reliqui dialecticorum modi plures sunt, qui ex disiunctionibus constant: Aut hoc aut illud; hoc autem; non igitur illud. Itemque: Aut hoc aut illud; non autem hoc; illud igitur. Quae conclusiones idcirco ratae sunt quod in disiunctione 57 plus uno verum esse non potest. Atque ex eis conclusionibus quas supra scripsi prior quartus posterior quintus a dialecticis modus appellatur. Deinde addunt coniunctionum negantiam sic: Non et hoc et illud; hoc autem; non igitur illud. Hic modus est sextus. Septimus autem: Non et hoc et illud; non autem hoc; illud igitur. Ex eis modis conclusiones innumerabiles nascuntur, in quo est tota fere διαλεκτική. Sed ne hae quidem quas exposui ad hanc institutionem necessariae.

58 Proximus est locus rerum efficientium, quae causae appellantur; deinde rerum effectarum ab efficientibus causis. Harum exempla, ut reliquorum locorum, paulo ante posui equidem ex iure civili; sed haec patent latius.

XV. Causarum enim [2] genera duo sunt; unum, quod vi sua id quod sub eam vim subiectum est certe

---

[1] dicis *added from Orator* 166.
[2] enim *codd*: igitur *Ofβ*.

---

[a] Ribbeck[3], *Trag. frag. incert.* 200 f. Warmington, *Remains of Old Latin*, ii, p. 620.

you believe to deserve reward? What you know is of no use; is what you do not know a hindrance? [a]

56 XIV. This kind of argumentation has doubtless a relation to your discussions when you give answers on legal problems, but it more closely concerns the philosophers, who share with orators that method of drawing a conclusion from contradictory statements which the logicians call the third form, and the teachers of rhetoric, the ἐνθύμημα (enthymema). There are several other methods used by the logicians, which consist of propositions disjunctively connected: Either this or that is true; but this *is* true, therefore that is not. Similarly, either this or that is true; but this is not, therefore that *is* true. These conclusions are valid because in a disjunctive state-

57 ment not more than one half can be true. Of the conclusions given above, the former is called by the logicians the fourth method and the latter, the fifth. Then they add a denial of the possibility of two statements being conjoined, thus: This and that are not both true; but this *is*, therefore that is not. This is the sixth form. The seventh is: This and that are not both true; this is not, therefore that is. From these forms innumerable conclusions are derived; in fact almost the whole of διαλεκτική (dialectice) consists of this. But not even those which I have explained are necessary for this treatise.

58 The next topic concerns efficient forces which are called causes, and secondly, things effected by efficient causes. I gave examples of these, as of other topics, from the civil law a little while ago; but these have a wider application.

XV. There are two kinds of causes: one which by its own force surely produces that effect which

425

efficit, ut : Ignis accendit ; alterum, quod naturam
efficiendi non habet sed sine quo effici non possit, ut
si quis aes statuae causam velit dicere, quod sine eo
59 non possit effici. Huius generis causarum, sine quo
non efficitur, alia sunt quieta, nihil agentia, stolida
quodam modo, ut locus, tempus, materia, ferramenta,
et cetera generis eiusdem ; alia autem praecur-
sionem quandam adhibent ad efficiendum et quaedam
afferunt per se adiuvantia, etsi non necessaria, ut :
Amori congressio causam attulerat,[1] amor flagitio.
Ex hoc genere causarum ex aeternitate pendentium
fatum a Stoicis nectitur.

Atque ut earum causarum sine quibus effici non
potest genera divisi, sic etiam efficientium dividi
possunt. Sunt enim aliae causae quae plane efficiant
nulla re adiuvante, aliae quae adiuvari velint, ut :
Sapientia efficit sapientis sola per se ; beatos efficiat
60 necne sola per sese quaestio est. Qua re cum in
disputationem inciderit causa efficiens aliquid necessario, sine dubitatione licebit quod efficitur ab
ea causa concludere. XVI. Cum autem erit talis
causa, ut in ea non sit efficiendi necessitas, necessaria
conclusio non sequitur. Atque illud quidem genus
causarum quod habet vim efficiendi necessariam
errorem afferre non fere solet ; hoc autem sine quo

---

[1] attulerat *codd. dett. Boethius* : attulerit *codd.*

depends on this force; for example, fire burns; the second which does not have the quality of producing an effect, but is that without which the effect cannot be produced; for example, if some one should call bronze the " cause " of a statue, because 59 the statue cannot be made without it. In this group, without which something is not produced, some causes are quiet, inactive, one might say, inert, as place, time, material, instruments, and other things of this type; others furnish a preparation for producing something, and add certain things which themselves give aid, although they are not necessary; for example: Meeting had given occasion for love, and love for crime. From this kind of causes following one another in an infinite series the Stoics have woven their doctrine of Fate.

Furthermore, just as I have distinguished the different kinds of causes without which something cannot be accomplished, so also may the efficient causes be distinguished. That is to say, there are some causes which clearly effect a result without aid from another source, and others which require assistance. For example, wisdom alone and unaided makes men wise, but it is a question whether or not it makes them happy, alone and unaided. 60 Therefore, when in a discussion one comes on a cause which inevitably produces an effect, one may without hesitation state as an inference what is effected by that cause. XVI. But when you have a cause such that it does not involve the necessity of effecting a result, an inevitable conclusion does not follow. Furthermore, the kind of cause which has the power of inevitably effecting a result does not usually lead to a mistake. But the cause without

non efficitur saepe conturbat. Non enim, si sine parentibus filii esse non possunt, propterea in parentibus causa fuit gignendi necessaria.

61 Hoc igitur sine quo non fit, ab eo in quo certe fit diligenter est separandum. Illud enim est tamquam

utinam ne in nemore Pelio—

Nisi enim " accedissent [1] abiegnae ad terram trabes," Argo illa facta non esset, nec tamen fuit in his trabibus efficiendi vis necessaria. At cum in Aiacis navim crispisulcans igneum fulmen iniectum est, inflammatur navis necessario.

62 Atque etiam est causarum dissimilitudo, quod aliae sunt, ut sine ulla appetitione animi, sine voluntate, sine opinione suum quasi opus efficiant, vel ut omne intereat quod ortum sit; aliae autem aut voluntate efficiunt aut perturbatione animi aut habitu aut natura aut arte aut casu: voluntate, ut tu, cum hunc libellum legis; perturbatione, ut si quis eventum horum temporum timeat; habitu, ut qui facile et cito irascitur; [2] natura, ut vitium in dies crescat; arte, ut bene pingat; casu, ut prospere naviget. Nihil horum sine causa nec quidquam omnino; sed huius modi causae non necessariae.

63 Omnium autem causarum in aliis inest constantia, in aliis non inest. In natura et in [3] arte constantia

---

[1] accidissent *AaV* : cecidissent *codd.*
[2] irascitur *Oc* : irascatur *codd.*
[3] in *omitted by ObL.*

---

[a] The opening lines of Euripides' *Medea* as translated by Ennius. A longer extract is given in *ad Her.* ii, 22, 34, and *Remains of Old Latin*, i, p. 312, and Vahlen's *Ennius*, 246–254.

[b] Ribbeck³, *frg. inc.* 36–37. Warmington, ROL, ii, p. 408, following a suggestion of Ribbeck in the notes, assigns it to Accius.

which something is not effected often gives rise to confusion. For example, if there cannot be sons without parents, it does not follow that there was in the parents a necessary cause of procreation.

61   This cause without which something does not occur must, therefore, be carefully distinguished from that by which something surely occurs. The former may be illustrated by the line:

Would that ne'er in Pelion's grove [a]

For unless " the beams of fir had fallen to earth," the Argo would not have been built; yet there was no inevitable efficient power in the beams. But when " the fiery bolt cutting a wavy furrow fell on the ship of Ajax," [b] the ship is inevitably set on fire.

62   There is a further difference in causes in that some effect their own work as it were without any eagerness of mind, without desire, without opinion; for instance, the rule that everything that is born must die. Others work through desire, or mental agitation, or disposition, or nature, or art, or accident: by desire, as in your case when you read this book; by agitation, as when some one might dread the outcome of the present crisis; by disposition, as when one is easily or quickly moved to anger; by nature, for instance it comes about that a vice grows day by day; by art that one should paint well; by accident, that one should have a successful voyage. None of these events is without its cause, nor for that matter is anything at all; but causes of this nature are not inevitable.

63   Looking at all causes we find that in some there is uniformity of operation, and not in others. There is uniformity in nature and art, but none in the rest.

est, in ceteris nulla. XVII. Sed tamen earum causarum quae non sunt constantes aliae sunt perspicuae, aliae latent. Perspicuae sunt quae appetitionem animi iudiciumque tangunt; latent quae subiectae sunt fortunae. Cum enim nihil sine causa fiat, hoc ipsum est fortuna, qui eventus obscura causa et latenter efficitur.[1] Etiam ea quae fiunt partim sunt ignorata partim voluntaria; ignorata, quae necessitate effecta sunt; voluntaria,
64 quae consilio.[2] Nam iacere telum voluntatis est, ferire quem nolueris fortunae. Ex quo aries subicitur ille in vestris actionibus: si telum manu fugit magis quam iecit. Cadunt etiam in ignorationem atque imprudentiam perturbationes animi; quae quamquam sunt voluntariae—obiurgatione enim et admonitione deiciuntur—tamen habent tantos motus, ut ea quae voluntaria sunt aut necessaria interdum aut certe ignorata videantur.

65 Toto igitur loco causarum explicato, ex earum differentia in magnis quidem causis vel oratorum vel philosophorum magna argumentorum suppetit copia; in vestris autem si non uberior, at fortasse subtilior. Privata enim iudicia maximarum quidem rerum in iuris consultorum mihi videntur esse prudentia. Nam et adsunt multum et adhibentur in consilia et patronis diligentibus ad eorum pru-

---

[1] fortuna, eventus qui . . . efficitur *Madvig*: fortunae eventus *codd.*
[2] *After* consilio *the MSS. have* Quae autem fortuna, vel ignorata vel voluntaria (What is accomplished by Fortune is either unintentional or voluntary): *bracketed by Schuetz.*

XVII. But of the causes which are not uniform in operation, some are evident and others are concealed. Those are evident which affect our impulses or judgement; those that are controlled by fortune are concealed. For since nothing happens without cause, this is exactly what Fortune is, an event which is the result of an obscure and unseen cause. Again, these results which are produced are partly unintentional, and partly due to our own volition. The unintentional are the product of necessity; those in our own volition are accomplished by design.

64 To illustrate, throwing a weapon is an act of the will, but hitting some one unintentionally is the act of Fortune. This distinction supplies the beam which you use to prop up a weak case in your pleadings: "Perchance he did not throw the weapon, but it slipped from his hand." Mental agitation belongs with acts performed in ignorance or lack of foresight. For though such a state of mind is voluntary—for these conditions yield to reproof and admonition— still they produce such violence of emotion that acts which are voluntary seem sometimes to be necessary and certainly unintentional.

65 We have now explained the topic of causes in full. From the great variety of them there is supplied a great store of arguments at least for the important discussions of orators and philosophers; in your profession, if they are less numerous, they are perhaps more subtle. At any rate private suits involving highly important issues seem to me to depend on the wisdom of the jurisconsults. For they frequently attend the trials and are invited to be members of the judge's advisory board, and supply weapons to diligent advocates who seek

66 dentiam confugientibus hastas ministrant. In omnibus igitur eis iudiciis, in quibus ex fide bona est
additum, ubi vero [1] etiam ut inter bonos bene
agier oportet, in primisque in arbitrio rei uxoriae, in
quo est quod eius aequius melius, parati eis esse
debent. Illi dolum malum, illi fidem bonam, illi
aequum bonum, illi quid socium socio, quid eum qui
negotia aliena curasset ei cuius ea negotia fuissent,
quid eum qui mandasset, eumve cui mandatum
esset, alterum alteri praestare oporteret, quid virum
uxori, quid uxorem viro tradiderunt. Licebit igitur
diligenter argumentorum cognitis locis non modo
oratoribus et philosophis, sed iuris etiam peritis
copiose de consultationibus suis disputare.

67 XVIII. Coniunctus huic causarum loco ille locus
est qui efficitur ex causis. Ut enim causa quid sit
effectum indicat, sic quod effectum est quae fuerit
causa demonstrat. Hic locus suppeditare solet
oratoribus et poetis, saepe etiam philosophis, sed
eis qui ornate et copiose loqui possunt, mirabilem
copiam dicendi, cum denuntiant quid ex quaque
re sit futurum. Causarum enim cognitio cogni-
tionem eventorum facit.

68 Reliquus est comparationis locus, cuius genus et
exemplum supra positum est ut ceterorum; nunc
explicanda tractatio est. Comparantur igitur ea
quae aut maiora aut minora aut paria dicuntur;
in quibus spectantur haec: numerus, species, vis,
quaedam etiam ad res aliquas affectio.

[1] vero *omitted by Odcf.*

66 succour in their skill. In all suits, then, in which the phrase " in good faith " appears in the formula, or the phrase " as one should deal honestly with honest men," and especially in arbitration over the return of dowry, where the principle " as is better and more equitable," is applied, the jurisconsults are bound to be ready (with their counsel). It is they who have defined fraud, good faith, equity, the duties of partner to partner, of an agent to his principal, of mandator and mandatee respectively, and of husband to wife and wife to husband. A careful study of the topics of arguments, therefore, will permit not only orators and philosophers, but even jurisconsults to discourse fluently on questions about which they have been consulted.

67 XVIII. Closely connected with the topic of causes is the topic of the effects of causes. For just as the cause shows what has been effected, so what has been effected points out what the cause was. This topic is wont to give a marvellous fulness of expression to orators and poets, and frequently even to philosophers (that is to those who can speak with elegance and fluency) when they declare what will be the outcome of each situation. For a knowledge of causes produces a knowledge of results.

68 There remains the topic of comparison; of this, as of the other, a definition and example were given above.[a] Now I must explain more fully how it is used. To begin then, comparison is made between things which are greater, or less or equal. And in this connexion the following points are considered: quantity, quality, value, and also a particular relation to certain things.

[a] § 23.

69 Numero sic comparabuntur, plura bona ut pauci-
oribus bonis anteponantur, pauciora mala malis
pluribus, diuturniora bona brevioribus, longe et late
pervagata angustis, ex quibus plura bona propagentur
quaeque plures imitentur et faciant.

Specie autem comparantur, ut anteponantur quae
propter se expetenda sunt eis quae propter aliud et
ut innata atque insita assumptis atque adventiciis,
integra contaminatis, iucunda minus iucundis, honesta
ipsis etiam utilibus, proclivia laboriosis, necessaria
non necessariis, sua alienis, rara vulgaribus, desidera-
bilia eis quibus facile carere possis, perfecta incohatis,
tota partibus, ratione utentia rationis expertibus,[a]
voluntaria necessariis, animata inanimis, naturalia
non naturalibus, artificiosa non artificiosis.

70 Vis autem in comparatione sic cernitur: efficiens
causa gravior quam non efficiens; quae se ipsis [1]
contenta sunt meliora quam quae egent aliis; quae
in nostra quam quae in aliorum potestate sunt;
stabilia incertis; quae eripi non possunt eis quae
possunt.

Affectio autem ad res aliquas est huius modi:
principum commoda maiora quam reliquorum;

[1] ipsis *Oef*: ipsa *codd.*

---

[a] Or, reasonable beings to those devoid of reason.

434

69 Things will be compared in respect to quantity as follows: more " goods " are preferred to fewer, fewer evils to more, goods which last for a longer time to those of shorter duration, those which are distributed far and wide to those which are confined in narrow limits, those from which more goods are generated, and those which more people imitate and produce.

In comparing things in respect to their quality we prefer those which are to be sought for their own sake to those which are desired because they make something else possible; also we prefer innate and natural qualities to acquired and adventitious ones, what is pure to what is defiled, the pleasant to the less pleasant, what is honourable to what is profitable itself, the easy task to the difficult, the necessary to the unnecessary, our own good to that of others, things which are rare to those that are common, desirable things to those which you can easily do without, the perfect to the incomplete, the whole to its parts, reasonable actions to those devoid of reason,[a] voluntary to necessary acts, animate beings to inanimate objects, the natural to the unnatural, that which is artistic to that which is not.

70 In regard to value, distinctions are drawn in comparison as follows: An efficient cause is weightier than one that is not; things which are sufficient in themselves are better than those that require help from others; we prefer what is in our own power to what is in the power of others; the stable to the uncertain; what cannot be taken from us to that which can.

Relation to other things is of this nature: the interests of leading citizens are of more importance than those of the rest; a similar value attaches to

itemque quae iucundiora, quae pluribus probata, quae ab optimo quoque laudata. Atque ut haec in comparatione meliora, sic deteriora quae eis sunt contraria.

71 Parium autem comparatio nec elationem habet nec summissionem; est enim aequalis. Multa autem sunt quae aequalitate ipsa comparantur; quae ita fere concluduntur: Si consilio iuvare cives et auxilio aequa in laude ponendum est, pari gloria debent esse ei qui consulunt et ei qui defendunt; at quod primum, est; quod sequitur igitur.

Perfecta est omnis argumentorum inveniendorum praeceptio, ut, cum profectus sis a definitione, a partitione, a notatione, a coniugatis, a genere, a formis, a similitudine, a differentia, a contrariis, ab adiunctis, a consequentibus, ab antecedentibus, a repugnantibus, a causis, ab effectis, a comparatione maiorum, minorum, parium, nulla praeterea sedes argumenti quaerenda sit.

72 XIX. Sed quoniam ita a principio divisimus, ut alios locos diceremus in eo ipso de quo ambigitur haerere, de quibus satis est dictum, alios assumi extrinsecus, de eis pauca dicamus, etsi ea nihil omnino ad vestras disputationes pertinent; sed tamen totam rem efficiamus, quandoquidem coepimus. Neque enim tu is es quem nihil nisi ius civile delectet, et quoniam haec ita ad te scribuntur ut

---

[a] § 8.

things that are pleasanter, that are approved by the majority, or are praised by all virtuous men. And just as these are the things which in a comparison are regarded as better, so the opposites of these are regarded as worse.

71 When equals are compared there is no superiority or inferiority; everything is on the same plane. But there are many things which are compared because of their very equality. The argument runs something like this: If helping one's fellow-citizens with advice and giving them active assistance are to be regarded as equally praiseworthy, then those who give advice and those who defend ought to receive equal glory. But the first statement is true, therefore the conclusion is also.

This is the end of the rules for the invention of arguments, so that if you have journeyed through definition, partition, etymology, conjugates, genus, species, similarity, difference, contraries, adjuncts, consequents, antecedents, contradictions, causes, effects, and comparison of things greater, less and equal, no region of arguments remains to be explored.

72 XIX. But since at the beginning *a* we divided topics into two groups, saying that some are intrinsic or inherent in the very nature of the subject which is under discussion (these we have discussed at sufficient length), and that others are extrinsic or brought in from without, let us say a few words about these topics from without, although they bear no relation to your discussions of the law. But now that we have begun, let us develop the whole subject. For you are not the person to take pleasure in nothing but the civil law, and since this book is written for you, but in such a form that it is going

437

etiam in aliorum manus sint ventura, detur opera,
ut quam plurimum eis quos recta studia delectant
prodesse possimus.

73   Haec ergo argumentatio, quae dicitur artis expers,
in testimonio posita est. Testimonium autem nunc
dicimus omne quod ab aliqua re externa sumitur ad
faciendam fidem. Persona autem non qualiscumque
est testimoni pondus habet; ad fidem enim faciendam auctoritas quaeritur; sed auctoritatem aut
natura aut tempus affert. Naturae auctoritas in
virtute inest maxima; in tempore autem multa
sunt quae afferant auctoritatem: ingenium, opes,
aetas, fortuna,[1] ars, usus, necessitas, concursio etiam
non numquam rerum fortuitarum. Nam et in-
geniosos et opulentos et aetatis spatio probatos
dignos quibus credatur putant; non recte fortasse,
sed vulgi opinio mutari vix potest ad eamque omnia
dirigunt et qui iudicant et qui existimant. Qui
enim rebus his quas dixi excellunt, ipsa virtute
videntur excellere.

74   Sed reliquis quoque rebus quas modo enumeravi
quamquam in his nulla species virtutis est, tamen
interdum confirmatur fides, si aut ars quaedam
adhibetur—magna est enim vis ad persuadendum
scientiae—aut usus; plerumque enim creditur eis
qui experti sunt. XX. Facit etiam necessitas fidem,
quae tum a corporibus tum ab animis nascitur. Nam

---

[1] fortuna *bracketed by Friedrich.*

to come into the hands of others, let us take pains to give all possible help to those who take pleasure in honourable studies.

73 This form of argumentation, that is said not to be subject to the rules of art, depends on testimony. For our present purpose we define testimony as everything that is brought in from some external circumstance in order to win conviction. Now it is not every sort of person who is worth consideration as a witness. To win conviction, authority is sought; but authority is given by one's nature or by circumstances. Authority from one's nature or character depends largely on virtue; in circumstances there are many things which lend authority, such as talent, wealth, age, good luck, skill, experience, necessity, and even at times a concurrence of fortuitous events. For it is common belief that the talented, the wealthy, and those whose character has been tested by a long life, are worthy of credence. This may not be correct, but the opinion of the common people can hardly be changed, and both those who make judicial decisions and those who pass moral judgements steer their course by that. As I was saying, those who excel in these things seem to excel in virtue.

74 But as for the rest of the qualities that I just now enumerated, although they have in them no kind of virtue, yet they sometimes strengthen conviction, if a person is shown to possess skill or experience; for knowledge has great influence in convincing, and people generally put faith in those who are experienced. XX. Necessity, too, wins conviction, and this necessity may be either physical or mental. For what men say when they have been worn down

et verberibus, tormentis, igni fatigati quae dicunt ea videtur veritas ipsa dicere, et quae perturbationibus animi, dolore, cupiditate, iracundia, metu, qui necessitatis vim habent, afferunt auctoritatem et fidem.

75 Cuius generis etiam illa sunt ex quibus verum nonnunquam invenitur, pueritia, somnus, imprudentia, vinolentia, insania. Nam et parvi saepe indicaverunt aliquid, quo id pertineret ignari, et per somnum, vinum, insaniam multa saepe patefacta sunt. Multi etiam in res odiosas imprudenter inciderunt, ut Staieno nuper accidit, qui ea locutus est bonis viris subauscultantibus pariete interposito, quibus patefactis in iudiciumque prolatis ille rei capitalis iure damnatus est. Huic simile quiddam de Lacedaemonio Pausania accepimus.

76 Concursio autem fortuitorum talis est, ut si interventum est casu, cum aut ageretur aliquid quod proferendum non esset, aut diceretur. In hoc genere etiam illa est in Palamedem coniecta suspicionum proditionis multitudo; quod genus refutare interdum veritas vix potest. Huius etiam est generis fama vulgi, quoddam multitudinis testimonium.

Quae autem virtute fidem faciunt ea bipertita sunt; ex quibus alterum natura valet alterum industria. Deorum enim virtus natura excellit, homi-

---

^a For Staienus, v. the *Brutus*, 241, and the speech *In Defence of Cluentius, passim*. According to Cicero he was a proper scoundrel, deeply involved in bribing juries.

^b Thucydides, I. 133–135.

^c For Palamedes, v. Vergil, *Aeneid* ii, 81–85, and Servius *ad loc.* A member of the Greek expedition against Troy, he was convicted by a chain of circumstantial evidence fabricated by Ulysses.

by stripes, the rack, and fire, seems to be spoken by
truth itself; and what they say under stress of mind—
grief, lust, anger or fear—lends authority and conviction, because these emotions seem to have the
force of necessity.

75 This class also includes those states or conditions
from which the truth is sometimes discovered, such
as childhood, sleep, inadvertence, intoxication and
insanity. Small children have often given some
information without knowing its pertinence, and
many facts have been revealed by persons asleep,
intoxicated or insane. Many men, too, have fallen
into disgrace through inadvertence, as lately happened to Staienus [a] who made incriminating statements within the hearing of some reputable citizens
concealed behind a wall. When these remarks of
his were published, and reported in court, he
was justly condemned on a capital charge. We
have heard a similar story about Pausanias, the
Lacedaemonian.[b]

76 The concurrence of fortuitous events is illustrated,
for example, by a chance interruption when something was being said or done which should be kept
secret. An instance of this sort is the mass of cir-
cumstantial evidence of treason which was heaped
on Palamedes.[c] Sometimes truth itself can scarcely
refute evidence of this sort. We may also put in
this class public opinion, which is a kind of testimony
of the multitude.

The testimony which produces conviction through
virtue is of two kinds; one sort gets its efficacy by
nature, the other acquires it by hard work. That
is to say, the surpassing virtue of the gods is the
result of their nature, but the virtue of men is the

441

77 num autem industria. Divina hace fere sunt testimonia: primum orationis—oracula enim ex eo ipso
appellata sunt, quod inest in [1] his deorum oratio—;
deinde rerum, in quibus insunt quasi quaedam opera
divina: primum ipse mundus eiusque omnis ordo
et ornatus; deinceps aerii volatus avium atque
cantus; deinde eiusdem aeris sonitus et ardores
multarumque rerum in terra portenta atque etiam
per exta inventa praesensio; a dormientibus quoque
multa significata visis. Quibus ex locis sumi interdum solent ad fidem faciendam testimonia deorum.

78 In homine virtutis opinio valet plurimum. Opinio
est autem non modo eos virtutem habere qui habeant,
sed eos etiam qui habere videantur. Itaque quos
ingenio, quos studio, quos doctrina praeditos vident
quorumque vitam constantem et probatam, ut
Catonis, Laeli, Scipionis, aliorumque plurium, rentur
eos esse qualis se ipsi velint; nec solum eos censent
esse talis qui in honoribus populi reque publica
versantur, sed et oratores et philosophos et poetas
et historicos, ex quorum et dictis et scriptis saepe
auctoritas petitur ad faciendam fidem.

79 XXI. Expositis omnibus argumentandi locis illud
primum intellegendum est nec ullam esse disputationem in qua [2] non aliquis locus incurrat, nec fere
omnis locos incidere in omnem quaestionem et

---

[1] in *A* : *om. codd.*
[2] in qua *codd.* : in quam *A vulg.*

77 result of hard work. The testimony of the gods is covered thoroughly enough by the following: first, utterances, for oracles get their name from the fact that they contain an utterance (*oratio*) of the gods; secondly, things in which are embodied certain works of the gods. First, the heavens themselves and all their order and beauty; secondly, the flight of birds through the air and their songs; thirdly, sounds and flashes of fire from the heavens, and portents given by many objects on earth, as well as the foreshadowing of events which is revealed by the entrails (of sacrificial animals). Many things also are revealed by visions seen in sleep. The testimony of the gods is at times adduced from these topics in order to win conviction.

78 In the case of a man, it is the opinion of his virtue which is most important. For opinion regards as virtuous not only those who really are virtuous, but also those who seem to be. And so when people see men endowed with genius, industry and learning, and those whose life has been consistent and of approved goodness, like Cato, Laelius, Scipio and many more, they regard them as the kind of men they would like to be. Nor do they hold such an opinion only about those who have been honoured by the people with public office and are busy with matters of state, but also about orators, philosophers, poets, and historians. Their sayings and writings are often used as authority to win conviction.

79 XXI. All the topics of argumentation have now been set forth, and it must be understood in the first place that there is no discussion in which there is not at least one topic involved, but that all topics scarcely ever occur in every inquiry, and that some

quibusdam quaestionibus alios, quibusdam alios esse
aptiores locos. Quaestionum duo genera sunt: [1]
alterum infinitum, definitum alterum. Definitum
est quod ὑπόθεσιν Graeci, nos causam; infinitum
quod θέσιν illi appellant, nos propositum possumus

80 nominare. Causa certis personis, locis, temporibus,
actionibus, negotiis cernitur aut in omnibus aut in
plerisque eorum, propositum autem aut in aliquo
eorum aut in pluribus nec tamen in maximis. Itaque
propositum pars est causae. Sed omnis quaestio
earum aliqua de re est quibus causae continentur,
aut una aut pluribus aut nonnunquam omnibus.

81 Quaestionum autem " quacumque de re " sunt
duo genera: unum cognitionis alterum actionis.

82 Cognitionis sunt eae quarum est finis scientia, ut si
quaeratur a naturane ius profectum sit an ab aliqua
quasi condicione hominum et pactione. Actionis
autem huius modi exempla sunt: Sitne sapientis
ad rem publicam accedere. Cognitionis quaestiones
tripertitae sunt; aut sitne aut quid sit aut quale sit
quaeritur. Horum primum coniectura, secundum
definitione, tertium iuris et iniuriae distinctione
explicatur.

Coniecturae ratio in quattuor partes distributa est,
quarum una est cum quaeritur sitne aliquid; altera
unde ortum sit; tertia quae id causa effecerit;
quarta in qua de commutatione rei quaeritur.
Sitne sic: [2] ecquidnam sit honestum, ecquid aequum

---

[1] genera sunt *Of*: generae *L*: sunt genera *V*.
[2] Sitne sic *Friedrich*: sit necne sit *codd.*: sitne necne
sit *A*.

---

[a] Literally, Is it? What is it? Of what sort is it?

topics are better suited to some inquiries than to others. There are two kinds of inquiry, one general and the other particular. The particular is what the Greeks call ὑπόθεσις (hypothesis), and we call cause or case; the general inquiry is what they call

80 θέσις (thesis), and we can call proposition. The hallmark of a case is that it involves definite persons, places, times, actions, or affairs, either all or most of these; a proposition involves one or several of these, but not the most important. Therefore a proposition is a part of a case. But every inquiry concerns some one of the subjects of which cases consist, that is, it concerns one or more or sometimes all of them.

81 Inquiries " about any possible subject " (i.e. general inquiries) are of two kinds: one theoretical,

82 the other practical. Theoretical inquiries are those of which the purpose is knowledge: for example, one may inquire whether law has its origin in nature or in some agreement and contract between men. The following is an example of the practical inquiry : Should a philosopher take part in politics? Theoretical questions fall into three groups; the question asked is either, Does it exist? or What is it? or What is its character? [a] The first of these is treated and answered by inference and conjecture, the second by definition, and the third by distinguishing between right and wrong.

There are four ways of dealing with conjecture or inference: the question is asked, first whether anything exists or is true; second, what its origin is; third, what cause produced it; fourth, what changes can be made in anything. As to existence, as follows : Is there really any such thing as honour

re vera; an haec tantum in opinione sint. Unde autem sit ortum: ut cum quaeritur, natura an doctrina possit effici virtus. Causa autem efficiens sic quaeritur, quibus rebus eloquentia efficiatur. De commutatione sic: possitne eloquentia commutatione aliqua converti in infantiam.

83 XXII. Cum autem quid sit quaeritur, notio explicanda est et proprietas et divisio et partitio. Haec enim sunt definitioni attributa; additur etiam descriptio, quam χαρακτῆρα Graeci vocant. Notio sic quaeritur: sitne id aequum quod ei qui plus potest utile est. Proprietas sic: in hominemne solum cadat an etiam in beluas aegritudo. Divisio et eodem pacto partitio sic:[1] triane genera bonorum sint. Descriptio, qualis sit avarus, qualis assentator ceteraque eiusdem generis, in quibus et natura et vita describitur.

84 Cum autem quaeritur quale quid sit, aut simpliciter quaeritur aut comparate; simpliciter: Expetendane sit gloria; comparate: Praeponendane sit divitiis gloria. Simplicium tria genera sunt: de expetendo fugiendoque, de aequo et iniquo, de honesto et turpi. Comparationum autem duo: unum de eodem et alio, alterum de maiore et minore. De expetendo

---

[1] sic *Of*: *omitted by codd.*

[a] *Cf.* Thrasymachus' definition of justice in Plato's *Republic*, 338c.

or equity, or are these merely matters of opinion?
As to origin: for example, the question may be
asked whether virtue can be engendered by nature
or by instruction. An instance of a question about
the efficient cause is: What produces eloquence?
Change is illustrated as follows: Can eloquence by
any change be transformed into want of eloquence?

83 XXII. When the question concerns what a thing
is, one has to explain the concept, and the peculiar
or proper quality of the thing, analyze it and enumerate its parts. For these are the essentials of
definition. We also include description, which the
Greeks call χαρακτήρ (character or hallmark). The
concept is inquired into in this way: Is justice that
which is to the advantage of the stronger?[a] An
example of inquiry into the peculiar or proper
quality of a thing is the following question: Is grief
incidental to man alone, or to the animals as well?
Analysis and enumeration are treated in the same
fashion: Are there three kinds of "goods?"
Description may be illustrated as follows: What
sort of person a miser or a flatterer is, and other
cases of the same sort, in which both a person's
character and his manner of life are described.

84 When the question is about the nature of anything, it is put either simply or by comparison;
simply as in the question: Should one seek glory?
—by comparison, as: Is glory to be preferred to
riches? There are three kinds of subjects for simple
questions: what to seek and what to avoid, what is
right and what wrong, what is honourable and what
base. Questions involving a comparison are of two
kinds: one about sameness and difference, the
other about superiority and inferiority. Questions

447

et fugiendo huius modi: Si expetendae divitiae,
si fugienda paupertas. De aequo et iniquo: Ae-
quumne sit ulcisci a quocumque iniuriam acceperis.
De honesto et turpi: Honestumne sit pro patria
85 mori? Ex altero autem genere, quod erat biparti-
tum, unum est de eodem et alio: Quid intersit inter
amicum et assentatorem, regem et tyrannum;
alterum de maiore et minore, ut si quaeratur
eloquentiane pluris sit an iuris civilis scientia. De
cognitionis quaestionibus hactenus.

86 Actionis reliquae sunt, quarum duo genera: unum
ad officium, alterum ad motum animi vel gignendum
vel sedandum planeve tollendum. Ad officium sic,
ut cum quaeritur suscipiendine sint liberi. Ad
movendos animos cohortationes ad defendendam rem
publicam, ad laudem, ad gloriam; quo ex genere
sunt querellae, incitationes, miserationesque flebiles;
rursusque oratio tum iracundiam restinguens, tum
metum eripiens, tum exsultantem laetitiam com-
primens, tum aegritudinem abstergens. Haec cum
in propositi [1] quaestionibus genera sint, eadem in
causas transferuntur.

87 XXIII. Loci autem qui ad quasque quaestiones
accommodati sint deinceps est videndum. Omnes
illi quidem ad plerasque, sed alii ad alias, ut dixi,
aptiores. Ad coniecturam igitur maxime apta quae
ex causis, quae ex effectis, quae ex coniunctis sumi
possunt. Ad definitionem autem pertinet ratio

---

[1] propositi *codex Bamberg.* MV 13 : propositis *codd.*

---

[a] Or taking *suscipere* in its technical sense, 'should children
be kept'?
[b] By which he means the class which he called adjuncts
(corollaries) above, §§ 11, 18, 50.

about what to seek and what to avoid are like
this: Should riches be sought? Should poverty
be avoided? A question about right and wrong:
Is it right to take vengeance on one who has wronged
you? A question about honour and baseness: Is
85 it honourable to die for one's country? In the other
class which we divided into two parts, one applies
to resemblance and difference, for instance: What
is the difference between a friend and a flatterer,
between a king and a tyrant? The second applies
to superiority and inferiority; for example, one
might ask whether eloquence or jurisprudence is
more valuable. So much for the theoretical
questions.

86   There remain the practical questions, and of these
there are two kinds: one has to do with our duty,
the other with arousing, calming or utterly removing
some emotion. A question of duty is: Should one
have children?[a] Under the head of arousing emotions
come exhortations to defend the state, and to seek
fame or glory. Here belong complaints, words of
encouragement, and tearful commiserations; and
again, speeches which now repress rage, now remove
fear, now restrain the transports of joy, and now wipe
away sorrow. All these types are used in inquiries
of a general nature, and may therefore be transferred
to particular cases.

87   XXIII. Our next task is to consider what topics
are suited to each question. As a matter of fact
all are suited to more than one, but as I said, some
are better adapted to one question, and some to
another. The topics which can be drawn from
causes, effects and conjuncts[b] are best fitted to
conjecture and inference. The knowledge and

449

et scientia definiendi. Atque huic generi finitimum
est illud quod appellari de eodem et de altero diximus, quod genus forma quaedam definitionis est; si
enim quaeratur idemne sit pertinacia et perse-
88 verantia, definitionibus iudicandum est. Loci autem
convenient in eius generis quaestionem consequentis,
antecedentis, repugnantis; adiuncti etiam eis qui
sumuntur ex causis et effectis. Nam si hanc rem
illa sequitur, hanc autem non sequitur; aut si huic
rei illa antecedit, huic non antecedit; aut si huic
rei repugnat, illi non repugnat; aut si huius rei
haec, illius alia causa est; aut si ex alio hoc, ex alio
illud effectum est: ex quovis horum id de quo
quaeritur idemne an aliud sit inveniri potest.

89 Ad tertium genus quaestionis, in quo quale sit
quaeritur, in comparationem ea cadunt quae paulo
ante in comparationis loco enumerata sunt. In
illud autem genus in quo de expetend ofugiendoque
quaeritur adhibentur ea quae sunt aut animi aut
corporis aut externa vel commoda vel incommoda.
Itemque cum de honesto turpique quaeritur, ad
unimi bona aut mala omnis oratio dirigenda est.
90 Cum autem de aequo et iniquo disseritur, aequitatis
loci colligentur. Hi cernuntur bipertito, et natura
et instituto. Natura partes habet duas, tributionem

science of defining is important for definition. Closely allied to this is what I said was called sameness and difference, this being a kind of definition. For if one should ask whether obstinacy and perseverance are the same, the matter would 88 have to be settled by definition. The topics of antecedence, consequence and contradiction are also suitable for a question of this sort; and those from cause and effect may be added to these. For if something follows this action but does not follow another; if it precedes this action but does not precede another; or if it is contradictory to this but not to another; or if this is the cause of this action, and that has a different cause; or if this is produced from one thing and that from another; from each of these contradictions we can find the solution of our question, *i.e.* whether we have here a sameness or a difference.

89   In respect to the third type of question, that in which the inquiry is directed to the nature of the thing, those points are useful for comparison which were enumerated shortly before under the topic of comparison. For the group which deals with questions of what to seek and avoid we use the advantages and disadvantages of mind, body or external circumstance. Likewise when the discussion turns on honour or baseness the whole speech must be directed to a consideration of the 90 virtues and defects of the mind. When, however, right and wrong are being discussed, the topics of equity will be brought together. These are of two kinds, the distinction being between natural law and institutions. Natural law has two parts, the right of every man to his own property, and the

sui cuique et ulciscendi ius. Institutio autem
aequitatis tripertita est: una pars legitima est,
altera conveniens, tertia moris vetustate firmata.
Atque etiam aequitas tripertita dicitur esse: una
ad superos deos, altera ad manes, tertia ad homines
pertinere. Prima pietas, secunda sanctitas, tertia
iustitia aut aequitas nominatur.[1] XXIV. De proposito satis multa, deinceps de causa pauciora
dicenda sunt. Pleraque enim sunt ei cum proposito
communia.

91 Tria sunt igitur [2] genera causarum: iudici, deliberationis, laudationis. Quarum fines ipsi declarant quibus
utendum locis sit. Nam iudici finis est ius, ex quo
etiam nomen. Iuris autem partes tum expositae, cum
aequitatis. Deliberandi finis utilitas, cuius eae partes
quae modo expositae.[3] Laudationis finis honestas,
92 de qua item est ante dictum. Sed definitae quaestiones a suis quaeque locis quasi propriis instru-
untur, . . . quae in accusationem defensionemque
partitae; in quibus exsistunt haec genera, ut accusator personam arguat facti, defensor aliquid op-
ponat de tribus: aut non esse factum aut, si sit
factum, aliud eius facti nomen esse aut iure esse
factum. Itaque aut infitialis aut coniecturalis prima
appelletur, definitiva altera, tertia, quamvis moles-

---

[1] Atque . . . nominatur *bracketed by Schuetz.*

[2] igitur *omitted by* O: enim *codd.*

[3] *After* expositae *the MSS. have* rerum expetendarum: (of
things to be sought) *bracketed by Friedrich.*

---

[a] § 90.   [b] § 89.   [c] § 89.
[d] There is a break in the text at this point; the words
in brackets fill out the sense, but are wholly conjectural.

right of revenge. The institutions affecting equity
are threefold: the first has to do with law, the
second with compacts, the third rests on long continued custom. Equity is also said to have three
parts: one pertains to the gods in heaven, the
second to the spirits of the departed, the third to
men. The first is called piety, the second respect,
the third justice or equity. XXIV. This is enough
about the general proposition. We must next treat
the special case, but in briefer compass; for it has
many points in common with the general proposition.
91 There are three kinds of speeches on special
subjects: the judicial, the deliberative, and the
encomiastic; and the "ends" of these three show
what topics are to be used. The end of the
judicial speech is justice, from which it also derives
its name. But the parts of justice were enumerated
when we discussed equity.[a] The end of a deliberative speech is advantage, and the divisions of this
subject have just now been enumerated.[b] The
end of an encomiastic speech is honour, and this,
92 too, was discussed above.[c] But particular inquiries
are built up of topics which are the peculiar property, as it were, of each one. [The first of these
particular inquiries is the judicial][d] which is divided
into accusation and defence; in which there are
the following classes: the prosecutor charges some
one with a crime, and the counsel for the defence
makes one of three replies, either that the crime
was not committed, or that, if it was committed,
it has a different name, or that it was justified. The
first, then, is called *infitialis* (denial) or *coniecturalis*
(based on inference or conjecture), the second
definitiva (involving definition) and the third (though

tum nomen hoc sit, iuridicialis vocetur. XXV.
Harum causarum propria argumenta ex eis sumpta
locis quos exposuimus in praeceptis oratoriis ex-
93 plicata sunt. Refutatio autem accusationis, in qua
est depulsio criminis, quoniam Graece στάσις dicitur
appelletur Latine status; in quo primum insistit
quasi ad repugnandum congressa defensio. Atque
in deliberationibus etiam et laudationibus idem
existunt status. Nam et negantur saepe ea futura
quae ab aliquo in sententia dicta sunt fore, si aut
omnino fieri non possint aut sine summa difficultate
non possint; in qua argumentatione status coniec-
94 turalis exsistit; aut cum aliquid de utilitate, honestate
aequitate disseritur deque eis rebus quae his sunt
contrariae incurrunt status aut iuris aut nominis;
quod idem contingit in laudationibus. Nam aut
negari potest id factum esse quod laudetur, aut
non eo nomine afficiendum quo laudator affecerit,
aut omnino non esse laudabile quod non recte, non
iure factum sit. Quibus omnibus generibus usus est
nimis impudenter Caesar contra Catonem meum.
95 Sed quae ex statu contentio efficitur, eam Graeci
κρινόμενον vocant, mihi placet id, quoniam quidem ad
te scribo, qua de re agitur vocari. Quibus autem

---

a Cicero's apology for using *iuridicialis*, a word newly-
coined as a translation of δικαιολογική (dicaeologicè).

b He may refer to his own Text-Book of Rhetoric (*de
Inventione*) or to any text-book of a similar kind.

c Both Latin *status* and Greek στάσις come from the root
sta, to stand. In the *de Inventione* Cicero used the older
term *constitutio*. It means the point on which the issue is
joined.

the word annoys me) [a] *iuridicialis* (involving right
and wrong). XXV. The proper arguments for
these cases, selected from the topics which we have
enumerated, have been developed in the rules for
93 oratory.[b] The reply to the accusation which con-
stitutes the denial of the charge, may be called in
Latin *status* since the Greeks call it στάσις (stasis): for
this is the place where the defence takes its stand, as
if it were coming to grips in a counter-attack.[c] The
same issues (*status*) come up in deliberative and
encomiastic speeches. For when some one has
given his opinion that certain things will happen,
the opponents deny that this is true, basing their
argument on the statement that these things
cannot be done at all, or only with the greatest
difficulty. And in this argument the conjectural
94 issue arises. Or when there is some discussion about
advantage, honour, or equity and their opposites,
we have the issue of justification and definition.
And the same holds true of encomiastic speeches.
For one can deny that the deed which is being
praised was done at all; or that it deserves the name
which the praiser gives it, or that it is at all praiseworthy, because it was immoral or illegal to do
it. All these arguments were brazenly used by
Caesar against my dear Cato.[d]
95   The debate which arises from the issue (*status*)
is called by the Greeks κρινόμενον (the thing being
decided), but I prefer to call it *qua de re agitur* (the
question at stake) especially in writing to you. The
arguments by which this " question at stake " is

[d] Cicero wrote an encomium of Marcus Porcius Cato
Uticensis, one of the last Republican leaders to hold out
against Caesar, and Caesar replied in his *Anticato*.

hoc qua de re agitur continetur, ea continentia
vocentur, quasi firmamenta defensionis, quibus
sublatis defensio nulla sit.

Sed quoniam lege firmius in controversiis dis-
ceptandis esse nihil debet, danda est opera ut legem
adiutricem et testem adhibeamus. In qua re alii
quasi status existunt novi, sed appellentur legitimae
96 disceptationes. Tum enim defenditur non id legem
dicere quod adversarius velit, sed aliud. Id autem
contingit, cum scriptum ambiguum est, ut duae
sententiae differentes accipi possint. Tum opponi-
tur scripto voluntas scriptoris, ut quaeratur verbane
plus an sententia valere debeant. Tum legi lex
contraria affertur. Ista sunt tria genera quae
controversiam in omni scripto facere possint: ambiguum, discrepantia scripti et voluntatis, scripta
contraria. XXVI. Iam hoc perspicuum est, non
magis in legibus quam in testamentis, in stipulationi-
bus, in reliquis rebus quae ex scripto aguntur, posse
controversias easdem existere. Horum tractationes
in aliis libris explicantur.

97 Nec solum perpetuae actiones sed etiam partes
orationis isdem locis adiuvantur, partim propriis,
partim communibus; ut in principiis, quibus[1] ut
benevoli, ut dociles, ut attenti sint qui audiant,
efficiendum est propriis locis; itemque narrationes
ut ad suos fines spectent, id est ut planae sint, ut
breves, ut evidentes, ut credibiles, ut moderatae,

---

[1] quibus *bracketed by Friedrich.*

---

[a] The use of technical terms here is at variance with *Part.
Orat.* 103, and *de Inv.* I, 13, 18. The confusion is too involved
for a discussion here; *v.* Thiele, *Hermagoras*, pp. 67–75.

supported are called *continentia* (supports); they are,
as it were, the foundation of the defence, for if these
are removed, there is no defence.[a]

But since there should be no firmer foundation
than law in settling disputes, we must be careful
to summon the Law as our helper and witness.
Hence there arise certain new quasi issues, but let us
96 call them disputes about a law. For instance,
sometimes the defence is made that the law does
not say what the opponent tries to make it say,
but something different. This occurs when the
law is ambiguous, so that two different meanings
can be got out of it. Again, the intent of the author
is shown to be opposed to the letter of the law, so
that the question is raised whether words or meaning
should prevail. Again, a law is cited which conflicts
with the law under discussion. These are the three
situations which can raise a controversy over any
written document; ambiguity, variance between
the letter and the intent, and conflicting documents.
XXVI. It is of course plain that such controversies
arise no more from laws than from wills, contracts,
and in any other matter which rests on a written
document. The methods of treating these are set
forth in other books.
97 Not only whole speeches, but also the several
parts of a speech receive help from these topics,
some of which are proper to each part, and some
are of use to all alike. The proper topics must be
used in the introductions to make the audience
well-disposed, receptive and attentive. The narra-
tives must receive similar treatment in order that
they may look to their goal, which is to be plain,
brief, clear, credible, restrained and dignified.

ut cum dignitate. Quae quamquam in tota oratione esse debent, magis tamen sunt propria narrandi.
98 Quae autem sequitur narrationem fides, ea persuadendo quoniam efficitur, qui ad persuadendum loci maxime valeant dictum est in eis in quibus de omni ratione dicendi. Peroratio autem et alia quaedam habet et maxime amplificationem, cuius effectus hic debet esse, ut aut perturbentur animi aut tranquillentur et, si ita affecti iam ante sint, ut aut
99 augeat eorum motus aut sedet oratio. Huic generi, in quo et misericordia et iracundia et odium et invidia et ceterae animi affectiones perturbantur, praecepta suppeditantur aliis in libris, quos poteris mecum legere cum voles. Ad id autem quod te velle senseram, cumulate satis factum esse debet
100 voluntati tuae. Nam ne praeterirem aliquid quod ad argumentum in omni ratione reperiendum pertineret, plura quam a te desiderata erant sum complexus fecique quod saepe liberales venditores solent, ut, cum aedes fundumve vendiderint rutis caesis receptis, concedant tamen aliquid emptori quod ornandi causa apte et loco positum esse videatur; sic tibi nos ad id quod quasi mancipio dare debuimus ornamenta quaedam voluimus non debita accedere.

---

^a §§ 6–24.
^b *Ruta caesa* covered minerals and timber already mined or cut, which the vendor of real estate reserved for himself and had a right to remove.
^c " In the last words Cicero probably referred to rocks or pebbles, or trunks of trees, not permanently affixed, but disposed by way of rustic ornament, or perhaps to wooden buildings not affixed to the soil, for such were counted among ruta et caesa." Roby, *Roman Private Law*, vol. II, p. 146, no. 1.

Though these qualities should prevail throughout the whole speech, they are more characteristic of 98 the narrative. The division of a speech which follows the narrative is the proof. Since this is accomplished by persuasion, this subject—that is the topics which are especially important for persuasion—has been covered in what was said about the whole theory of oratory.[a] The peroration among other topics makes especial use of amplification; the effect of this should be to excite the spirits of the audience or calm them, and if they have already been so affected, to heighten their feelings or quiet them 99 still more. Rules for this division of a speech, in which pity, anger, hatred, envy and other emotions are aroused, are given in other books, which you can read with me when you wish. But for the object which you had in mind, this should be enough 100 and more than enough to satisfy your desires. For in order not to omit anything which had to do with the discovery of arguments in any fashion, I have included more than you requested, and have done what liberal sellers are wont to do; when they sell a house or farm, reserving title to minerals and timber,[b] they make a concession to the buyer and allow him to keep something which seems to be put in the right spot as an ornament.[c] So in addition to what we were bound to sell you, as it were, we wished to give you some ornaments not called for in the contract.

INDEX

I = *de Inventione*, Book I; II = *de Inventione*, Book II; O = *de Optimo Genere Oratorum*; T = *Topica*. Arabic numbers refer to sections, indicated on the margins.

461

INDEX

INDEX

INDEX

464

INDEX

INDEX